MEXICAN-AMERICANS
IN
COMPARATIVE PERSPECTIVE

MEXICAN-AMERICANS
IN
COMPARATIVE PERSPECTIVE

Edited by
Walker Connor

An Urban Institute Book

THE URBAN INSTITUTE PRESS·WASHINGTON, D.C.

*Publication of this volume was made possible
by financial support from the Weingart Foundation.*

Library of Congress Cataloging in Publication Data
Main entry under title:

Mexican-Americans in comparative perspective.

   1. Mexican Americans—Addresses, essays, lectures.
I. Connor, Walker, 1926–
E184.M5M514   1985   305.8′6872073   85-11052
ISBN 0-87766-389-0
ISBN 0-87766-390-4 (pbk.)

Printed in the United States of America

9 8 7 6 5 4 3 2 1

THE URBAN INSTITUTE is a nonprofit policy research and educational organization established in Washington, D.C., in 1968. Its staff investigates the social and economic problems confronting the nation and government policies and programs designed to alleviate such problems. The Institute disseminates significant findings of its research through the publications program of its Press. The Institute has two goals for work in each of its research areas: to help shape thinking about societal problems and efforts to solve them, and to improve government decisions and performance by providing better information and analytic tools.

Through work that ranges from broad conceptual studies to administrative and technical assistance, Institute researchers contribute to the stock of knowledge available to public officials and to private individuals and groups concerned with formulating and implementing more efficient and effective government policy.

Conclusions or opinions expressed in Institute publications are those of the authors and do not necessarily reflect the views of other staff members, officers or trustees of the Institute, advisory groups, or any organizations that provide financial support to the Institute.

ADVISORY COMMITTEE

Henry G. Cisneros, Mayor of San Antonio, Texas

Leobardo F. Estrada, Associate Professor of Architecture and Urban Planning, University of California, Los Angeles

Nathan Glazer, Professor of Education and Sociology, Harvard University

Francine Rabinovitz, Vice President, Hamilton, Rabinovitz, Szanton, & Alschuler, Inc.; joint appointment, School of Public Administration and School of Urban and Regional Policy, University of Southern California

CONTENTS

FOREWORD

During the 1970s, according to the U.S. census, immigrants accounted for more than one out of four persons added to the U.S. population—evidence of a significant new wave of immigration in the history of the United States. With the continued growth of non-English-speaking communities in the United States during the 1980s, immigration has become a subject of national attention and controversy. In 1984, congressional efforts to reform immigration law made front-page news. In May 1985, major reform legislation was again introduced in Congress. The legislative momentum to limit immigration derives from rising public concern about immigration's effects, both real and imagined, on the economic, educational, social, and linguistic systems of the United States. Scholars and policymakers at all levels of government have been grappling with questions about these effects for years. In some cases, research has yielded facts to replace assumptions. In other cases, serious questions remain unanswered.

Most attention to immigration in the United States has focused on people of Mexican origin (including U.S. citizens, permanent and temporary residents, and undocumented workers). Mexican-Americans constitute by far the largest single component of the new immigration wave. In addition, growth of this population is facilitated by the porosity and length of the 2,000-mile border shared by the United States and Mexico.

One concern repeatedly raised by people who advocate an end to immigration flows is that immigrants are taking jobs from U.S.-born workers. Numerous studies refute this contention. For other concerns, however, such as the political and cultural effects of immigration, conclusive findings do not exist. The increasing size of the Mexican-American population and its concentration in a few regions of the country, most notably the Southwest, have intensified these concerns and the need for objective information.

The papers in this volume investigate some of these concerns. They are the result of a conference initiated by The Urban Institute and the Weingart Foundation to broaden the base of knowledge about the Mexican-American community in the United States in the 1980s. The conference, entitled "Lessons from Other Societies: Mexican-Americans in Comparative Perspective," took place March 14–16, 1984, in Los Angeles, California.

The conference agenda and the selection of experts to prepare papers were designed to shed light on the key issues that dominate immigration debate by relating the applicable immigration experiences of other countries and societies to the experience of the United States. The comparative approach of the conference clarified some significant common misconceptions about Mexican-Americans in the United States, and provided some new vantage points from which to assess the factual, policy, and ethical concerns uppermost in the minds of many U.S. citizens. The major issues raised and the author's conclusions are briefly summarized below.

Walker Connor introduces the conference papers with an essay that puts the ethnic heterogeneity of the United States into a global perspective and discusses some important terms and concepts. He points out that the political entities called "states" rarely coincide with the cultural entities called "nations" or "ethnic groups," and that these discrepancies result in great potential for conflict. Most political states encompass two or more ethnic groups, each with its own language and culture. Furthermore, political borders divide many ethnic groups, often splitting the land that a group considers its ancestral homeland.

In attempting to make meaningful comparative analyses between the experiences of other political states and the situation of Mexican immigrants in the United States, Connor distinguishes among three types of states: the nation-state, the multinational state, and the immigrant state. The nation-state comes closest to having political borders coterminous with those of a single ethnic group or "nation" that considers the territory its ancestral homeland. The multinational state contains two or more ethnic groups within its political borders, each of which probably perceives at least part of the territory it occupies to be a homeland. The immigrant state effectively has no homelands; almost the entire population has migrated there from somewhere else. That the United States is an immigrant state is critically important in interpreting relations among ethnic groups in this country and in attempting to translate the experiences of other nations into predictions for the United States.

Turning his attention to Mexican-Americans, Connor concludes that the Mexican-American population is quite heterogeneous. Most do not perceive themselves as part of a Mexican "nation"; nor do they perceive the Southwest as their ancestral homeland despite their knowledge that it once belonged to Mexico. All these factors strongly suggest a low probability of ethnic conflict involving persons of Mexican origin in the United States.

J. Milton Yinger describes in his paper the experiences of numerous immigrant groups in the United States. He presents the U.S. side of the "comparative" perspective. He also provides some important theoretical concepts for thinking about assimilation.

Yinger stresses that assimilation is often a two-way exchange, that it is a gradual process, not an event, and that the process encompasses several dimensions. A group can be almost totally assimilated on one dimension, partially assimilated on another, and virtually unassimilated on yet another. His analysis enriches our understanding of how immigrant groups move along the continuum of assimilation.

Structural assimilation reflects the degree to which a group's members are integrated into the full range of a society's associations, institutions, and regions. When an ethnic group has been assimilated into a society's structures, its members hold the same jobs, live in the same neighborhoods, and belong to the same political parties as the large society. By this measure, Mexican-Americans are partially assimilated and are becoming more so.

Cultural assimilation indexes the extent to which an ethnic group holds the same range of norms and values as the rest of the population. Psychological assimilation, or identification, refers to an ethnic group's sense of belonging to the political state in which they live. By both these measures, Mexican-Americans are quite well integrated into American life. Yinger's final component of assimilation is biological— as measured by the degree of intermarriage between ethnic group members and nonmembers. Several papers in this volume attest to the increasing rates of intermarriage involving Mexican-Americans.

Yinger concludes with an assessment of assimilative and dissimilative factors affecting Mexican-Americans. His data indicate that the assimilative factors outweigh the dissimilative ones in both the short and the long run.

Donald L. Horowitz, drawing on his extensive knowledge of societies in which ethnic conflict abounds and exploring conditions that engender such conflict, concludes that the Mexican-American situation does not suggest a high probability of severe ethnic conflict. He contrasts the ways in which the Mexican-American experience resembles the experience of other immigrant groups in the United States with the ways it resembles the experience of the black population. Although Mexican-Americans have encountered discrimination just as black Americans have, Horowitz marshals considerable evidence that suggests certain parallels to the experience of the European immigrant groups. He notes, however, that many aspects of the earlier immigrant experience are no longer replicable.

A supraethnic "American" identity allows immigrants to maintain aspects of their culture while still perceiving themselves as well-integrated members of American society. One mechanism for this integration is social-occupational and geographical mobility. Americans, including immigrants, are expected to "do better" with each generation, and to consider the entire country their terrain for upward mobility. Mexican-Americans increasingly exhibit both types of mobility.

Horowitz also examines the ability of the American political system and that of other states to contain and reduce ethnic conflict. America's federal system, like the systems of other federally organized states, allows a great deal of potential ethnic conflict to be played out at the state and local levels. Newly arrived immigrant groups have achieved power and control over their immediate environment without escalating ethnic conflict to a national level. Because American political parties are essentially nonideological, newly arrived groups have been able to attach themselves to whichever party can do the most for them, sometimes switching parties when they perceive they would thereby gain influence.

Finally, Horowitz explores the advantages and disadvantages of recent developments in the American electoral system and compares them with the electoral mechanisms other countries use to accommodate ethnic aspirations. He looks at the creation of political districts based strictly on population. He suggests that while an ethnic group remains geographically concentrated, district elections may best serve its interests. However, as the group disperses, at-large elections may provide it with more political influence.

John Stone compares and contrasts the recent West European experience of migrant workers (*gastarbeiter*) with that of the latest wave of Mexican immigrants to the United States. Both groups include large numbers of migrants motivated almost entirely by economics and destined, at least initially, for the lowest ranks of the host country's economy. However, important differences are also apparent—such as the relative ethnic homogeneity of the European host countries before the migrant flow (unlike the heterogeneity found in the United States and the fact that the European host countries never intended to grant citizenship, or even permanent residence, to its *gastarbeiter* groups (although some previous colonial and Commonwealth subjects automatically acquired such privileges). As a result, most European states were unprepared for the social and political consequences of this migration and for the establishment, in the second and subsequent generations, of permanent racial and ethnic minorities.

Stone also explores three theories—assimilation, internal colonialism, and neo-Marxism—to explain the empirical relations between ethnicity and stratification. He is interested in the degree to which ethnicity must be used in addition to class to explain patterns of employment, educational attainment, residential segregation, attitudes, and values. He concludes that an analysis that recognizes the influence of several factors—class, race, ideology, and the structure of political control—best accommodates the evidence of both the European and the Mexican-American experiences.

Myron Weiner presents a detailed example from Assam, India, and two other examples from the Horn of Africa and the Baluchi homeland in Pakistan, Afghanistan, and Iran to explore the often tension-ridden situation in which members of an ethnic group live on two sides of an international border. Because the transborder situation of Mexican immigrants (heightened by their residing largely in areas of the United States that once belonged to Mexico), coupled with the size of the migration flow, is unique in the U.S. immigrant experience, Weiner's observations shed much light on the potential for conflict.

Weiner's paper makes it clear, however, that Mexican-Americans do not exhibit the usual warning signs of potential transborder conflict. They do not seriously regard the southwestern United States as their homeland, and they do not make irredentist claims that this region should be returned to Mexico. They are not interested in secession, regional autonomy, or creation of a separate state encompassing their own ethnic homeland. They have arrived in a country in which the existing citizens, from all ethnic groups, have increasingly shown a willingness to share power (at least since the Voting Rights Act of 1965 and its reauthorizations). Moreover, Mexican-Americans—especially second- and subsequent-generation Mexican Americans—are increasingly successful educationally and occupationally; this success reduces the correlation between their ethnicity and their position in U.S. society. Finally, their growing geographical dispersion beyond the southwestern states further dilutes the potential for a regionally based Mexican-American political movement along ethnic lines.

Rosemarie Rogers focuses primarily on economically motivated migration streams, rather than those generated by cultural or political causes, because the Mexican migration to the United States has been largely economically motivated since at least the 1930s. She examines structural and proximate causes of migration and cites research that attempts to determine why some people are motivated to emigrate, while others are not.

She then analyzes various types of migration, including year-round migration, seasonal migration, border commuting, "irregular" (illegal or undocumented) migration, and refugee movements. She illustrates that isolating a single type of migration for study is inappropriate because the same persons often hold several different migrant statuses over a period of time. When host countries cut off year-round migration (a system in which migrants are permitted to renew their initial entry permits annually without first having to leave the country, but are not granted permanent residency) after a migration stream has become well established, the migrant flow may diminish less than expected. Would-be immigrants know the loopholes and have contacts enabling them to enter the country by classifying themselves according to other migrant categories (or by entering illegally).

Rogers also discusses circulatory migration. She points out that the United States stands virtually alone among developed countries in failing to document out-migration—including both people who return permanently to their home countries and people who repeatedly come to the United States to work, going back home only periodically. This failure seriously impairs the ability of the United States to document net migration flows and skews U.S. perceptions of "irregular" migrants.

Rogers points out that voluntary returns to the sending country decrease when host countries tighten entry procedures. For example, migrants who would otherwise return home when seasonal work ends tend to remain in the host country for fear that they will be denied reentry. Thus, tightening entry requirements may have exactly the opposite effect from that which is intended—encouraging rather than discouraging permanent settlement.

Finally, Rogers describes the seeming inevitability of permanent settlement by migrants regardless of the desires or policies of host countries to the contrary. Initially, host countries may refuse entry to families and may restrict services, civil rights, and housing for migrants. But as more migrants stay on, the sending countries typically begin to put pressure on the host countries to loosen their restrictions. However, most host countries try to stanch (or stabilize) the flow of migrants, liberalized policies attract the families of migrants already present, and many illegal entrants will have established contacts in the host country. Questions of eligibility for services and rights of migrants soon arise, as well as civil rights issues, especially where citizenship is not granted to the children born to migrants in the host country (a condition true of most European host countries). Whereas some of these issues are not relevant to the American immigration experience, others are. Efforts to end firmly established migration streams have met with little success on either side of the Atlantic.

Three papers in this volume are devoted to the issue of Mexican-American participation in U. S. politics. Nathan Glazer raises, then lays to rest, the issue of Mexican-American loyalty to the United States. Rodolfo de la Garza describes the current political realities for Mexican-Americans; he shows that, despite more than a century of active discrimination and exclusion from the political process, the Mexican-Americans' use of the American political system increasingly parallels the behavior of other Americans. Harry P. Pachon challenges the appropriateness of comparing the political experience of Mexican-Americans with that of either European immigrants or blacks.

Glazer cites five conditions that differentiate the present wave of Mexican immigration from previous waves of European immigration to the United States. These are (1) the shared U.S.-Mexican border, (2) the history of the Southwest as conquered territory, (3) the extreme discrepancy in economic development between the United States and Mexico, (4) the geographical concentration of Mexican-Americans, and (5) changed U.S. conditions that do not force immigrants to acquire knowledge of English (for example, bilingual ballots and antidiscrimination laws). Nevertheless, of the three traditional forces of assimilation, he finds two—American popular culture and the two-party system—to be as strong as ever. The third major force, the public schools, he finds considerably weakened. He concludes that, despite all the dissimilarities, Mexican-Americans appear to be following a path very similar to that taken by previous waves of European immigrants.

De la Garza details the racism and discrimination, literacy tests in English, poll taxes, residency requirements, and repression to which Mexican-Americans have been subjected since the United States won the Mexican-American War. He then expresses incredulity that the loyalty of Mexican-Americans to the United States is questioned on the basis of their historically lower levels of political participation in comparison with the participation of other immigrant groups. He notes that nearly half of the resident Mexican-origin population is ineligible to vote. (Slightly more than 20 percent are not citizens, and another 20 percent are too young.) At the same time, he presents data showing a surge in registration and electoral participation following enactment of the Voting Rights Act. Finally, he argues that Mexican-American political attitudes and values closely resemble those of the beliefs of the mainstream. He concludes that, even with a major increase in political involvement, Mexican-American political activities will not alter much in substance.

To de la Garza's list of discriminatory actions against Mexican-Americans, Pachon adds gerrymandering of political districts and suppression of political participation by threats, economic sanctions, subterfuge, and violence. He also notes that the tendency of Mexican-Americans in the past to use multipurpose organizations to achieve political (as well as cultural and welfare) goals partially obscured their political activism from the view of mainstream political scientists looking for (and failing to find) single-purpose political organizations.

Pachon believes the Mexican-American experience differs from the European immigrant experience in three important ways: (1) the Europeans were not discriminated against on a racial basis, whereas Mexican-Americans have been; (2) Mexican-Americans were associated in the public eye with American Indians, "a subordinate conquered population," another factor not faced by the Europeans; and (3) Europeans came to eastern United States cities at a time when there were effective political machines that they could use to pursue their interests. Most Mexican-Americans in the Southwest have not had access to such machines; but where they have, they had already achieved early political gains. Pachon attributes the improving political fortunes of Mexican-Americans to the civil rights movement, bootstrap operations within the Mexican-American community, and the growing mainstream perception of Mexican-Americans as a "swing" vote that could affect elections.

Finally, Pachon differentiates the assimilation experience of Mexican-Americans from that of black Americans, noting that the color-race barrier has been much less extreme for Mexican-Americans. Increasingly diffuse residential patterns attest to their greater acceptability to other Americans. Moreover, a less distinct color line for some members of the group allows them to avoid being identified as Mexicans, should they wish to do so.

Few aspects of ethnic group relations stimulate more conflict worldwide than language policies. Countries have used language policies to promote national unification, modernization, the smooth functioning of public institutions, and the fortunes of one people over another. These policies have met widely different reactions of acceptance and resistance. The last three papers in this volume address language issues.

Shirley Brice Heath distinguishes between *language maintenance* (government policymaking with regard to language) and *language retention* (the ability of individuals, families, and communities to continue speaking a language). For example, a host country that wants immigrant workers to return home would not insist they learn the language of the host country and might actively discourage such learning. Alternatively, many states encompassing peoples speaking a multitude of languages have, in the interest of creating a national consciousness, chosen a national language and taken pains to make all citizens use it. These are examples of language policies. Heath examines Mexico's attempt to establish language policies that favor Spanish over numerous Indian languages.

Heath then turns her attention to the United States, noting that the United States has never had an official policy declaring English to be the national language. She discusses the growing tendency for public institutions to accommodate people who speak only Spanish, then looks at the struggle in the United States during the decade over the meaning of bilingual education. Here she notes a rhetorical shift from the idea of bilingual education as a help to non-English-speaking children in elementary school to the idea that such education should also help children in the higher grades retain both their non-English language and their culture. While the latter idea is popular among professional bilingual educators, it is not heavily endorsed by the average Mexican-American.

Reynaldo F. Macías examines English and Spanish language abilities among Mexican-Americans. He sees a pattern of Spanish language increase over time, at the same time that the numbers of English monolinguals and bilinguals increase. He notes that these language changes result from the interaction of retention factors such as the large size of the group, its relative linguistic homogeneity, continued in-migration, relative social isolation, Spanish-language mass media, the intergenerational stability of the Mexican extended family, and the negative or language-loss factors such as the continuing intolerance of non-English language retention by the U.S. monolingual population (for example, the "English only" movement).

Patterns of English acquisition, according to Macías, are patterns of bilingualism of the population (Spanish language retention while adding English), as well as patterns of English monolingualism (native English language acquisition). Among Mexican-Americans born in Mexico, 54 percent consider themselves bilingual, as do 63 percent of Mexican-origin people born in the United States. Higher education and younger age correlate with more English dominance; increased English facility, bilingualism, and more schooling correlate with higher income. Clearly, the issues of language retention, bilingualism among the Mexican-origin population, and language discrimination are complex and delicate, as are the public policies affecting these issues.

Joshua Fishman explores the phenomena of "sidestream ethnicity" and the ethnic revival of the 1960s and early 1970s. During this period, ethnic and area studies (including Slavic, Chicano, and black studies) flourished in American universities. Many Americans sought their roots and heritage in their immigrant past. More third-generation immigrants claimed to speak a non-English "mother tongue" than did second-generation immigrants, and people revived "old country" customs and returned to visit the lands from which their ancestors had come.

Although this ethnic revival has somewhat abated in recent years, Fishman believes that many Americans will continue their quest for some type of ethnic identification. From a global perspective, the United States provides the relatively rare opportunity for people to fully identify with the larger political entity as "American" while continuing to cherish a unique cultural heritage as a Polish-American, Italian-American, Irish-American, or Greek-American. In this context, attempts by Mexican-Americans to retain their native language appear compatible with their acquisition of English language proficiency and adoption of American values and aspirations.

Walker Connor reiterates in the last paper that the goal of the conference was to work toward a better understanding of the Mexican-American community in the 1980s, not to make recommendations for public policy. As noted at the outset of this volume, the papers were written to show policymakers and others how a comparative perspective might be used to enrich our knowledge of the Mexican-American community with regard to selected topics including assimilation, the potential for intergroup conflict, stratification, language retention, political mobilization. Perhaps the most important insight that this volume offers policymakers is that the Mexican-Americans are not a single, homogeneous group—not ethnically, socioeconomically, or politically.

Connor draws attention to several significant dimensions of the Mexican-American drama that were not addressed by the authors. He also notes an important consensual thread running through the analyses. Given the emphasis that all the authors of the papers place on the unique and diverse features of the Mexican-American community, perhaps the biggest surprise is the agreement among them that the Mexican-Americans are following an integrationist pattern similar to that followed by earlier immigrant groups. Although not ruling out the possibility of deviation in the future, the authors concur that alterations in the pattern have thus far reflected differences of tempo rather than of direction.

This volume should be of considerable interest to the general public as well as to scholars, legislators, specialists in education and immigration, and others involved in Mexican-American issues. It is hoped that the publication of these conference papers will enlarge the forum for discussion of these issues and encourage attitudes that reflect more accurately the reality of the Mexican-American situation. If this is accomplished even partially, the volume will have contributed toward a better informed public.

William Gorham
President
The Urban Institute

PREFACE

What follows is the result of an experiment. All the authors of papers presented in this book are scholars with extensive experience in bringing a comparative focus to bear upon the study of group dynamics, in some cases having employed the United States as their framework, while in others having utilized cross-country data. They were therefore not specialists on the Mexican-American community. For some, that community had hitherto entered their work only marginally. For others, not at all.

The decision to have comparativists rather than specialists prepare papers for the conference was not due to a dearth of qualified authorities on the Mexican-American community. There is a voluminous literature dealing with that community. In the early 1970s, for example, the Latin American Studies Center at Michigan State University compiled a two-volume, 1,400-page bibliography on this people, and even bibliographies of bibliographies of Mexican-American materials exist. Although much of this literature, particularly that which appeared in the late 1960s and early 1970s, was exhortatory rather than clinical and was aimed at raising group consciousness rather than at dispassionate analysis, the literature has also included an impressive number of articles and books that are models of clinical analysis.

What, then, had we hoped to achieve by adding still more to this already voluminous literature? Our goal was quite modest. We sought to bring a comparative perspective to bear upon selected aspects of the Mexican-American experience; our premise was that analogies might provide additional insight into some facets of that community.

In adopting this procedure, we were heeding the advice of several outstanding scholars who, over the decades, have stressed that issues involving ethnicity and national consciousness are most efficaciously studied from a comparative perspective. As Hans Kohn, one of the most prolific writers on ethnonationalism, noted some forty years ago: "A study of nationalism must allow a comparative method, it cannot remain confined to one of its manifestations; only the comparison of the different nationalisms all over the earth will enable the student to see what they have in common and what is peculiar to each, and thus allow a just evaluation" (Hans Kohn, *The Idea of Nationalism: A Study in Its Origins and Background,* Macmillan, 1944, pp. ix–x).

But although the comparative method is therefore broadly accepted as the best method for analyzing ethnicity and nationalism, we were fully cognizant that it is nonetheless a most imperfect analytical tool. It is necessarily imperfect because of the absence of ideal analogues: all peoples enjoy a measure of uniqueness. As a result, purportedly comparative works that consist of a series of case histories of peoples seldom satisfy. The reader is customarily more impressed by the dissimilarities than by the similarities among the several groups. Yet if one wants to assess the impact that some characteristic of a people is apt to exert upon that people's behavior, consideration of other groups that share that characteristic may be suggestive. For example, the French-Canadian community within the United States is obviously quite different in several respects from the Mexican-American community. But if one wants to assess the impact that the transborder location of Mexico is apt to exert upon culture maintenance among Mexican-Americans, the experience of the French-Canadian community in the northeastern United States may indeed prove instructive.

For this reason we adopted a topical rather than a case-study approach. A planning committee selected eight themes encountered in the literature on Mexican-Americans that could be examined in a broader comparative framework. In briefest outline, the selected topics were as follows:

1. *Migration theory and practice:* Transstate migration patterns since World War II and their social and political consequences for both sending and receiving countries.

2. *Transborder peoples:* Situations in which a political border dissects a people and treats such issues as divided loyalties in terms of a wide range of variables.

3. *Ethnicity and political mobilization:* Patterns of political mobilization followed by ethnic groups in terms of commonly encountered catalysts, conditioners, channels, strategies, and results.

4. *Acculturation and assimilation in the United States:* Contrasts among the different rates of acculturation and assimilation of major immigrant groups and analysis of the factors accounting for the variation.

5. *Conflict management in a multiethnic society:* The reasons some states have been much more successful than others at peacefully accommodating ethnic aspirations.

6. *Ethnicity and stratification:* Surveys of how intragroup and intergroup stratification are apt to influence integration into the recipient society.

7. *Language, identity, and political loyalty:* History of language maintenance in the United States within a broad, global framework.

8. *Language policies:* An assessment of the language policies of various countries, including the United States.

Having reached agreement on this eightfold agenda, we then sought the assistance of scholars who had published on these topics from a comparative perspective. The authors were given total discretion with regard to content. The sole condition was that they become familiar with the appropriate literature on Mexican-Americans and that references to the experiences of that community be woven into their papers.

We recognized, of course, that a crash course in the history of Mexican-Americans was no substitute for years of sustained study. If transgroup analysis is to proceed beyond the superficial, the comparativist must utilize the detailed knowledge and particular insight of the specialist, gleaned through years of familiarity with (and perhaps membership in) the group. The relationship between comparativist and specialist is therefore a symbiotic one. As the quotation of Hans Kohn suggests, a broad, analogical approach should ideally provide the specialist some guidelines for (1) differentiating trivia from essence, (2) determining what in fact is unique and not unique to a particular environment or group, and (3) anticipating the patterns of future group behavior. But comparativists, in turn, necessarily stand on the shoulders of specialists. Were it not for the effort of skilled specialists, comparative analyses would necessarily be sterile.

Beyond requesting authors of the papers to familiarize themselves with the literature, our plans for ensuring sufficient input by specialists called for requesting acknowledged authorities on Mexican-Americans to serve as commentators. (The division between specialists and comparativists was hardly hermetical—some of the specialists had undertaken comparative work, and some of the comparativists had published work focused on Mexican-Americans. Nonetheless, the distinction remained valid because the commentators were known *primarily* for their work on Mexican-Americans or on Mexican-U.S. affairs.) To ensure a transborder perspective, we also invited two scholars from the Colegio de Mexico to serve in this capacity. In addition, the audience invited to the conference consisted of people with expertise on some aspect of the Mexican-American community. Both commentators and audience were urged to focus on the relevance of the papers to a better understanding of the Mexican-American experience and to suggest ways in which the papers might be further honed in this regard.

Another consideration in selecting both authors and commentators was to ensure that a variety of disciplines was represented. The final list of participants included persons trained in anthropology, demography, law, linguistics, political science, psychology, or sociology.

As the person scheduled to chair the conference, I confess to an attack of preconference jitters. As a result of previous experiences in dealing with one-people, one-country, or one-region authorities, I had come to expect that scholars who had spent years in developing an expertise on a topic would tend to view the comparativist as a resented interloper. My fears proved groundless, however. We "carpetbaggers" encountered an atmosphere characterized by collegiality and reasoned give-and-take. Sharply divergent perceptions and interpretations were certainly articulated, but always in the spirit of intellectual dialecticalism. The commentators merit particular mention for their key contributions to this circumambience. They were Tomas Amalguer, Carlos Arce, Gilberto Cardeñas, Manuel Garcia y Griego, Rodolfo de la Garza, José Limon, David Lopez, Reynaldo Macías, Margarita Melville, Joan Moore, Harry Pachon, Amado Padilla, Fernando Peñalosa, and Rodolfo Stavenhagen. Papers later submitted by three of the commentators—de la Garza, Macías, and Pachon—are included in this conference volume.

Publication of the conference papers by The Urban Institute had been considered a likely prospect from the outset. The decision to publish was confirmed at the conference, and some of the commentators—de la Garza, Macías, and Pachon—later submitted papers for inclusion in this volume.

As noted, sharply divergent opinions were aired at the conference. For this reason as well as the fact that the contributors to this volume have not seen the revised papers of other participants, it should be stressed that the authors are alone responsible for their respective contributions. Agreement among the authors should not be inferred.

Walker Connor
Editor
Singapore, September 1984

ACKNOWLEDGMENTS

A large number of people, in addition to the authors whose papers appear in this book, have made significant contributions. The relative feasibility of designing a conference dedicated to examining the Mexican-American community within a broad comparative framework was originally raised by William Gorham, president of The Urban Institute. Milton Esman, Arturo Munoz, and Robert Reischauer attended the first planning meeting, at which they offered essential guidance on specific aspects of the Mexican-American experience that might best lend themselves to comparative analysis. The Weingart Foundation generously financed the conference on Mexican-Americans in comparative perspective; without this foundation's support, this book would not have been written. All participants at the conference—the authors of papers, the commentators, and the general audience—contributed substantially to the intellectual cross-fertilization and cordial climate that characterized the proceedings. Joan Moore should be particularly commended for her willingness to act as last-minute substitute for another speaker. Martha Burt of The Urban Institute served as key coordinator throughout all stages of the project, from its inception as an idea to publication of this book. A major debt is owed to Mary Connor for unrecorded hours of effort spent compiling a working bibliography for the contributors and serving as preliminary copy editor of all manuscripts in this volume.

Finally, the support of the Weingart Foundation is gratefully acknowledged. To one and all: *¡Gracias!*

A NOTE ON THE LANGUAGE

The Spanish expressions used in text throughout this book are according to *Diccionario de la Lengua Española,* 2 vols. (Madrid: Real Academia Española, 1984); Spanish in citations appearing in footnotes is according to the published work as cited by the author of the respective paper. Hyphenation throughout the book of the term Mexican-American follows a consolidation of advice from numerous authorities including the *United States Government Printing Office Style Manual,* rev. ed. (Washington, D.C., 1984); *The New York Times Manual of Style and Usage* (New York: Quadrangle/The New York Times Book Company, 1976); and Roy Copperud, *American Usage and Style: The Consensus* (New York: Van Nostrand Reinhold Company, 1980). Other terms for which no official standard usage or definition has been established—such as Chicano, Latino, Mexican-origin, Spanish-origin, and so on—are according to the authors' interpretations as described in their respective papers.

MEXICAN-AMERICANS
IN
COMPARATIVE PERSPECTIVE

CHAPTER ONE

Ethnic heterogeneity is a nearly universal characteristic of states. Only a handful of countries—less than 10 percent of the total—can be classified as essentially homogeneous, and the number is dwindling as a consequence of recent intercountry labor- and refugee-flows. The level of heterogeneity varies dramatically among states, however. In many multiethnic states, a single national group clearly predominates (examples include the Bulgars within Bulgaria, Han Chinese within China, English within the United Kingdom, Malays within Malaysia, Thais within Thailand, and Turks within Turkey). But in some forty states, the largest group fails to account for even a bare majority. Similarly, while the number of significant groups within the state may be as few as two (Belgium, Cyprus, Finland), in over fifty states the population is divided into more than five significant groups, and in some cases (Nigeria and the Soviet Union are examples) into more than one hundred.

Over the past two decades, this pattern of ethnic heterogeneity has been a (if not *the*) major cause of political instability. More than 50 percent of all countries have been troubled by ethnically inspired unrest. Yugoslavian Albanians, Israeli Arabs, Armenians, Assamese, Irani Azerbaijanis, Basques, Baluchis, Bengalis, American blacks, Catalans, Corsicans, Croats, Flemings, Ibos, the Irish within Northern Ireland, Karens, Kashmiris, Kurds, Mizos, Nagas, Ndebeles, Quebecers, Shans, Sikhs, Slovaks, Sri Lankan Tamils, and Cypriot Turks represent but a small fraction of the peoples who have unambiguously expressed acute displeasure with the status quo. This global tremor of ethnic disquiet has, in turn, triggered an outpouring of articles and monographs dealing with ethnic heterogeneity within a broad range of environments. The person who wants to set the Mexican-Americans against a comparative background will therefore not lack case studies. However, as Walker Connor maintains in the following essay, proper heed must be given to the issue of comparability. The nature of the particular peoples under scrutiny and of their parent political societies must be ascertained and respected if comparisons are to be valid.

2

WHO ARE THE MEXICAN-AMERICANS?

A Note on Comparability

Walker Connor

The validity of comparative analyses concerned with the attitudes and behavior of peoples has all too often been undermined by (1) the improper use of key terms, such as *nation* and *ethnic group,* (2) the failure to differentiate whether the group under study is living within or without its ethnic homeland, and (3) the failure to differentiate the country in which the group under study is living, according to whether it is a *nation-state, multination-state,* or *immigrant state.* A few words concerning each of these pitfalls may therefore be advisable.

Nations and Ethnic Groups

In its pristine sense, *nation* refers to a group who share a myth of common descent. It derives from the past participle of the Latin verb *nasci* ("to be born"). Hence the Latin noun *nationem,* which connoted breed or race. The myth, of course, need not be grounded in fact. Thus, an old European saw defines the nation as "a group of people united by a common error about their ancestry and a common dislike of their neighbors."

Unfortunately the term *nation* is habitually misued as a synonym for (1) a state (consider the League of Nations or the United Nations) or (2) the population or citizenry of a state without regard to its ethnonational composition (consider the widely used expression "the British nation," despite the fact that the British people are composed, inter alia, of the Cornish, English, Manx, Scottish, and Welsh nations). "The American nation," whether used in reference to the country called the United States or to the polygenetic citizenry of that country, is also a misnomer.

The author is indebted to Arturo Munoz for an informed and informative critique of an early draft of this paper.

The term *ethnic group* has also been fatally compromised. Sociologists use the term loosely to describe any minority, whether of a religious, linguistic, national, or still other variety. Thus, one dictionary of sociology defines ethnic group as "a group with a common cultural tradition and a sense of identity which exists as a sub-group of a larger society."[1] Historically, however, the term was derived from the Greek word *ethnos,* which, like *nationem,* conveyed the notion of an ancestrally related group. Consonant with this etymology, Max Weber defined *ethnic groups* as "those human groups that entertain a subjective belief in their common descent. . . . This belief must be important for the propagation of group formation; conversely, it does not matter whether an objective blood relationship exists. Ethnic membership *(Gemeinsamkeit)* differs from the kinship group precisely by being a presumed identity."[2]

An evident danger associated with the tendency to ignore this pristine meaning of ethnic group and to use it as an umbrella term to cover nearly any type of minority is that the term's application to a series of generically unrelated groups will cause the unwary to assume that all groups can be considered essentially the same for comparative purposes. Thus, while the 1980 U.S. census professed to use *ethnic group* in its pristine sense of an ancestrally related people, it is evident that this definition was not honored in practice.[3] State citizenry rather than kinship was reflected in such entries as Belgian, Swiss, Iranian, Lebanese, Ethiopian, Ghanian, Nigerian, Asian Indian, Indonesian, Pakistani, and Jamaican. Interspersed with such identities were true ethnonational categories, such as Czech and Slovak (rather than Czechoslovakian) and English, Manx, Scottish, and Welsh (rather than British).[4]

---

1. George Theodorson and Achilles Theodorson, *A Modern Dictionary of Sociology* (New York: Thomas Y. Crowell Co., 1969), p. 135. A similar definition is offered by H. S. Morris, under the entry "Ethnic Groups" in *The International Encyclopedia of the Social Sciences* (New York: Macmillan and Free Press, 1968).

2. Max Weber, *Economy and Society,* vol. 1, Guenther Roth and Claus Wittich, eds. (New York: Bedminster Press, 1968), p. 389. Elsewhere (p. 395), Weber made clear the close relationship he perceived between the nation and the ethnic group: "The concept of 'nationality' (or 'nation') shares with that of the 'people' *(Volk)*—in the 'ethnic' sense—the vague connotation that whatever is felt to be distinctively common must derive from common descent."

3. See U.S. Department of Commerce, Bureau of the Census, *1980 Census of Population: Ancestry of the Population by States: 1980,* Supplementary Report PC80-S1-10 (Washington, D.C.: U.S. Government Printing Office, April 1983), p. 1 and particularly footnote 1: "In this report, the terms 'ancestry' and 'origin' (and ancestry group and ethnic group) are used interchangeably."

4. The confusion was guaranteed by the instructions to the respondents for answering the question, "What is this person's ancestry?" The instructions read, "Print

A second peril in grouping such vitally different phenomena under a single rubric of ethnic groups is that the analyst will be lulled into assuming as fact that which may most demand questioning. Thus, the census would appear to signify that all Belgians consider themselves to be blood-related in the same way that all Czechs and all Slovaks (but not all Czechoslovaks) do.[5] Mexican-Americans were also listed as an ethnic group in the census, and they are quite regularly described and treated as such in the scholarly literature.[6] But again, this categorization may preempt the potentially vital question: are Mexican-Americans agreed that they constitute an ancestrally related group?"[7]

A group's perception of itself as a kinship group possesses important ramifications for its attitudes and behavior. Commencing with Napoleon, an array of political leaders has demonstrated appreciation of the strategic value of appealing to ethnopsychology as a means of mobilizing the masses. Thus Bismarck, when exhorting the people, over the heads of their several princes, to unite into a single state, urged all Germans to "think with your blood." And Marxist-Leninists also have not hesitated to appeal to blood links as a technique of mass mobilization, as witness Mao Tse-tung's 1931 attempt to appear as the defender of the great Han (Chinese) family: "Brothers! Sisters! Can we allow the reactionary rule to connive freely with imperialism to carve us up like sheep? Can we watch our land being forcefully taken away by Japanese imperialism? Can we silently watch our own brothers being whipped, killed, and slaughtered? Can we unfeelingly watch our sisters being molested, insulted, and raped? No! No! Ten thousand times no!"[8]

And in 1937 the Central Committee of the Chinese Communist Party addressed "all fathers, brothers, aunts, and sisters" as follows: "We know that in order to transform this glorious future into a new

---

the ancestry group with which the person *identifies*. Ancestry (or origin or descent) may be viewed as the nationality group, the lineage, or the country in which the person or the person's parents or ancestors were born before their arrival in the United States," ibid., p. 9. Given the complex multiethnic composition of most countries, this encouragement to substitute country for ancestry was certain to invalidate the results.

5. Belgium, of course, has been riven by ethnonational rivalry between its Flemish and Walloon components.

6. The census first inquired, "Is this person of Spanish/Hispanic origin or descent?" If answered affirmatively, the respondent had a choice of answers, one of which was "Yes, Mexican, Mexican-American, Chicano." U.S. Department of Commerce, *1980 Census: Ancestry.*

7. The question is addressed below.

8. Mao Tse-tung, *Selected Works of Mao Tse-tung,* vol. 3 (Peking: Foreign Languages Press, 1975), p. 38.

China, independent, free, and happy, all our fellow countrymen, every single zealous descendent of Huang-ti [the legendary first emperor of China] must determinedly and relentlessly participate in the struggle. . . ."9

Through such speeches and common allusions to themselves as the protectors of "our race and nation," Mao's movement successfully transferred the Hans' loyalty to itself.

A shared sense of ancestral ties can also become intermeshed in foreign policy and raise the issue of divided loyalties if important segments of the group are separated by political borders. Hitler's appeals in the name of the *Volksdeutsch* to all Germans living within Austria, the Sudetenland, and Poland are well known. More recently, Albania has claimed the right to act as the protector of Albanians within Yugoslavia on the ground that "the same mother that gave birth to us gave birth to the Albanians in Kosovo, Montenegro, and Macedonia"; China has proclaimed its right to Taiwan on the ground that "the people of Taiwan are our kith and kin"; and Kim Il Sung has declared the need to unify Korea in order to bring about the "integration of our race."10 But again, whether such appeals are addressed to an internal or external audience, people's receptivity to them is conditional upon the existence or nonexistence of a sense of consanguinity.

Homelands

As illustrated in ethnographic atlases, most of the populated land masses of the world are divided into ethnic homelands—territories whose names reflect a particular people. Armenia, Catalonia, Croatia, Finland, Iboland, Kurdistan (literally "land of the Kurds"), Nagaland, Pakhtunistan, Pol(e)land, Scotland, Somaliland, Swaziland, Uzbekistan, and Zululand constitute but a small sampling. To the people who have lent their name to the area, the homeland is much more than territory. The reverential, emotional attachment is reflected in such widely used descriptions as the native land, the fatherland, this sacred soil, the ancestral land, this hallowed place, the motherland, this blessed plot, land of our fathers, land where our fathers died, and, not least, the *home*land.

9. Conrad Brandt, Benjamin Schwartz, and John Fairbank, *A Documentary History of Chinese Communism* (London: Allen and Unwin, 1952), pp. 245–47.

10. See Robert King, *Minorities under Communism* (Cambridge, Mass.: Harvard University Press, 1973), p. 144; *New York Times*, September 1, 1975; and *Atlas* (February 1976), p. 19.

As concisely summed up in the nineteenth-century German phrase *Blut und Boden,* blood and soil become mixed in popular perceptions. Members of the homeland people are convinced that they possess an inalienable and exclusive proprietary title to the homeland. Nonmembers of the homeland may be tolerated or even encouraged as sojourners (consider the guest workers in Germany, for example), but they remain an alien presence in the eyes of the more indigenous element. The cry of "alien, go home!" can be raised at any time and can be aimed at compatriots as readily as at foreigners. To cite a few of the many current examples, the call of "Russian, go home!" has been heard in Estonia, Lithuania, and Uzbekistan; "Punjabi, go home!" in Baluchistan and Sind; "Frenchman, go home!" in Corsica; "Han, go home!" in (East) Turkestan; "Albanian, go home!" in Slovenia and Serbia; "Persian, Arab, and Turk, go home!" in Kurdistan; "Bengali, go home!" in Assam; "Castilian, go home!" in Euzkadi (Basqueland); and "Ethiopian, go home!" in both Tigre and the Ogaden district of Somaliland.

A people's sense of a plenary claim to a homeland is, of course, more dependent upon sentient than actual history, more dependent upon myth and popular perception than upon fact. In some cases, two peoples may possess conflicting claims to the same homeland. What to Israelis is "the homeland of the Jews" is part of Arabdom in Arab perceptions. Moreover, a relatively few generations may suffice to give rise to the *Blut und Boden* linkage. Thus the case of the Parti Quebecois for cultural and political autonomy—sloganized as *Maitres Chez Nous* ("Masters in our Home")—rests upon a primal sense of homeland rendered no less powerful by the fact that no Frenchman had resided in the region prior to the sixteenth century.

The patterns of attitudes and behaviors of people living within their homeland are significantly different from those of people living outside. An impressive number of studies conducted within the multihomeland Soviet Union confirm patterns observed elsewhere. The Soviets have discovered that residence within or without the homeland exerts a perceptible influence upon, inter alia, willingness to learn a second language, willingness to enter into interethnic marriage, the choice of ethnonational identity on the part of children of interethnic marriages, and attitudes toward members of other ethnonational groups.[11] Residents of the homeland manifest greater hostility toward other groups and greater resistance to acculturation and assimilation.

---

11. For a review of Soviet studies, see Walker Connor, *The National Question in Marxist-Leninist Theory and Strategy* (Princeton: Princeton University Press, 1984), chapter 11.

Nation-States, Multinational States, and Immigrant States

Although scholars commonly refer to all states as nation-states, the true nation-state, as its name implies, is that relatively rare phenomenon of a country that demonstrates a very high level of homogeneity from an ethnonational viewpoint—that is, a situation in which a nation (in the pristine sense of an ancestrally related people) has its own state. Contemporary examples of nation-states include Japan (99.4 percent Japanese), Poland (98 percent Polish), and Sweden (93 percent Swedish). In these cases, political and ethnonational borders closely coincide. In some instances, however, although a state might be quite homogeneous and therefore qualify as a nation-state, the homeland extends well beyond its borders. Such situations, referred to as irredentist, frequently give rise to a clamor for unifying the homeland.[12]

Easily the most common type of state is the multinational variety, whose population consists of at least two significant elements with different ethnonational backgrounds. As in the case of India and Nigeria, it may contain scores. The borders of a multinational state may coincide fairly closely with an ethnic homeland if the state's heterogeneity is due to the immigration of a nonhomeland people (Sri Lanka is an illustration). Far more typically, however, the multinational state contains several, or segments of several, homelands. Iran, for example, contains all of Persia and segments of Arabdom, Azerbaijan, Baluchistan, Kurdistan, and Turkmenia. The Soviet Union contains several homelands in their entirety (for example, Estonia, Ukraine, and Georgia), and segments of several others (Azerbaijan, Turkmenia, and Tadzhikistan).

The immigrant state is the rarest form of polity. It is a state essentially devoid of homelands, with a highly variegated population in terms of ethnonational ancestry. It is not disqualified if a small fraction of its area is composed of homelands within which dwell a small percentage of the population. The United States, for example, is clearly an immigrant state, despite the presence of American Indian and Eskimo homelands.

When analogizing concerning group behavior, it is dangerous to cross the dividing lines separating nation-states, multinational states, and immigrant states. Failure to distinguish the experiences of the immigrant state from the other two classifications has been a partic-

---

12. The desire of the Somali Democratic Republic to incorporate those parts of Somaliland currently within Djibouti, Ethiopia, and Kenya is a current case in point. For details, see the chapter in this volume by Myron Weiner.

ularly common and pernicious practice. Many reputable scholars have erroneously drawn upon the history of acculturation and assimilation of immigrant groups within the United States as a guide to the path that peoples ensconced in their own homelands within a multinational state could be anticipated to follow. Thus, they conclude that since Germans, Poles, and the like have become "Americans," Walloons and Flemings can be expected to become "Belgians," and Ibos and Hausa-Fulani to become "Nigerians."[13]

Such analogies are deficient on a number of grounds. The immigrant society, as noted, is a nonhomeland state, and the complex of attitudes and behavior of the population toward newcomers, although falling far short of "the Golden Rule," is qualitatively different from that of homeland peoples. There may be resistance to immigration, but it is not suckled by a broadly held, intuitive sense of a prehistoric and exclusive claim to the land. As set forth in the lyrics to a popular folk song, this land may indeed be "my land," but it is also true, as the lyrics add forthwith, that "this land is your land." Given the officially and popularly endorsed image of the society as "a nation of immigrants," the exclusion of individuals from any activity on the basis of ethnic heritage would necessarily undermine the society's most cherished self-held image. Thus, slavery and its aftermath, "Jim Crowism," being diametrically opposed to this image, had either to trigger the implosion of the image or to be vanquished by it. Neither could indefinitely coexist with the image; nor could various nativist movements, the application of prejudicial national origin quotas to immigrants, and Oriental exclusion acts.

The influence of the immigrant society's self-held image of a people composed of several strains is not restricted to the reception accorded to immigrants. It pertains as well to the attitudes of newcomers toward acculturation and assimilation. It is one thing, for example, for a member of the Korean minority in Japan to contemplate Nipponization and quite another for a Korean-American to contemplate Americanization. The latter can be undertaken with one's emotional memory bank intact, because the new identity is ethnically neutral. Americanization does not require one to deny or hide his or her ancestry. There is nothing inconsistent between Americanization and pre-American national ancestry. The same

---

13. Karl Deutsch and Alfred Cobban are among the better known scholars to have fallen prey to this faulty analogy. For details, see Walker Connor, "Self-Determination: The New Phase," *World Politics*, vol. 20 (October 1967), pp. 30–53; and "Nation-Building or Nation-Destroying?" *World Politics*, vol. 24 (April 1972), pp. 319–55.

cannot be said for Nipponization. Moreover, as Milton Yinger notes
in his chapter in this book, Americanization is a graduated process,
a continuum characterized by "more-or-less" rather than "either-or."
The far more traumatic, clear-cut decision of the above example to
either retain one's identity as Korean *or* to attempt to assume the
identity of a Nipponese need not be faced. Indeed, Americanization
for most affected people has been more the result of a barely perceived
daily process than the result of a premeditated decision.

Implications for the Comparative Study of Mexican-Americans

It is apparent from the foregoing that there are at least two
analytical frameworks within which the Mexican-American community might be placed. First, Mexican-Americans might be viewed as
a geographic extension of a Mexican nation, separated from the
larger segment by the U.S.-Mexican border. In such case, the framework will be global, with the analyst drawing on the experiences of
several peoples in Africa and Eurasia who are similarly divided among
two or more states. Second, the Mexican-American community might
be viewed as an immigrant ethnic element within the framework of
the United States, with analogies drawn from the experiences of
German-Americans, French Canadian Americans, and the like. The
two approaches need not be mutually exclusive. When properly
conditioned by an appreciation of the unique features of the Mexican-
American community (and this community's variance from each of
these ideal models is substantial), both approaches promise added
insight concerning the Mexican-American community, and both
approaches are employed in the following papers. However, the
relative validity of either approach will be materially affected by the
group's ethnonational self-perception.

A Mexican Nation?

As noted, the first approach would conceptualize the Mexican-
Americans as an extension of the Mexican nation. But this presupposes
the existence of a Mexican nation, a presupposition that requires
examination.

Mexico is a mestizo-state, that is to say, a state in which people
of joint European-Indian ancestry form the politically dominant
element. The mestizo-states of Latin America have traditionally posed
severe problems of classification and analysis to those engaged in the

comparative study of ethnonationalism. If the ethnonational image that is commonly endorsed and propagated today by the governments of these states were to approximate the self-held view of their entire populations, these states would merit classification as nation-states. According to the image, a new breed or race has come forth from the melding of the European (a near synonym for Castilian) and the Indian, a breed that is not less self-perceptively homogeneous because of its antecedents than is, say, the English nation because of its Angle, Briton, Norman, and Saxon inputs. Thus throughout Latin America what is celebrated in the United States as Columbus Day is honored as *El Dia de la Raza*, "the Day of the Race," or advent day for the mestizo race.[14]

The image of its populace propagated by a mestizo-state's government is therefore one in which the various indigenous Indian peoples have been fused with one another and with lesser numbers of Spanish people to form a basically undifferentiated whole. The image further maintains that from this homogeneous base has evolved a nation that is coterminous with the state—that is, a Guatemalan, Peruvian, or Mexican nation.[15]

The image of a Mexican nation is blemished by a number of contrary considerations, however, To begin with, there is a serious question concerning the degree to which the indigenous peoples have surrendered earlier ethnonational identities to a Mexican *mestizaje*. Estimates of the percentage of Mexico's population represented by Indians, in contradistinction to mestizos, range from 5 to 44 percent.[16]

---

14. The principal inspiration for the notion of a new race was a book written by Jose Vasconcelos, *La Raza Cosmica* (Barcelona: Agencia Mundial de Libreria, 1925). For a sympathetic account of Vasconcelos's ideas on the new race, see John Haddox, *Vasconcelos of Mexico* (Austin: University of Texas Press, 1967), pp. 53–71. For highly critical accounts, see Carlos Rangel, *The Latin Americans: Their Love-Hate Relationship with the United States* (New York: Harcourt Brace Jovanovich, 1976), particularly pp. 91–99; and Leo Grebler, Joan Moore, and Ralph Guzman, *The Mexican-American People* (New York: Free Press, 1970), pp. 379–80.

15. See, for example, the speech of Rios Montt, former president of Guatemala, in *Foreign Broadcast Information Service*, vol. 26 (July 1982), p. P8: "We Guatemalans . . . are a dark-skinned people. We are not Anglo-Saxons. . . . Ours is an Indian country. This is our nation. . . . Our Indian is more of a man when he works more, when he can do his job better, when he can do two jobs better. We should learn to be his kind of man, a Guatemalan man, not a gringo or Russian but Guatemalan."

16. See *Area Handbook for Mexico*, 2d ed., Department of the Army Pamphlet 550-79 (Washington, D.C.: U.S. Government Printing Office, 1975), p. 88. A major contributing element to the broad range of estimates is that contrary to the conceptualization of the mestizo as a new cosmic race, mestizo often has more of a cultural than an ethnonational basis. Indigenous peoples have become mestizos over time by adopting the Spanish language, non-Indian garb, and possibly a Spanish surname. The reverse procedure is also possible.

A popular source describes the ethnic composition of Mexico as 10 percent Caucasian, 55 percent mestizo, and 29 percent American Indian.[17] Whatever the correct figure, the number of Indians is certainly substantial.

It is also certain that the Indians remain the objects of severe discrimination. Contrary to the myth of *la raza cósmica* as the happy comingling of two equally esteemed ethnic stalks, the Indian is popularly perceived and treated as a lower species. As one anthropologist who has done field work among the Indians of Mexico has noted: "Generally speaking, Ladinos [mestizos] consider Indians as inferior beings, or children from whom it is proper to demand subordination and obedience. They believe that they themselves represent the 'superior culture'—another *raza* (race). Until recently only Ladinos were permitted to mount a horse. . . . Intermarriage between Ladinos and Indians is likewise exceptional and looked upon with great disgust."[18]

In the words of another scholar: "The Indian is someone who is denied recognition as a full member of the human community, one who is thought to be naturally inferior."[19] Still another observes, "The Indio identity is strongly stigmatized as 'backwards' and 'inferior.' "[20]

Many Mexican mestizos have in fact come to deny that *la raza* incorporates any Indian blood. As one observer concluded from his field interviews and observations: "Originally, the term 'Mestizo' was used to refer to the Hispanized Indians or those of Spanish and Indian blood, or 'mixed blood.' But now the Mestizos claim, sometimes too vehemently, that they have no hereditary connections with Indian ancestors. . . . This claim is often expressed by their use of the label *raza blanca* (white race) to refer to themselves."[21]

And a handbook on Mexico notes that mestizo culture "values 'white blood' and deprecates Indian ancestry."[22] It adds: "Perceived

---

17. *The World Almanac and Book of Facts 1983* (New York: Newspaper Enterprise Associations, 1982), p. 544.

18. Henning Siverts, "Ethnic Stability and Boundary Dynamics in Southern Mexico," in Fredrik Barth, ed., *Ethnic Groups and Boundaries: The Social Organization of Culture Differences* (London: George Allen and Unwin, 1970), p. 110.

19. Julian Pitt-Rivers, "Race in Latin America: The Concept of 'Raza'," *European Journal of Sociology*, vol. 14 (1973), pp. 12–30. Reprinted in John Stone, ed., *Race, Ethnicity, and Social Change* (North Scituate, Mass.: Duxbury Press, 1977). The citation can be found on p. 320.

20. Edwin Almirol, "Economic Strategies and Ethnic Alternatives," *Human Relations*, vol. 31 (1978), p. 368.

21. Ibid., p. 364.

22. *Area Handbook for Mexico*, p. 103. This fixation with blood recalls a much older obsession of Spaniards with what was once termed *limpieza de sangre* (purity of blood).

racial difference is the oldest and most tenacious element affecting interethnic relationships. In some ways it is also the most pervasive. Rural ladinos and mestizos distinguish themselves from their Indian neighbors through ascribed superiority of race, blood, and genealogy. They attribute certain superior cultural qualities to their white race and blood, and they undervalue the Indian's dark skin and alleged mixture of races. Mestizos perceive cultural differences as a consequence of natural inferiority on the part of the Indian, and from the Indian point of view they represent distinctions that are natural and indelible, based on biological heredity."[23]

With Indian blood and heritage held in such low esteem, visible gradations of admixture become important within the mestizo group itself. Not just Indians, but mestizos with more evident Indian characteristics, become the target of prejudice.[24] This tendency toward further self-differentiation provides a constant reminder to its members that the mestizo community is not per se a homogeneous, ancestrally related national group.

In this setting of "us-them" cleavage between mestizo and Indian, the Indian communities within Mexico cause that country to more closely resemble a multinational state than a nation-state. And in passing, it is worth noting that in a series of other mestizo-states, Indian peoples have been adopting an increasingly assertive political stance. Antimestizo sentiments on the part of Indian peoples are already a key element in the guerrilla struggles within Guatemala

---

It was popularized during the period of the Inquisition to differentiate the faithful from the infidel Moors and Jews. It was later employed in the New World to differentiate those of pure Spanish (Castilian) ancestry from those with American Indian background. Its more recent adoption (in content, if not in name) by members of a cosmic race, defined as an admixture of two races, in order to deny any ancestral connection to one of the two constituent races is indeed a paradox, but the sort of psychological paradox with which issues involving ethnonational identity abound.

23. Ibid., p. 104. For two other accounts of the prejudice practiced by Mexican mestizos toward Indian compatriots, see Pablo Gonzales Casanova, *Democracy in Mexico* (London: Oxford University Press, 1970), pp. 94–103; and Rodolfo Stavenhagen, *Between Underdevelopment and Revolution: A Latin American Perspective* (New Delhi: Abhinav Publications, 1981), particularly p. 65. Given all the evidence and numerous accounts of the ubiquity of this discrimination, the glancing references to it in the case study of Mexico found in Jose Dominguez et al., *Enhancing Global Human Rights* (New York: McGraw-Hill, 1979) on pp. 69–71 and 83–84 are surprisingly meager.

24. See, for example, Joan Moore, *Mexican Americans*, 2d ed. (Englewood Cliffs, N.J.: Prentice Hall, 1976), p. 114: "(Thus the myth of 'pure blood' was not invented in the United States.) Mexicans of mixed Spanish-Indian blood or of pure Indian ancestry have long suffered from discrimination and exploitation in their own country." A mestizo with strong Indian features is apt to be sarcastically referred to as an *indio revestado,* (a "redressed Indian"), that is to say, one who has simply changed his clothes but cannot thereby hide his non-Latino Indianness.

and Peru, and threaten to become so within Bolivia, Ecuador, and other Latin American states.[25] Thus, the so-called mestizo-states are experiencing the same challenges to their legitimacy as are multinational states elsewhere.

Such popular repugnance toward Indians and things that are Indian would at least superficially appear to be in sharp contrast to the official *indigenista* policies of several mestizo-states. In theory, *indigenismo* stresses the Indian stalk of the mestizo's twin heritage. And in the form of anthropological and archeological museums, the graphic arts (particularly murals and statuary), and the restoration of ancient ruins, pre-Columbian indigenous culture has indeed been promoted by a number of governments. However, far from fostering the society's adoption of Indian culture or even fostering a system of cultural pluralism, *indigenista* policies have sought the hastened integration and acculturation of the Indian peoples into the mestizo culture. The motto of Mexico's National Indian Institute, *"Redimir al indio es integrar la patria"* ("To redeem the Indian is to integrate the Fatherland"), is a case in point. What is intended by the Indian's redemption is his "civilizing" or Hispanization, as has been made clear by the institute's director:

> The purpose is still integration and in no way to develop in [the Indians] an ethnic consciousness that separates them from the rest of the nation. . . . The indigenous societies—rural and isolated within their self-sufficient economy and technological backwardness—try to conserve modes of life which they consider acceptable, but which constitute an obstacle to the integration of a common nationality and nation. . . . If the regional and parochial populations of Mexico do not share in a national consciousness, the changes which they experience as the inevitable consequence of their contact with modern culture could bring them—as has happened in the nations we mention—to the organization of a panindian movement that could lead them to the formation of a second nationality. As such a goal is contrary to goals of national formation the education for integration carried out among the Indian population should complement the education of the dominant population.[26]

---

25. The Maoist *Sendero Luminoso* (Shining Path) movement within Peru is Indian (Quechuan) based. For the proclamation of a movement dedicated to the obliteration of the Bolivian-Peruvian-Ecuadorian borders and the establishment of a state along the geographic lines of the old Inca Empire, see *Keesing's Contemporary Archives* (1982), p. 31308. Demands for increased autonomy have recently been pressed by a number of Indian peoples within Panama, and separatist/autonomous aspirations on the part of the Miskito Indians have become an important element in the Nicaragua saga. In the literature that these movements have spawned, the Day of the Race is termed "the Day of Misfortune."

26. The statements were made by Gonzalo Aguirre Beltran during 1972 and 1973 and are cited in Alicia Barabas and Miguel Bartolome, *Hydraulic Development and Ethnocide: The Mazatec and Chinantec People of Oaxaca, Mexico* (Copenhagen: International Work Group for Indigenous Affairs, 1973), IWGIA Document 15, pp. 16–17.

Indigenismo therefore becomes a euphemism for acculturation and assimilation of the Indians. As one scholar has noted with regard to Peru: "*Indigenismo* is an ideology for *Mestizos.*"[27] Whereas colonial powers were often accused of pitting one ethnonational group against another as part of a strategy of divide and rule, this stratagem of trying to convince the Indian peoples that they are part of a larger cosmic race might be termed a strategy of unite and rule. But, as noted, the growth of Indian consciousness and movements strongly suggests that this strategy is not succeeding and that Mexico, as other mestizo states generally, is taking on the coloration of a multinational entity.[28]

Yet another body of evidence that blurs the image of the Mexican people as sharing a strong sense of nationhood and as perceiving the Mexican state as the political expression of that nation consists of attitudinal surveys that disclose a remarkable lack of identification among the Mexican people with the Mexican state and its political institutions. One such study disclosed that more than one-third of the population was not at all affected by the Mexican state apparatus and only a tenth considered themselves as participants in the system.[29] Moreover, in Almond and Verba's highly publicized comparative study, fully two-thirds of the respondents stated that the central government had no effect whatsoever upon their daily life.[30] As was generally true of all of the case studies in the Almond and Verba book, the ethnic factor was simply ignored, but it can safely be assumed that the Indian peoples are among the most alienated.[31]

A portrait of Mexico as a nation-state would therefore be a highly overdrawn one. Some unknown percentage of mestizos unquestionably do consider themselves part of a Mexican nation in the sense of

---

27. François Bourricaud, as cited by Pitt-Rivers, "Race in Latin America," p. 323. See also Stavenhagen, *Between Underdevelopment and Revolution*, particularly p. 67.

28. See Rodolfo Stavenhagen, "Indian Ethnic Movements and State Policies in Latin America," paper prepared for the VII World Conference of the World Future Studies Federation, Stockholm, Sweden, June 6-8, 1982.

29. *Area Handbook for Mexico*, p. 226.

30. Gabriel Almond and Sidney Verba, *The Civic Culture* (Boston: Little, Brown & Co., 1965), p. 46.

31. A recent criticism of the Almond and Verba work states that, if anything, the study painted a more homogeneous picture of Mexico than was warranted because its sample did not reflect "the pronounced differences among regions in that country in terms of economic development, land-tenure patterns, occupational structure, *ethnicity*, religiosity, political participation, relationship with the federal government, and other dimensions." See Ann Craig and Wayne Cornelius, "Political Culture in Mexico: Continuities and Revisionist Interpretations," in Gabriel Almond and Sidney Verba, eds., *The Civic Culture Revisited* (Boston: Little, Brown & Co., 1980), p. 337 (emphasis added).

an ancestrally related group. But the Indian component certainly does not. Nor do a large but incalculable percentage of mestizos who are dissuaded from identifying themselves with a Mexican nation because of commonly encountered denigration of their ethnic roots. By definition, such attitudes characterize a *trans*national, not an *intra*national relationship. An inkling of the growing significance of interethnic relations within Mexico was offered by the current president of Mexico during the 1982 presidential campaign when, in a "first" for Mexican leaders, he publicly acknowledged that Mexico was a multinational state.[32] His action suggested that dissension among the Indian peoples had become too pronounced to be any longer hidden or ignored.

A Homeland People?

Refocusing on our primary concern—those people of Mexican background living north of the U.S.-Mexican border—raises the question of the degree to which Mexican-Americans perceive of themselves as living within an extension of the Mexican homeland. There are two quite different, although not contradictory, cases that are made for such a transborder homeland. One is mythological in nature, holding that what is now the southwestern United States was once *Aztlán*, the legendary original homeland of the ancient Aztecs. Belief that a particular territory constituted the original cradle of one's people is the more powerful for being mythical and unprovable, and the militant Chicano movement of the late 1960s and early 1970s made liberal use of this emotion-laden term when attempting to raise ethnic consciousness among Mexican-Americans.[33]

The other justification for declaring the region part of a Mexican homeland involves the fact that people from Mexico began to settle in the area in the late sixteenth century and were there before the coming of "Americans." It is probably not important that the only numerically large settlement before the U.S. annexation had been in what is now New Mexico and that many of the early settlers subsequently moved south of the newly established border.[34] Nor is it of vital significance that these early Mexican settlements testify that

---

32. Stavenhagen, "Indian Ethnic Movements," p. 12.
33. Its use extended to entitling a journal *Aztlán*.
34. The most commonly employed estimates hold that at the time of U.S. annexation, there were approximately 60,000 Mexicans in present-day New Mexico, but only 7,500 in California, 5,000 in Texas, and 1,000 in Arizona. These statistics are customarily based upon those first offered by Carey McWilliams, *North from Mexico* (Philadelphia: J.B. Lippincott, 1949).

Mexicans were not native to the area and that the area could therefore not be their homeland.[35] Perceptions are again the key, and some Mexican-Americans perceive that they have a plenary right to the land because it was part of their heritage before it was wrested away by the invaders.[36]

Mexican-Americans are, of course, intently aware of this aspect of the region's history. Daily reminders of previous Mexican ownership abound in the plentiful presence of Spanish place names (El Paso, Los Angeles, San Antonio), Spanish names for the region's outstanding natural phenomena (Sierra Nevada Mountains, Colorado River), and examples of early Spanish and Mexican architecture. This knowledge that the region was once Mexican has a psychological dimension, inspiring a special sense of a historically derived right to live in the region, a right that immigrants from an overseas ancestral homeland cannot feel (such as those of Swedish descent living within Minnesota, with its plethora of names derived from the American Indians for places and natural phenomena. One manifestation of this feeling among Mexican-Americans is the popular eschewing of the adjective *illegal* to refer to those who have crossed the border without U.S. authorization. Whereas the expression *illegal immigrants* is most commonly used by others, Mexican-Americans have tended to describe such migrants as merely *undocumented*.

Despite this special historic connection, however, there is ample evidence that most Mexican-Americans do not feel that they possess a plenary and exclusive right to this territory, which has been described above as the hallmark of a homeland people. Separatist sentiments and cries of "Anglos, go home!" have been rare and have failed to elicit broad support. Even the militantly ethnonational party *La Raza Unida*, which realized some highly localized electoral successes in the early 1970s, projected its goals within a continuing U.S. framework. As a position paper noted, the party "must symbolize the creation of

---

35. The approximately 70,000 Mexican settlers were outnumbered by some 120,000 American Indians of the area. See Moore, *Mexican Americans*, p. 12.

36. Steiner, for example, states flatly that the Mexican-Americans are native to the area: "One of the distinguishing characteristics of the Mexican American people is that it is one of the two indigenous minorities; the other being the American Indians. The saying is: We did not come to America, America came to us!" See Stan Steiner, *The Mexican Americans* (London: Minority Rights Group, 1979), p. 14. One author has suggested that the area was not so much conquered as it was lost through neglect. He draws on an extensive body of primary and secondary literature to conclude that Mexico City's disinterest caused the people dwelling in the area to perceive the United States as a more responsive alternative. See David Weber, *The Mexican Frontier, 1821–1846: The American Southwest under Mexico* (Albuquerque: University of New Mexico Press, 1982).

a nation within a nation, a spiritual unification for effective action of all persons of Mexican descent in the United States."[37] The concept of national self-determination was part of the party's program but, as described by two students of the party's history, it was "self-determination interpreted not as secession from the United States but as the gaining of control of existing institutions and the creation of new ones where necessary."[38]

As noted earlier, studies conducted in a number of other societies establish that residence within the homeland tends to buttress the maintenance of ethnonational identity. But group self-identification studies establish that most people who, or whose ancestors, came to the United States from present-day Mexico do not consider themselves to be Mexican. In three careful surveys carried out in the mid-1970s, respondents were asked the most appropriate group designation for themselves. The *combined totals* for those replying Mexican, Mexicano, or Chicano were only 16 percent, 28.5 percent, and 31 percent of all interviewees in the respective surveys.[39] All other respondents identified themselves either as Mexican-American or by a group nomenclature that contained no reference whatsoever to Mexican background. Similarly, when offered the opportunity in the 1980 census to designate themselves as "Mexican, Mexican-American, [or] Chicano," nearly 1.25 million people living within the five states that are commonly considered to constitute the homeland (Arizona, California, Colorado, New Mexico, and Texas) opted instead for a category ("Spanish/Hispanic") which denied any hint of Mexican ancestry.[40]

---

37. Cited in Carlos Munoz and Mario Barrera, "La Raza Unida Party and the Chicano Student Movement in California," *Social Science Journal*, vol. 19 (April 1982), p. 113.

38. Ibid., p. 111. For additional avowals that the Chicano movement, including La Raza Unida party, was integrationist, see Fred Cervantes, "Chicanos as a Post-Colonial Minority: Some Questions Concerning the Adequacy of the Paradigm of Internal Colonialism," pp. 129, 130, 131, and 132; and Tatcho Mindiola, "Marxism and the Chicano Movement: Preliminary Remarks," pp. 179 and 185; both in Reynaldo F. Macías, ed., *Perspectivas en Chicano Studies I* (Los Angeles: National Association of Chicano Social Science, 1975). Both writers note that there were those who were unhappy with this integrationist posture.

39. In the same order: Philip Lampe, "Ethnic Self-Referent and the Assimilation of Mexican Americans," *Journal of Comparative Sociology*, vol. 19 (September-December 1978), p. 262; John Garcia, "Yo Soy Mexicano . . .: Self-Identity and Sociodemographic Correlates," *Social Science Quarterly*, vol. 62 (March 1981), p. 90; and Nicholas Lovrich and Otwin Marenin, "A Comparison of Black and Mexican American Voters in Denver," *Western Political Quarterly*, vol. 29 (June 1976), p. 291. Geographic differences and differences in the questions (specific categories versus free choice) skew the results.

40. Department of Commerce, *1980 Census: Ancestry*, p. 9 and table 3 pp. 28 et seq. For additional comment on these "Spanish/Hispanics," see the discussion below under the heading "An Ethnic Community within the U.S. Context?"

The matter of group self-referent is extremely important, for research has established that employing *American* as part of one's group name is a good index of behavior. Those who use it are more apt to have a positive view toward integration into the society and a more positive view toward other ethnic groups.[41] In other words, use of the term *Mexican-American* is correlated with behavior and attitudes that are the opposite of those that comparative studies have found associated with residence in a homeland. And, again, most of the community under study refer to themselves as Mexican-Americans, while a substantial number reject all reference to a Mexican heritage.

Even the percentage figures for that small fraction who identify themselves as Mexican or Mexicano may not necessarily possess ethnonational overtones but may be analogous to Ibos or Hausas identifying themselves as Nigerian when outside of the country, or persons of Flemish or Walloon background reporting themselves as Belgian in the U.S. census. In this context it is pertinent to note that when asked to choose from a list of attributes those aspects of the Mexican heritage they would like to preserve in their children, only 5 percent of the respondents in Los Angeles and only 3 percent in San Antonio selected "identity as Mexican" and only 2 percent and 1 percent, respectively, selected "patriotism, Mexican nationalism."[42] Moreover, employing a substantial data base, John Garcia has determined that more than half of the U.S. minority who describe themselves as "Mexican" (56.2 percent) and three-quarters of those

---

41. Lampe, "Ethnic Self-Referent," particularly p. 267. The difference in attitudinal patterns is not just between those who identify themselves as Mexican-American and those who identify themselves as Mexican or Mexicano. Some rather sharp differences can be found between self-identified "Mexican-Americans" and "Chicanos." As Lampe has more recently reported: "Finally, differences have been found to exist between those who self-identify as Mexican Americans and those who self-identify as Chicanos, with the latter exhibiting significantly more anti-Anglo feelings and anti-establishment orientation in addition to greater anger, hostility and militancy." Philip Lampe, "Ethnic Labels: Naming or Name Calling?" *Ethnic and Racial Studies*, vol. 5 (October 1982), p. 546.

42. Grebler et al., *Mexican-American People*, p. 384. "Spanish language" (51 percent and 32 percent) was the most popular choice, followed by "manners and customs" (33 percent and 38 percent). Significantly, 15 percent and 28 percent stated that they wish to preserve nothing of the Mexican heritage in their children. The interviews were conducted during 1965 and 1966. In 1972 Ambrecht and Pachon reinterviewed 51 of the original 759 respondents in the Los Angeles area. See Biliana Ambrecht and Harry Pachon, "Ethnic Political Mobilization in a Mexican American Community: An Exploratory Study of East Los Angeles 1965-1972," *Western Political Quarterly*, vol. 27 (September 1974), p. 508. They found an increase in what they termed "Mexican identity, culture, pride" (21 percent). However, given (1) the small sample, (2) the addition of culture and pride to "identity as Mexican," and (3) the failure to include the category of "patriotism, Mexican nationalism," there appears to be a lack of comparability between the two studies.

identifying themselves as "Mexicano" (74.6 percent) were born south of the U.S.-Mexican border.[43] And newly arrived members of any group would be those most expected to describe themselves as German, Chinese, Mexican, or what have you.[44]

Data on intermarriage further attest to the weakness of a homeland psychology. Comparative studies, as noted, disclose a resistance to intermarriage on the part of those living within a homeland. But a 1965–66 survey found that 82 percent of Mexican-Americans living within San Antonio and 88 percent living within Los Angeles did not frown upon intermarriage. The credence of these figures is lent powerful support by increasingly high rates of group intermarriage. Geography and urban or rural domicile exert great influence, but the rate of intermarriage in nearly every locale, and most assuredly the rate for Mexican-Americans as a whole, is well above that normally associated with an endogamous group. For example, in San Antonio the percentage of exogamous marriages among Mexican-Americans progressively increased from 17 percent in 1940–55 to 27 percent in 1973; in Albuquerque, the percentage went from 22 percent in 1945 to 48 percent in 1967;[45] in Los Angeles the exogamy rate jumped from 17 percent in 1924–33 to 40 percent in 1963 and has remained slightly above 50 percent in California as a whole for the past two decades.[46] As with other groups in the

43. Garcia, "Yo Soy Mexicano," p. 92. By contrast, 94.3 percent of those identifying themselves as Mexican American and 99.1 percent of those selecting "Other Spanish" were born in the United States. Those replying *Chicano* were also overwhelmingly U.S.-born (96.3 percent). However, those identifying themselves as Chicanos accounted for the smallest percentage of the total sample (4.0 percent, as contrasted with 20.1 percent responding *Mexican* and 4.4 percent responding *Mexicano*). Moreover, there is a close association between Chicano identity and membership in La Raza Unida party, and, as we have seen, that party, although militantly ethnonational, defined its goals within a U.S. context.

44. Given the high percentages of foreign born among those reporting themselves as Mexican or Mexicano, it is also probable that the sample contains a number of undocumented migrants who consider their stay in the United States as temporary. Studies of undocumented workers and data gathered by the U.S. Immigration Service record a great deal of circular migration between the two countries.

45. A subsequent study in 1971 indicated a sharp drop to (the still very high rate of) 39 percent. However, as later studies in other Mexican-American communities have indicated, the 1971–73 period represented a deviation from the norm. This was a period of intense Chicano militancy, particularly among those of marrying age. On this point, see Alverado Valdez, "Recent Increases in Intermarriage by Mexican American Males: Bexar County, Texas, from 1971 to 1980," *Social Science Quarterly*, vol. 64 (March 1984), p. 139.

46. For a helpful summary of the findings of a number of intermarriage studies, see Edward Murguia, *Chicano Intermarriage: A Theoretical and Empirical Study* (San Antonio: Trinity University Press, 1982), pp. 48–49. The lowest figures recorded have been for Hidalgo County in Texas, a nonmetropolitan area in a state with a traditionally

United States, studies of Mexican-Americans show that exogamy increases significantly with each subsequent generation. Given the fact that the Mexican-American community has a large percentage of new arrivals and that the influx continues, these rates of exogamy become even more striking.[47]

The pattern may be duplicated with regard to language maintenance. Basing his study on language use in Los Angeles, David Lopez has concluded that when the impact of continuing mass migration is controlled for, the rate of attrition in language maintenance is comparable to the attrition rate experienced by earlier European immigrants: "The inescapable conclusion is that were it not for new arrivals from Mexico, Spanish would disappear from Los Angeles nearly as rapidly as most European immigrant languages vanished from cities in the East."[48] Minimally, it can be said that the intermarriage and language maintenance patterns of Mexican-Americans do not reflect those associated with homeland peoples.

Yet another indication of a lack of consciousness of homeland is the increasing tendency for Mexican-Americans to disperse widely outside the five states that are generally described as comprising the homeland. The numerical size of the California and Texas components, which alone account for 26 percent of all Mexican-Americans, tends to hide the scope of this diffusion. Today, Mexican-Americans in Illinois alone more than double the number in either Colorado or New Mexico and roughly equal the numbers in Arizona. There are now important pockets of Mexican-Americans in such geographically dispersed states as Michigan, Washington, Florida, Indiana, and Kansas. At the time of the 1980 census, more than a million Mexican-Americans (15 percent of the total) were living outside of the five southwestern states, and the trend was definitely in the direction of greater dispersal.[49]

---

higher level of intergroup tensions than California or New Mexico. However, even here exogamous marriages nearly doubled from 5 to 9 percent during the 1960s. For a recent study of intermarriage not covered by the table in Murguia, see Valdez, "Recent Increases in Intermarriage."

47. For comments on the impact of generation, see Grebler et al., *Mexican-American People*, pp. 409–10. Murguia, *Chicano Intermarriage*, detects some leveling off in the rate of intermarriage, but this perception is seemingly due to a disregard for the closely interrelated phenomena of intergenerational differences and the continuing huge influx of first-generation immigrants. For additional commentary on intermarriage, see the chapter by Milton Yinger in this volume.

48. David Lopez, "Chicano Language Loyalty in an Urban Setting," *Sociology and Social Research*, vol. 62 (January 1978), p. 276.

49. All the figures would be altered if those who described themselves in the 1980 census as "Spanish/Hispanic" were included in the calculations.

A final consideration concerning the image of a homeland people concerns the views that Mexican-Americans hold toward further immigration across the U.S.-Mexican border. In fact, these attitudes show little deviation from those of the U.S. populace as a whole. According to Gallup, 75 percent of people of Hispanic descent agree that the hiring of undocumented workers should be decreed an illegal act, and precisely the same percentage support a proposal requiring citizens and legal (documented) residents to carry internal "passports" that would have to be presented as a prerequisite for employment.[50] The corresponding figures for the entire population were 79 percent and 66 percent. Another poll recorded that 60 percent of all Hispanics within the United States and 66 percent of those Hispanics holding U.S. citizenship were in favor of "penalties and fines for employers who hire illegal aliens."[51] Spokesmen for Mexican-American organizations have generally lobbied against such legislation, but a 1984 poll indicated that even the leaders of the Mexican-American community were badly split on the issue, with 40 percent favoring sanctions against employers of undocumented migrants.[52]

Overall, then, the data show that Mexican-Americans do not broadly conceptualize themselves as a homeland people. Mexican-Americans are unquestionably aware that the southwestern United States was once part of Mexico, and this awareness tends to lead to a feeling that people from Mexico consequently possess a claim to the land—a claim that, because of its longer history, is superior to any claim that could be made by someone of English, German, or Irish descent. But judging by their attitudes and behavior, most Mexican-Americans perceive this claim more in chronological and historic-legal terms than in the spiritual-mythological terms of an ancestrally created linkage between blood and soil.[53] While even the former type of claim has psychological and emotional dimensions,

---

50. *New York Times*, November 15, 1983. Although the report did not further break down "respondents of Hispanic descent" in the 1980 census, Mexican-Americans accounted for nearly three-quarters (72 percent) of all people of Hispanic background who furnished a country of origin for themselves or their ancestors. (Extrapolated from Department of Commerce, *1980 Census: Ancestry*, p. 14.)

51. See the letter by the executive director of the Federation for American Immigration Reform, in "Letters to the Editor," *New York Times*, May 7, 1984.

52. *Wall Street Journal*, June 11, 1984.

53. Thus, some of the more publicized and bitter episodes arising from ancient claims to the land by Mexican-Americans have been predicated upon the legality of centuries-old land grants from the Spanish and Mexican authorities, rather than upon claims to a homeland. See, for example, the article entitled "Ethnic Tensions Rise in New Mexico after Arson," *New York Times*, July 16, 1982.

the data demonstrate that it is vitally different from the latter in the patterns of attitudes and behavior to which it gives rise.

A much smaller percentage of Mexican-Americans, some incalculable fraction of that minority of the community who identify themselves as Mexican or Mexicano, do conceive of themselves as an extension of a Mexican nation. In addition, an unknown percentage of the undocumented migrants unquestionably think of themselves as Mexican. The undocumented element represents a not insignificant consideration. Given the present U.S. government's estimate of some 3.5 to 6 million undocumented aliens, these people possibly account for from 37 to 51 percent of all people of Mexican background currently within the United States.[54] (If the sometimes-encountered figure of 12 million undocumented aliens were used, they would account for two-thirds of the total Mexican-American population.)[55] Nevertheless, no evidence was encountered to contradict the conclusion of Rodolfo de la Garza that "though they feel strong cultural ties to Mexico, Chicanos overall feel almost no political attachment to Mexico."[56]

An Ethnic Community within the U.S. Context?

Aside from that fraction of Mexican-Americans who consider themselves a homeland people, can one comparatively treat the remainder as equivalent to other ethnically defined immigrant groups, such as the Polish-Americans? Polish-Americans, of course, conceptualize themselves as ancestrally related. By contrast, many people who are treated in the literature as Mexican-Americans emphatically deny any Mexican ancestry, insisting that they are of purely Spanish (by which is usually meant Castilian) ancestry. Many of these people trace their history back to the earlier settler families in the Southwest.

---

54. For a statement by Attorney General William French Smith to the effect that during 1983 an additional 500,000 illegal aliens were expected to join the 3.5 to 6.0 million already here, see the *Christian Science Monitor,* March 1, 1983.

55. These estimates are based on the assumption that Mexican-Americans account for the lion's share of undocumented immigrants. It is also based upon an assumption of some 5.5 million Mexican-Americans who are citizens or documented residents. The latter figure was derived by subtracting the 2,047,000 illegal immigrants who were counted in the 1980 census from the census figure of 7,692,619 Mexican-Americans. For the source of the 2,047,000 figure, see "Estimates of Aliens Baffle U.S.," *New York Times,* June 19, 1983. Again, these calculations do not consider those who identified themselves as "Spanish/Hispanic" in the 1980 census.

56. Rodolfo de la Garza, "Chicano-Mexican Relations: A Framework for Research," *Social Science Quarterly,* vol. 63 (March 1982), p. 121; see also his "Chicanos and U.S. Foreign Policy: The Future of Chicano-Mexican Relations," *Western Political Quarterly,* vol. 33 (December 1980), pp. 571-82.

Apparently vexed by this renunciation of Mexican ancestry, a number of writers have taken pains to establish that only a small handful of families can legitimately make such a claim. But this type of criticism again ignores the fact that in matters of group identity, it is the perception and not the fact that shapes attitudes and behavior. If people delude themselves into believing that they are not of Mexican descent, they will be deaf to calls in its name.

The 1980 census indicates that the number of people shunning a claim to Mexican ancestry is quite substantial. In addition to the categories of "Mexican, Mexican-American, Chicano" and "Spanish/ Hispanic," the census made allowance for people to declare themselves Argentinean, Bolivian, Chilean, Colombian, Costa Rican, Cuban, Dominican, Ecuadoran, Guatemalan, Honduran, Nicaraguan, Panamanian, Peruvian, Puerto Rican, Salvadoran, Spaniard, Uruguayan, and Venezuelan. It is therefore safe to assume that those who opted for the "Spanish/Hispanic" category were largely those who are customarily grouped statistically with Mexican-Americans but who prefer to stress a pure Spanish, non-Mexican heritage. As indicated in table 1, those who spurned the offered category of "Mexican, Mexican-American, [or] Chicano" in favor of "Spanish/Hispanic" accounted for more than 15 percent of those customarily grouped with Mexican-Americans. More than 500,000 "Hispanics" in California alone denied any Mexican ancestry. In Colorado, those who chose "Spanish/Hispanic" were nearly as numerous as those indicating a Mexican background. And in New Mexico, Hispanics denying Mexican roots substantially outnumbered those who acknowledged them.

It can further be assumed that many people who chose the "Mexican, Mexican-American, Chicano" category were indicating thereby a country of ancestral origin, rather than an ethnonational unit. It has been shown that Mexico does not contain an ethnically homogeneous population and that, from a combination of choice and rebuff, Indians and dark-skinned mestizos have maintained a sense of identity distinct from that of the dominant group. Not surprisingly, these same considerations play a role north of the border.[57] One is seriously handicapped in pursuing this matter, however, by an almost total absence of data, for, as Carlos Arce has noted, "The function and impact of color and race [read ancestry] among Chicanos has been seriously neglected."[58] There is, for example, no firm basis for

57. For an excellent treatment of this issue, see chapter 16, "Ethnic Perceptions and Relations: Ingroup and Outgroup" in Grebler et al., *Mexican-American People*.

58. Carlos Arce, "A Reconsideration of Chicano Culture and Identity," *Daedelus*, vol. 110 (Spring 1981), p. 180.

TABLE 1
ANCESTRAL SELF-REFERENT IN THE 1980 CENSUS

State	Mexican, Mexican-American, Chicano	Spanish/Hispanic	Ratio of First Column to Second Column
Arizona	368,259	48,495	0.13
California	3,361,773	539,285	0.16
Colorado	160,548	154,396	0.96
New Mexico	153,960	281,189	1.82
Texas	2,495,035	221,568	0.09
Totals	6,539,575	1,224,933	0.19

estimating the number of Indians among the Mexican-American community. One commonly cited set of figures holds that Mexican-Americans are 40 percent full-blooded Indians, 55 percent mestizos, and 5 percent people of purely European ancestry, but the basis for these figures is not clear.[59] Arce adds that the class profile and geographic source of migrants make it likely that the percentage of American Indians among the Mexican-American community is larger than that among the population of Mexico: "The overwhelmingly lower class, rural, Central Mexican origin of Chicanos suggests that Mexicans in the United States are more likely to be of Indian than European ancestry, or if they are *mestizos* (part Indian, part European), to be genotypically more Indian than Mexicans south of the border."[60]

In any case, it is not figures indicating ancestry but rather figures indicating perceptions of ancestry that are required. Moreover, treating the Mexican-American community as a triad composed of Castilians, mestizos, and Indians does not do justice to the community's complexity, for *Indian* is itself a transethnic category. In bemoaning the lack of key data concerning the various identities of Mexican-American peoples, one source has cogently noted: "Another facet of which there are curious hints in many interviews is the symbolic significance of particular Indian strains. Being part Tarahumara is very different in meaning from being part Tarrascan, just as Hopi is from Sioux. These differences in meaning would be more strongly felt in Indian-conscious Mexico, of course, than in the United States.

59. These figures were first used by Jack Forbes, "Mexican-Americans," in John Burma, ed., *Mexican-Americans in the United States* (Cambridge, Mass.: Schenkman Publishing Co., 1970), p. 15. The 5 percent European figure would be greatly out of line with the number reporting themselves "Spanish/Hispanic" in the 1980 census. For a related article by the same author, see Jack Forbes, "Race and Color in Mexican-American Problems," *Journal of Human Relations*, vol. 16 (1968), pp. 55–68.

60. Arce, "A Reconsideration of Chicano Culture," p. 180.

But it is also a matter of special interest in the United States among a population whose legal "whiteness" is symbolically important."[61]

Future research will therefore presumably confirm that sociopolitically important divisions predicated upon perceptions of ancestry exist at the intra-Indian level of the Mexican-American community.

Although it is therefore oversimplified, the tripartite division into Castilian, mestizo, and Indian does reflect the dominant self-held view of the key divisions within the Mexican-American community. The low regard in which Indian blood is held is evident in the aforementioned tendency of large numbers to hold fervently to a fictional, purely Castilian account of their ancestry.

Quite inadvertently, the militant Chicano movement of the late 1960s and early 1970s provided a hint of the social distance between the larger community and those of predominantly Indian heritage. In an attempt to propagate a single ethnonational identity among all Mexican-Americans, the movement emphasized the Indian roots common to the entire community. Aspects of its campaign included (1) the popularization of the group self-referent *Chicano* (formerly considered a pejorative); (2) appeals to a separate and unifying consciousness on the basis of a presumed difference in skin pigmentation between the dominant society and the community ("brown power," the brown berets); (3) the dichotomous division of the society into "us" and "them," all "them" being regularly described as "Anglos"; and (4) the development of a common sense of nationhood by the ubiquitous venerating of *La Raza*. In his not unsympathetic account of the Chicano movement, Edward Murguia describes the impact of the movement upon its converts as follows:

> Expressions of antagonism toward Anglos as well as toward anglicized Mexican Americans are heard. There is an attempt by those in the movement to become very Mexican. One begins to speak Spanish more and more on every occasion that presents itself. On purpose, one begins to eat tortillas, enchiladas, tamales and beans very often. One becomes very racially and culturally aware of what others in the decolonization movement are doing. One begins to pay attention to the struggles of *La Raza* as an oppressed people in the United States nationally, regionally and locally. Instead of the more "guero" (light-skinned) Mexican Americans being favored, the more Indian physical type is favored. Instead of wishing that they looked more guero, those in the movement find themselves wishing that they looked more Indian.[62]

61. Grebler et al., *Mexican-American People*, pp. 381–82. In correspondence with this writer, Arturo Munoz wrote that he has encountered numerous people on either side of the U.S.–Mexican border who took great pride in claiming descent from the Yaqui Indians, a formerly warlike people from northern Mexico.

62. Edward Murguia, *Assimilation, Colonialism and the Mexican American People*, Monograph Series 1 (Austin: University of Texas Center for Mexican American Studies, 1975), p. 85. Stoddard succinctly describes how some Mexican-Americans who

Here, then, was a call to unity predicated upon Indianness. But the Chicano movement's star, which never shined very brightly, soon went into eclipse. Its party, *La Raza Unida,* was never able, despite great effort, to acquire even one-third of the necessary 66,000 registrants to qualify as a legally recognized political party in California.[63] And the group designation of Chicano is still far more popular among those who write about the Mexican-Americans than it is within that community.[64] In John Garcia's survey of Mexican-Americans, only 4 percent described themselves as Chicano, and in a survey in Denver undertaken by Nicholas Lovrich and Otwin Marenin, only 10 percent did so.[65] In sum, appeals to an Indian heritage failed to elicit broad support.[66]

---

were formerly "reluctant to openly proclaim their Indian heritage" suddenly began to emphasize it. (See Ellwyn Stoddard, *Mexican Americans* (New York: Random House, 1973), pp. 60ff.

63. Munoz and Barrera, "The Raza Unida Party," pp. 112 and 115.

64. The movement received its primary impetus from intellectuals and university students, which may help to account for its lack of mass support in the barrios.

65. Garcia, "Yo Soy Mexicano," p. 90; and Lovrich and Marenin, "A Comparison of Black and Mexican American Voters," p. 291. In their dangerously small sample taken in Los Angeles, Ambrecht and Pachon ("Ethnic Political Mobilization," p. 571) found that only 2 percent of Spanish-speaking and 2 percent of English-speaking Mexican-Americans referred to themselves as "Chicano." Given the prejudice toward Indianness to which I earlier alluded, the tendency to equate Chicano with Indian may partially explain the finding of Miller that those who chose the self-referent of "Mexican-American" felt a strong dislike both for the appellation of Chicano and for those who self-consciously bore it. See M. V. Miller, "Mexican Americans, Chicanos and Others: Ethnic Self-Identification and Selected Social Attitudes of Rural Texas Youths," *Rural Sociology*, vol. 41 (Summer 1976), pp. 234–37.

66. "Indianness" possessed serious handicaps as a focus for common identity among Mexican-Americans. In addition to encountering the prejudice toward Indianness that infects many members of the community, it also faced the previously mentioned hurdle that common Indianness is itself a transethnic category. Several earlier trans-Indian movements within Mexico had floundered on the unwillingness of various Indian peoples to cooperate. (See, for example, Siverts, "Ethnic Stability and Boundary Dynamics," p. 116.)

The significance that American Indians ascribe to their national (usually described as tribal) identity was demonstrated in a study of intertribal relations in southwestern United States. It found that each of the region's five major "tribes" felt a greater animosity toward some other Indian people than it did toward "the white man." See Joe Fagan and Randall Anderson, "Intertribal Attitudes among Native American Youth," *Social Science Quarterly,* vol. 54 (June 1973), pp. 117–31. This study would suggest that attempts to get American Indians to impute greater significance to racial divisions than to ethnic divisions is doomed to disappointment. Indeed, the racial perceptions of American Indians are quite complex. In the 1980 census, 1.9 million people claimed to be totally American Indian and 4.8 million people claimed partial American Indian ancestry. But on the racial question, only 1.4 million respondents circled "Indian (Amer.)." The remainder circled "White." (See U.S. Department of Commerce, *1980 Census: Ancestry,* pp. 9 and 14.) Emphasizing "brownness," as did the Chicano movement, may have therefore triggered more perplexity than emotion.

The failure of the Chicano label, or any other group self-designation, to find broad favor casts yet another shadow across the image of the Mexican-Americans as a single ethnic community. Upon first introduction to the Mexican-American literature, the comparativist is struck by what has been aptly termed "the Battle of the Name."[67] Surveys document that the designations American and Americano, Chicano, Hispano, Latin-American, Latino, Mexican and Mexicano, Mexican-American, Spanish, Spanish-American, and Spanish-speaking all have their devotees. Because choice of name indicates the ancestral family to which one feels one belongs—or from which one wishes to clearly disassociate oneself—the battle of names has been waged with great fervor and has often prevented cooperative action among organizations.[68] One finds nothing remotely comparable among Armenian, Croatian, German, Irish, Japanese, and Ukrainian-Americans, each of whom is defined by a collective sense of common ancestry.

Two Frameworks

Mexican-Americans therefore represent a far more heterogeneous people than their common grouping under a single rubric would suggest. This heterogeneity possesses substantive implications for comparative analysis. To the degree that Mexican-Americans consider themselves part of an uninterrupted homeland people, they can be placed within a global framework and validly contrasted with transborder ethnic groups. To the degree that Mexican-Americans consider themselves an ancestrally related immigrant group, they can be validly contrasted with other such groups in the United States. As noted at the outset, both these approaches will be encountered in the following chapters. But what should not be lost sight of is that there are many people, commonly grouped under the collective title of Mexican-Americans, who do not share in either perception.

---

67. Grebler et al., *Mexican-American People*, p. 385.

68. Stoddard, *Mexican Americans*, p. 64; Garcia, "Yo Soy Mexicano," p. 89; Lampe, "Ethnic Self-Referent," p. 259; and Grebler et al., *Mexican-American People*, pp. 385–87. In his chapter in this volume, Rodolfo de la Garza cites a study suggesting that differences in class between earlier and more recently arrived immigrants from Mexico are viewed as more important than a sense of shared cultural characteristics. Such an ordering is much more typical of an international than an intranational situation.

CHAPTER TWO

The United States represents the immigrant society par excellence. During the two centuries of its existence, more than 50 million settlers have been officially admitted. The relative magnitude of this migration is suggested by the fact that even today, following three decades of what has been popularly termed the global population explosion, only fifteen states (less than 10 percent of the total) have a population in excess of 50 million.

The ethnic, geographic, linguistic, and religious diversity reflected in this diaspora can be gleaned from responses to the 1980 U.S. census questions concerning ancestry. More than 130 classifications of responses were ultimately published. Even the 30 most popular responses (those that were selected by more than 500,000 people as partially or totally describing their ancestry) highlight the variety characterizing the roots of the American people. In descending numerical order, Americans described their ancestry as English, German, Irish, French, Italian, Scottish, Polish, Mexican, Dutch, Swedish, Russian, Spanish-Hispanic, Czech, Norse, Hungarian, Welsh, Puerto Rican, Portuguese, Swiss, Greek, Austrian, Chinese, Filipino, Japanese, French Canadian, Slovak, Lithuanian, Ukrainian, Finnish, and Cuban. And to this list must be added those who claimed total or partial descent from the nonmigrant classifications of Afro-American (20 million) and American Indian (6.7 million).

As Milton Yinger explains, we are still far from satisfactorily comprehending that network of processes, popularly termed assimilation, by which such an ethnically variegated agglomerate has become "American." As he notes, Americanization can vary in form, degree, and tempo among groups. He provides an anatomy of assimilation and a listing of those group characteristics that are most apt to influence the assimilation equation, and he discusses the implications of this scheme of things for the Mexican-American community.

ASSIMILATION IN THE UNITED STATES

The Mexican-Americans

J. Milton Yinger

So much has been written and said about assimilation, and from such a variety of perspectives, that it is difficult to use it as an analytic construct suitable for study across time and groups. In an effort to reduce that difficulty, I believe it is essential to keep two characteristics of assimilation firmly in mind:

First, *assimilation refers to a process.* Much of the disagreement surrounding the study of assimilation is due to the failure to see it as a process and to examine the effects of various degrees of assimilation. "Complete assimilation" or "complete separation" rarely occurs within the context of contemporary states.

As a variable, assimilation can range from the smallest interactions and cultural exchanges to the fusion of groups. Contrary to commonly stated judgments, assimilation can exist alongside pluralism, except in extreme cases. Pluralism is the recognition of the legitimacy and even the value of some cultural and associational variation. As defined, assimilation and pluralism are to some degree mutually limiting, but they are not mutually contradictory. Indeed, pluralism as a value and as a policy is unlikely to appear until some assimilation occurs.

Second, *assimilation is a multidimensional process.* The various aspects of that process, which I describe below, are highly interactive; but they vary separately, propelled by somewhat different sets of causes; they change at different rates and in different sequences.

Within the context of these principles, then, assimilation can be defined as a process of boundary reduction that can occur when members of two or more societies, ethnic groups, or smaller social groups meet.[1] When carried to completion, "an assimilated ethnic

---

1. Elsewhere I have noted that the study of assimilation is simultaneously the study of its antithesis. To study the conditions under which cultural lines of division within a society are weakened is to study the conditions under which they are reinforced. For a detailed discussion, see J. Milton Yinger, "Toward a Theory of Assimilation and Dissimilation," *Ethnic and Racial Studies,* vol. 4 (July 1981), pp. 249–64.

population is defined operationally as a group of persons with similar foreign origins, knowledge of which in no way gives a better prediction or estimation of their relevant social characteristics than does knowledge of the behavior of the total population of the community or nation involved."[2]

The Subprocesses of Assimilation

An adequate comparative study of the extent of assimilation requires data on the strength of the four subprocesses of which it is constituted: structural (integration), cultural (acculturation), psychological (identification), and biological (amalgamation).[3]

An empirical science of ethnicity will develop only as reliable and valid instruments are designed for measuring these processes, data are accumulated by the use of those instruments, and conditions are identified under which various levels of intensity in each of the processes exist. Much has been done along those lines, even if not in the formal sense suggested here. The advantage of a formal statement of the research task is that scholars can see themselves working on a common set of problems and can contribute to a shared enterprise.

In the absence of such an approach, a common and powerful vocabulary cannot be developed, research gaps are not readily identified, old issues are repeatedly examined (sometimes by disregarding one's predecessors or emphasizing their presumed one-sidedness), and ideological perspectives more readily intrude into analysis. The result, despite substantial research, is a slow rate of cumulation. In recent years, few topics in the social sciences have been the subject of more doctoral dissertations than ethnicity. Research centers, individual scholars, and national and international conferences abound. In this context of strong scholarship but inadequate research focus, it may be of value to analyze the several dimensions of one of the most important and controversial concepts related to ethnicity—assimilation.

2. Stanley Lieberson, *Ethnic Patterns in American Cities* (New York: Free Press, 1963), p. 10.
3. I have not included three additional factors to which Gordon refers, along with four factors similar to those I have listed. What he calls "absence of prejudice," "absence of discrimination," and "absence of value and power conflict" seem to me to be better noted as both causes and consequences of given levels of assimilation than as aspects of it. See Milton Gordon, *Human Nature, Class and Ethnicity* (New York: Oxford University Press, 1978), p. 169.

Integration

As I use the term, a group is integrated (one of the four aspects of assimilation) to the degree that its members are distributed across the full range of associations, institutions, and regions of a society in a pattern similar to that of the population as a whole. In politics, for example, this would mean similar rates of registration and voting and similar ratios and levels of office holding. The boundaries of political movements and parties would not be coterminous with ethnic or other group boundaries.

By these criteria, Americans of Mexican descent are only moderately well integrated politically. Immigrants exhibit relatively low levels of naturalization;[4] as citizens they register and vote in lower proportion than the black population;[5] and, partly as a result, they are less well represented among officeholders. Although "nationalistic" political organizations may receive more attention in the press than they receive support among Mexican-Americans, there is little doubt they have grown in importance in the past twenty years.[6] The political situation seems highly volatile, however, with integrative tendencies growing in importance. Nine Hispanics were elected to the House of Representatives in 1982—eight of them from the Southwest. The number of Hispanic mayors, state legislators, and city council members has increased greatly in the last decade. The process of political activation that began several years earlier among black Americans seems likely to grow in strength among the Hispanics.

In economic matters, full integration would mean that occupational and income distributions of an ethnic group matched those of the whole society; rates of work-force participation would be similar when age profiles were taken into account; and work places would be shared, not segregated.

Recent data on these items present a mixed picture of economic integration among Mexican-Americans. Median family income for

---

4. John A. Garcia, "Political Integration of Mexican Immigrants: Explorations into the Naturalization Process," *International Migration Review*, vol. 15 (Winter 1981), pp. 608–25.

5. George Antunes and Charles M. Gaitz, "Ethnicity and Participation: A Study of Mexican-Americans, Blacks, and Whites," *American Journal of Sociology*, vol. 80 (March 1975), pp. 1192–1211; Cary Davis, Carl Haub, and JoAnn Willette, "U.S. Hispanics: Changing the Face of America," *Population Bulletin*, vol. 38 (June 1983).

6. Gaynor Cohen, "Alliance and Conflict among Mexican Americans," *Ethnic and Racial Studies*, vol. 5 (April 1982), pp. 175–95; Herbert Hirsch and Armando Gutierrez, *Learning to be Militant: Ethnic Identity and the Development of Political Militance in a Chicano Community* (San Francisco: R&E Research Associates, 1977); and Edward Murguia, *Assimilation, Colonialism, and the Mexican American People* (Austin: University of Texas Press, 1975), pp. 88–97.

TABLE 1
OCCUPATIONS OF MEXICAN-AMERICANS AND ALL WORKERS, BY SEX, 1981
(Percent)

Occupation	All Workers		Mexican-American Workers	
	Men	Women	Men	Women
Professionals and technicians	15.9	17.0	5.7	8.0
Managers and administrators	14.6	7.4	6.3	4.3
Sales personnel	6.1	6.8	2.6	5.2
Clerical workers	6.3	34.7	5.0	32.4
Craft and kindred workers	20.7	1.9	20.9	2.5
Operatives except transport	11.1	9.7	20.2	21.6
Transport equipment operatives	5.5	0.7	6.8	0.5
Nonfarm laborers	7.1	1.3	12.7	2.2
Service workers	8.9	19.4	12.2	21.1
Farm workers	3.9	1.1	7.5	2.5

SOURCE: Adapted from Cary Davis, Carl Haub, and JoAnn Willette, "U.S. Hispanics: Changing the Face of America," *Population Bulletin*, vol. 38 (June 1983), p. 36. Figures are rounded.

Hispanics in 1982 was 70 percent of the median for all U.S. families; unemployment rates were about 50 percent higher (for Hispanics the unemployment rate was 11.6 percent in December 1983, compared with 7.1 percent for non-Hispanic whites and 17.8 percent for blacks); participation in the labor force by Hispanics over nineteen years of age is 62 percent, the same as that of all non-Hispanics.[7] Although there has been some improvement in occupational status, there is still a significant gap between Mexican-American workers and all workers, as shown in table 1. Using the simple white-collar/blue-collar distinction, Mexican-American men are underrepresented in each of the white-collar job categories and overrepresented in each of the blue-collar job categories. With one small exception, this is also true of Mexican-American women, although they more nearly match the occupational profile of all women than Mexican-American men match the profile of all men. It should not be overlooked, however, that a substantial industrial working class has developed, that a fifth of Mexican-American men and half of the women hold white-collar

7. Dennis M. Roth, "Hispanics in the U.S. Labor Force: A Brief Review," in Congressional Research Service. *The Hispanic Population of the United States: An Overview* 1983; U.S. Bureau of the Census, "Money Income and Poverty Status of Families and Persons in the United States, 1981," *Current Population Reports*, series P–60 (July 1982); Davis, Haub, and Willette, "U.S. Hispanics."

jobs, and that only a small fraction are farm workers—all indications of substantially more economic integration than was the case a generation ago.

The rate of intermarriage is widely regarded as the clearest measure of the extent of integration. However, to an important degree it reflects the influence of other assimilative processes. There is now a substantial amount of research on intermarriage that indicates, in the United States and elsewhere, the conditions under which it is most likely to occur, the existence of higher rates of acceptance, and increased numbers (or in some instances, correction of previous underestimation of the number).[8]

The definition of intermarriage is not self-evident. Studies that use national or other survey data are limited by the one-variable categories available, so that Catholics who marry Protestants or Mexican-Americans who marry Anglos are considered intermarried, however similar they may be in other ways. I do not examine that problem here,[9] but note that a multivariable description is needed, and in its absence the significance of intermarriage must be interpreted with caution.

---

8. See, for example, Richard D. Alba, "Social Assimilation among American Catholic National-Origin Groups," *American Sociological Review*, vol. 41 (December 1976), pp. 1030–46; Richard D. Alba, "The Twilight of Ethnicity among American Catholics of European Ancestry," *Annals of the American Academy of Political and Social Science*, vol. 454 (March 1981), pp. 86–97; Richard D. Alba and Ronald C. Kessler, "Patterns of Interethnic Marriage among American Catholics," *Social Forces*, vol. 57 (June 1979), pp. 1124–40; Jon P. Alston, "Review of the Polls: Three Current Religious Issues: Marriage of Priests, Intermarriage, and Euthenasia," *Journal for the Scientific Study of Religion*, vol. 15 (March 1976), pp. 75–78; Peter M. Blau, Terry C. Blum, and Joseph E. Schwartz, "Heterogeneity and Intermarriage," *American Sociological Review*, vol. 47 (February 1982), pp. 45–62; Steven M. Cohen, "Socioeconomic Determinants of Intraethnic Marriage and Friendship," *Social Forces*, vol. 55 (June 1977), pp. 997–1010; Noel P. Gist and Anthony G. Dworkin, eds., *The Blending of Races: Marginality and Identity in World Perspective* (New York: John Wiley and Sons, 1972); Douglas T. Gurak and Joseph P. Fitzpatrick, "Intermarriage among Hispanic Ethnic Groups in New York City," *American Journal of Sociology*, vol. 87 (January 1982), pp. 921–34; Peter R. Jones, "Ethnic Intermarriage in Britain," *Ethnic and Racial Studies*, vol. 5 (April 1982), pp. 223–28; Edward Murguia, *Chicano Intermarriage: A Theoretical and Empirical Study* (San Antonio, Texas: Trinity University Press, 1982); Ceri Peach, "Which Triple Melting Pot? A Reexamination of Ethnic Intermarriage in New Haven," *Ethnic and Racial Studies*, vol. 3 (January 1980), pp. 1–16; Ernest Porterfield, *Black and White Mixed Marriages* (Chicago: Nelson-Hall, 1978); Robert Schoen and Lawrence E. Cohen, "Ethnic Endogamy among Mexican American Grooms: A Reanalysis of Generational and Occupational Effects," *American Journal of Sociology*, vol. 86 (September 1980), pp. 359–66; and J. Milton Yinger, "On the Definition of Interfaith Marriage," *Journal for the Scientific Study of Religion*, vol. 7 (Spring 1968), pp. 104–07.

9. See J. Milton Yinger, "A Research Note on Interfaith Marriage Statistics," *Journal for the Scientific Study of Religion*, vol. 7 (Spring 1968), pp. 97–103.

Intermarriage can be defined as marriage across a socially significant line of distinction. Not all will agree, however, that a given line ought thus to be regarded. In Honolulu I once asked one friend of Japanese descent and another of Chinese background whether a marriage between a Japanese-American and a Chinese-American was an intermarriage. Both said, "Of course." When I asked if marriages between Americans of English and German background were intermarriages, both said, "Of course not." On the whole, studies of intermarriages in the United States deal with the generally acknowledged "of course" variety; but one needs to be aware of the unexamined assumptions on which that designation rests.

Attitudes of the majority are not an entirely reliable indicator of the probable rate of intermarriage in a society, since only a small percentage of the majority that intermarry will have a substantial impact on the percentage of a minority who intermarry. In Britain, about 80 percent of the population oppose interracial marriages, yet approximately 20 percent of Britain's blacks and Asians marry white partners.[10] By 1984, according to the Gallup poll, 43 percent of white Americans (63 percent of those eighteen to nineteen years of age) approved of white-nonwhite marriages. At present, some 30 percent of American Indians, 10 to 25 percent of Asian-Americans (depending upon the country of origin), and 2 percent of black Americans have white spouses. In most instances the percentages are higher for younger cohorts. The relatively high intermarriage rates of Asian-Americans have been influenced by U.S. military and political relations with the Philippines, Korea, Vietnam, and Japan. Tens of thousands of service men have brought Asian wives to the United States (more than 65,000 from Japan alone between 1947 and 1975).[11] This situation creates an exception to the more common pattern of white wives with nonwhite husbands.

The extent of religious intermarriage in the United States now greatly weakens the "triple melting pot" thesis of a few decades ago.[12] A comparison of data from the Detroit Area Studies of 1958 and 1971 found a substantial decrease in preference for homogamy by

---

10. Jones, "Ethnic Intermarriage in Britain"; Vaughan Robinson, "Patterns of South Asian Ethnic Exogamy and Endogamy in Britain," *Ethnic and Racial Studies,* vol. 3 (October 1980), pp. 427–43; Christopher Bagley, G. K. Verma, Kanka Mallick, and Loretta Young, *Personality, Self-Esteem and Prejudice* (London: Saxon House, 1979).

11. Bok-lim C. Kim, "Asian Wives of U.S. Servicemen: Women in Shadows," *Amerasia,* vol. 4 (1977), pp. 91–115.

12. Ruby Jo Reeves Kennedy, "Single or Triple Melting Pot? Intermarriage in New Haven, 1870–1950," *American Journal of Sociology,* vol. 58 (July 1952), pp. 55–59. The theory held that intermarriage tended to be restricted to intrareligious contours.

religion[13]—a change matched by the rates of intermarriage. About 40 percent of both Catholic and Jewish marriages are now interreligious. Of course, the number of Protestant individuals in interreligious marriages is as large because most of the partners of Catholics and Jews are Protestants, but the percentage is much lower—about 18 percent—reflecting the fact that more than two-thirds of the American population are nominally Protestants. Even if every Catholic and Jew married a Protestant, fewer than half of all Protestants would have intermarried.

In thinking about these intermarriage rates one must understand that the proportion of individuals from a given group that has intermarried (the individual rate) is not the same as the proportion of intermarriages (intermarriage rate). It takes two individuals who are members of the some group to make an *intra*marriage, but only one person from a particular group to make an intermarriage for that group. For example, there would be 120 Catholic or Jewish persons in 60 intramarriages and 40 in 40 intermarriages. This means that if 40 percent of the marriages are intermarriages (40 out of 100), only 25 percent of the individuals from each group (40 out of 160) are intermarried.[14]

In assessing the implications of these data for assimilation, we must add another complication—the rate of conversion of one spouse to the other's religion. In one study, the rate of conversion to Judaism among non-Jews married to Jews was 36 percent.[15] In national survey data sets, the Jewish sample is too small to allow a reliable estimate. Data from the 1980 General Social Survey of the National Opinion Research Center indicate that 59 percent of Catholic men and 68 percent of Catholic women were married to persons who had been reared as Catholics. At the time of the survey, however, 80 percent of the Catholic men and 83 percent of the women were married to Catholic spouses, indicating that nearly half of the non-Catholic spouses had converted. Among Protestants, 84 percent of the men and 80 percent of the women were married to persons who had been reared as Protestants; but 92 percent of their wives and 88 percent of their husbands were Protestants at the time of the survey, indicating that about half of the non-Protestants had also converted.

---

13. James A. McRae, "Changes in Religious Communalism Desired by Protestants and Catholics," *Social Forces*, vol. 61 (March 1983), pp. 708–30.

14. The transposition can be made by use of the following formulas, where x is the group rate and y the individual rate: $x = 200y/100 + y; y = 100x/200 - x$.

15. *New York Times*, October 16, 1983.

Numerous studies examine the rates of ethnic intermarriage (ethnicity usually being defined simply as national origin). Comparing 1930 with 1960, Bulgelski found that persons of Italian and Polish background in Buffalo exhibited sharply increasing rates of ethnic intermarriage, going from 12 percent to 50 percent for the Polish individuals (the intermarriage percentages for the group were 21 and 67 percent), and from 17 percent to 56 percent for Italian individuals (29 percent to 72 percent for the group).[16] Using 1975 data from New York City, Gurak and Fitzpatrick found high rates of ethnic intermarriage among five Hispanic groups.[17] (The extent to which these marriages were also interreligious and interracial cannot be determined from the data.) The individual rates ranged from 29.5 percent among Puerto Ricans to 63.4 percent among Cubans. The intermarriage rates for the group ranged from 45.8 percent (Puerto Ricans) to 77.6 percent (Cubans). About half of this ethnic (national origin?) intermarriage was with members of other Hispanic groups. However, the incidence of intermarriages among second-generation Hispanics (including intermarriage with non-Hispanics) was much higher than for the first-generation Hispanics. The Puerto Ricans were an exception to this generalization. Their intermarriage rates fell slightly in the second generation, a pattern that fits the Blau, Blum, and Schwartz formula precisely: large size and low level of heterogeneity (indicative of segregation) are associated with homogamy.[18]

Alba reports that two-fifths of Italian and Polish Catholics born after World War II report mixed ancestry, a proportion that is repeated among German Catholics and British Protestants. Fully half of those identified as Irish Catholics have ancestry other than Irish as well.[19] In a sample of American Catholics ages twenty-three to fifty-seven, Alba found mixed-ancestry rates (different national origins) ranging from 79.8 percent (English) to 8.8 percent (Hispanic), and intermarriage rates ranging from 93.2 percent (English) to 19.7 percent (Hispanic).[20] When generational controls are introduced, the differences among the groups are sharply reduced. Alba concluded that "the picture conveyed by these data is one of extensive and

---

16. B. R. Bulgelski, "Assimilation through Intermarriage," *Social Forces*, vol. 40 (December 1961), pp. 148–53.
17. Gurak and Fitzpatrick, "Intermarriage among Hispanic Ethnic Groups."
18. Blau, Blum, and Schwartz, "Heterogeneity and Intermarriage."
19. Alba, "Twilight of Ethnicity."
20. Alba, "Social Assimilation."

increasing social assimilation, even as long ago as 1963 when they were collected."[21]

The importance of the generational control is especially important in the analysis of integration among groups with large proportions of newcomers. Using data for Los Angeles County in 1963, Mittelbach and Moore found that 13.3 percent of first-generation Mexican-American men had married non-Hispanic women. The rates were 23.4 percent for the second generation and 30.2 percent for the third. Intermarriage rates were particularly high (40.4 percent) for persons in high-status jobs compared with those in middle- and low-status jobs (22.1 percent and 21.4 percent).[22] When the two variables are combined, one finds that 48.5 percent of third-generation Mexican-American men with high-status jobs married non-Hispanics.[23]

In his recent thorough study, *Chicano Intermarriage*, Murguia emphasizes the need for taking account, not only of time period, but of rural-urban differences and class, county, and state differences. In the three states for which the most studies are available (and which contain more than two-thirds of the Mexican-American population), the lowest rates of exogamous individuals are found in Texas and New Mexico, and the highest in California. Using only studies since 1970, one finds that rates of exogamous individuals range from 5 to 16 percent in Texas, from 15 to 24 percent in New Mexico, and from 34 to 38 percent in California. Referring to intermarriages rather than individual rates, I note that the rates range from 9 to 27 percent in Texas, from 27 to 39 percent in New Mexico, and from 51 to 55 percent in California.[24]

Mexican-American intermarriage rates are somewhat lower in the Southwest, 22.5 percent, than in the United States as a whole, 28.9 percent. (The individual rates are 12.7 and 16.9 percent, respectively.)[25] The rates may have stabilized for now, indicating the net effects of offsetting forces. Urbanization, along with occupational

21. Ibid, p. 1045.

22. Calculated from Frank G. Mittelbach and Joan W. Moore, "Ethnic Endogamy—the Case of Mexican Americans," *American Journal of Sociology*, vol. 74 (July 1968), pp. 50–62.

23. For analyses of the comparative influence of job status and generation on the Mexican-American intermarriage rate, see Robert Schoen and Lawrence E. Cohen, "Theory and Method in the Study of Ethnic Endogamy among Mexican American Grooms," *American Journal of Sociology*, vol. 87 (January 1982), pp. 939–42; Schoen and Cohen, "Ethnic Endogamy"; Richard D. Alba, "A Comment on Schoen and Cohen," *American Journal of Sociology*, vol. 87, (January 1982), pp. 935–39.

24. Murguia, *Chicano Intermarriage*, pp. 48–49.

25. U.S. Bureau of the Census, "Persons of Spanish Origin in the United States, March 1977," *Current Population Reports*, series P–20, no. 329 (1978), pp. 44–45.

and educational gains, tends to increase intermarriage. At higher levels of education, school populations become more heterogeneous. Education also affects values, which tends to make persons more cosmopolitan and, for some, creates a new kind of group "akin to an ethnic community" that draws different exogamous and endogamous lines.[26] The growing size of the Mexican-American population, however, tends to reduce the rate of intermarriage. The existing residential patterns have a mixed influence. Although "a barrio experience is far from universal, or even prevalent, among Hispanics in the southwest,"[27] large, predominantly Mexican-American communities and schools are far from uncommon. Residential segregation continues to be the most persistent barrier to integration for ethnic and racial groups generally.[28] Because Mexican-American segregation results from class differences as well as from discrimination, we will see its reduction in the years ahead to the degree that the class profile of Mexican-Americans continues to become more similar to the class profile of the population as a whole.

Acculturation

An ethnic group is acculturated to the degree that the range of values and norms held by its members (the blueprints for action on cognitive, aesthetic, and ethical questions) fall into a pattern similar to that of the general population. Whether such convergence as exists is a result of a one-way or two-way process is not indicated in the definition but requires empirical study in each instance. One can only say that smaller, less compact, more heterogeneous, and resource-poor groups are less likely to contribute cultural influences than are groups with the opposite characteristics.[29]

Anthropologists and historians have long emphasized the extent to which the cultures of almost all societies—the United States in

---

26. S. Cohen, "Socioeconomic Determinants," p. 1008.

27. Douglas S. Massey, "Research Note on Residential Succession: The Hispanic Case," *Social Forces*, vol. 61 (March 1983), pp. 825–33.

28. See Lieberson, *Ethnic Patterns in American Cities;* Wilfred G. Marston and Thomas L. VanValey, "The Role of Residential Segregation in the Assimilation Process," *Annals of the American Academy of Political and Social Science*, vol. 441 (January 1979), pp. 13–25; and John Yinger, "Prejudice and Discrimination in the Urban Housing Market," in Peter Mieszkowski and Mahlon Straszheim, eds., *Current Issues in Urban Economics* (Baltimore: Johns Hopkins University Press, 1979), pp. 430–68.

29. For classic studies of acculturation, see M. J. Herskovits, *Acculturation: The Study of Culture Contact* (New York: Augustin, 1938); and Ralph Linton, ed., *Acculturation in Seven American Indian Tribes* (New York: Appleton-Century, 1940). For a valuable recent collection of studies, see Amado M. Padilla, ed., *Acculturation: Theory, Models, and Some New Findings* (Boulder, Colo.: Westview Press, 1980).

particular—are the result of the convergence of many cultural streams. That process continues. Even casual observation in regions outside as well as inside their major concentrations reveals the cultural effects, for example, of Jewish-Americans, black Americans, American Indians, Hispanics, and Italian-Americans on the total cultural repertoire of the country. I know no way of measuring those effects; and they are certainly smaller for more recently arrived and less powerful groups than is the influence of the dominant culture on the members of those groups. Here I want only to illustrate questions related to the study of cultural convergence.

It is important to distinguish between additive and substitutive acculturation. Some cultural traits, such as religious and political ideologies, are mutually exclusive. One cannot become a Christian while remaining a Buddhist (although one should not forget the frequency with which religious and political ideologies absorb new elements). Much acculturation, however, is not substitutive but additive. Many Americans pride themselves on the range of their culinary, musical, literary, and linguistic skills and tastes. In ideological discussions, acculturation is often treated simply as a process of giving up something, of impoverishment. To some extent it can be seen as a process of cultural enrichment, unless one sees a given cultural complex as integral and complete. We are a long way from knowing, however, which cultural traits and complexes tend to be additive, which ones substitutive, and what their various consequences are for all the persons involved. As a general principle one can say that cultural groups separated by many traits that could be exchanged only by substitution will have low rates of cultural assimilation and the process will often be conflictual. For example, those American Indian tribes whose economies were built around the bison could not simply add settled agriculture; nor could the settlers adopt the Indian economy.

To illustrate the importance of acculturation as one of the dimensions of assimilation, I examine "the culture of poverty," a topic widely discussed in connection with the extent of acculturation of Mexican-Americans. Although Oscar Lewis surely intended, by his discussions of the concept,[30] to contribute to the sympathetic or at least the objective study of a life style that seemed to depart significantly

---

30. Among the works of Oscar Lewis, see "The Culture of Poverty," *Scientific American,* vol. 215 (October 1966), pp. 19–25; *Five Families: Mexican Case Studies in the Culture of Poverty* (New York: Basic Books, 1959); *La Vida: A Puerto Rican Family in the Culture of Poverty* (New York: Random House, 1966); and *The Children of Sanchez* (New York: Random House, 1961).

from the dominant values and norms, he had another kind of influence as well. Drawing his material primarily from his studies of Mexicans, Mexican-Americans, and Puerto Ricans, Lewis sought, by the use of the culture-of-poverty idea, to describe "in positive terms a subculture of Western society with its own structure and rationale, a way of life handed on from generation to generation along family lines. The culture of poverty is not just a matter of deprivation or disorganization, a term signifying the absence of something. It is a culture in the traditional anthropological sense in that it provides human beings with a design for living, with a ready made set of solutions for human problems, and so serves a significant adaptive function."[31]

If poverty is so deeply rooted in a traditional way of life as Lewis believed, then it has imposed, among those socialized to it, a major obstacle to acculturation to the values of a mainly middle-class, competitive, future-oriented society. Those inclined to explain poverty as due not to the structure of society or to discrimination but to the individual characteristics of the poor and their shared values were attracted to the concept of a culture of poverty. It was used, for example, by Banfield, first with reference to Italian villagers and then to American cities.[32] It is also in harmony with many aspects of U.S. government policy in the early 1980s.

I will not examine here the culture of poverty debate.[33] The concept sharply challenges the emphasis on opportunity and the structures of contact that both preceded it[34] and followed it.[35] Those most critical of the concept see it as nothing more than "blaming the victim."[36] Others criticize it as a superficial "cultural" explanation of what is, in reality, a "value-stretch,"[37] a "shadow culture,"[38] an

31. Oscar Lewis, "The Culture of Poverty," p. 19.
32. Edward C. Banfield, *The Moral Basis of a Backward Society* (Chicago: University of Chicago Press, 1958); Edward C. Banfield, *The Unheavenly City: The Nature and Future of Our Urban Crisis* (Boston: Little, Brown, 1968).
33. See George E. Simpson and J. Milton Yinger, *Racial and Cultural Minorities*, 5th edition (New York: Plenum Publishing, forthcoming), chap. 6.
34. Allison W. Davis and Robert J. Havighurst, *Father of the Man: How Your Child Gets His Personality* (Boston: Houghton-Mifflin, 1947) and Robert L. Sutherland, *Color, Class, and Personality* (Washington, D.C.: American Council on Education, 1942).
35. For example, see Michael Lewis, *The Culture of Inequality* (Amherst, Mass.: University of Massachusetts Press, 1978); Charles A. Valentine, *Culture and Poverty* (Chicago: University of Chicago Press, 1968); and Chaim I. Waxman, *The Stigma of Poverty: A Critique of Poverty Theories and Policies* (New York: Pergamon, 1977).
36. William Ryan, *Blaming the Victim* (New York: Vintage Books, 1971).
37. Hyman Rodman, "The Lower-Class Value Stretch," *Social Forces*, vol. 42 (December 1963), pp. 205–15.
38. Elliot Liebow, *Tally's Corner: A Study of Negro Streetcorner Men* (Boston: Little, Brown, 1967).

adaptation to extremely limited opportunities.[39] Thus a point of view that was first expressed to lend support to cultural pluralism and to affirm the dignity of the life styles of lower classes and minority groups is now used, according to these critics, to support conditions that perpetuate poverty and discrimination.

I agree substantially with these critics. Students of poverty need to recall, however, the story of the blind men and the elephant. In my judgment, people who emphasize the presumed culture of poverty and its effects on character have seized the tail. To say that an elephant is very much like a rope does not take us very far; yet one should not forget the element of truth that it contains. People who emphasize the structure of opportunities are touching the body of the problem, even if they call it a wall. A full assessment, however, must take account of many factors.

Lest I become tangled even more in this analogy, let me say simply that poverty experienced through several generations, in a context of limited opportunities and discrimination, must influence values and norms. This effect, if the conditions persist, feeds back into the system that produced it, reinforcing it. Current research demonstrates, however, that this effect is surprisingly small. Results and interpretations of "guaranteed income experiments" are complex; but few disagree with the finding that the great majority of the poor want to work—they share the work ethic.[40] Hill and Ponza have recently shown that children raised in families that are heavily dependent on welfare are themselves dependent on welfare in only a very small percentage of cases.[41]

---

39. Troy Abell and Larry Lyon, "Do the Differences Make a Difference? An Empirical Evaluation of the Culture of Poverty in the United States," *American Ethnologist*, vol. 6 (August 1979), pp. 602–20; Barbara E. Coward, Joe R. Feagin, and J. Allen Williams, Jr., "The Culture of Poverty Debate: Some Additional Data," *Social Forces*, vol. 52 (June 1974), pp. 621–34; Richard L. Della Fava, "The Culture of Poverty Revisited," *Social Problems*, vol. 21 (June 1974), pp. 609–21; Richard L. Della Fava, "Success Values: Are They Universal or Class-Differentiated," *American Journal of Sociology*, vol. 80 (July 1974), pp. 153–69; Gerald D. Suttles, *The Social Order of the Slum: Ethnicity and Territory in the Inner City* (Chicago: University of Chicago Press, 1968); and Bettylou Valentine, *Hustling and Other Hard Work: Life Styles in the Ghetto* (New York: Free Press, 1978.)

40. See David Kershaw and Jerilyn Fair, *The New Jersey Income-Maintenance Experiment*, vol. 1 (New York: Academic Press, 1976); Harold W. Watts and Albert Rees, eds., *The New Jersey Income-Maintenance Experiments*, vols. 2 and 3 (New York: Academic Press, 1977); Robert E. Haveman, ed., *A Decade of Federal Antipoverty Programs; Achievements, Failures, Lessons* (New York: Academic Press, 1977); and Vincent T. Covello, ed., *Poverty and Public Policy: An Evaluation of Social Science Research* (New York: Schenkman, 1980).

41. Martha S. Hill and Michael Ponza, "Poverty and Welfare Dependence across Generations," *Economic Outlook USA* (Summer 1983), pp. 61–64.

A full understanding of the extent to which—and the ways in which—recently rural, poorly educated, relatively unskilled persons are acculturated to the norms and values of a rapidly changing urban society, with its escalating skill requirements, has important public policy implications. I believe that the present level of public understanding is modest at best, with the result that policies ostensibly designed to reduce proverty often help perpetuate it instead.

Identification

The "identification" aspects of assimilation are the most difficult to conceptualize and are the least well measured. Each person has several identities, the salience of which varies from situation to situation. Even ethnic identities are not self-evident. Which of various possibilities is dominant at a particular time depends in part on other people, on individual choice, and on the pattern of groups in a situation. Alex Haley investigates his "roots" in Africa, but also, on third or fourth thought, in Ireland as well.

Identities can be inherited, chosen, assigned, or merely inferred from some bit of evidence. Not much is known about the salience of racial or ethnic identifications from the single fact of a census classification. That a high percentage of the American population claims to know where the majority of their grandparents or more distant ancestors were born reveals little about their most important identities. Researchers need to distinguish carefully between self-identification and identities given by others. Above all, behavioral measures are needed that make possible some estimate of the significance of a given identity, whether self-selected or assigned. Identification is powerfully influenced by the opportunity structures of the surrounding society. Participation in a Chicano movement, broadly defined, or a sense of strong identification with *la raza*, for example, expresses a situation in which slowly expanding opportunities fail to keep pace with rapidly increasing levels of aspiration. Walker Connor in chapter 1 of this book cites a number of studies that indicate not only the variety of ways by which Americans of Mexican background identify themselves, but also how these differences affect behavior.[42]

Social psychologists traditionally measure self-identification by asking respondents to answer, perhaps twenty times, "Who are you?"

---

42. See also Margarita B. Melville, "Ethnicity: An Analysis of its Dynamism and Variability Focusing on the Mexican/Anglo/Mexican Interface," *American Ethnologist,* vol. 10 (May 1983), pp. 272–89.

The answers range widely—often encompassing physical characteristics, roles, group memberships, and global identities. Such a procedure could well be adapted to the study of racial, national, or ethnic
groups. Perhaps we can persuade some national research center to
ask a group of respondents to rank, in order of importance, a list of
possible identities (age, sex, citizenship, ethnic group, race, occupation,
etc.) by giving several answers to the question "Who are you?"[43]

We noted previously that one can think of acculturation as
substitutive or additive. The same issue needs to be raised in connection with identities. Are they zero-sum, that is, if a person takes
on one, another must be dropped? Or are they additive, allowing a
person to add identities without setting aside or downgrading others?
Perhaps most probably, some identities are mutually inconsistent or
competitive; an increase in the salience of one entails a decrease in
the salience of the other; other combinations, however, may be
compatible, allowing a person to build up more complex structures
of identity. If this is the most useful way to pose the problem, the
critical question for us is this: with what other identities are ethnic,
racial, and national identities compatible or incompatible, and at what
levels of salience?

Nisbet believes that increasing emphasis on ethnicity (along with
an increase in fundamentalism and the rise of the "cultural left") is
in part the result of the repudiation of the political state. "Throughout
recorded history there is a high correlation between alienation of
individual loyalties from dominant political institutions and the rise
of new forms of community—ethnic, religious, and others—which
are at once renunciations of and challenges to these political institutions."[44] In many instances, of course, one would need to speak not
of new but of persistent or renewed forms of community. Donald
Horowitz makes a related point, but in the form of a broader and
more objective principle: "An identity tends to expand with an
expanding context, often shaped by expanding territorial boundaries,
it tends to contract with a contracting context, again often defined
by contracting territorial boundaries. . . . As the importance of a
given political unit increases, so does the importance of the highest
available level of identification immediately *beneath* the level of that

---

43. While working on this paper I asked two groups of students of rather diverse
backgrounds to rank their identities from among ten suggested. Seldom was ethnicity
in the top three. This exercise had no substantive value, but it helped to test the
method.

44. Robert Nisbet, *Twilight of Authority* (New York: Oxford University Press, 1975),
p. 12.

unit, for that is the level at which judgments of likeness are made and contrasts take hold."[45]

One can think of several ways to define "identification" assimilation operationally. Only research can show which ones lead to the most creative questions. For example, those persons who give the society their first rank are assimilated by identification. That may seem too "soft" a test. One could add the phrase "and who place no other cultural or ancestral group or polity in the top three (or five) ranks. Or one could develop profiles of identification based on several choices and seek to determine the causes and consequences of those profiles. Studies of disidentification and of the absence of certain kinds of identification would also be of value.

Amalgamation

In a strictly biological sense, two or more groups are amalgamated when the genetic makeup of their members has been drawn from the same gene pool. When stated as a variable, this definition indicates that groups are amalgamated *to the degree that* the genetic makeup of their members is drawn from the same gene pool. A more limited definition, however, is appropriate to our interests: groups are amalgamated when no *socially visible* genetic differences separate their members.

The blurring of genetic distinctions has been taking place in many parts of the world for thousands of years, opening up for societies a variety of ways in which they can draw lines distinguishing "genetically different" groups and individuals. These ways change with shifts in the degree and kind of sensitivity to differences in ancestry, class, and culture. Before 1850, Williamson notes, free mulattoes in the United States constituted a kind of third class. Relationships with whites "had a distinct West Indian flavor."[46] He notes, for example, that in South Carolina and Louisiana there were some mulatto-white intermarriages. As tensions over slavery mounted, however, whites rejected this ambiguous way of drawing the line between African and European, a rejection that holds quite firm in most parts of the country even today. In 1983 the courts upheld a Mississippi law which classified a person with one thirty-second or more of African heritage as a Negro. (A few months later, however,

45. Donald L. Horowitz, "Ethnic Identity," in Nathan Glazer and Daniel P. Moynihan, eds., *Ethnicity: Theory and Experience* (Cambridge, Mass.: Harvard University Press, 1975), p. 137.

46. Joel Williamson, *New People: Miscegenation and Mulattoes in the United States* (New York: Free Press), 1980.

the law was repealed.) After millennia of contact among Europeans, Middle Easterners, and Africans, and after centuries of black-white contact in North America, hundreds of thousands and probably millions of "white" Americans would be classified as Negroes by this criterion.

Amalgamation may begin early in contact between two groups. A conquering or invading group may exploit the women of the conquered group; or a highly imbalanced sex ratio may lead to increased sexual contact across racial or cultural lines. At later stages of contact, intermarriage plays a more important part.

In common usage, amalgamation refers only to racial blending. This is due not so much to the assumed larger genetic differences involved, but to the fact that early racial contacts were correlated with large differences in culture—in religion, language, and custom. Amalgamation must be studied as part of the assimilation process, in fact, because this historical background has made visible genetic differences almost everywhere an important factor in the nature of contact between groups.

I do not examine here the myths and conflicts surrounding the term *race*. Most of the criteria by which the human species is genetically differentiated today can be detected and measured only by use of sophisticated instruments and analysis. On the basis of these criteria, Dobzhansky lists thirty-four races, some of them the result of recent blends.[47] Perhaps it is sufficient here to say that the U.S. population contains very large—and internally diverse—numbers of people from three categories or clusters of races which, based on their ancestral backgrounds, I call simply African, Asian, and European. Such crude categories are least satisfactory for the Asians, since the ancestors of more than two-thirds of them migrated to the Western Hemisphere ten thousand to twenty thousand years ago. To describe our population in this simple-minded way, I am hoping, will remind us how arbitrary our conceptions of amalgamation can be.

All these groups are genetically blended to an important degree. About 80 percent of persons classified as being of predominantly African background have European or (in fewer instances) Asian ancestors as well. Current rates of intermarriage between "Europeans" and American Indians, Hispanics, and recent migrants from Asia (rates that average, as noted, between one-quarter and one-third) indicate that the American multiracial population is continuing to

---

47. Theodosius Dobzhansky, *Mankind Evolving* (New Haven, Conn.: Yale University Press, 1962).

expand. A large proportion of migrants from the West Indies are of mixed ancestry. The distribution of Indians, mestizos, and Europeans in Mexico is not well established (perhaps 30 percent, 60 percent, and 10 percent, respectively), and the ancestry of Mexican-Americans is even less clearly understood; but few would doubt that 50 percent or more of the latter have both European and Indian ancestors.

The number of Americans of predominantly European background who also have Asian or African ancestors is least well known. Twenty-five years ago Edward Dozier, an American Indian anthropologist, told me his studies had convinced him that there were more Americans with some Indian ancestry living as whites than as identified Indians. Asian and Hispanic ancestry among the "socially white" will grow quite rapidly, from an unknown base, if present rates of intermarriage continue. Estimates of the number of "white" Americans with African ancestry vary widely.[48] Only a small number of blacks "passing" as white in each generation, however, have an expanding influence on each succeeding generation.

I am trying to suggest with these crude estimates that the amalgamation aspect of the assimilation process in the United States deserves careful attention. Current rates among several groups are quite high; and the impact is cumulative. If one assumes (1) that the offspring of the intermarried do not simply marry among themselves, but marry proportionately persons from their two parental lines, and (2) that the difference in the birthrates of the intra- and intermarried is relatively small, then, even with no increase in rates of intermarriage, more than three-fourths of the offspring in the smaller group (for example, Mexican-American) would be of mixed ancestry by the third generation.

The rather high rates of intermarriage of American Indians and of Mexican-Americans (who in a majority of cases also have Indian ancestors) indicate clearly that some generalized "racial difference" factor is of little help in accounting for the extent of intermarriage. Historical, cultural, demographic, and status factors are the critical ones. Some of these factors are now becoming more commonly associated with intermarriage in the United States, with the result that some racial lines are continuing to become less clear; amalgamation continues.

It seems probable also that amalgamation need not be biologically complete (that is, no difference in ancestry between persons in

---

48. Stuckert calculates the proportion to be 19.5 percent. See Robert Stuckert in Peter Hammond, ed., *Physical Anthropology and Archaeology* (New York: Macmillan, 1964), p. 195.

formerly distinctive groups) before socially visible genetic differences fade. As the other assimilative processes continue, the inherited lines that divide one group from another are likely to shift. More and more persons of European background, for example, will see those who have one American Indian, Asian, or Hispanic grandparent as "amalgamated." This process will be slowest for those of predominantly African background. During the past twenty years, blacks have paid less attention to differences in racial mixture among themselves. This may have reenforced the attitudes of the most prejudiced whites. Other whites, however, have developed a more differentiated picture of black Americans on the basis of variation in education, occupation, and ancestry.

The different effects of partial amalgamation are seen throughout the world. In Japan and Korea the children of American servicemen and Asian mothers who have remained with their mothers have faced great discrimination. There are many circumstances under which the marginality of those of mixed inheritance and the discrimination they experience has led them to prefer more strongly a single identity.[49]

Variables That Affect the Extent and Speed of Assimilation

Having discussed the four subprocesses of assimilation, it is now necessary to examine in a more systematic way the factors that influence them. I treat those factors as variables, with influences that range from highly assimilative to highly dissimilative. Table 2 details a number of the factors that influence both the degree and tempo of the assimilation process.

Undoubtedly other variables could be added to this list that would enrich our understanding of the assimilation process.[50] I note, moreover, that the variables included are highly interactive, so that their patterning is important. For example, a small group speaking

49. Noel P. Gist and Anthony G. Dworkin, eds., *The Blending of Races: Marginality and Identity in World Perspective* (New York: John Wiley, 1972).

50. For comments on various combinations of these variables, see Won Moo Hurh, Hei Chu Kim, and Kwange Chung Kim, *Assimilation Patterns of Immigrants in the United States: A Case Study of Korean Immigrants in the Chicago Area* (Washington, D.C.: University Press of America, 1979); George E. Simpson, "Assimilation," *International Encyclopedia of the Social Sciences*, vol. 1 (New York: Macmillan and Free Press, 1969), pp. 438–44; Murguia, *Assimilation, Colonialism, and the Mexican American People;* Blau, Blum, and Schwartz, "Heterogeneity and Intermarriage"; and S. Cohen, "Socioeconomic Determinants."

TABLE 2
VARIABLES THAT AFFECT THE EXTENT AND SPEED OF ASSIMILATION

Assimilative Influence	*Dissimilative Influence*
1. Belongs to a small group (relative to total population)	Belongs to a large group
2. Is residentially scattered (by region and community)	Is residentially concentrated
3. Has resided in a given society a long time (low proportion of newcomers)	Has resided in a given society a short time (high proportion of newcomers)
4. Return to homeland is difficult and infrequent	Return to homeland is easy and frequent
5. Speaks the majority language	Speaks a different language
6. Adheres to one of majority religions	Adheres to a different religion
7. Belongs to the same race as the majority	Belongs to a different race
8. Entered voluntarily	Entered by conquest or forced migration
9. Comes from a culturally similar society (in terms, for example, of literacy, urbanization, and so on) to the receiving society	Comes from a culturally different society
10. Is repelled by political and economic developments in homeland	Is attracted to those developments
11. Is diverse in class and occupation	Is homogeneous in class and occupation
12. Has a high average level of education	Has a low average level of education
13. Experiences little discrimination	Experiences much discrimination
14. Resides in an open-class society	Resides in a society with little social mobility

a foreign language is under greater pressure to change than a large foreign-language group. The variables noted here may suffice, however, to allow one to think systematically about assimilation in the United States. Some variables are difficult to quantify; for others, there is little evidence. Because some of the variables are of most importance in the early years of residence in a new society and others are of continuing importance, change over time must be taken into account. Collectively the variables have effects that themselves become causes—new variables that affect the rate of assimilation. Such cybernetic processes are common in human experience, complicating theories of cause and effect. The balance of influences at one time may lead, for example, to only a few intermarriages. Those having occurred, however, other changes may take place—shifts in residence, occupation, and attitude—that lead to higher rates of intermarriage.[51]

Without rich data and precise definitions (How does one measure levels of discrimination? What constitutes a low average level of education?), application of these assimilation variables can only be exercises in imagination. These exercises, however, can be valuable early steps in the application of a theory of assimilation. My illustrations will apply primarily to the experience of Mexican-Americans.

The first three variables in table 2 refer to demographic items, the collective impact of which is likely to be neither assimilative nor dissimilative during the rest of the century. The number of Mexican-Americans will certainly grow from the present 11 million (this includes an estimated 2 million who are uncounted and undocumented) to at least 15 million by the year 2000. Assuming a fairly slow decline in the birth rate, a legal immigration rate of about 60,000 per year (it averaged 56,700 during the 1970s), and an influx of 60,000 undocumented migrants per year, then about half of the growth will result from births and about half from new migrants. These estimates may be far off the mark, of course, because political, economic, and demographic conditions in Mexico and in the United States will significantly affect the outcomes.

Although the Mexican-American population will grow significantly both in absolute terms and relative to the total U.S. population during the rest of this century (a dissimilative factor), the proportion of newcomers among the group will decline slightly and, if present trends continue, Mexican-Americans will be more widely dispersed throughout the country (assimilative influences).

In 1980, 76 percent of the Hispanics or 11.1 million persons reported to the census that they spoke Spanish at home. This does not reveal, however, how many also speak English at school or on the job. One-quarter of Hispanic children in public primary and secondary schools know little or no English.[52] Use of English by the

---

51. On such processes, see Thomas C. Schelling, *Micromotives and Macrobehavior* (New York: W. W. Norton, 1978).

52. Davis, Haub, and Willette, "U.S. Hispanics," p. 33.

third generation, however, occurs at about the same rate for Hispanics as for other immigrant groups. Perhaps the most important question is the degree of effective literacy in either language, as indexed by the level of education. In 1981, 45.5 percent of Hispanic males and 43.6 percent of Hispanic females had completed at least four years of high school. By comparison, 53.2 percent of black males and 52.6 percent of black females had completed this amount of schooling, as had 70.3 percent of the total male population and 69.1 percent of the total female population.[53] Black gains in educational level during the preceding decade were more than 50 percent greater than Hispanic gains. It should be noted that the low percentages of high school graduation among Mexican-Americans are strongly influenced by the educational situation in Mexico. As that improves, and as the proportion of Mexican-Americans reared in the United States increases, educational levels will rise, adding to the influence of educational, economic, and residential changes also taking place in the United States.

The influence of language and education on assimilation of Mexican-Americans thus seems to be mixed. If economic and political opportunities are going to be expanded, the rates of improvement in education will need to be accelerated and more rigorous training in the language of their polity as well as in the "language of their intimacy," to use Fishman's phrase, is required.

The ninth variable in table 2 relates to acculturation. It is sometimes stated that certain cultural values interfere with education or with occupational and political activity. In a well-known study, Florence Kluckhohn argued that some of the fundamental value orientations of Mexico—"being" rather than "doing," present-time orientation, strong attachment to the wider kin group, and the like—hindered the acculturation of Mexican-Americans into American society.[54] I noted above how the concept of a "culture of poverty" has been interpreted in the same way. This is in sharp contrast with interpretations of Japanese culture, which many observers have seen as particularly well suited to rapid acculturation to the American educational, economic, and political situation, even though Japanese-Americans retain many traditional Japanese qualities.[55]

53. Ibid., p. 3.
54. Florence Kluckhohn, "Dominant and Variant Value Orientations," in Clyde Kluckhohn, H. A. Murray, and David Schneider, eds., *Personality in Nature, Society, and Culture*, rev. ed. (New York: Knopf, 1953), pp. 342–57.
55. Darrell Montero, "The Japanese-Americans—Changing Patterns of Assimilation over Three Generations," *American Sociological Review*, vol. 46, (October 1981), pp. 829–39; Eric Woodrum, "An Assessment of Japanese Assimilation, Pluralism, and Subordination," *American Journal of Sociology*, vol. 87, (July 1981), pp. 157–69; and

Such emphasis on culture underestimates, in my judgment, the influence of structural conditions, such as patterns of discrimination and levels of opportunity. It also overlooks the currents of cultural change in the society as a whole. Despite some renewed emphasis on competition, economic growth as a primary value, and individualism, other trends that were especially evident in the 1960s persist. These include emphasis on "being," harmony with nature, cooperation, and "hanging loose." Many Americans in the dominant groups as well as among the disadvantaged are experiencing cultural modification.

It would be a mistake to dismiss the cultural factor; but dogmatic interpretations are difficult to make because of interaction with the structures of opportunity, discrimination, and demographic influences. Lieberson argues convincingly that Americans of European background made faster educational and occupational gains than black Americans not because of more congruent cultural values but because they faced lower levels of discrimination.[56] Moore analyzes the Mexican-American situation similarly.[57] Mexican-Americans working in the same jobs as Anglo-Americans show little evidence of cultural effects on performance.[58]

Relatively slow growth in the number of jobs on the lower rungs of the occupational ladder[59] —rungs that were crucial for older immigrant groups in the United States—has resulted from technical change and developments in the world economic system. Lack of such jobs and persistent discrimination seem to be more significant than cultural disharmonies in retarding the growth of income and occupational status among Mexican-Americans, and to an even greater degree among black Americans.

I have made estimates—some of them quite rough—showing how the variables affecting the extent and speed of assimilation listed in table 2 apply to Mexican-Americans (see table 3). An argument could be made for shifting each of my estimates, or at least for placing them on a five- or seven-step, rather than a three-step, scale. Perhaps

John W. Connor, *Tradition and Change in Three Generations of Japanese Americans* (Chicago: Nelson-Hall, 1977).

56. Stanley Lieberson, *A Piece of the Pie: Blacks and White Immigrants Since 1880* (Berkeley: University of California Press, 1980).

57. Joan W. Moore, *Homeboys: Gangs, Drugs, and Prisons in the Barrios of Los Angeles* (Philadelphia: University of Pennsylvania Press, 1978).

58. Charles N. Weaver and Norval D. Glenn, "The Job Performance of Mexican-Americans," *Sociology and Social Research*, vol. 54 (July 1970), pp. 477–94.

59. Thomas Muller, *The Fourth Wave: California's Newest Immigrants: A Summary* (Washington, D.C.: Urban Institute, 1984), table 2.

TABLE 3

APPLICATION TO MEXICAN-AMERICANS OF THE VARIABLES THAT AFFECT THE
EXTENT AND SPEED OF ASSIMILATION

Mainly Assimilative	*Of Mixed or Neutral Influence*	*Mainly Dissimilative*
1. . . .	. . .	Size of the group is large and growing.
2. . . .	Population is still concentrated in the Southwest, but is increasingly dispersed.	. . .
3. . . .	Immigration is extensive, but proportions of second- and third-generation group members are increasing.	. . .
4. . . .	. . .	For many, return to homeland is easy and frequent.
5. . . .	Use of Spanish language continues, but English is the main language by the third generation.	. . .
6. Most share a majority religion; church segregation is decreasing.	. . .	. . .
7. . . .	Many belong to a minority race, but racial line is increasingly blurred and of decreasing importance.	. . .
8. Most entered voluntarily; but early entrants were forced by annexation.	. . .	. . .
9. . . .	Mexico is becoming increasingly urban (that is, similar to U.S. society).	. . .

TABLE 3 (*Continued*)

Mainly Assimilative	Of Mixed or Neutral Influence	Mainly Dissimilative
10. There is no strong pull toward political and economic developments of homeland.	. . .	. . .
11. Class and occupation are increasingly deverse.	. . .	. . .
12. . . .	Educational gap is significantly reduced by third generation.	. . .
13. . . .	Discrimination persists but is declining.	. . .
14. Many experience fairly extensive social mobility in the United States.	. . .	. . .

less subject to argument is the need for thinking about assimilation in the context of some such set of variables as this.

Conclusion

So long as one uses assimilation as an "either-or" categorization and assumes it to be one-directional (rather than carefully investigating the direction of flow), it will not be possible to think clearly about it. The strength of society's moral and policy actions will also be weakened. Ethnic and racial lines are not going to disappear in the foreseeable future.[60] "Affective ethnicity"[61] will persist alongside structural assimilation. "Sidestream ethnicity," to use Fishman's term, will continue. A clearly distinguishable Mexican-American and a more

---

60. See Thomas J. Archdeacon, *Becoming American: An Ethnic History* (New York: Free Press, 1983), especially chaps. 7 and 8.

61. See Thomas F. Pettigrew, "Three Issues in Ethnicity: Boundaries, Deprivations, and Perceptions," in J. Milton Yinger and Stephen J. Cutler, eds., *Major Social Issues: A Multidisciplinary View* (New York: Free Press, 1978), pp. 30–31.

nearly symbolic[62] pan-ethnic Hispanic group will be important parts of the American scene for many generations, as will other ethnic and racial groups. This should not be a subject of concern, but a situation to welcome. What we should be concerned about is the relationship of this continuing distinctiveness to the larger society and to the world as a whole.

Three questions suggest may own perspectives and values about this relationship. First how can the present connections between the ethnic and racial order and discrimination be broken, the inequalities eliminated? Second, what is needed to keep our ethnic and racial identities subordinate to our humanwide identities, our identities as persons, and identities as members of multinational states and societies? When racial and ethnic identities dominate thought and action, they are divisive and often tragic. It may be that a society is not injured when some few make ethnicity their "vocation." It surely suffers, however, when significant cross-cutting memberships are destroyed and subgroup memberships become preeminent for large numbers. Third, how can support for cultural diversity be maintained without encouraging the tendency in each group to treat its traditional ways as sacrosanct? Ethnic variation brings richness to a society and to individuals if it occurs in a context that brings unity to a society and to humankind and allows some freedom of choice to individuals. Cultures may contain many glorious elements, but they may also be encumbered with the flotsam and jetsam of the historical passage. This is certainly true of the dominant American culture. What is needed is cultural exchange and change, as well as renewal, adapted to life on this small and crowded planet.

---

62. Herbert J. Gans, "Symbolic Ethnicity: The Future of Ethnic Groups and Cultures in America," *Ethnic and Racial Studies*, vol. 2 (January 1979), pp. 1–20.

CHAPTER THREE

In the introduction to Walker Connor's first chapter in this volume it was noted that ethnic heterogeneity characterizes most states and that ethnically inspired unrest is today a global phenomenon. No category of state has proven immune to ethnic tensions: old (France) and new (Malaysia); rich (Canada) and poor (Sudan); large (Nigeria) and small (Fiji); developed (Belgium) and undeveloped (Chad); Communist (the Soviet Union) and non-Communist (Pakistan); binational (Cyprus) and multinational (Yugoslavia); democratic (Switzerland) and authoritarian (Iraq); Buddhist (Burma), Christian (the Republic of South Africa), Hindu (India), Islamic (Iran), and Jewish (Israel); first world (the United Kingdom), second world (Romania), and third world (Ethiopia)—all have been afflicted. Moreover, no state can unchallengingly boast of having discovered a perfect formula for ensuring the peaceful accommodation of ethnic heterogeneity. Thus, although Marxist-Leninist states officially claim to have "solved" what they term their *national question,* through the application of "Leninist national policy," ethnic tensions are matters of serious concern for the governments of Bulgaria, Cambodia (Kampuchea), Czechoslovakia, Laos, Romania, the Soviet Union, Vietnam, and Yugoslavia.

Although no state has discovered a magic formula for exorcising all interethnic tensions, it cannot be gainsaid that some multiethnic states have been far more tranquil than others. Some situations appear inherently resistant to conflict management: cases, for example, involving rival claims to the same homeland (as in Israel) or those involving lengthy histories of virulent, feud-like, intergroup animosity (as between Greeks and Turks on Cyprus). However, the experience of states such as Finland, Singapore, and Switzerland suggests that a combination of propitious circumstances and appropriate policies may result in the accommodation of ethnic diversity without excessive tension or violence.

Is the immigrant state most apt to provide such a constellation of propitious circumstances? In the following essay, Donald L. Horowitz evaluates the United States as an environment for the regulation of ethnic conflict, paying particular attention to relations between Mexican-Americans and the larger community. He employs two frameworks for analysis, contrasting the experiences of the United States with those of other states and then contrasting the experiences of Mexican-Americans with those of other groups both inside and outside the United States. While doing so, he adds materially to our profile of the Mexican-Americans in the 1980s, a portrait of a people in rapid flux.

CONFLICT AND ACCOMMODATION

Mexican-Americans in the Cosmopolis

Donald L. Horowitz

Every dogma has its day, and the dogmas associated with ethnic relations in the United States would fill a multiyear calendar. There is, for example, the dogma that color makes black-white differences unique in their ability to generate conflict or to produce reliable identifications of every group member. I have elsewhere called this dogma, which has no firm basis in comparative evidence, the figment of the pigment.[1] There is the equally prevalent American notion that ethnic relations are always hierarchical, that they always entail superiors and subordinates, so that the main question is who is on top, and everything else follows from that. Yet, in world perspective, most groups cannot be ordered hierarchically, and it is a distraction to search for ranked subordinates everywhere. There is the further article of faith that the United States cannot really be compared fruitfully to other societies, because our experience has been so different. Quite the contrary, for I shall suggest that, while the experience of the United States is genuinely different from that of many other societies, the differences are far more instructive than they are misleading.

With respect to the Mexican-Americans, there are some special dogmas. Chicanos are either expected to follow in the footsteps of black Americans and act the part of a ranked subordinate group seeking to escape ethnic hierarchy or to follow in the path of the nineteenth- and twentieth-century European immigrants and act the part of an upwardly mobile, "assimilating" group ready to submerge its identity completely in the rewarding, wider American identity. These constricting alternatives obviously pose choices that ignore some rather important historical and conceptual distinctions. The analogy to the black experience takes no account of the powerful

The author is indebted to Jana Fleming for research assistance in gathering materials for this essay.

1. Donald L. Horowitz, "Three Dimensions of Ethnic Politics," *World Politics*, vol. 23 (January 1971), p. 244.

impact of capture, transportation, slavery, and Jim Crow in producing an unusually rigid form of ascriptive subordination that is unlikely to be replicated where ethnic pluralism is created principally by voluntary labor migration. The model of the European immigrant is, of course, premised on a doubtful, all-or-nothing depiction of assimilation, as well as an assumption that no difficulties stand in the way of generalizing from one period of American ethnic history to another, much later period. That Mexican-Americans "fit into" wider and larger American patterns somehow or other, there is no doubt— though they will also help to create the new, emerging patterns. But the alternatives, as given, are just too rigid to be useful in that form.

That is not to say that analogies are unhelpful or that the two experiences I have referred to are irrelevant. Far from it. I shall suggest that some of the important issues concerning Mexican-Americans relate to the presence or absence of ascriptive ranking, the ability to maintain ethnic and supraethnic (in this case, "American") identities simultaneously, and the extent to which interethnic relations are characterized by severe conflict. On all these questions, the experience of black Americans and of European Americans will help inform the analysis. But, at the same time, it is important to escape the constricting choices into which the culturally conditioned channels of our mind force us. If only for this purpose, a comparative venture of this kind, reordering our understanding of group relations by changing the angle of vision, is worthwhile.

Consequently, the task here is really the double one of placing the American experience in comparative perspective and, in turn, placing the Mexican-American experience in both the wider American and comparative contexts. All this is as true of conflict management techniques as it is of other aspects of ethnicity. But conflict management brings with it a special danger to be averted: the danger of prescribing before diagnosing. And so, while I shall attend ultimately, albeit briefly, to the matter of conflict management, I shall first deal in detail with the raw evidence of the conflict that is arguably to be managed. For there is, in social policy as in medicine, very little to be said for a priori prescription and much to be gained from careful examination. What the United States manifestly does not need is pill-pushing doctors of ethnic relations.

The American Cosmopolis in Comparative Perspective

When Wyndham Lewis remarked some decades ago that America was not a territory but an idea, he was one in a long line of foreign observers who have found a distinctive spiritual unity in the United States. Lewis's further observation that any two Americans think more alike than do a Yorkshireman and a Dorsetman was surely hyperbole, but it was hyperbole with a certain ring of truth. Membership in the American community has always been defined in some considerable measure by adherence to a set of ideas about politics.[2] Implicitly, too, membership in the community was not conferred primarily by birth, at least so far as groups of European origin were concerned. With some notable exceptions, the United States was a community defined not by ascription but by subscription.

By world standards, the United States is a remarkably successful multiethnic society, but that is partly because, on this matter, world standards are so abysmally low. There has always been a duality in the American experience between ethnic differentiation and the wider American identification; there has also been a dialectic between group conflict and the limits imposed by the distinctive American ideology and its institutions.

As early as the period immediately preceding independence, several colonies were embroiled in conflicts involving ethnic and religious groups that helped determine the position of elites on the question of independence. In Pennsylvania, for example, Anglicans and Scottish Presbyterians alike sought to displace the politically dominant Quakers, who reacted to this threat by opposing independence.[3] Yet, just as parochial ethnic antipathies were affecting the choice of Loyalist or Revolutionary alignments within colonies, a study of newspapers of the period finds a notable increase in "American" symbolism transcending such conflicts.[4] Even today, by contrast, in severely divided societies, open-ended survey questions that ask "What is your nationality?" elicit overwhelmingly ethnic responses, even when the set before the question is fixed on "national" rather than ethnic identity.[5]

The founding myth, with its emphasis on migration to achieve freedom, reinforced by the actual migration of many groups for precisely that purpose, reduced the extent to which conflict could

---

2. Wyndham Lewis, *America and Cosmic Man* (Port Washington, N.Y.: Kennikat Press, 1969; originally published in 1949), pp. 21, 27.

3. Janet Merrill Alger, "The Impact of Ethnicity and Religion on Social Development in Revolutionary America," in Wendell Bell and Walter Freeman, eds., *Ethnicity and Nation Building* (Beverly Hills: Sage, 1974), pp. 327–40.

4. Richard L. Merritt, *Symbols of American Community, 1735–1775* (New Haven: Yale University Press, 1966).

5. I have collected a number of these in my book, *Ethnic Groups in Conflict* (Berkeley and Los Angeles: University of California Press, 1985), chap. 1.

occur over who owns the country. Typically, English-descended inhabitants of particular localities received a rather mild acknowledgment of their priority as a "charter group" entitled to consideration as *primus inter pares*.[6] To be sure, there were also ugly episodes of nativism that coincided with surges of immigration, beginning with the Know Nothing movement in the 1850s and culminating with restrictive immigration legislation in 1924.[7] Nativism is a persistent theme in American social life, but it is not now the force it once was, and overall it has not been the force in the United States that it is in many other countries. In comparative perspective, what stands out is the inability to dichotomize sharply between indigenes and immigrants.[8] Elsewhere, relations between groups viewed, respectively, as indigenous and immigrant have been the cutting edge of some of the most severe ethnic conflicts in the contemporary world.

This is not a matter of the actual history of migration but of ideas about migration. Pretensions to prior occupation of the land have given rise to exclusionary claims on the part of groups that might reasonably have thought themselves to be immigrants. Instead, they claim indigenousness against descendants of later migrants long after the latter might in turn have been thought to have established themselves securely. In countries such as Malaysia and Sri Lanka, in several Indian states, and in many other countries at the regional and local level, identification of a putatively indigenous group with the territory has produced claims to priority and policies that favor the indigenes on this basis. The Malay name for Malaya means literally "land of the Malays," and the Malays are referred to as "sons of the soil." Such claims and policies were formulated notwithstanding the facts that, in both Malaysia and Sri Lanka, there were aboriginal groups with antecedent claims, that many of the so-called indigenes in Malaysia are actually immigrants from Indonesia who came much more recently than nearly all the so-called immigrants from China, and that the Ceylon Tamils, sometimes regarded in Sri Lanka as relatively recent arrivals, migrated on the average about a thousand years ago.

No such powerful exclusionary claims to ownership could be made in the United States, despite the fact that, as in other countries,

---

6. Elin Anderson, *We Americans; A Study of Cleavage in an American City* (Cambridge, Mass.: Harvard University Press, 1937).

7. See John Higham, *Strangers in the Land: Patterns of American Nativism* (New Brunswick, N.J.: Rutgers University Press, 1955).

8. For a similar view, see Stephan Thernstrom, "Ethnic Groups in American History," in Lance Liebman, ed., *Ethnic Relations in America* (Englewood Cliffs, N.J.: Prentice-Hall, 1982), p. 7.

immigration came in discernible waves and the early British settlers might have been identified as the exclusive sons of the soil. The failure to recognize group legitimacy by virtue of indigenousness, of course, cut both ways, for it also implied a reciprocal unwillingness to recognize the claims of American Indians and Mexicans to priority in the territories they occupied. But, for the moment, I want to stress the comparative weakness of ethnic claims to priority in the United States on the basis of earlier migration or, for that matter, any other ethnically exclusive foundation.

Except for color, of course. But then the slaves did not migrate for freedom; they were captured for bondage, and this made, obviously, for a completely different relationship. Indeed, as I have already intimated, the history of subordination is the critical difference between black-white relations and relations among the groups of European origin. Here, too, a comparative framework helps.

In a severely divided society, ethnic group conflict can take two rather different forms. Where ethnic groups are ordered in a hierarchy, where stratification is synonymous with ethnicity, and where social mobility is restricted by group identity, it is appropriate to speak of *ranked* ethnic groups. Interethnic relations entail conceptions of superordinate and subordinate status. Interactions partake of caste etiquette; subordinate groups are stigmatized as dirty and inferior. Indeed, they do the dirty work of the society, and they are unable to escape from it. Where, on the other hand, groups are not ordered hierarchically but are cross-class, it is possible to speak of relations between *unranked* groups. These are not ascriptively defined components of a single society but rather incipient whole societies. Social mobility does not necessarily imply that the prevailing system of ethnic relations is about to be undermined, which is what it does imply in ranked systems. Whereas conflict between ranked groups has a class coloration, and in extreme cases takes a revolutionary form, severe conflict between unranked groups concerns not the politics of subordination and certainly not the politics of class. On the contrary, where groups are unranked, politics is markedly conservative. Unranked groups come into conflict over political inclusion and exclusion, over identification of the state with particular ethnic groups rather than with all groups on equal terms. In its most extreme forms, such conflicts involve attempts to homogenize the composition of the state by excluding some groups from a share of power or by expelling or exterminating them.

Like many societies, the United States has experienced both forms of ethnic conflict. Needless to say, there have been inequalities among unranked groups in the United States, as there are elsewhere. Not inequality alone, but ascriptive subordination, characterizes ethnic ranking. For very good historical reasons, American experience with conflict between ranked groups—black-white relations—has been much more severe than American experience with conflict among unranked groups of European origin. In this respect, the experience of the United States has been comparable to that of many other societies struggling with ascriptive stratification, from Japan with its Burakumin to India with its scheduled castes to Brazil with its color categories. On the other hand, a good many societies, including Canada, Belgium, Northern Ireland, Nigeria, and Malaysia, have far more serious conflict among unranked than among ranked groups. Some, including India, have both types of conflict.

Some peculiarly American institutional features have also inadvertently operated to limit ethnic conflict among European-derived ethnic groups. Among these features, federalism has been profoundly important. American federalism has meant that many conflicts were not inflated to the national level but were played out on a much smaller, local stage. Again, a comparative perspective is instructive. On a world scale, states that have experienced the most severely destabilizing ethnic conflict have been those in which ethnic cleavages tend to bifurcate the society at the national level of politics. This was the situation that produced the Nigerian civil war of 1967 to 1970, and it is the situation in which Northern Ireland and Sri Lanka find themselves. By contrast, India, with its federal system and its proliferation of groups, is able to withstand a good deal of ethnic conflict that occurs at the state level of politics. Not every federal system has provided insulation against conflict; Nigeria's federalism did not serve it well in the 1960s. In the United States, however, migration patterns combined with federalism to quarantine much ethnic conflict within state boundaries. With dispersed power and decentralized institutions, the United States remained for a long time a two-tier polity. "Within such a loosely knit society," writes the historian John Higham, "many dissimilar ethnic adjustments could find lodgement."[9]

Two tier is probably too simple, for many of the most important developments occurred at the still-lower level of the city, where newly arriving groups met earlier immigrants and worked out some relationship. Here that other great American innovation, the urban political machine, contributed to the integration of groups that might

---

9. John Higham, "Disjunction and Diversity in American Ethnic History," unpublished colloquium paper (Woodrow Wilson International Center for Scholars, Washington, D.C., April 20, 1977), p. 14.

otherwise have seen their interests in conflict.[10] Made possible by the nonideological, decentralized character of American political parties, political machines, using patronage jobs and welfare handouts, had an important impact in the Northeast and the Midwest. Moreover, because ideology played a minor role in party choice, a group could respond to a party that did not make adequate room for its participation by turning to the opposing party. In New Haven, for example, when the Democratic party was controlled by an Irish machine, Italian voters finally deserted it and became Republicans.[11] The result was a redoubled effort by Democrats to capture valuable Italian votes. The coalitional character of the parties and the openness of their boundaries facilitated the accommodation of ethnic groups and their leaders.

Ideology and institutions thus combined to soften the conflicts that might have attended the reception of so many immigrants between 1850 and 1924. The lack of a firm birth basis for membership in the polity and the explicitly immigrant foundation of the society facilitated the emergence of an evolving "American" supraethnic identity alongside particular ethnic identities. These forces impeded the development of conceptions of territorial ownership, ultimately undermining the nativism that did arise. Federalism and nonideological parties—the latter in part the product of high levels of ideological agreement to begin with[12]—also fostered ethnic inclusion. None of this had much impact on black Americans, however, except for federalism, which plainly propped up ethnic subordination by making Jim Crow a local or regional problem. When black-white relations became a national policy issue, first during Reconstruction and then after 1954, this was at the expense of the prevailing federal-state balance and not because of it.

Several implications flow from this depiction of the American system of ethnic relations. These can be clustered under the headings of (1) social mobility, (2) group boundaries and identity, (3) political culture and behavior, and (4) relations of groups to territory. All have a single common theme: fluidity.

First of all, the United States system of ethnic relations might be expected to provide considerable opportunities for the educational and occupational mobility of members of unranked groups. In fact,

---

10. See Robert Dahl, *Who Governs? Democracy and Power in an American City* (New Haven: Yale University Press, 1961), pp. 33–36.

11. Raymond Wolfinger, "The Development and Persistence of Ethnic Voting," in Lawrence H. Fuchs, ed., *American Ethnic Politics* (New York: Harper & Row, 1968), pp. 163–93.

12. See Louis Hartz, *The Liberal Tradition in America* (New York: Harcourt, Brace, 1955).

it goes further and provides positive encouragement for mobility. There is room for intergroup variation on this score, but a group that seems "stagnant" may be viewed as presenting a problem. This is rather different from the conventional understandings of most other societies, but it finds root in, among other things, the bourgeois mythology of the American system, embodied in the Horatio Alger stories. The Americanization of immigrants becomes entangled with the quest for material success, as Louis Hartz has made so convincingly clear.[13] Moreover, the myth is congenial to intergenerational measures of mobility. The Alger myth does not promise immediate gratification. The aspiring American begins with manual labor and is prepared to wait for opportunity to knock.

The myth turns out to have a substantial basis in fact. As of the early 1970s, for example, an impressive array of immigrant groups—Japanese, Irish Catholics, Jews, Italians, Poles, and other Slavic Catholics—were all above the national mean in family income. In education, Jews, Japanese, Chinese, Irish Catholics, and German Catholics were all above the mean. Italians were at the mean, and Poles and other Slavic Catholics were just a shade beneath it in years of schooling.[14] On the whole, groups that immigrated in the nineteenth and twentieth centuries, including groups often regarded as over-whelmingly blue collar, had acquired significantly more income and education than many groups that arrived earlier from the British Isles and northern Europe.

Plainly, this pattern of mobility does not apply to ranked sub-ordinates. It is not surprising to find that blacks had family incomes significantly below the mean in the early 1970s, by far the greatest negative deviation, and they also were below the mean in education.[15]

Second, the relations among ethnic identity, group boundaries, and intergroup conflict are perhaps more complex, but here, too, what stands out is the mutability of cultures and boundaries in the American setting. Home languages were lost by virtually all European immigrant groups, and exogamy rates were between 30 and 60 percent for these groups by the 1960s, ranging from about 30 percent for Jews to about 40 percent for Italians, Poles, and French Canadians

13. Louis Hartz, *The Founding of New Societies* (New York: Harcourt, Brace, & World, 1964), pp. 103–11.
14. Harry H. L. Kitano, "Asian-Americans: The Chinese, Japanese, Koreans, Pili-pinos, and Southeast Asians," *The Annals*, vol. 454 (March 1981), pp. 125–38; Andrew M. Greeley, "Making It in America: Ethnic Groups and Social Status," *Social Policy* (September–October 1973), pp. 21–29.
15. Andrew M. Greeley, *Ethnicity in America: A Preliminary Reconnaissance* (New York: John Wiley & Sons, 1974), pp. 64–67.

to about 60 percent for Irish and German Catholics.[16] These rates were significantly higher for members of the third and fourth generations, however. Among persons thirty years old or younger in 1963, large majorities of Irish, German, Polish, and Italian Catholics had married exogamously.[17] Overall Catholic exogamy was in the 30 percent range in the 1960s, so that members of Catholic groups who practiced exogamy often retained their religious affiliation; more than 40 percent of Catholics born after World War II, however, married non-Catholics.[18] The same pattern holds for Chinese and Japanese. By the early 1970s, a third of young Chinese and a half of young Japanese in the United States were marrying non-Asians.[19] These are extremely high rates of exogamy, rates that, as I shall explain later, are too high to be compatible with patterns of severe ethnic conflict.

In spite of these trends, there are strong indications of persisting ethnic identifications. In a survey of Irish and Italians in Providence, Rhode Island, to take just one example, 50 percent of both groups in the first and second generations identified themselves ethnically, but 70 percent in the third generation did so.[20] This, despite the fact that 63 percent of the third generation had married exogamously, compared to 15 percent of the first generation. But while ethnic identification may have continuing significance, it bears no necessary relation to conflictual attitudes. Almost 90 percent of the Italians and 80 percent of the Irish exhibited no hostile attitudes toward the other group. Hostility declined with generational change; indications of social distance between the two groups were virtually nonexistent by the third generation. And, finally, strong ethnic identification does not get in the way of belief in open opportunity in the American system: strong, though decreasing, majorities of all three generations attested to such a belief.

Once again, the pattern for black Americans is different. The incidence of interracial marriage for black Americans doubled between 1963 and 1970, but the 1970 rate was only 1.2 percent.[21] One can hardly speak of permeable ethnic boundaries under these cir-

---

16. Leonard Dinnerstein and David M. Reimers, *Ethnic Americans: A History of Immigration and Assimilation* (New York: Harper & Row, 1975), p. 147.

17. Richard D. Alba, "The Twilight of Ethnicity among American Catholics of European Ancestry," *The Annals,* vol. 454 (March 1981), p. 93.

18. Ibid., p. 95.

19. Thernstrom, "Ethnic Groups in American History," p. 23.

20. John M. Goering, "The Emergence of Ethnic Interests: A Case of Serendipity," *Social Forces,* vol. 49 (March 1971), pp. 379–84.

21. Thernstrom, "Ethnic Groups in American History," p. 25.

cumstances. These are rates of exogamy quite compatible with high levels of ethnic conflict, and indeed surveys of black respondents in the early 1970s elicit high levels of distrust of whites and of political authorities, attitudes that contrasted markedly with white attitudes.[22]

Third, the United States has escaped a number of the political characteristics of severely divided societies, such as Northern Ireland or Nigeria or Sri Lanka. In such societies, ethnic affiliations repeatedly preempt alternative bases of political association. Ethnic antipathies are strong; they are revealed in attitudes of exclusivity and hostility and in behavior, including, typically, the formation of ethnically based parties, high rates of voting for such parties, and episodes of collective interpersonal violence. In American society, as I have noted, ethnic identity among European-origin groups seems compatible with low levels of exclusivity and hostility; ethnic parties are not unheard of but are not a predominant form of electoral expression; and large-scale interethnic violence directed primarily at persons has been largely absent since the first quarter of the twentieth century.[23]

Fourth, the American system is presumably conducive to geographic mobility and a variety of ethno-political arrangements flowing from mobility. The absence of acknowledged claims to indigenousness should facilitate spatial mobility. It is often not recognized just how common are the restraints on geographical mobility in severely divided societies, where groups entertain a sense of territoriality. Unlike many countries, the United States has no designated *sabon gari* or "strangers' quarters," no regions "protected" from migration, no ethnic restrictions on landholding (though it once had these), and no internal visa requirements. Although housing discrimination and residential segregation are practiced, they do not constitute a bar to interstate mobility. The history of American cities in particular has been characterized by the ephemeral quality of ethnic neighborhoods. For well over a century, residential and occupational succession has been the rule.[24] Despite a general consistency of ethnic concentration by regions over the decades, the United States has experienced a staggering amount of spatial mobility. The cultural homogenization of the country—all the way from public school curricula to McDonald's

---

22. Joel D. Aberbach and Jack L. Walker, *Race in the City* (Boston: Little, Brown & Co., 1973), pp. 165, 183–84.

23. The black riots of the 1960s fall into a quite different category. See Donald L. Horowitz, "Racial Violence in the United States," in Nathan Glazer and Ken Young, eds., *Ethnic Pluralism and Public Policy* (London: Heinemann, 1983), pp. 187–211.

24. See, for example, Stephan Thernstrom, *Poverty and Progress: Social Mobility in a Nineteenth Century City* (Cambridge, Mass.: Harvard University Press, 1964), pp. 84–90.

cuisine—is largely due to the free flow of people across the land. The most important precondition for this has been the unthinkability of equating any given territory with any particular ethnic group.[25]

Much social mobility in the United States is attributable to the ability to move freely in quest of opportunities. There are few geographic impediments to equilibration of factors of production. Groups feel free to exploit differentials in the price of labor by moving from one region to another, as blacks have in this century. A political consequence of this absence of impediment is that there has been no strong regional claim to indigenousness in the United States. So, too, has there been none of the strong ethno-territorial separatism that characterizes ethnic conflict nearly everywhere that ethnic groups are concentrated in particular territories.[26] Hospitable though it has been to regional difference, the thrust of American ethnic politics has been markedly centripetal.

Fluidity in ethnic group social mobility, fluidity in ethnic boundaries, fluidity in political alignments and behavior, and fluidity in regional boundaries and spatial mobility—these seem to me the great themes in American ethnic relations among unranked groups. All of them are consistent with comparatively low levels of intergroup conflict, and all seem to lead back to a chemical interaction among several features: the weakness of claims to priority; the evolving supraethnic, largely nonascriptive "American" identity coexisting with particular ethnic identities; and the permeation of that American identity with a decidedly modern view about the mastery of nature through human will and an unequivocally bourgeois acquisitiveness. Wyndham Lewis sensed something critical in the lesser role accorded to blood and territory in the shaping of American national identity.

Mexican-Americans in the American Ethnic System

How the Mexican-Americans relate conceptually to the broader framework of ethnic relations in the United States is a matter that has puzzled a number of writers,[27] for good reason. The history of Mexicans in the United States has two sides, and both are important.

---

25. For two different but converging perspectives on this, see Nathan Glazer, *Affirmative Discrimination* (New York: Basic Books, 1975), pp. 22–25; Richard D. Lambert, "Ethnic/Racial Relations in the United States in Comparative Perspective," *The Annals*, vol. 454 (March 1981), pp. 199–201.

26. See Donald L. Horowitz, "Patterns of Ethnic Separatism," *Comparative Studies in Society and History*, vol. 23 (April 1981), pp. 65–95.

27. For example, Lambert, "Ethnic/Racial Relations in the United States in Comparative Perspective."

The first is that a fairly small but significant Mexican population was encapsulated within the expanding United States. Whether the expansion took place by conquest or purchase, what followed was consistent with the treatment of a conquered population. There was a good deal of land grabbing, fraud, violence, and coercion practiced against the Mexican population of the Southwest in the second half of the nineteenth century, and there is evidence of downward social mobility as a result.[28] There were, no doubt, state-to-state variations, but they cut both ways. The Hispanic population was able to retain a better position in New Mexico than elsewhere, but by the same token there was a spillover from anti-black racism in Texas, where the great majority of new settlers had come from the South. Consequently, it is not wholly fatuous to regard Mexican-Americans in the Southwest, at least initially, as ranked subordinates. Ranked systems tend to originate in conquest, and it is not surprising to find elements of ascriptive hierarchy in the interaction of so-called Anglos and Mexican-Americans from Texas to California.

Nonetheless, there is another, later, arguably more important side: voluntary migration. Except in New Mexico, the Mexican population of the Southwest was small, relative both to the non-Mexican population at the time of American expansion and relative to the migratory flow that was to come in the twentieth century. Moreover, the reasons for the later migration are precisely the sort that are associated in comparative ethnic relations with the creation of systems of unranked ethnic relations. The first great period of immigration coincided with the Mexican Revolution, beginning in 1910. Migratory motives for this period are fairly well established. The revolution, which went on for more than a decade, created the unsettled conditions characteristic of internal warfare. Migrants such as Ernesto Galarza, whose family odyssey is beautifully chronicled in his book, *Barrio Boy*,[29] moved from town to town in Mexico to escape the fighting and the threat of conscription. As both became more difficult to escape, as hardships grew, and as making a living became more problematic, the final move was across the border, in his case to Sacramento. Others no doubt had more purely economic reasons. By the turn of the century, the disparity in national income was

28. Among many sources, see Leobardo F. Estrada et al., "Chicanos in the United States: A History of Exploitation and Resistance," *Daedalus*, vol. 110 (Spring 1981), pp. 103–31; Carlos E. Cortes, "Mexicans," in Stephan Thernstrom et al., eds., *Harvard Encyclopedia of American Ethnic Groups* (Cambridge, Mass.: Harvard University Press, 1980), pp. 697–719; Thomas J. Durant, Jr., and Clark S. Knowlton, "Rural Ethnic Minorities: Adaptive Response to Inequality," in Thomas R. Ford, ed., *Rural USA: Persistence and Change* (Ames: Iowa State University Press, 1978), p. 153.
29. Galarza, *Barrio Boy* (New York: Ballantine Books, 1972).

substantial, and the railroads (which crossed the border) were especially attracting labor.[30]

What is more, the exclusion of Japanese and Chinese immigrants from the United States coincided with the Mexican Revolution, thereby opening up new opportunities in an expanding economy.[31] In the first three decades of the century, close to a million Mexicans immigrated. In this respect, the history of Mexican-American immigration parallels that of the great voluntary migrations of Europeans, which took place for the most part somewhat earlier. Both push and pull, both political and economic incentives played a part.

The experience of Mexican-Americans reflects their dual origins in the United States. Attempts were made to enforce ascriptive subordination on them—for example, in the informal extension of segregation designed for blacks in east Texas to Mexican-Americans in west Texas. On the other hand, there is the immigration experience, in which, as Galarza and others testify, Mexican newcomers were subjected to a more or less thoroughgoing "Americanization" in the public schools and the more spontaneous acculturation that took place in the polyglot working-class neighborhoods where they settled.[32] No doubt this experience was far more intense for those who went directly to cities than for those who engaged in agricultural labor, but, sooner or later, nearly all Mexican-Americans ended up in cities. In terms of social mobility, group boundaries and identity, political culture and behavior, and the relation of groups to territory, once controls are instituted for continuing migratory influx, Mexican-American patterns are not replicas of black American patterns so much as they are consistent with the general fluidity of the American ethnic system.

Social Mobility

The overall picture is clear. Mexican-Americans have less education than black Americans, but higher income. Their generally low levels of education are improving over time, albeit not dramatically, and they display modest educational aspirations. There is also evidence of both rising occupational aspirations and convergence of aspiration level between Mexican-Americans and other Americans.

30. Dinnerstein and Reimers, *Ethnic Americans*, p. 95; Ciro Sepulveda, "Una Colonia de Obreros: East Chicago, Indiana," *Aztlán*, vol. 7 (Summer 1976), p. 329.

31. Dinnerstein and Reimers, *Ethnic Americans*, p. 95.

32. Galarza, *Barrio Boy*, pp. 206–07. For scholarly confirmation, see June Macklin and Alvina Teniente de Costilla, "*La Virgen de Guadalupe* and the American Dream: The Melting Pot Bubbles on in Toledo, Ohio," in Stanley A. West and June Macklin, eds., *The Chicano Experience* (Boulder: Westview, 1979), p. 116.

Education. Mexican-Americans have acquired significantly less education than most other ethnic groups have. Of the population over age 24, only 38 percent had completed high school or a year of college, compared to 89 percent of non-Hispanic white Americans and 55 percent of black Americans as of 1974.[33] Those figures, however, do not say anything about rates of change. Nor do they distinguish by age cohort, by country of origin, or by generation in the United States. Once such distinctions are introduced, a less extreme picture emerges.

A recent survey of East Los Angeles and San Antonio, in which noncitizens were excluded from the analysis, showed high levels of education among younger respondents. Whereas more than half of the over-45 age group had less than an eighth-grade education, only one in five in the under-45 group was in that position, and fully 58 percent had completed some college.[34] Nationwide trends were similar. Of Mexican-Americans who reached college age between 1968 and 1972, 52 percent had graduated from high school.[35] That was below the level of black Americans (72 percent) and the level of non-Hispanic white Americans (85 percent), but Mexican-Americans had the same rate of increase as non-Hispanic whites did. For that same cohort, only 17 percent of Mexican-Americans completed a year of college, compared to 27 percent of blacks and 43 percent of Anglos, but the Mexican-American rate of change was as high as the black rate and significantly higher than the Anglo rate.

Comparable results obtain for median years of schooling.[36] As of 1970, the overall figure for the United States was 12.1. Texas was lower, with a median of 11.6. With a large Mexican-American population, El Paso was at the national level, but Mexican-Americans in El Paso were at 8.6. El Paso, however, contains a heavily working-class population, many of whom were born in Mexico, where they received little education. A rough examination of census tracts containing concentrations of middle-class Mexican-Americans in El

---

33. Carlos H. Arce, "Chicanos in Higher Education," *Integrated Education,* vol. 14 (May–June 1976), pp. 14–18. For some Midwest figures, see Jim D. Faught, "Chicanos in a Medium-Sized City," *Aztlán,* vol. 7 (Summer 1976), p. 311.
34. Rodolfo O. de la Garza and Robert R. Brischetto, "The Mexican American Electorate: A Demographic Profile," Occasional Paper 1, Mexican American Electorate Series (Center for Mexican American Studies, University of Texas at Austin, 1982), p. 13.
35. Arce, "Chicanos in Higher Education," p. 15.
36. Clark S. Knowlton, "Changing Patterns of Segregation and Discrimination Affecting the Mexican Americans of El Paso, Texas," in Z. Anthony Kruszewski et al., eds., *Politics and Society in the Southwest: Ethnicity and Chicano Pluralism* (Boulder: Westview Press, 1982), pp. 150–51.

Paso reveals median levels of 13 to 15 years of schooling.[37] More recent figures show Mexican-Americans between the ages of 20 and 24 with 12.2 median years of school, a significant increase.[38] This is not surprising. Earlier intercensal increases in years of schooling for Mexican-Americans nationwide ran in the 30 percent range.[39] Rates of increase in Texas were higher.[40]

There are hints of qualitative increases in education as well. From 1975 to 1980, reading scores of Latinos increased at rates more than double the national average, though Mexican-Americans are not broken out separately.[41] There is no doubt that Mexican-Americans overall have low levels of education, but these are in large part an artifact of ongoing immigration of uneducated adults from Mexico, and they also mask the much higher levels prevailing in younger age cohorts.

Income. Education and income are not necessarily related directly. Italian-Americans, as we have seen, have low average levels of education but higher than average levels of family income. Black Americans, on the other hand, are rapidly closing the educational gap between them and the median for the society, but not the income gap, which remains substantial. Education is not automatically convertible to income in the United States. There is variation not accounted for by years of schooling. Quality of education, the structure of opportunity, the local economy, the level of achievement motivation, and the prevalence of discrimination are among the variables that bear on the relation of education and income. I shall return to the education-income connection shortly.

In 1977, the median family income for Mexican-Americans was 75 percent of the income of all families in the United States.[42] The

---

37. Ibid.

38. Harry P. Pachon and Joan W. Moore, "Mexican Americans," *The Annals*, vol. 454 (March 1981), pp. 111–24, at p. 120.

39. Median years of schooling from 1950 to 1960 increased from 5.4 to 7.1.

40. Richard A. Garcia, "Political Ideology: A Comparative Study of Three Chicano Youth Organizations," mimeographed paper (San Francisco, 1977), pp. 30–31. For California, see Fernando Peñalosa, "The Changing Mexican-American in Southern California," *Sociology and Social Research*, vol. 51 (July 1967), p. 412.

41. Wayne A. Cornelius et al., "Mexican Immigrants and Southern California: A Summary of Current Knowledge," Research Report 36 (Center for U.S.-Mexican Studies, University of California, San Diego, 1982), p. 77.

42. Morris L. Newman, "A Profile of Hispanics in the U.S. Work Force," *Monthly Labor Review*, vol. 101 (December 1978), p. 10. See also U.S. Department of Labor, Bureau of Labor Statistics, *Workers of Spanish Origin: A Chartbook* (Washington, D.C.: U.S. Government Printing Office, 1978), p. 41; Robert M. Jiobu, "Earnings Differentials between Whites and Ethnic Minorities: The Cases of Asian Americans, Blacks, and Chicanos," *Sociology and Social Research*, vol. 61 (October 1976), pp. 24–38.

comparable figure for black Americans was 60 percent. Black family income, in other words, was only four-fifths that of Mexican-Americans. Chicanos are a predominantly blue-collar group, but many are employed in fairly well-paid craft occupations, such as construction and mechanical work. Rates of Mexican-American unemployment also lie between those of black Americans and Anglos, but Mexican-Americans have unusually short periods of unemployment, suggesting considerable persistence and success in finding work.[43]

Once again, it is important to examine changes over time, over age cohorts, and over generations in the United States. A recent summary of research reports considerable intragenerational and intergenerational change.[44] First-generation immigrants experience little occupational mobility but much improvement of income level in the course of working lives. For example, Mexicans who immigrated before 1959 have wage rates 20 to 25 percent higher than the most recent immigrants, a rate of income progress significantly higher than that of comparable, time-lagged Puerto Rican immigrants.[45] A California study shows intergenerational occupational mobility to be common: 15 percent of the first generation of Mexican-Americans were in white-collar jobs, compared to 27.4 percent of the second generation and 36.7 percent of the third.[46] Third-generation median income as of 1970 was 74 percent higher than first-generation median income.[47] California, it was found, offers less discrimination toward Mexican-Americans and generally higher levels of opportunity than do other southwestern states, particularly Texas, and California is the preferred destination of Mexican immigrants to the United States.[48]

Age cohort analysis performed on the East Los Angeles-San Antonio sample shows marked differences in family income for 1981–82.[49] More than half the cohort aged 66 and over had incomes under $5,000, and more than half of the 56–65 cohort was under $10,000. However, more than half of the 36–55 group was over $15,000, with substantial fractions higher. In the 18–55 age range, 13 percent had incomes over $30,000. Median family income for the United States in 1981 was $19,074.

---

43. Newman, " A Profile of Hispanics in the U.S. Work Force," p. 7.
44. Cornelius et al., "Mexican Immigrants and Southern California," pp. 77–82.
45. George J. Borjas, "The Earnings of Male Hispanic Immigrants in the United States," *Industrial and Labor Relations Review*, vol. 35 (April 1982), pp. 348–49.
46. Cornelius et al., "Mexican Immigrants and Southern California," p. 78.
47. Ibid., p. 79.
48. Ibid., pp. 13, 79. For a similar verdict on California, see Peñalosa, "The Changing Mexican-American in Southern California," p. 411.
49. De la Garza and Brischetto, "The Mexican American Electorate," p. 14.

Focusing on trends over time, a mixed picture emerges from the fragmentary evidence available. From 1930 to 1970, the proportion of Chicano men in professional and technical occupations rose from less than 1 percent to more than 6 percent; more significantly, those in skilled crafts trebled, from 7 to 21 percent, and those in white-collar occupations increased from 8 to 22 percent.[50] In a midwestern city, three out of every four Mexican-American high school graduates were employed in nonmanual occupations as of 1974.[51] The number of Hispanic-origin teachers in California more than doubled between 1967 and 1980, an increase much more rapid than the black American increase.[52] Mexican-Americans also experienced gains in state civil service employment and dramatic gains in federal government employment. Between 1964 and 1974, Hispanic employees in federal offices in the five Southwest states nearly doubled. As usual, California had the highest rate of increase (55 percent); the increase in Texas was much smaller.[53] There are also hints that the private sector may offer marginally more useful avenues of mobility to Mexican-Americans than the public sector, which is more helpful to blacks.[54]

Having noted all these trends, questions remain about the significance of the improvements. For one thing, the overall ratio of Mexican-American earnings to Anglo earnings changed rather little during the 1970s,[55] but of course this was a decade of enormous migration from Mexico, which would exert a downward pull on earnings in the first instance. Perhaps more revealing is the impact of increased education on earnings, and here the evidence is equivocal. Earnings differentials between Hispanics and Anglos are explained about equally by two sets of variables: productivity variables (such as education, age, and time worked) and nonproductivity variables (including discrimination).[56] Disaggregation into various Hispanic

50. Cortes, "Mexicans," pp. 712–13.

51. Faught, "Chicanos in a Medium-Sized City," p. 319.

52. Craig Richards, "Bilingualism and Hispanic Employment," Project Report 83-A16 (Institute for Research on Educational Finance and Governance, School of Education, Stanford University, July 1983), p. 9.

53. U.S. Civil Service Commission, A Profile of Hispanic Employment, 1974–1976 (Washington, D.C.: U.S. Government Printing Office, 1978), p. 3.

54. Cf. Richards, "Bilingualism and Hispanic Employment," table 3; Rufus P. Browning et al., "Blacks and Hispanics in California City Politics: Changes in Representation," Public Affairs Report, vol. 20 (Bulletin of the Institute of Governmental Studies, University of California, Berkeley, June 1979), p. 4; Santiago Rodriguez, "Affirmative Action and the Hispanic Community," Civil Service Journal, vol. 18 (October–December, 1977), pp. 18–22.

55. Pachon and Moore, "Mexican Americans," p. 118.

56. James E. Long, "Productivity, Employment Discrimination, and the Relative Economic Status of Spanish Origin Males," Social Science Quarterly, vol. 58 (December 1977), pp. 365–67.

groups, however, produces the interesting finding that productivity variables were a bigger factor in explaining Mexican-American differentials than in explaining differentials for other Hispanic groups;[57] for black Americans, discrimination was a much more significant component of the differentials. Given equal productivity attributes, in other words, Mexican-Americans had higher ratios of earnings to Anglo earnings than did Puerto Ricans and Cubans, and much higher ratios than blacks. This, it should be stressed, does not mean that education is worth as much in earnings to Chicanos as it is to Anglos. To be precise, one study using California data from 1970 found that an additional year of education was worth $522 in annual earnings to non-Hispanic whites, $340 to Chicanos, and only $284 to blacks.[58]

Put differently, there is still discrimination against Mexican-Americans that limits earnings, but it seems to be slightly less than discrimination against Cubans and Puerto Ricans and significantly less than discrimination against blacks. Higher earnings for Cubans are accounted for heavily by education, for Cubans invested much more heavily than Mexicans in accumulating education *after* their arrival in the United States.[59] A Cuban who immigrated between 1965 and 1969 had 10.6 percent higher wages in 1976 than a Mexican who immigrated at the same time with the same initial level of schooling, because that Cuban, on the average, obtained more education after arrival. "Differences in the rate of human capital accumulation while in the United States," concludes George J. Borjas in a recent study, "are an important source of earnings differentials among the various Hispanic immigrant groups."[60]

Increases in education may therefore be expected to reduce further the earnings differentials between Mexican-Americans and non-Hispanic whites.[61] But this may not be so easy to accomplish, for it has been argued—using Japanese and Mexican-American income contrasts—that large family size and relatively early marriage reduce the ability of Mexican-Americans to finance the education of their children.[62] As I shall note below, however, in at least one study

---

57. Ibid., p. 371.
58. Jiobu, "Earnings Differentials between Whites and Ethnic Minorities," p. 29.
59. Borjas, "The Earnings of Male Hispanic Immigrants in the United States," pp. 348–51.
60. Ibid., p. 352.
61. This is another way of interpreting the otherwise pessimistic conclusions of Dudley L. Poston, Jr., et al., "Earnings Differentials between Anglo and Mexican American Male Workers in 1960 and 1970: Changes in the 'Cost' of Being Mexican American," *Social Science Quarterly*, vol. 57 (December 1976), pp. 618–31.
62. Peter Uhlenberg, "Demographic Correlates of Group Achievement: Contrasting Patterns of Mexican-Americans and Japanese-Americans," *Demography*, vol. 9 (February 1972), pp. 119–28.

Mexican-Americans reported no difficulty financing fairly high levels of education for their children.

Aspirations. Mexican-American attitudes have long been oriented toward achievement. As early as the mid-1960s, it was noted that Mexican-American high school students in Los Angeles had high levels of upwardly mobile aspirations.[63] Only 5 percent of the fathers of students sampled had attended college, but 44 percent of the sons expected to attend college. Some 2 percent came from homes with fathers in professional or semiprofessional occupations, but 35 percent aspired to such occupations. Only 13 percent of the fathers owned their business or practice, whereas 41 percent of the sons thought that they themselves would eventually do so. Although these ambition levels were actually lower than those in the overall sample, the intergenerational disparity was much greater for Mexican-American students.[64]

Subsequent studies report a significant convergence in the occupational aspirations of Mexican-American, black Americans, and Anglo students in a variety of regional locations. In a Texas sample, Mexican-American students are reported to have the strongest intensity of occupational aspiration, coupled with higher expectations of occupational realization than students from other groups.[65] To be sure, in a longitudinal study of Mexican-Americans, blacks, and Anglos in Wisconsin, Chicanos had college aspirations for their children at rates lower than blacks or Anglos, though the differential closed a good bit over a decade.[66] Bear in mind, however, that this is the older generation speaking of what might be appropriate for the younger, which, in an intergenerationally changeable population, is less relevant than what the younger generation itself thinks. In any case, on virtually every other measure of aspirations and career-relevant values, the trend over time was strongly toward convergence with the wider society. Mexican-American parents raised their educational sights by 50 percent between 1960 and 1971, more than

---

63. Celia Stopnicka Heller, "Class as an Explanation of Ethnic Differences in Mobility Aspirations: The Case of Mexican Americans," *International Migration Review*, vol. 2 (Fall 1967), pp. 31–39.

64. Ralph Turner, *The Social Context of Ambition* (San Francisco: Chandler Publishing, 1964), pp. 35–44.

65. William P. Kuvlesky and Everett D. Edington, "Ethnic Group Identity and Occupational Status Projections of Teenage Boys and Girls," in Kruszewski et al., *Politics and Society in the Southwest*, pp. 67–102.

66. Judith L. McKim et al., "Becoming 'We' Instead of 'They': The Cultural Integration of Mexican-Americans and Negroes," *Urban Education*, vol. 13 (July 1978), pp. 147–78.

black parents did. More Mexican-Americans than blacks, and almost as many as Anglos, said they could afford post-high school education for their children. In that intervening decade, Mexican-Americans and blacks both assumed a much more personally activist posture with respect to planning, shaping their future, expecting a good life, and determining their own fate, whereas Anglos either became less activist on these dimensions or rejected passivity at slower rates of change. "All of this," say the investigators, "suggests that Negroes and Mexican-Americans have come to perceive the [occupational] world around them more and more as do Anglos."[67] These results square with surveys of work attitudes that show growing interethnic convergence in the structure of reward preferences.[68]

Mobility and Subordination. In all, then, the studies show higher income for Mexican-Americans than for black Americans; increasing levels of income, held back, however, by, among other things, persistent discrimination and low levels of education; growing educational and occupational aspirations; and rather clear differences in education and income by generation and migration status. Two subjects that I have not touched on yet but that have major effects on education and income levels are linguistic facility and regional variation. So far there is evidence of fluidity of the sort expected for unranked groups in the American system. Needless to say, this does not rule out conflict among unranked ethnic groups. But these levels of social mobility, however modest, are quite incompatible with ascriptive subordination.

Group Boundaries and Identity

The relationship among group culture, group boundaries, group identity, and ethnic conflict is by no means straightforward. High levels of cultural change are quite compatible with the maintenance of group boundaries. The distinction between acculturation and assimilation needs to be taken seriously. Cultures may change dramatically without undermining group identity, which is largely a function of the preexisting mix of groups in a given territorial

---

67. Ibid., p. 156.
68. Charles E. Davis and Jonathan O. West, "Job Reward Preferences of Mexican-American and Anglo Public Employees," *Public Productivity Review,* vol. 4 (September 1980), pp. 199–209. Cf. Ruth Chavez and Albert Ramirez, "Employment Aspirations, Expectations, and Attitudes among Employed and Unemployed Chicanos," abstracted in *Journal of Social Psychology,* vol. 119 (Fall 1983), pp. 143–44.

context.[69] It is a mistaken view of ethnicity that sees group identity threatened by acculturation. Furthermore, although some theories of ethnic conflict have been cast in terms of cultural divergence, cultural convergence is not inimical to the pursuit of ethnic conflict.[70] And, finally, the maintenance of ethnic group identity is not dependent on the persistence of rigidly ascriptive boundaries. Boundaries may become quite permeable without necessarily obliterating intergroup distinctions. Very permeable boundaries do typically signal, however, a fairly modest level of interethnic conflict.

All of this is pertinent to the experience of Mexican-Americans. They have undergone a substantial degree of cultural change without the loss of group identity. These changes appear to be adaptations to the exigencies of competition in the wider society. At the same time, group boundaries have become more and more permeable, less and less ascriptive, without producing assimilation. The rate at which this is happening, however, appears inconsistent with a politics of severe ethnic conflict.

Language and Culture. There is much discussion in the literature by and about Mexican-Americans of the decline of extended families and of such institutions as *compadrinazgo* (godparenthood and the obligations deriving from it). There is now also abundant evidence of language change. The most careful study is by David E. Lopez of 1,129 couples in Los Angeles.[71] Both husband and wife were of Mexican descent, and the respondents were women. Both of these factors might have been thought to bias the results against English. Women may be in less frequent contact with English, and, as we shall see shortly, many Mexican-Americans have spouses who are not of Mexican descent; they were not in the sample. Nevertheless, the shifts to English are striking. Of those born and raised in Mexico, 84 percent speak mostly Spanish at home. By the third generation, 84 percent use mostly English. Most of the rest are bilingual, and only 4 percent use mostly Spanish.

The key variable is generation. The full extent of language shift in the group as a whole is thus masked by continuing immigration.

---

69. See Donald L. Horowitz, "Ethnic Identity," in Nathan Glazer and Daniel P. Moynihan, eds., *Ethnicity: Theory and Experience* (Cambridge, Mass.: Harvard University Press, 1975), pp. 111–40; Donald L. Horowitz, "Cultural Movements and Ethnic Change," *The Annals*, vol. 433 (September 1977), pp. 6–18.

70. See Donald L. Horowitz, "Multiracial Politics in the New States: Toward a Theory of Conflict," in Robert J. Jackson and Michael B. Stein, eds., *Issues in Comparative Politics* (New York: St. Martin's Press, 1971), pp. 164–80.

71. David E. Lopez, "Chicano Language Loyalty in an Urban Setting," *Sociology and Social Research*, vol. 62 (January 1978), pp. 267–78.

Comparable results have now been obtained for Chicago high school students; as in Los Angeles, no significant differences were explained by social class.[72] A longitudinal study of high school students in south Texas showed a 10 percent change from Spanish to English in usage with parents in the course of six years.[73] The overall trend toward English, with particularly rapid shifts to English in recent years, is simply not in doubt.[74]

None of this means that the Mexican-American identity is in jeopardy. Lopez is careful to note that English-speaking Mexican-Americans maintain their group affiliation, their Mexican friends, co-workers, and neighbors: "shifting to English does not imply anything about loosening ethnic bonds."[75] Language change is, however, likely to go hand in hand with other forms of acculturation. What some of these might be is suggested by alterations in ritual and festival practices, as reported for the Mexican-American community in Toledo, Ohio, for example. When dormant customs were to be revived by aspiring families, the parents made a trip to Mexico "to 'research' the ritual in order to do it 'correctly.' "[76] Those who cannot practice revived authenticity make some accommodation between received practices and local milieux, much as other ethnic groups have done.[77]

Students of language change tend to use self-reporting of shifts to English, which is probably reliable, but they do not purport to measure adequacy of the command of English. In one 1975 survey, some 2.2 million Hispanics (not, it should be emphasized, Mexican-Americans alone) described themselves as having "difficulty in English."[78] Such a figure raises the intriguing question of the relationship between facility in English and income. This bears on the relationship between language shift and the maintenance of group boundaries. In the United States, with its low levels of native English speakers who have facility in a second language, it would seem reasonable to suppose

72. Ellen Bouchard Ryan and Miguel A. Carranza, "Language Attitudes and Other Cultural Attitudes of Bilingual Mexican-American Adolescents," *Ethnicity*, vol. 7 (June 1980), pp. 191–202.

73. Victoria P. Morrow and William P. Kuvlesky, "Bilingual Patterns of Nonmetropolitan Mexican-American Youth," in Kruszewski et al., *Politics and Society in the Southwest*, pp. 3–24.

74. Cornelius et al., "Mexican Immigrants and Southern California," pp. 74–78.

75. Lopez, "Chicano Language Loyalty in an Urban Setting," p. 275.

76. Macklin and Teniente de Costilla, *"La Virgen de Guadalupe* and the American Dream," p. 134.

77. Ibid., p. 136.

78. Abigail Thernstrom, unpublished manuscript on the Voting Rights Act, chapter 5, p. 64.

that Spanish speakers would find it economically rewarding to shift to English but that such a pattern of change would imply nothing about the renunciation of one ethnic identity for another.

The income hypothesis turns out to be virtually unchallengeable. A recent study prepared for the United States Department of Labor contains some startling findings on language and income.[79] The investigators constructed a measure of "English-language deficiency" (ELD) and administered the instrument to a large Hispanic and Anglo sample. Once years of schooling, age, and region of residence are controlled, deficiencies in English account for all statistically significant differentials in earnings between immigrant and native-born Hispanics. More dramatic still is the finding of no significant wage differentials between Anglos and Hispanics in the most English-proficient categories.[80] Negative effects of ELD on income are greater in skilled than in unskilled occupations; in other words, they retard income most where wages are otherwise the highest.[81]

At the low end, a Hispanic male with maximum English-language deficiency, 12 years of schooling, and 20 years of work experience will earn a wage 35 percent below that earned by a comparable Hispanic male with no English-language deficiency, and he will earn even less if located outside a metropolitan area. Consequently, the average differential between the highest and lowest ELD categories, otherwise similarly situated, is 43 percent—a very high price to pay for English-language deficiency.[82]

What predicts maximum English-language deficiency? For immigrants, recency of arrival in the United States and arrival after receiving substantial schooling in the country of birth. Minimal deficiency is, of course, predicted by arrival as a preschool child and by birth in the United States.[83]

Taken together with the Borjas and Lopez studies discussed above (and assuming the findings hold up when "Hispanic" is disaggregated into Mexican-American and other Hispanic categories), it is easy enough to paint an optimistic hypothetical picture of the long-term income future of those Mexican-Americans born in the United States. As English language transmission increases across

79. Walter McManus et al., "Earnings of Hispanic Men: The Role of English Language Proficiency," paper prepared for U.S. Department of Labor, Office of the Assistant Secretary for Policy, 1983. Cf. de la Garza and Brischetto, "The Mexican American Electorate," pp. 17–18.
80. McManus et al., "Earnings of Hispanic Men," p. 23.
81. Ibid., p. 30.
82. Ibid., p. 25.
83. Ibid., p. 27.

generations and education levels also rise, income should increase rapidly. But such trends, obviously, would not affect the situation of immigrants, and indeed one can hypothesize, with continuing immigration, a more prominent intergenerational income and status bifurcation within the Mexican-American community than has so far occurred.

Marriage. Changes in language thus affect income more than they do group identity. Perhaps the same may be said of intermarriage. In a Los Angeles sample from the early 1960s, 40 percent of Chicano marriages were exogamous.[84] More than half of Mexican-American women marrying high-status men married exogamously. Occupational mobility was clearly significant in explaining Mexican-American exogamy. So, however, was generation. In the second and third generations, both women and men were more likely to marry Anglos than immigrants from Mexico. In the third generation, the probability of marriage between a Mexican-American and an Anglo was higher than between a Mexican-American and either a first- or second-generation Mexican-American.

It is now a generation later, and exogamy in California has proceeded apace, to about the 50 percent mark.[85] Studies elsewhere also report high and increasing levels of Chicano exogamy. In San Antonio, as of 1973, 27 percent of all Chicano marriages were exogamous, and in Albuquerque in 1971 the figure was 39 percent.[86] In Toledo, from 1974 to 1977, 60 percent of Mexican-American marriages were exogamous.[87] By generation, the increase in Toledo was striking. Nearly all the Mexican-born males married endogamously. More than half of the Texas-born males married exogamously, though only 20 percent of the females did. Two-thirds of the Ohio-born males married exogamously, and nearly 40 percent of the females did. In the somewhat more isolated Mexican-American communities of western New York, exogamy rates were 71 percent, but rose to 92 percent for those born in New York state.[88]

Even such high rates of exogamy as those reported for some northern cities do not inevitably result in assimilation. It seems likely that some group members are lost as a result—and since they are

---

84. Frank G. Mittelbach and Joan W. Moore, "Ethnic Endogamy—the Case of Mexican Americans," *American Journal of Sociology*, vol. 74 (July 1968), pp. 50–62.
85. See chapter 1 by Walker Connor in this volume.
86. Ibid.
87. Macklin and Teniente de Costilla, *"La Virgen de Guadalupe* and the American Dream," pp. 129–30.
88. George Rivera, Jr., and Juventino Mejia, "Mas aya del ancho rio: Mexicanos in Western New York," *Atzlán*, vol. 7 (Fall 1976), pp. 505–06.

lost their exact numbers are, in the nature of things, obscure—but researchers are nonetheless able to identify significant numbers of Mexican-Americans who are the progeny of exogamous marriages.

As Macklin and Teniente de Costilla observe most aptly, exogamy proved possible because Mexican-Americans did not "occupy a caste-like position."[89] The contrast with black Americans, whose rates of exogamy are in the range of 1 to 2 percent,[90] could hardly be clearer.

There is a further contrast that exogamy rates of 25 to 50 percent and upward suggest—the contrast with unranked but severely divided societies, where exogamy is an unusual event. Except at the extremes, not much is known about the relation of exogamy to ethnic conflict. But the meaning of the extremes is very clear. In severely divided societies, efforts are generally made to maintain the birth bases of ethnic groups. Since completely free choice of marriage partners would undermine ascription, there are strong pressures against exogamy. As ethnic conflict accelerates, exogamy often declines sharply. In Kenya, for example, when ethnic relations grew tense, there was a virtual halt to Kikuyu-Luo cohabitation and intermarriage.[91] Rates of exogamy for severely divided societies typically run below 10 percent, and probably lower if only unions between the two most-conflicted groups are counted. In a Kampala, Uganda, survey the rate of exogamy was 8.2 percent, and no marriage crossed the major fault lines of the society.[92] In Singapore, the exogamy rate in the 1960s was 5.1 percent, but Malay-Chinese unions were much rarer.[93] Exact figures are not available for Lebanon before the civil war of the mid-1970s, but there is enough evidence to show that exogamy ran much below 10 percent.[94] And if these figures do not suffice to make the point, a comparison of the Irish Republic with Northern Ireland surely will. As early as 1961, estimates of Protestant-Catholic

---

89. Macklin and Teniente de Costilla, *"La Virgen de Guadalupe* and the American Dream," p. 131.

90. Despite recent increases. See Martin Kilson, "Whither Integration?" *American Scholar,* vol. 45 (Summer 1976), p. 369. Compare Peter R. Jones, "Ethnic Intermarriage in Britain," *Ethnic and Racial Studies,* vol. 5 (April 1982), pp. 223–28.

91. David Parkin, "Congregational and Interpersonal Ideologies in Political Ethnicity," in Abner Cohen, ed., *Urban Ethnicity* (London: Tavistock Publishers, 1974), p. 142.

92. R. D. Grillo, "Ethnic Identity and Social Stratification on a Kampala Housing Estate," in Cohen, ed., *Urban Ethnicity,* p. 168.

93. Riaz Hassan, "Interethnic Marriage in Singapore: A Study in Interethnic Relations," Occasional Paper 21 (Institute of Southeast Asian Studies, Singapore, May 1974).

94. David R. Smock and Audrey C. Smock, *The Politics of Pluralism: A Comparative Study of Lebanon and Ghana* (New York: Elsevier, 1975), p. 92.

intermarriage ran at about the 25 percent level in the Republic; exogamy in the conflict-prone North, on the other hand, was so close to zero that Catholics and Protestants there were described as "two endogamous groups more separated from each other in sexual matters than most white and negro groups in societies that supposedly abhor miscegenation."[95]

Societies with more moderate levels of ethnic conflict sometimes have higher rates of exogamy, particularly if sex-ratio imbalances accompany recent migration. Ghana has overall exogamy rates ranging from 8 to 18 percent, depending on how groups are counted, and the rate is probably higher for immigrant groups like the Mossi.[96] In Philippine cities, exogamy runs as high as 15 or 20 percent.[97] Yet, in Morocco, with a strong ethos of tolerant ethnic relations, by one count only 11.3 percent of all marriages crossed Arab-Berber lines.[98]

The figures for the United States need to be contrasted with these, for they are simply not in the same range. Where ethnic loyalties are strong, the ethnic group rests on kinship connections and marriage is even more urgently than usual a family matter. Where ethnic conflict is low, exogamy becomes possible even for groups with fairly strong family ties. The exceptionally high rate of intermarriage in Hawaii has long been noted. In 1980, 59 percent of Japanese in Hawaii married out.[99] But now the pattern is more widespread. In Los Angeles in 1979, half of all Japanese not only married exogamously but married non-Asians.[100] Of course, endogamy-exogamy is not only a function of high or low levels of ethnic conflict, for family structure is also pertinent.[101] But at the level of necessary (as opposed to sufficient) conditions, ethnic conflict is a major constraint. Severe conflict renders exogamy uncomfortable at best, dangerous at worst. Low levels of conflict reduce social distance,

---

95. For the Republic, see Harold Jackson, "The Two Irelands—A Dual Study of Intergroup Tensions," Minority Rights Group Report 2 (London, January 1971), p. 20. The quotation on the North is from Rosemary Harris, *Prejudice and Tolerance in Ulster* (Manchester: Manchester University Press, 1972), p. x.

96. Smock and Smock, *The Politics of Pluralism*, p. 307; Enid Schildkrout, "Ethnicity and Generational Differences among Urban Immigrants in Ghana," in Cohen, ed., *Urban Ethnicity*, pp. 209–10.

97. Rodolfo Bulatao, *Ethnic Attitudes in Five Philippine Cities* (Quezon City: University of the Philippines Social Research Laboratory, 1973), p. 34.

98. Lawrence Rosen, "The Social and Conceptual Framework of Arab-Berber Relations in Central Morocco," in Ernest Gellner and Charles Micaud, eds., *Arabs and Berbers* (Lexington, Mass.: Lexington Books, 1972), p. 163.

99. Michael Banton, *Racial and Ethnic Competition* (Cambridge, England: Cambridge University Press, 1983), p. 143.

100. Ibid.

101. For a discussion, see Hassan, "Interethnic Marriage in Singapore."

facilitate intergroup interactions in the full range of social settings, remove the constraint of hostile in-group opinion, and may even act subtly to provide an incentive to exogamy—namely, the satisfaction that derives from being in tune with the ideals of the society. Whatever the mechanism, there is no way to square Mexican-American exogamy rates with the conception of the United States as a severely conflict-prone society. As I have said, black-white exogamy is an altogether different matter; and that is because it pertains to all of the taboos historically associated with ranked subordination and inferiority and, more recently, to black reactions to those taboos.

Political Culture and Behavior

When Almond and Verba conducted their five-country survey of political culture around 1960, their results in Mexico were interesting. They found positive attitudes toward the political system coupled with low expectations of favorable outputs from that system. High system affect they attributed to the Mexican Revolution and to the new links it created between the population and the regime. Low output affect, on the other hand, they attributed to actual experience with governmental performance.[102]

In some ways, the many attitudinal studies of Mexican-Americans show traces of a comparable pattern. Orientations toward the political system are fairly favorable, but demands and expectations of it are quite limited, and rates of political participation, although rising, remain low. It would be a major mistake to view second- and third-generation Mexican-Americans as blindly carrying with them into the American polity views held by former generations in Mexico. But it is not wholly unreasonable to wonder, for what is mainly a post-revolution migratory pattern, whether some portion of these political attitudes did not survive, just as a variety of cultural patterns survive in modified form among the descendants of migrants everywhere.

Whatever careful study ultimately discloses on this issue—and the Almond and Verba data themselves have been challenged—the moderate quality of Mexican-American political attitudes can scarcely be gainsaid. At the most general level, Mexican-American and Anglo schoolchildren in East Los Angeles exhibit similar levels of pride in

---

102. Gabriel A. Almond and Sidney Verba, *The Civic Culture: Political Attitudes and Democracy in Five Nations* (Princeton: Princeton University Press, 1963), pp. 414–15, 495–96. The Almond and Verba findings on Mexico have been challenged. See Ann L. Craig and Wayne Cornelius, "Political Culture in Mexico: Continuities and Revisionist Interpretations," in Almond and Verba, eds., *The Civic Culture Reconsidered* (Boston: Little, Brown & Co., 1980), pp. 325–93.

being American. More Mexican-American students than Anglo students (67.5 to 64.7 percent) agree that "the United States of America is the best country in the world," and overall there are only small attitudinal differences between the two groups of students.[103] By contrast, black students show increasingly negative affective orientations toward the political system with age.[104] Even among Mexican-American youth gangs in El Paso, a striking degree of political affect was reported: 40 percent of the members of one gang responded "yes" to the question, "Is America close to being a perfect society?"[105] Most members of that gang were first- or second-generation Americans; members of two other gangs, generationally older, exhibited lower levels of support for this extreme proposition. All three gangs displayed low levels of support for ethnic separatism, measured by responses to questions about the desirability of keeping to one's own group and working only with groups members; between 63 and 93 percent, depending on the gang, thought such exclusive practices undesirable.[106] These findings are consistent with Ambrecht and Pachon's careful surveys of East Los Angeles in 1965 and 1972, in which majorities of Mexican-Americans (albeit declining majorities) thought assimilation was a good thing (82 and 67 percent) and likely to occur (75 and 55 percent).[107] The point is not whether the respondents were right. What is revealing is the terms in which they were thinking.

Even after the turmoil of the preceding decade, in 1972 Ambrecht and Pachon found a strong preference for "orderly, legitimate" political action and an antipathy to political violence.[108] Community problems should be solved by electing people of Mexican background to office (90 percent), by appointing them to government jobs (98 percent), and by working within the Democratic and Republican parties (71 percent), but not by forming separate parties (44 percent) or by joining street demonstrations (36 percent) or by rioting (22

103. F. Chris Garcia, "Orientations of Mexican American and Anglo Children toward the U.S. Political Community," *Social Science Quarterly*, vol. 53 (December 1973), pp. 814–29.
104. Edward S. Greenberg, "Children and the Political Community: A Comparison across Racial Lines," *Canadian Journal of Political Science*, vol. 2 (December 1969), pp. 471–92.
105. Richard A. Garcia, "Political Ideology," p. 74.
106. Ibid., p. 77.
107. Biliana C. S. Ambrecht and Harry P. Pachon, "Ethnic Political Mobilization in a Mexican American Community: An Exploratory Study of East Los Angeles, 1965–72," *Western Political Quarterly*, vol. 27 (September 1974), pp. 500–19.
108. Ibid. See also the conservative attitudes among Mexican-American college freshmen, reported by Arce, "Chicanos in Higher Education," p. 16.

percent). The contrast with black attitudes is interesting. About half of all black respondents after the riots of the 1960s felt sympathy for the rioters, and substantial minorities advocated violence as "the best" or "necessary" means to achieve equality.[109] Two-thirds of the Mexican-Americans in a Denver survey disagreed that violence is sometimes necessary to overcome barrio conditions; a majority of black Americans agreed with the statement for ghetto conditions.[110] The contrast in political attitudes is fairly consistent. Mexican-Americans display high levels of trust in the national government: between 71 and 74 percent of a Nebraska sample expected equal treatment by federal government officials.[111] Among black Americans, as we have seen, levels of political trust and expectations of equal treatment are lower.[112] Blacks are also less satisfied than whites with municipal services. In an Omaha survey, Mexican-Americans displayed high levels of satisfaction with government—in the 68 to 94 percent range, among those who had had contact with government.[113] These are far closer to Anglo levels of satisfaction than to black, although whether Omaha typifies a larger universe is an open question. A Texas survey also showed much less political alienation among Mexican-Americans than among blacks.[114]

Perceptions of discrimination run in the same direction. In surveys, blacks report discrimination in hiring, promotion, police treatment, and government services at levels some twenty-five percentage points above comparable reports by all Hispanics.[115] Consciousness of discrimination increases with length of stay among Mexican immigrants and with generation as well, but the levels to which it rises are comparatively modest.[116] The same is true for

---

109. The studies are summarized in Horowitz, "Racial Violence in the United States," p. 195.
110. Nicholas P. Lovrich, Jr., and Otwin Marenin, "A Comparison of Black and Mexican American Voters in Denver: Assertive versus Acquiescent Political Orientations and Voting Behavior in an Urban Electorate," *Western Political Quarterly*, vol. 29 (June 1976), p. 291.
111. Susan Welch et al., "Political Participation among Mexican Americans: An Exploratory Explanation," *Social Science Quarterly*, vol. 53 (December 1973), p. 806.
112. Aberbach and Walker, *Race in the City*, p. 184.
113. John C. Comer, " 'Street Level' Bureaucracy and Political Support: Some Findings on Mexican Americans," *Urban Affairs Quarterly*, vol. 14 (December 1978), p. 216.
114. Clifton McClesky and Bruce Merrill, "Mexican American Political Behavior in Texas," *Social Science Quarterly*, vol. 53 (December 1973), p. 796.
115. A convenient summary can be found in "Data Track 6" (Social Research Services, American Council of Life Insurance, Washington, D.C., n.d.), p. 39.
116. Cornelius et al., "Mexican Immigrants and Southern California," pp. 73–74. Compare Rivera and Mejia, "Mas aya del ancho rio," p. 508 (majorities of those replying report no discrimination).

formal complaints of discrimination. Hispanics in general file many fewer charges with the Equal Employment Opportunity Commission than blacks do, and the charges they do file are more frequently closed without remedy to the charging party (84 percent for Hispanics versus 49 percent for blacks). Of the entire EEOC litigation caseload in 1983, only 2.5 percent alleged discrimination on the basis of national origin.[117]

Views of interethnic social distance are generally congruent with perceptions of discrimination. A careful survey of blacks, non-Hispanic whites, and Mexican-Americans in Houston found that blacks perceived Anglos to be more strongly determined to maintain social distance than in fact they were.[118] Anglos exhibited a willingness to have considerably closer relations with Mexican-Americans than with blacks. Speaking hypothetically, only 8.4 percent of the Anglos would admit a black to the family through marriage, whereas 41.6 percent would admit a Mexican-American. Anti-black attitudes do not transfer automatically to other groups, even in Texas. More important for present purposes was the Mexican-American perception of Anglo attitudes. Inaccurate black perceptions magnified the social distance, on the average almost doubled it. But, in general, Mexican-American perceptions accurately reflected the attitudes revealed by white respondents, and on a few dimensions imputed less social distance to whites than was actually present. In short, Anglos feel more hostility to blacks than to Mexican-Americans,[119] and blacks sense even greater hostility than Anglos feel. Anxiety-laden perceptions of threat are a good indicator of serious ethnic conflict; their absence among Mexican-Americans is not conclusive evidence that there is no serious conflict, but it tends to suggest a much lower intensity.[120]

One other attitudinal comparison bears mention; it is drawn from the longitudinal survey in Racine, Wisconsin.[121] Gaps between parental resources and educational aspirations are narrower for Mexican-Americans than for blacks, both because resources are

---

117. *Labor Relations Reporter,* vol. 114, no. 33 (December 26, 1983), p. 2.
118. George Antunes and Charles M. Gaitz, "Ethnicity and Participation: A Study of Mexican Americans, Blacks, and Whites," *American Journal of Sociology,* vol. 80 (March 1975), pp. 1204–06.
119. Cf. Steven G. Cole and James B. Goebel, "Mexican-American and White Reactions to Same and Different Race Stimulus Persons as a Function of Knowledge of Beliefs," *Ethnicity,* vol. 3 (June 1976), pp. 124–32.
120. I discuss this aspect of interethnic hostility at some length in *Ethnic Groups in Conflict,* chap. 4.
121. McKim et al., "Becoming 'We' Instead of 'They,'" pp. 159, 163, 173.

greater and because aspirations are lower. More than a third of Mexican-Americans continued to be content seeing their children receive only a high school education (35.9 percent in 1960, and 33.7 percent in 1971), but 75 percent of the parents surveyed in 1971 said they could afford more than a high school education, compared to 35 percent in 1960. For blacks, the relationship is reversed. About seven in eight preferred more than a high school education for their children (83.5 percent in 1960, and 87.0 percent in 1971), but only two-thirds could afford more than high school (57 percent, 1960, and 66 percent, 1971). This is a shortfall not evident in the Mexican-American figures. When educational aspirations outrun income capabilities for a group, there is a built-in source of dissatisfaction for the next generation. It should be emphasized that the next generation of Mexican-Americans may seek more education than their parents seek for them, for their aspirations are rising, but so is the reported ability to fulfill them. In the United States, the interethnic disparity in capacity to fulfill expectations would seem to be a revealing comparative indicator of potential group discontent.

The political ideology of Mexican-Americans is distinctly more conservative than that of blacks. In a Denver study of both groups, blacks were found to have more homogeneous views and to be more critical of their environmental conditions, which were actually better than those of Mexican-Americans.[122] Blacks pay more attention to politics, belong to more associations, and are more "liberal." Forty-one percent of the Mexican-Americans in the Denver sample refused to apply ideological labels to themselves, twice the refusal rate of blacks. Similar results were obtained in a Texas survey, where 29 percent of Mexican-Americans called themselves "liberal" and 23 percent "conservative"; comparable black figures were 47 and 14 percent.[123] A sample survey of four Texas cities found middle-class Chicano respondents most favorably disposed toward the most conservative Mexican-American organizations.[124] In Texas, Mexican-Americans are overwhelmingly Democrats, as they are nationwide; but, in verbal statements and in voting patterns, they are less committed to the party than blacks are.[125]

---

122. Lovrich and Marenin, " A Comparison of Black and Mexican American Voters in Denver," p. 290.
123. McClesky and Merrill, "Mexican American Political Behavior in Texas," p. 793.
124. Raymond H. C. Teske, Jr., and Bardin H. Nelson, "Middle Class Mexican Americans and Political Power Potential: A Dilemma," *Journal of Political and Military Sociology*, vol. 4 (Spring 1976), p. 115.
125. McClesky and Merrill, "Mexican American Political Behavior in Texas," p. 789.

Nor, for that matter, are Mexican-Americans committed strongly
to ethnic voting, in either precept or practice. A bare majority in
Denver—51 percent—approved of voting for ethnically kindred
candidates, and large minorities voted for Anglo candidates running
against Mexican-Americans in council elections.[126] Similar patterns
were found in Tucson.[127] In short, ethnically cohesive political
ideology and behavior are not prominently displayed.

For the rest, it is well known that Mexican-American rates of
political participation, measured in terms of awareness and discussion
of politics, contact with government, voting, campaigning, and officeholding, seem low.[128] There have, however, been few efforts to
sort out participation rates by citizenship rather than by population.
There are recent indications of increased voter registration,[129] but
previous surges in minority electoral interest have not benefited
prospective Mexican-American officeholders to the same extent as
they have black candidates. In a study of ten large northern California
cities that had no minority representatives in the 1960s, it was found
that by the mid-1970s black officeholders were proportionate to the
black share of the 1970 adult population, whereas Hispanics had 42
percent of such a proportionate share.[130] Statewide, the Hispanic
percentage was much lower.[131] There were similar results in a national
survey of 264 cities with significant black or Mexican-American

126. Lovrich and Marenin, "A Comparison of Black and Mexican American Voters
in Denver," p. 288.
127. John A. Garcia, "An Analysis of Chicano and Anglo Electoral Patterns in School
Board Elections," *Ethnicity*, vol. 6 (June 1979), pp. 168–83.
128. Antunes and Gaitz, "Ethnicity and Participation," p. 1201; Rufus P. Browning et
al., "Minorities and Urban Electoral Change: A Longitudinal Study," *Urban Affairs
Quarterly*, vol. 15 (December 1979), pp. 206–28; A. Jay Stevens, "The Acquisition of
Participatory Norms: The Case of Japanese and Mexican American Children in a
Suburban Environment," *Western Political Quarterly*, vol. 28 (June 1975), pp. 281–95;
Susan Welch et al., "Political Participation among Mexican Americans: An Exploratory
Examination," *Social Science Quarterly*, vol. 53 (December 1973), p. 806; Garcia, "An
Analysis of Chicano and Anglo Electoral Patterns in School Board Elections," p. 173;
Comer, " 'Street Level' Bureaucracy and Political Support," p. 214; McClesky and
Merrill, "Mexican American Political Behavior in Texas," pp. 788–89; U.S. Bureau of
the Census, "Voting and Registration in the Election of November 1980," Advance
Report, *Current Population Reports*, series P-20, no. 359 (Washington, D.C.: U.S.
Government Printing Office, 1981), pp. 2–3; Luis M. Salces and Peter W. Colby,
"Mañana Will Be Better: Spanish-American Politics in Chicago," *Illinois Issues*, February
1980, pp. 19–21.
129. *Congressional Quarterly Weekly Report*, October 23, 1982, pp. 2707–09.
130. Browning et al., "Minorities and Urban Electoral Change."
131. Stan Steiner, "The Mexican Americans," *Minority Rights Group Report* 39 (London,
1979), p. 5.

populations.[132] From 1972 to 1978, black elected officeholders as a fraction of total black population in a city rose from 53 percent to 71 percent; the comparable figures for Mexican-Americans in 1973 and 1978 were 34 percent and 44 percent. Furthermore, black education and income were strongly correlated with strength of black representation on councils,[133] but the same correlation was not found for Mexican-Americans. In fact, in the California study, a negative correlation was found between Hispanic income and council representation.[134]

The usual explanation for such findings is low electoral participation, low sense of political efficacy (about the same level as the black level), and a failure to internalize participant role expectations.[135] Moreover, it is said, such "passive" orientations are stable by social class.[136]

There are, however, alternative lines of explanation. Surveys of Mexican-Americans report a perception of increasing political influence, even when other conditions are said to be worsening.[137] This perception can be squared with the officeholding figures. Even when Chicanos do not elect a Mexican-American candidate, their marginal vote may secure them more effective representation than that obtained by more cohesive voting behavior. There is evidence of Anglo candidate appeals to Mexican-American voters, based precisely on their willingness to vote for non-Chicanos.[138] Moreover, Mexican-Americans are much less geographically segregated within cities than blacks are.[139] Hence it will be more difficult for Chicanos to match black officeholding where elections are conducted on a ward basis.[140] That does not, of course, foreclose substantial officeholding. In Texas, for example, although Mexican-Americans formed a majority in only

132. Albert K. Karnig and Susan Welch, "Sex and Ethnic Differences in Municipal Representation," *Social Science Quarterly*, vol. 60 (December 1979), pp. 465–81.
133. Ibid., pp. 467, 470.
134. Browning et al., "Minorities and Urban Electoral Change," pp. 208–09.
135. McClesky and Merrill, "Mexican American Political Behavior in Texas," p. 795; Stevens, "The Acquisition of Participatory Norms," p. 291.
136. Stevens, "The Acquisition of Participatory Norms," p. 291.
137. Ambrecht and Pachon, "Ethnic Political Mobilization in a Mexican American Community"; Cornelius et al., "Mexican Immigrants and Southern California," pp. 73–74, citing the work of John A. Garcia.
138. Lovrich and Marenin, "A Comparison of Black and Mexican American Voters in Denver," p. 288; Garcia, "An Analysis of Chicano and Anglo Electoral Patterns in School Board Elections," pp. 174–75.
139. Joan W. Moore and Frank G. Mittelbach, "Measuring Residential Segregation in 35 Cities," in Rudolph Gomez, ed., *The Changing Mexican American* (n.p.: Pruett, 1972), pp. 81–82.
140. Karnig and Welch, "Sex and Ethnic Differences in Municipal Representation," p. 470; Salces and Colby, "Mañana Will Be Better," p. 19.

21 of 254 counties, they were far better represented among office-holders as of 1971 than blacks were—by a margin of more than 700 to 50, despite the fact that there were almost two-thirds as many blacks as Mexican-Americans in the state.[141] But, clearly, a minority that is not geographically compact within cities will be disadvantaged in officeholding where elections are organized territorially.

More fundamentally, however, there is a distinction between officeholding and representation. Where the environment is hostile to minority interests, a compact neighborhood minority may elect a council member or two on a ward-election basis and yet have no impact whatsoever on legislative output.[142] A citywide minority, as I have just indicated, may affect the results of elections for several seats without electing a single minority council member. Such a group would be likely to be better represented than the group that elects a single ward representative, if ordinary electoral incentives prevail, for the marginal utility of its votes would be greater. Needless to say, the data do not provide evidence of this kind of effective representation, for they only measure the more readily measurable indicator of officeholding and automatically equate it with representation. It is, in fact, a curiously naive conception of representation that equates it with mere officeholding and an equally naive expectation that, under normal or "equitable" conditions,[143] a group will be proportionately represented in offices held, regardless of its territorial concentration or dispersion or the territorial or at-large basis of elections.

Finally, something needs to be said about the much-discussed political "passivity" of Mexican-Americans. Here intergroup comparisons are necessary.

First of all, below-median levels of political activity are not surprising insofar as first-generation immigrants are concerned. It is known from their income figures that their energies are directed toward the all-consuming task of earning a living. A good many are not citizens, and, of these, some undetermined number may not be lawfully in the country.

---

141. McClesky and Merrill, "Mexican American Political Behavior in Texas," p. 786, n. 5.
142. This has happened in California. See Browning et al., "Minorities and Urban Electoral Change," p. 222.
143. Karnig and Welch, in "Sex and Ethnic Differences in Municipal Representation," use the term *equity* to denote proportional representation of a group in an elected body. Unlike Browning et al., "Minorities and Urban Electoral Change," who use the term *parity* for such representation, Karnig and Welch fail to measure equity in terms of adult population, thereby permitting age skewing of the underlying populations to bias the result.

Second, we know that levels of political activity among ethnic groups vary widely by generation. Many descendants of European immigrants vote at above-median levels, but this is uneven by ethnic group. For some, it peaks in the second generation and trails off later; for others, there is a slower, linear, rather than curvilinear, relationship.[144] There is no particular level of political activity that qualifies as "normal" across groups and generations. Various groups, like various individuals, make differing accommodations between the spheres of public and private concern that command their attention.

Third, it is well established that lower levels of education correlate with lower levels of most forms of political awareness and participation.[145] Because Mexican-Americans have below-median levels of education, it is not surprising that they have below-median levels of political participation.

Fourth, the attitudinal evidence speaks eloquently to the moderate quality of Mexican-American political demands and aspirations. That, too, is not surprising for a group of somewhat recent and continuing immigrant origin. Migrants and at least some of their descendants typically measure their progress by how far they have come, not by some abstract standard, and they may entertain quite modest aspirations for improving their conditions. The more modest their aspirations are, the more easily they will be satisfied.[146] In one interesting survey, no correlation was found between system affect and output affect—Chicanos did not condition their general support for the system on satisfaction with its particular products. Equally significant, only trivial correlations were found between satisfaction and political participation.[147] Whether deprivation translates into discontent and hostility—or into political participation—is a subjective and not an objective matter.[148] This is all rather well documented in the comparative literature, but it is not always remembered.

---

144. Lyman A. Kellstedt, "Ethnicity and Political Behavior: Intergroup and Intergenerational Differences," *Ethnicity*, vol. 1 (December 1974), pp. 393–416.

145. For example, ibid., p. 411. See also Samuel P. Huntington and Joan M. Nelson, *No Easy Choice: Political Participation in Developing Countries* (Cambridge, Mass.: Harvard University Press, 1976), pp. 80–81; Joan M. Nelson, *Access to Power: Politics and the Urban Poor in Developing Nations* (Princeton, N.J.: Princeton University Press, 1979), pp. 30–40.

146. See Joan M. Nelson, "Migrants, Urban Poverty, and Instability in Developing Nations," Occasional Papers in International Affairs 22 (Cambridge, Mass.: Harvard University Center for International Affairs, September 1969).

147. Comer, " 'Street Level' Bureaucracy and Political Support," pp. 218–22.

148. I have made this point in connection with the black riots of the 1960s, compared to the quiescence of the 1950s and 1970s, in Horowitz, "Racial Violence in the United States," pp. 193, 201–02.

Ethnicity and Territory

"We did not come to America," runs a theme in Chicano political discourse. "America came to us!"[149] Mexican-Americans "were conquered and forced to be citizens." Those who migrate north "simply are 'returning'. . . ."[150] There is, then, a certain claim to indigenousness that can be made; it is based on the Mexican population in the Southwest antedating the incorporation of those territories in the United States. It is a claim that, I have said, fits uncomfortably with the immigrant ethos in the United States and its emphasis on spatial mobility. And it is a claim not likely to be made by the much-later migrants and their descendants who comprise the great bulk of the Mexican-American population.

The association of Chicanos with the Southwest is, in any event, undergoing significant change. Like other Americans, Mexican-Americans have migrated far from home in quest of opportunity, from rural to urban areas, and from the Southwest to the Midwest. In spite of the earlier association of Mexicans with farm labor—and, ironically, perhaps because the *bracero* program of the 1950s helped push established Mexican-Americans out of agriculture[151]—Mexican-Americans were, by 1970, 85 percent urbanized, a change of twenty percentage points in twenty years. By the same token, surplus labor and concomitant low wages in the Southwest, especially in Texas, provided substantial incentives for northward migration, above all to the railroad yards, steel mills, and meat-packing and automobile plants of the industrial cities of the Midwest. The great majority of Mexican-Americans still resides in the Southwest, but at least 10 percent of all Mexican-Americans live in the Midwest. The fraction may be larger, because in recent decades the midwestern Chicano population has been growing at an intercensal rate of about 50 percent.[152] There are forecasts that, by the end of the decade, only

---

149. Steiner, "The Mexican Americans," p. 14.
150. Garcia, "Political Ideology," pp. 9–10.
151. Peñalosa, "The Changing Mexican American in Southern California," p. 413. For some other forces for migration, see Kenneth R. Weber, "Ecology, Economy, and Demography: Some Parameters of Social Change in Hispanic New Mexico," *Social Science Journal*, vol. 17 (January 1980), pp. 53–64.
152. Gilbert Cardenas, "Mexican Migration to the Midwest," in West and Macklin, *The Chicano Experience*, p. 35. See also Cardenas, "Mexican Labor: A View to Conceptualizing the Effects of Migration, Immigration and the Chicano Population in the United States," in Charles H. Teller et al., eds., *Cuantos Somos: A Demographic Study of the Mexican-American Population* (Austin: University of Texas Center for Mexican American Studies, 1977), pp. 159–82.

half of all Mexican-Americans will live in the Southwest.[153] If this happens, most of the remainder will be located in the upper Midwest, in cities like Chicago and South Bend, Detroit and Milwaukee. These are prospects that should be taken seriously. In 1910, almost 90 percent of all black Americans lived in the South. Fifty years later, that figure was about 50 percent. For Mexican-Americans, a sense of territorial origin in the Southwest may not disappear, but it obviously will be much diluted in the interest of spatial mobility.

Estrada and others describe Chicanos outside the Southwest as "a vanguard."[154] There are many ways in which this is true, but one interesting line of speculation involves treating space as a surrogate for time and thinking about the Midwest as representing a substantial part of the future of Mexican-Americans.

There has been much discussion about whether the Midwest provides better income and occupation opportunities for Mexican-Americans than the Southwest does. When the question is put this way, the answer is indeed equivocal. Some studies find midwestern Chicano incomes higher than southwestern incomes, and some do not.[155] But that is the wrong question, because midwestern Mexican-Americans do not come equally from all over the Southwest, and they especially do not come from California, where Mexican-American incomes are highest. On the contrary, California is a destination state for migrants from the Midwest as well as from Mexico. In fact, California receives more than half of Spanish-origin migrants from the Midwest to the Southwest and contributes only 7 percent of Spanish-origin migrants going in the opposite direction. Rather, Texas is the largest source state: more than 80 percent of those migrating from the Southwest to the Midwest are from Texas.[156]

Here the comparisons are extremely clear. Illinois is not much ahead of California in median Spanish-origin income (though the large Puerto Rican population in Chicago complicates the comparison), but median Hispanic income, even in Illinois, is nearly twice that of Texas, and the differences between Indiana, Michigan, and Ohio, on the one hand, and Texas, on the other, are even greater. Among Hispanic males aged 16 and over, the contrast among states

153. Estrada et al., "Chicanos in the United States," p. 128.
154. Ibid.
155. Compare Julian Samora and Richard A. Lamanna, "Mexican-Americans in a Midwest Metropolis: A Study of East Chicago," Advance Report 8, U.C.L.A. Graduate School of Business Administration, Mexican-American Study Project, July 1967, p. 101; and Durant and Knowlton, "Rural Ethnic Minorities," p. 156; with Welch et al., "Political Participation among Mexican Americans," p. 802.
156. Cardenas, "Mexican Migration to the Midwest," pp. 53–54.

was stark in 1970. In Michigan and Indiana, 23 percent earned more than $10,000; in Ohio, it was 21 percent; in California, 14 percent; in Colorado and New Mexico, 7 percent; and in Texas, 5.5 percent.[157] Spatial mobility was tantamount to social mobility.

Data from particular cities bear out the regional disparity. Median 1970 income for Mexican-Americans in Detroit was $9,672; in Toledo, $8,633. In Fremont, Ohio, with a working-class, ex-farmworker, Chicano community, it was $6,261. But in south Texas, it was $3,793. Fifteen percent of the Mexican-American labor force in Detroit was professional or managerial, and there were discernible trends for such people to move "into the Anglo suburbs."[158] Even as of 1970, of course, these are not figures that suggest great ease or comfort for midwestern Mexican-Americans, for most were hardworking and wage-earning. As we have come to expect, they are higher than black figures and much lower than Anglo. How much lower depends very much on the city.[159] What the numbers do suggest is a significant improvement over Texas and most of the rest of the Southwest and, for some, what Estrada calls "a strong economic base for an emerging middle class."[160]

One interregional contrast that does not show up is in education. With the exception of Texas, with its unusually low years of schooling, Mexican-Americans in the Southwest and the Midwest are not far apart in educational attainment.[161] Income and occupational mobility in the Midwest were gained despite, not because of, the educational levels of the Chicano community.

Impressionistic evidence also suggests that facility in English is greater in the Midwest than in the Southwest,[162] even though a significant fraction of midwesterners earlier came directly from Mexico or from Texas border towns.[163] It may well be that linguistic

---

157. Leobardo F. Estrada, "A Demographic Comparison of the Mexican Origin Population in the Midwest and Southwest," *Aztlán*, vol. 7 (Summer 1976), p. 228.
158. John R. Weeks and Joseph Spielberg Benitez, "The Cultural Demography of Midwestern Chicano Communities," in West and Macklin, *The Chicano Experience*, pp. 236–41 (quotation on p. 236). See also Louise Año Nuevo de Kerr, "Chicano Settlements in Chicago: A Brief History," *Journal of Ethnic Studies*, vol. 2 (Winter 1975), p. 28.
159. Compare Macklin and Teniente de Costilla, "*La Virgen de Guadalupe* and the American Dream," in West and Macklin, *The Chicano Experience*, p. 120; Samora and Lamanna, "Mexican-Americans in a Midwest Metropolis," pp. 79, 101.
160. Estrada, "A Demographic Comparison of the Mexican Origin Population in the Midwest and Southwest," p. 227.
161. Ibid., p. 221.
162. See Comer, " 'Street Level' Bureaucracy and Political Support," p. 213; Macklin and Teniente de Costilla, "*La Virgen de Guadalupe* and the American Dream," p. 116.
163. See, for example, Año Nuevo de Kerr, "Chicano Settlements in Chicago," p. 22.

or generational self-selection for interregional migration is at work here. And it seems very clear, too, that programs to "Americanize" immigrants, which were very common in the polyglot Midwest, with its masses of central European immigrants in all the major industrial cities, had an impact on Mexican-Americans in the first third of the century, providing instruction in English and fostering a good deal of cultural amalgamation.[164] The reception accorded black migrants to the Midwest in the teens and twenties was far more hostile and violent.[165] Exactly how all this worked and what relation it had to Chicano income, exogamy, and interethnic relations remain fertile fields for inquiry. But it does suggest a different midwestern pattern. As Cardenas says, "some aspects" of the European "immigrant analogy approach . . . may be applicable in the Midwest."[166] For it is there, above all, that Mexican-Americans report, not merely success, but also a measure of satisfaction.[167]

How much social mobility the Midwest experience portends for Mexican-Americans overall, I do not presume to know. The population and income disparity figures show that Mexican-Americans now have a strong place outside the Southwest. They have lived in the Midwest in some numbers through nearly all of this century. It will no longer do to consider Chicanos, or for Chicanos to consider themselves, a regional minority with a narrow territorial base. With migration trends such as we have already observed, interregional income disparities will continue to pull Mexican-Americans out of Texas and other low-income states and into higher-income states. There is precedent in the Mexican-American experience for large-scale, rapid migratory movement, as the rural-to-urban figures so palpably show. And there are at least hints that Mexican-Americans who are prepared to go further afield may reap more significant rewards. In western New York, the end of the midwestern line, the percentage of Mexican-Americans holding white-collar jobs ranged from 21 percent for those born in Mexico to 38 percent for those born in New York; educational attainment was also high.[168] A

---

164. See ibid., p. 24; and especially Macklin and Teniente de Costilla, "*La Virgin de Guadalupe* and the American Dream," pp. 115–16.

165. See, for example, Elliott M. Rudwick, *Race Riot at East St. Louis* (Carbondale, Ill.: Southern Illinois University Press, 1964).

166. Gilbert Cardenas, "Los Desarraigados: Chicanos in the Midwestern Region of the United States," *Aztlán*, vol. 7 (Summer 1976), p. 158.

167. For example, see Rivera and Mejia, "Mas aya del ancho rio," p. 508; McKim et al., "Becoming 'We' Instead of 'They' "; Comer, " 'Street Level' Bureaucracy and Political Support."

168. Rivera and Mejia, "Mas aya del ancho rio," p. 504.

nationwide field of opportunity is ultimately what the Midwest model substitutes for identification with a particular region. Comparable nationwide fields have done much the same for formerly territorially concentrated ethnic groups all over the world. In comparative perspective, the maintenance of such nationwide fields has been an inhibitor of severe ethnic conflict of a territorial sort.

The Context of Conflict Management

Since the close of the "old immigration" in 1924 and the opening of the "new immigration" in 1965, important changes in the structure of ethnic conflict management have occurred in the United States, as they have elsewhere. These changes concern access to education and employment, the federal-state-local balance, and the relation of ethnicity to electoral systems.

Comparatively, the same categories are implicated in ethnic conflict management. In an array of countries, provisions are made against discrimination in admission to schools or recruitment to jobs, or these goods are apportioned by ethnic criteria, either proportionately or preferentially for underrepresented groups. Territorial arrangements are likewise employed to mitigate ethnic conflict, through devolution to local authority, through regional autonomy, or through federalism, using either more or less homogeneous or more or less heterogeneous state units. Electoral systems are utilized to overrepresent some ethnic groups, or to forge ties between groups, or to limit the influence of particularly powerful groups. In the tools of conflict management, therefore, the United States is very much in tune with currents elsewhere.

The music, however, is quite different in the United States. Where states like Malaysia or Sri Lanka have had some second thoughts about preferential admissions to universities—and in the latter case have tried, with partial success, to abolish them—in the United States such admissions now seem fairly firmly established. Where India's federalism seems causally connected to its capacity to endure high levels of ethnic conflict in the states, and where Belgium, Canada, and the Sudan conceive of federalism or regional autonomy as central to conflict management techniques, none of this seems true any longer in the United States. And, at the local level, the integrating political machine is largely dead in this country. Where Nigeria, Sri Lanka, and Lebanon seem destined, despite the present difficulties of each, to continue using the electoral system flexibly for conflict management objectives, the electoral system in the United States is in a completely different position. The Voting Rights Act of 1965 resulted in an enormous enfranchisement of blacks, and subsequent amendments have facilitated the electoral participation of Mexican-Americans and other Hispanics, but judicial interpretation of the act, coupled with the earlier legislative reapportionment cases, limits the ability of American policymakers to use the electoral system flexibly for ethnic conflict management objectives. The tools, then, are the same, but the craftsmen use them completely differently.

Having opened up such a large subject, I now need to limit it. I shall say nothing further about proportional or preferential policies, such as affirmative action, largely because they are the subject of such extensive investigation in the United States and elsewhere.[169] I shall have a little to say about federalism vis-à-vis the Mexican-American situation and rather more to say about electoral systems and ethnic conflict, for that is the subject on which, it is not too strong to say, Americans wear ideological blinders that keep out any knowledge of the rest of the world.

In the United States, state boundaries are by now firmly fixed, and, as I have said earlier, the notion of states formally identified with particular groups is not really an open question. What the states do is to create possibilities for diversity that are affected by the balance of ethnic and religious forces, but they hardly provide arenas for decentralized ethnic domination in the way they sometimes do elsewhere. The Mormons are powerful in Utah, as the Irish and Italians are in Rhode Island, but constitutional restrictions, conditions attached to federal funds, and the general shift to centralized power limit the possibilities open to ethnic groups operating in states where they are concentrated. In cities, too, black or Hispanic mayors may be elected, but they typically rely on the support of some fraction of voters of other groups and practice a politics of interethnic compromise. Of course, New Mexico and Texas, Los Angeles and San Antonio constitute arenas in which Mexican-Americans can gain

---

169. India is the most carefully studied country. See Myron Weiner, *Sons of the Soil: Migration and Ethnic Conflict in India* (Princeton, N.J.: Princeton University Press, 1978); Mary Fainsod Katzenstein, *Ethnicity and Equality: The Shiv Sena Party and Preferential Policies in Bombay* (Ithaca, N.Y.: Cornell University Press, 1979); Myron Weiner and Mary Fainsod Katzenstein, *India's Preferential Policies: Migrants, the Middle Classes and Ethnic Equality* (Chicago, Ill.: University of Chicago Press, 1981); Marc Galanter, *Competing Equalities: Law and the Backward Classes in India* (Berkeley and Los Angeles: University of California Press, 1984). I have also undertaken a wide-ranging comparative evaluation in Donald L. Horowitz, "Ethnicity and Development: Policies to Deal with Ethnic Conflict in Developing Countries," a report to the U.S. Agency for International Development, March 1981.

greater recognition through officeholding and, what is more important, through more general representation. But the idea of devolution
of power to an ethnic group by devolving power formally on the
territory in which that group predominates—an idea that is alive and
well in much of the world—is no longer possible in American
federalism.[170] And, even if it were, the growing dispersion of Mexican-
Americans around the United States, coupled with Sunbelt migration
of Anglos to the Southwest, would limit the ethnic utility of such a
practice.

The electoral system is an altogether different matter. In other
multiethnic societies, a wide range of electoral devices is employed
for ethnic conflict management. Proportional representation by party
has been used to keep mere ethnic-party pluralities from becoming
electoral majorities. Multimember constituencies, with reserved seats
but multiethnic electorates and interethnic ticket requirements, have
been imposed in order to maximize interethnic appeals to the
electorate. Alternative or preferential voting systems have been
enacted for the purpose of heightening the marginal impact of
minority votes. Regional distribution requirements have been superimposed on majority or plurality requirements for election; the dual
requirements temper majority support with interethnic appeals and
at least a modicum of minority support. Devices such as these do not
exhaust the range of innovations.

The United States, that most experimental society, has, on this
question, closed the door to experimentation and is on the verge of
locking it altogether. We have long assumed that single-member
constituencies and candidates elected on a first-past-the-post (plurality) formula are the natural order of things in elections. Onto this
set of British-derived assumptions, the reapportionment cases grafted
the requirement of "one person, one vote," thereby eliminating
constituency size as a variable available for policy manipulation.
Beginning in 1969, the Voting Rights Act began to be reinterpreted
to require, not merely access to the ballot—which, of course, was its
purpose—but rather delimitation of constituencies and electoral
formulae that appeared to produce electoral results reasonably favorable to prospective black officeholders.[171] Multimember constituencies fell under the scrutiny of the courts, and so did at-large
elections for municipal office. The assumption has been that, under

170. Cf. Nathan Glazer, "Federalism and Ethnicity: The Experience of the United
States," *Publius*, vol. 7 (Fall 1977), pp. 71–88.
171. See, for example, *White* v. *Regester*, 412 U.S. 755 (1973); *Allen* v. *State Bd. of
Elections*, 393 U.S. 544 (1969).

nondiscriminatory conditions, a minority constituting, say, 20 percent of a city's population would elect 20 percent of its council members. (I am not, incidentally, speaking here of section 5 of the Voting Rights Act, which applies to "covered" jurisdictions, those with a history of discrimination; I am referring to section 2, which applies to all jurisdictions across the country.)

In 1981, the House of Representatives passed an amendment to the act that would have made electoral "results" the test of the discriminatory character of an electoral arrangement. There was much opposition to the "results test" in the Senate,[172] and a compromise was ultimately enacted which muddied the language of the act but essentially provided that whether an arrangement was unlawful would depend on all the circumstances. This passed the problem to the courts, but in the end it will probably mean that a results test has been adopted *sub silentio*.

The most prominent impact of such a change—and the one with greatest bearing on Mexican-Americans—will, at least in the short run, be on at-large elections at the municipal level: city councils, school boards, county commissions, and the like. Lower courts have tended to find that at-large elections constitute unlawful discrimination if they result in the election of few or no minority council members.[173] Where they find such discrimination, the courts can order new elections to be held on a ward or territorial basis, with constituencies demarcated to maximize black electoral power. In city after city, the days of at-large elections seem numbered. Local diversity of formal electoral arrangements is thus no longer a major mode of interethnic adjustment. As in other cases, uniformity will be called for.

As I explained earlier, Mexican-American municipal officeholding runs at proportionately much lower levels than black officeholding. Mexican-Americans vote less cohesively than blacks. More important, however, Mexican-Americans are, in every southwestern city and in most other cities, much less segregated residentially then blacks are. The most careful multicity study done so far shows that district, rather than at-large, elections will not increase Mexican-American officeholding.[174] Nor are cities with ward elections more responsive

---

172. See U.S. Senate, Committee on the Judiciary, Subcommittee on the Constitution, *Voting Rights Act: Hearings on S. 53, S. 1761, S. 1975, S. 1992, and H.R. 3112*, 97th Cong., 2d sess. (U.S. Government Printing Office, 1982), vols. 1–2.
173. See *Jones* v. *City of Lubbock*, 727 F.2d 364 (5th Cir. 1984); *Boykins* v. *City of Hattiesburg*, Civ. No. H77–0062(C) (S.D. Miss. March 2, 1984).
174. Karnig and Welch, "Sex and Ethnic Differences in Municipal Representation," pp. 470–73.

to minority interests than cities with at-large elections; indeed, there is a bit of evidence the other way.[175] The impending demise of at-large elections, even for blacks, runs the risk of segregating minority votes in order to achieve minority officeholding, at the likely expense of diminishing minority voter influence. Anglo candidates, who might have bid for minority votes under an at-large system, need only bid for the votes of members of their own ethnic group under a ward system. And, finally, of course, given the increased geographic mobility that seems the only reasonable forecast for Mexican-Americans, there is a good chance that wider use of ward rather than at-large elections will not have simply no effect but a negative effect on their political influence.

The broader point here is not merely that this is a misguided change, or that it is based on simple-minded notions equating representation with officeholding, or that it assumes that ethnically proportional officeholding is the appropriate standard, or that it takes no account of the different spatial distribution of various ethnic groups—though it is and does all these things. The point is that, by law, we have progressively locked ourselves into an electoral strait-jacket and disqualified ourselves from using the electoral system nimbly and creatively for the genuine alleviation of underrepresentation and the management of ethnic group conflict. American inventiveness has failed us here.

To some extent, Mexican-American political behavior can be expected to counteract such forces. In presidential elections and in congressional elections, Mexican-Americans vote at a rate about half the rate for Anglos and about 60 percent the rate for blacks. But the low rates for blacks and Mexican-Americans have different roots. Blacks register, but often do not vote; Mexican-Americans often fail to register.[176] Between 1976 and 1981, however, Mexican-American registration in Texas nearly doubled.[177] Such tendencies would seem to presage a significant increase in electoral participation. The less solid partisan alignment of Mexican-Americans and their less stable

---

175. Susan Welch, "The Impact of Urban Riots on Urban Expenditures," *American Political Science Review*, vol. 19 (November 1975), pp. 756–57; Joe R. Feagin and Harlan Hahn, *Ghetto Revolts: The Politics of Violence in American Cities* (New York: Macmillan, 1973), pp. 255–57; Harlan Hahn, "Civic Responses to Riots: A Reappraisal of Kerner Commission Data," *Public Opinion Quarterly*, vol. 34 (Spring 1970), pp. 101–07.
176. U.S. Bureau of the Census, "Voting Registration in the Election of November 1980," p. 2. Note that these are undifferentiated "Spanish origin" figures.
177. *Congressional Quarterly Weekly Report*, October 23, 1982, p. 2709. For evidence of increasing turnout, see Steve Padilla, "Latinos Wield Political Clout in Midterm Election," *Nuestro* (November 1982), pp. 28–30.

pattern of ethnically cohesive voting suggest a great deal of latitude for Anglo candidates to bid for Chicano electoral support by representing Mexican-American interests, in much the same way as aspiring Chicano candidates, unable to count on solid support among Mexican-American voters, have had to make inroads among Anglo voters. All this augurs more Mexican-American representation than might prevail under other conditions and at the same time fewer zero-sum outcomes than ethnic politics in severely divided societies so generally produces.

A National Arena

"America is not a boardinghouse," Theodore Roosevelt admonished the European immigrants three-quarters of a century ago. Neither is it a countinghouse, in which ethnic groups merely compete for proverbial shares of epigrammatic pies composed of goods and services. The Chicano slice of the pie has so far been rather thin, and yet this has not translated into the level of discontent or hostility that a countinghouse conception of ethnic competition would have predicted. Nowhere, in fact, is ethnic politics reducible to ethnic economics. The Mexican-American case is consistent with comparative experience on this score.

In terms of domestic comparisons, it is abundantly clear that the Mexican-Americans will not retrace the footsteps of black Americans or of European immigrant Americans or of anybody else. The contrasts with the black experience are pronounced—in exogamy; in education and income, and in the interrelations of the two; in political participation and officeholding; in perceptions of discrimination, of social distance, and of the political system. The European immigrant experience, to the extent that it depended on local politics to achieve mobility—most prominently for the Irish—is hardly replicable. Local politics now counts for less, the party system has changed, and by the time Mexican-American political participation is at a sufficiently high level, continuing migration will have spread the population out much further than it already is. What help comes from government is far more likely to come from the national level that was, at best, indifferent to the European immigrants than from the local level that gave them sustenance. Neither the corrupt big-city politics of six or seven decades ago nor the local diversity that the American system once permitted seems of much relevance for Mexican-Americans.

Quite the opposite, for Mexican-Americans began long ago to consider the whole of the United States as an arena for mobility. Curiously enough, what may be relevant is not the actual experience of any other group but something much closer to the American ideal of success through hard work and community membership through belief. Perhaps that is effing the ineffable, as Peter De Vries would say, but the data seem to say somewhat the same thing.

CHAPTER FOUR

A major danger inherent in drawing comparisons predicated upon aggregate group data is that the analyst risks drawing unwarranted conclusions about the nature and causes of uncovered discrepancies. Thus, comparisons of income between black and white people in the United States show a significant gap in favor of the latter. But, as William Wilson *(The Declining Significance of Race)* and others have documented, this type of aggregate analysis masks the rise of a significant and growing class of well-off black Americans, and obscures the fact that, in absolute terms, there are more than twice as many white as black Americans living below the officially defined poverty line. Concentration upon groups qua groups had led numerous scholars, reporters, government authorities, and black leaders to overlook significant dynamics at work in the situation (the rise and expansion of a black middle class) and to perceive in the gross data prima facie evidence of a caste-system type of discrimination.

Stratification, by definition, involves the horizontal division of a society into layers according to wealth, income, occupation, status, and the like. Ethnic groups, by contrast, represent vertical divisions of a society and are therefore usually internally crosscut by lines of stratification. That is to say, a single ethnic group will typically reflect substantial gradations in the level of education, wealth, and status among its members. As in the case of black Americans, this need not preclude significant overall differences between the group and the remainder of the society. But the disaggregated data will seldom support a perception of a dichotomic relationship between groups within a single society. Where such a dichotomic relationship exists over a lengthy period of time, its maintenance is likely fostered by public policy and traditional institutions and values popularly endorsed by the dominant group. Current examples include the disparities between blacks and whites in the Republic of South Africa, between Hutu and Tutsi in Burundi, between the outcaste Burakumin and the Japanese in Japan, and between various castes in India (the last situation being an example of perpetuation of discrimination despite contrary official policy). But again, such cases are rare.

When large numbers of a group, fleeing poverty, emigrate to a wealthier country in search of employment, there arises at least a temporary situation in which lines of stratification closely correspond to ethnic divisions. Thus, newly arrived immigrant groups from Europe and the Far East have customarily occupied the lower-paying and lower-status positions in United States society. The overall rate of subsequently "making it" in America has varied among these groups, but all have done so to a sufficient degree to invalidate the current application of the dichotomic model to which we earlier alluded.

The data involving occupation and income of Mexican-Americans provided in this volume by J. Milton Yinger and Donald L. Horowitz depict a community in transition. Significant differences between it and the larger community exist. Yet, as both Yinger and Horowitz document, a significant fraction of Mexican-Americans has "made it." Are the Mexican-Americans therefore following the pattern set by earlier immigrant groups from Europe and Asia? Or are the socioeconomic discrepancies between the smaller and larger community apt to persevere? John Stone suggests that the analysis of stratification in any situation should be prefaced by a review of the contending theories of the causes of stratification. And in his search for relevant analogies outside of U.S. history, he discovers a number of similarities between Mexican-American immigrants and the "guest workers" of Western Europe. Although the latter come from several states and have settled in several others, he feels that, properly conditioned, the experience of the *gastarbeiter* can shed important light on that of the Mexican-Americans.

ETHNICITY AND STRATIFICATION

Mexican-Americans and European *Gastarbeiter*

John Stone

"There are only two families in the world, my old grandmother used to say, the *haves* and the *have-nots*." (Cervantes, *Don Quixote*)

To the European observer of race and ethnic relations in the United States, there are certain interesting parallels between the substantial inflow of Mexican migrants during the past few decades and the postwar movement of migrant laborers to the countries making up the European Economic Community (EEC). Although all cross-national comparisons pose serious problems when the details of specific cases are being considered, nevertheless, if used with caution, they may provide valuable insights not always readily apparent to the specialist focusing exclusively on a single area or ethnic group. In these two extremely complicated situations—which, for convenience, I will refer to as the Chicano and *gastarbeiter* (guest worker) cases—there are a series of important similarities that have significant implications for the development of ethnic and racial stratification. The fact that social and political scientists attempting to describe and interpret these movements have made use of a similar range of models suggests that a number of important common features are shared by two of the most dramatic migrations of the postwar era.[1]

A first major similarity relates to the absolute size of the groups involved. This immediately raises the significant fact that, in both cases, our knowledge of what should be simple demographic details is based on rough estimates rather than accurate statistical data. Several factors account for this situation: inadequacies in the techniques of gathering official information; definitional problems concerning the groups and the categories involved; and the prevalence

---

1. For a general discussion of migrant labor movements, see Michael J. Piore, *Birds of Passage: Migrant Labor and Industrial Societies* (Cambridge, England: Cambridge University Press, 1979).

of illegal or "undocumented" migration, whether across the Rio Grande or across the political boundaries of the EEC. According to the Immigration and Naturalization Service, Hispanic migrants regularly contributed about one-third of the total legal flow of immigrants into the United States throughout the 1960s and 1970s.[2] Approximately half of this figure, about 14 percent of all new immigrants, came from Mexico during the period.[3] According to the 1980 census, 7,692,619 people of "Mexican descent" live in the United States,[4] but this is generally considered to be a gross underestimation of the real size of the Mexican-American community.[5]

Attempts to determine the number of migrant workers living in the EEC are equally complex and controversial, but a figure of 12 million in the early 1980s is usually regarded as a realistic compromise between the lower and upper estimates of 10 and 15 million.[6] Most of these migrants are concentrated in the major industrial societies of West Germany, France, Britain, the Netherlands, and Belgium and make up between 5 and 10 percent of the respective labor forces.[7] Although it is obviously true that the diverse origins of these groups make them more heterogeneous than their Chicano counterparts, a major point of comparison is that they are migrants—lacking economic resources and political power and destined to join the lowest echelons of the stratification system of their new societies. Furthermore, differences among the countries of Europe in the legal rights and treatment given to migrant workers—although probably more significant than variations between Arizona, Texas, California, and New Mexico—do not seem to have produced markedly different outcomes. As Castles has recently observed, "The pattern is the same, whether

2. Douglas G. Massey and Kathleen M. Schnabel, "Recent Trends in Hispanic Immigration to the U.S.," *International Migration Review*, vol. 17 (Summer 1983), pp. 212-31.

3. For estimates of the number of "undocumented" foreigners, see Jorge A. Bustamante, "The Mexicans Are Coming: From Ideology to Labor Relations," *International Migration Review*, vol. 17, (Summer 1983), p. 329. The role of undocumented workers in sectors of the Los Angeles automobile industry is discussed in Rebecca Morales, "Transitional Labor: Undocumented Workers in the Los Angeles Automobile Industry," *International Migration Review* vol. 17 (Winter 1983–84), pp. 570–96.

4. This figure represents those who reported at least one parent as being of Mexican background.

5. For further discussion of these issues, see Carlos E. Cortes, "Mexicans" in Stephan Thernstrom, ed., *Harvard Encyclopedia of American Ethnic Groups* (Cambridge, Mass.: Harvard University Press, 1980), p. 697.

6. Malcolm Cross, *Migrant Workers in European Cities: Concentration, Conflict and Social Policy*, Working Paper on Ethnic Relations 19, (Social Science Research Council and Research Unit on Ethnic Relations (SSRC-RUER), 1983.

7. Ibid., p. 4.

one looks at Notting Hill or Kreuzberg, St. Denis or St. Pauls, Sodertalje or the Frankfurt Bahnhofsviertel: around the business centres of Europe's great cities are areas of slum housing . . . ghettos of the under-privileged strata of Western European society, where ethnic minorities are the largest group."[8]

The development of similar patterns of ethnic and racial stratification is a direct consequence of the fundamentally economic nature of the migrant labor movements in both Europe and the United States. Throughout the postwar period, strategic labor shortages, particularly for unskilled manual workers, have been generated by the expansion of European capitalist industry as well as by the growth of the public service sector.[9] Peach's study of West Indian migration to Britain during the 1950s and early 1960s demonstrates how the flow of migrant workers depended on the economic demands of the British economy.[10] Much the same is also true for the other major European economies, although the source of the migrant labor has varied from country to country. The British have attracted most of their immigrants from South Asia and the West Indies; the French particularly from Algeria, Morocco, and Tunisia; and the Germans from Turkey, Yugoslavia, and Italy. Similarly the migration from Mexico to the United States has been characterized as "a response to conditions of the international market for manual labour in which the rules imposed by 'the demand' [side have] predominated."[11]

Another common economic feature of these migrations can be seen in the important role played by capital remittances sent by migrant workers from one society to another. Van Amersfoort and his colleagues note that "in Turkey and Morocco, particularly, the migrants' money plays a substantial part in the national economy."[12] With reference to the Mexican migration, Cornelius estimates that "some 13.6 million Mexicans, or 21.3 percent of the present total population of Mexico, depend to some extent on U.S. earnings in

---

8. Ibid., p. 14.

9. In Britain systematic recruitment drives were held to encourage West Indian immigrants to work in the state sector, particularly in nursing and public transport. Ironically, one of the ministers responsible for this policy was Enoch Powell. See Douglas Schoen, *Enoch Powell and the Powellites* (London: Macmillan, 1977).

10. Ceri Peach, *West Indian Migration to Britain* (London: Oxford University Press, 1968).

11. Jorge A. Bustamante, "The Mexicans Are Coming," p. 324.

12. Hans van Amersfoort, Philip Muus, and Rinus Penninx, "International Migration, The Economic Crisis and The State: An Analysis of Mediterranean Migration to Western Europe" *Ethnic and Racial Studies*, vol. 7 (April 1984), pp. 238–68.

any given year."[13] This interconnection between labor and capital flows has attracted many scholars toward explanatory models with a strong materialist emphasis. These include a variety of neo-Marxist perspectives incorporating dependency theories, the interaction between "cores" and "peripheries" within a world economic system, and a range of colonialist, neocolonialist and "internal" colonialist approaches.

Despite the undeniable centrality of economic factors, however, important political variables complicate the analysis. Opposition to migrant labor has varied in intensity and has come from different segments of the "host" societies. It has generally been muted during times of full employment.[14] In Europe the political pressure for immigration restrictions, which has often been couched in crudely racial terms, has become increasingly strident with the onset of the world recession in the aftermath of the oil crisis of the early 1970s. The political platforms of the National Front in Britain, the Centrum Partij in the Netherlands, the Front National in France, and the various neo-Nazi groups in West Germany have all chosen the migrant laborer as a central target of attack. Frequently these anti-immigrant views are articulated by right-wing politicians, sometimes by left-wing trade unionists, and on certain occasions by an unholy alliance of the two ends of the orthodox political spectrum. The march of East End dockworkers to the House of Commons in support of Enoch Powell's anti-immigrant speeches and the considerable backing given to Jean-Marie Le Pen's candidates in the 1983 municipal by-elections in the so-called red belt around Paris illustrate the complex political expression of racist sentiments in contemporary European society.[15]

Recent demands for the "repatriation" of migrant workers (and generally their locally born children) parallel the obsession among some political groups with illegal migration to the United States. Even though most primary migration had ceased throughout the EEC by 1974, the continuing movement of dependents has helped to sustain,

---

13. Wayne A. Cornelius, "Mexican Immigration: Causes and Consequences For Mexico," in Roy Simon Bryce-Laporte, ed., *Sourcebook on The New Immigration* (New Brunswick N.J.: Transaction Books, 1980), p. 81.

14. Jorge A. Bustamante, "Immigration From Mexico: The Silent Invasion Issue," in Bryce-Laporte, *Sourcebook,* p. 140.

15. It is interesting to compare the Front National slogan used in the November 1983 campaigns in Villeneuve-St-Georges and Aulnay-sous-Bois ("Two million unemployed; two million immigrant workers") with earlier election speeches by the leader of the French Communist party, Georges Marchais ("It is inadmissible to allow immigrant workers into France when two million French and immigrant people are on the dole.") See *Times* (London) November 8, 1983 and January 12, 1981.

in certain circles, an illusion of an unarmed invasion. These newcomers, it is argued, threaten to swamp the indigenous population and create an alien wedge of unassimilable individuals who will gradually change the social fabric of West European societies. The myth of continuing migration, like the migrants' myth of return, persists in popular perceptions long after it has ceased to have any basis in fact. Nevertheless, the consequences of this political insecurity for ethnic stratification are very important. Although it is true that not all migrant workers have been passive recipients of prejudice and discrimination,[16] political hostility has almost certainly been a major variable contributing to their concentration in the lower levels of the system of social stratification.

I have stressed certain similarities in the demography, economics, politics, and social stratification of the *gastarbeiter* and Chicano cases, but I am not implying that the differences are unimportant. European migrants are far more heterogeneous than migrants from Mexico: a shared language and similar cultural traditions act as a major force promoting Chicano identity and serve as a potential resource for political mobilization. In Europe it is the experience of economic deprivation, combined with social and political discrimination, which forms a bond between groups that often have little else in common.

Another crucial difference is the sense of historical continuity, which is entirely missing in the European case. It is true that blacks from the West Indies were living in London during the eighteenth century[17] and colonial connections have certainly played their part in the development of European migration and politics,[18] but nonetheless there is no serious claim from the *gastarbeiter* groups that they have been dispossessed from their ancestral lands. The slogan, "We are over here, because you were over there," is a reminder to racist Europeans of the moral legacy of colonial exploitation. It is a rather different assertion from that of the Chicano nationalist who argues that the Southwest of the United States was forcibly taken from Mexico as a consequence of American imperial expansion. As Walker

---

16. Mark J. Miller, "The Political Impact of Foreign Labor: A Re-evaluation of the Western European Experience," *International Migration Review*, vol. 16 (Spring 1982), pp. 27-60.

17. Kenneth L. Little, *Negroes in Britain: A Study of Racial Relations in English Society* (London: Routledge, 1948).

18. See John Rex's comment: "In a very real sense the slave plantations of the Caribbean in the seventeenth and eighteenth centuries were part of the social structure of modern Britain." "A Working Paradigm For Race Relations Research," *Ethnic and Racial Studies*, vol. 4 (January 1981), p. 3.

Connor has been careful to emphasize, the distinction between "migrant" and "homeland" peoples is an important one.[19]

Three Models of Ethnic Stratification

Three basic types of analysis are generally employed to explain the development of ethnic stratification resulting from the two cases of migration described above. These may be broadly termed the *assimilationist,* the *internal colonialist,* and the *neo-Marxist* models. Within these categories many variations in the emphasis are placed on different components of the models, but because neo-Marxist explanations have assumed considerable prominence in recent years, I will devote most of my attention to them. The first two are certainly worth considering, however, because no single approach gives a totally convincing or comprehensive account of the dynamics of stratification in either the Chicano or the *gastarbeiter* cases.[20]

Assimilationist assumptions were implicit in the initial attempts by social scientists to interpret the pattern of stratification emerging in the postwar European situation. During the 1950s and early 1960s, several leading analysts of British race relations adopted what became known as the "stranger" hypothesis.[21] These writers were influenced by Park's notion of a race relations cycle, which proposed a steady transitional process in which new immigrants passed through a set of fairly predictable stages: contact, competition, accommodation, and assimilation.[22] It was suggested that once West Indians learned the subtle norms and values of British society, they would be accepted into full citizenship on much the same basis as the Jews and Irish

---

19. See chapter 1 in this volume by Walker Connor.

20. In a recent survey article, Morrissey selects three major analytical perspectives on Chicano stratification for scrutiny: "internal colonialism." "class," and "international world system and Marxian." See Marietta Morrissey, "Ethnic Stratification and the Study of Chicanos," *The Journal of Ethnic Studies,* vol. 10, (1983), pp. 73-99.

Considering the West German case, Schmitter evaluates "Marxist," "split-labor Market," and "cultural division of labor" models. See Barbara E. Schmitter, "Immigrant Minorities in West Germany: Some Theoretical Concerns," *Ethnic and Racial Studies,* vol. 6, (July 1983), pp. 308-19.

21. See, for example, Sheila Patterson, *Dark Strangers* (London: Tavistock, 1963) and *Immigrants in Industry* (London: Oxford University Press, 1968).

22. Robert E. Park, *Race and Culture* (New York: Free Press, 1950) pp. 149–51. How important the concept of a race relations cycle was for Park's own analysis of race relations is a matter of debate. See Barbara B. Lal, "The 'Chicago School' of American Sociology, Symbolic Interactionism and Race Relations Theory," (unpublished document provided by Lal (Department of Social Science and Administration, University of London, Goldsmiths' College, March 1984), p. 4.

who had arrived at the turn of the century. The pervasive nature of institutional racism in British society was only generally recognized in the mid-1960s, producing alternative explanatory paradigms, based on the legacy of colonialism and the dynamics of the capitalist economy.

In France and the Netherlands, an assimilationist tradition was also apparent in the early postwar years. France's colonial policy, at least in terms of its dominant ideology, had been one of cultural and political incorporation, while in the period before World War II the French state had admitted a large number of European immigrants, particularly from Italy, Spain, and Russia. This influx was so significant that one scholar has referred to France as "Europe's melting pot."[23] Just as France's regional diversity had for so long been buried under the Jacobin philosophy of a "one and indivisible" French state, so its immigrant groups tended to be submerged in a similar "strategy of silence."[24] The bitter legacy of the Algerian war of independence and the revival of autonomist movements helped to undermine any facile claim that assimilation was a necessary part of the French way of life.

The remarkable ease with which the Dutch had accepted the repatriation of a substantial number of excolonial immigrants from Indonesia, combined with the pluralistic structure of Dutch society and the consociational nature of the Dutch political system, seemed to favor, if not an assimilationist, at least an integrationist interpretation of the Netherlands' migrant policy. However, subsequent experience with the Moluccans, Surinamese, Moroccans, and Turks has forced a reevaluation of minority group formation in even this relatively tolerant European society.[25] By the time of the economic recession of the 1970s, most West European states exhibited similar characteristics as far as their immigrant populations were concerned. This was as true for Germany and Switzerland, whose governments had never accepted that migrant laborers were anything more than

23. Don Dignan, "Europe's Melting Pot: A Century of Large-Scale Immigration into France," *Ethnic and Racial Studies*, vol. 4, (April 1981), pp. 137–52. The author notes, "During the 1920s, when the United States ended its open door immigration policy, France became for a while the leading immigration receiving country on a *per capita* basis, and second only to the United States in absolute terms. From 1921 to 1926 France absorbed 515 immigrants for every 100,000 inhabitants compared with 492 in the United States" (p. 138).

24. Christian Coulon, "French Political Science and Regional Diversity: A Strategy of Silence," *Ethnic and Racial Studies*, vol. 1 (January 1978), pp. 80–99.

25. Hans van Amersfoort, *Immigration and Minority Group Formation: The Dutch Experience 1945–1975* (Cambridge, England: Cambridge University Press, 1982).

temporary guest workers,[26] and thereby rejected an assimilationist philosophy from the outset, as it was for the other industrial societies, where colonial traditions had fostered a myth of "motherland" acceptance.

Assimilationist views have also played a central part in the analysis of American race and ethnic relations.[27] With respect to most white and some Asian ethnic groups, there is a considerable element of plausibility in this perspective, despite the so-called ethnic revival of the 1970s, which Gans has set in context as a largely symbolic phenomenon.[28] But assimilationist models have proved to be inappropriate and often highly confusing with reference to the established racial minorities of blacks and American Indians. A comprehensive account of the experiences of the complete range of American minority groups requires a theory that recognizes both assimilation and dissimilation.[29] Overemphasis on the former merely serves to highlight the disparities between the universalistic ethos of the American creed and the particularistic practices of American society. Such shortcomings have been generally appreciated by analysts looking at the historical and contemporary position of Mexican-Americans and have been dismissed by certain Chicano scholars as simplistic and misleading.[30] Not surprisingly, therefore, colonialist and neo-Marxist perspectives have appeared to shed more light on the development of ethnic stratification in the Southwest of the United States.

The history of conquest and dispossession that has characterized the evolution of Chicano stratification from the middle of the nineteenth century has particularly lent itself to a colonialist interpretation.[31] Scholars such as Blauner, Moore, Acuna, and Barrera have pointed to many key features that might justify the use of an

---

26. Ray C. Rist, "Guestworkers in Germany: Public Policies as the Legitimation of Marginality," *Ethnic and Racial Studies*, vol. 2 (October 1979), p. 413.

27. See Milton M. Gordon, *Assimilation in American Life: The Role of Race, Religion and National Origins* (New York: Oxford University Press, 1964); and Harold J. Abramson, "Assimilation and Pluralism" in Stephan Thernstrom, ed., *Harvard Encyclopedia of American Ethnic Groups* (Cambridge, Mass.: Harvard University Press, 1980), pp. 15–60.

28. Herbert J. Gans, "Symbolic Ethnicity: the Future of Ethnic Groups and Cultures in America," *Ethnic and Racial Studies*, vol. 2 (January 1979), pp. 1–20.

29. J. Milton Yinger, "Toward a Theory of Assimilation and Dissimilation," *Ethnic and Racial Studies*, vol. 4 (July 1981), pp. 249–64.

30. Marietta Morrissey, "Ethnic Stratification and the Study of Chicanos," *The Journal of Ethnic Studies*, vol. 10 (1983), p. 73.

31. Mario Barrera, *Race and Class in the Southwest: A Theory of Racial Inequality* (Notre Dame, Ind.: University of Notre Dame Press, 1979), pp. 1–103.

"internal colonial" analogy.[32] Conquest, segregation, a dual wage structure, and dominant administrative control are all familiar aspects of colonial regimes. A major strength of this approach is its proper recognition of the role of racism and racial categorization which, as I argue below, tends to be the Achilles' heel of many neo-Marxist analyses. Significantly, many who claim to be writing in a neo-Marxist tradition subject it to precisely this criticism. Enda Bonacich, for example, argues: "My major disagreement with this perspective is that it takes ethnic or racial categories for granted. It assumes, for example, that "whites" in the United States have colonized "blacks." In doing so, it ignores class struggle within each racial group. Indeed the "class question" is shunted aside, and it is assumed that racial and national oppression take its place. All whites benefit from racial oppression and all blacks lose by it."[33]

This seems to me to be based on a somewhat stereotyped version of classical colonial systems that in fact almost always had complex class divisions intersecting their various racial groupings. An internal colonialist approach need not necessarily ignore class: it is just that it does not assume a priori that class will always be the dominant and overriding variable. Barrera's attempt to synthesize the colonial and class models is one logical way out of this dilemma.[34]

In European societies the internal colonialist perspective has been applied mainly to an analysis of regionalist movements, following Michael Hechter's influential book, *Internal Colonialism: The Celtic Fringe in British National Development.*[35] Some situations certainly seem to fit this model rather well as, for example, Reece found in the case of Brittany,[36] but its relevance to other regions[37] and to the position of *gastarbeiter* groups is more difficult to sustain. In a recent attempt

---

32. Robert Blauner, *Racial Oppression in America* (New York: Harper & Row, 1972); Joan Moore, "Colonialism: The Case of Mexican-Americans," *Social Problems*, vol. 17 (Spring 1970), pp. 463–72.; Rodolfo Acuna, *Occupied America* (San Francisco: Canfield, 1972); Mario Barrera, Carlos Munoz, and Charles Ornelas, "The Barrio as Internal Colony," in Harlan Hahn, ed., *People and Politics in Urban Society* (Los Angeles: Sage, 1972), pp. 465–98.

33. Edna Bonacich, "The Past, Present and Future of Split Labor Market Theory," in Cora B. Marrett and Cheryl Leggon, eds., *Research in Race and Ethnic Relations: A Research Annual* vol. 1 (Greenwich, Conn.: JAI Press, 1979), p. 41.

34. Barrera, *Race and Class*, pp. 212–18.

35. Michael Hechter, *Internal Colonialism: The Celtic Fringe in British National Development, 1536–1966* (London: Routledge, 1975).

36. Jack E. Reece, "Internal Colonialism: The Case of Brittany" *Ethnic and Racial Studies*, vol. 2 (July 1979), pp. 275–92.

37. John Stone, "Internal Colonialism in Comparative Perspective," *Ethnic and Racial Studies*, vol. 2 (July 1979), pp. 255–59.

to assess the value of the three major models of ethnic stratification in relation to immigrant minorities in West Germany, Schmitter concluded that Hechter's later formulation of a "cultural division of labor" provided the most perceptive analysis of the facts. This approach places a greater stress on the minority group's own response than either the standard Marxian focus on conflicts between capitalists and workers, or the "split-labor market" emphasis on the power of organized labor.[38] Although colonial elements are apparent in the early years of migration, the strength of the analogy seems to become diluted as migrants become permanently resident minorities and a second generation begins to emerge.

Some Neo-Marxist Perspectives

At this point it is appropriate to consider the various neo-Marxist analyses of the two cases. As with any discussion of Marxism, complications arise because of the diversity of interpretations that claim to fall within this particular tradition. Marx's famous retort that he did not wish to be considered a Marxist reveals the extent to which his ideas had already become the subject of bitter debate during his own lifetime. When one looks at the writings of prominent neo-Marxists in recent years, this complex problem of relating class, race, and ethnicity is apparent. Two typical examples illustrate this point. Frantz Fanon, the theorist of the Algerian War of Independence, can be seen wrestling with the connection between national liberation strategies and socialist revolutions, both in Africa and in the rest of the third world, and concluded that Marxism had to be "slightly stretched" in the colonial context. And Herbert Marcuse, a leading member of the Marxist-influenced, Frankfurt School, argued that racial minorities, rather than the working classes of classical Marxism, would be in the vanguard of the revolutionary struggle to overthrow American capitalism.

Part of the problem lies with Marx's own analysis of these questions, which, for a prolific author writing over a period of some forty years, not surprisingly contained a number of ambiguities. Marx's principal preoccupation was with the nature of capitalist society and the manner in which it would be transformed, through the struggle between the owners of the means of production and the

---

38. Barbara Schmitter, "Immigrant Minorities in West Germany: Some Theoretical Concerns," *Ethnic and Racial Studies*, vol. 6 (July 1983), p. 316.

workers, into a socialist society. This was part of a broad evolutionary scheme, typical of much nineteenth-century social thought, which postulated a series of historical stages through which all societies must pass on the road to communism. The ancient world leads into feudalism, which is subsequently overcome by capitalism, which, in its turn, will collapse in the face of the socialist revolution.

An obvious objection to this approach is its heavy emphasis on European historical experience and its dismissal of vast tracts of the world, such as India and China, on the grounds that they belonged to a separate and totally undynamic category that Marx called the "Asiatic mode of production." As Avineri comments, "Stated bluntly it implies that Marx is aware of the fact that his philosophy of history does not account for the majority of mankind since it is relevant only to the European experience."[39]

Even within European societies, however, Marx's writings display considerable difficulties in reconciling the activities of racial, ethnic, and national groups with his class-based model of social change. Marx's ambivalence in his analysis of the relation between Irish nationalism and the English socialist movement is well known: he originally believed that an English proletarian revolution would produce a liberated Ireland, but later he switched to the argument that Irish nationalism would act as the catalyst that would ignite a class revolution in England. The impatience of Marx and Engels with such ethnic and national complications to the class war is probably best captured in the latter's notorious outburst against the Irish worker in Manchester: "His crudity places him little above the savage."[40] Subsequent distinctions drawn between the "historic nations" of West Europe and the "ruins of peoples" to be found in East Europe, as well as on the periphery of West European states, give little assistance in trying to assess the strength of attachment to various nationalist forces. Thus, as one authority rightly concludes, "Marx and Engels left their followers little guidance in matters of nation and nationalism," and much the same is also true concerning race and ethnicity.[41]

This problem has become more apparent only in the present century with Lenin's attempt to analyze imperialism as the "highest

---

39. Shlomo Avineri, *Karl Marx on Colonialism and Modernization* (New York: Doubleday, 1968), p. 11.

40. Quoted in Paul Foot, *Immigration and Race in British Politics* (Harmondsworth, England: Penguin, 1965), p. 82.

41. Hélène Carrère d'Encausse, "The Bolsheviks and the National Question (1903–1929)," in Eric Cahm and Vladimir C. Fišera, eds., *Socialism and Nationalism* (Nottingham, England: Spokesman, 1980), p. 114.

stage" of capitalism, often resulting in a deplorable but very evident split in the labor movement, and Stalin's efforts to define, and later brutally resolve, the "national question" in Soviet society. It would seem, then, that Marxist analysis can easily founder on the rocks of racism and nationalism, but this does not mean that Marxist scholars have either ignored these issues or failed to make useful contributions to the debates that have been engendered by them. The distinction made between "open Marxism" and the simplified, dogmatic materialism, often referred to as "vulgar Marxis," is helpful in differentiating between those Marxists who are prepared to recognize the complexity of racial and ethnic dynamics and those who simply dismiss the issues as irrelevant epiphenomena, a smokescreen disguising the "objective" class relations that are the one and only cause of all social conflict. As Blauner argued with respect to the United States:

> Colonial forms of racial domination were entrenched in the matrix of a developing capitalism. A racial structure and a class structure were both produced. Races and classes coexist and interpenetrate. Racial division has influenced class formation and class factors have affected racial dynamics in a manner that a deterministic Marxism could not seriously investigate.[42]

An influential attempt to present a Marxist interpretation of the *gastarbeiter* case was provided by Castles and Kosack in their book *Immigrant Workers and Class Structure in Western Europe*, which viewed this massive migration as part of the process of international capitalist development. Migrant workers were merely another element in the class structure of the host societies, forming a bottom stratum of the working class because of their concentration in the least desirable manual occupations.[43] Ethnic differences between the very diverse sources of this migration are regarded as insignificant compared with their common structural location among the working classes. Ethnic consciousness is dismissed as false consciousness, and working class racism is depicted as a deliberately contrived mechanism of the ever-present and all-powerful ruling classes to subvert the cause of working class solidarity.[44] The evident entrepreneurial goals of several of these groups are largely ignored, since "objectively" they are defined as a "working class fraction" that should not aspire to become assimilated as part of the self-employed bourgeoisie.

---

42. Robert Blauner, "Marxist Theory, Nationality and Colonialism," unpublished document provided by Blauner (University of California, Berkeley, Sociology Department, 1973), p. 35.

43. Stephen Castles and Godula Kosack, *Immigrant Workers and the Class Structure in Western Europe* (London: Oxford University Press, 1973), pp. 2–8.

44. Ibid., pp. 450–56.

It is quite true that many immigrant workers do share characteristics and conditions of the indigenous working classes. They may
be trade union members; vote for labor, socialist, or communist
parties; and view their interests in class terms. But this does not mean
that class rather than ethnicity will always be the more salient feature
of the immigrant workers' organizational structure. Nor does it imply
that the indigenous (white) working classes will not define immigrants
in racist terms and believe, no matter how strong the evidence to the
contrary, that they are the cause rather than the victims of economic
and social problems.

A direct attempt to respond to these questions is provided by
Phizacklea and Miles in their study of black and white workers in
Willesden, an inner-city area of northwest London.[45] They are critical
of what they call the "race-relations approach" of much sociological
analysis of blacks in British society, singling out the work of Rex and
his collaborators for specific attack.[46] This is somewhat ironic as Rex
clearly regards his own work as a "class analysis" and constantly
repeats the claim, thereby emphasizing my early point about the
diversity of materialistic perspectives.

Phizacklea and Miles are also critical of the attempts by neo-
Marxists such as Poulantzas to incorporate intraclass divisions within
a Marxist analysis of contemporary capitalism, understandably feeling
that the finer distinctions between "categories," "fractions," and
"strata" are ill-defined and often positively confusing.[47] Nevertheless,
they still argue that migrant labor in Britain must be seen as a
"fraction of the working class," but unfortunately they too fail to
define clearly and unambiguously what a "fraction" actually is. The
implication and continual assertion is that class will always override
fractional alignments, although they qualify this by recognizing the
extent of racial discrimination and racism, not least among white
workers.[48] The authors accept that these experiences of prejudice
and discrimination may persuade black workers that "their position
as a racialized fraction of the working classes should serve as the basis
for independent political action" and that this would be "paralleled

45. Annie Phizacklea and Robert Miles, *Labour and Racism* (London: Routledge,
1980).
46. John Rex and Robert Moore, *Race Community and Conflict: A Study of Sparkbrook*
(London: Oxford University Press, 1967); and John Rex and Sally Tomlinson, *Colonial
Immigrants in a British City: A Class Analysis* (London: Routledge, 1979).
47. N. Poulantzas, *Classes in Contemporary Capitalism* (London: New Left Books,
1975).
48. Phizacklea and Miles, *Labour and Racism*, pp. 23, 156–57.

by the development of a particular form of political consciousness which we [will] . . . call *racial consciousness.*"[49]

Far from demolishing the value of a race relations perspective on British racial and ethnic minorities, Phizacklea and Miles have demonstrated what an important qualification it provides to any class analysis. Furthermore, if their sample evidence had not been so heavily based on the work relations of the first generation of West Indians and had focused more on other groups (such as the Asians), other areas (such as housing and education), and other generations (such as the British-born youth), their position would have been even more difficult to sustain. In the conclusion to their study they virtually concede the case when they argue: "We are therefore referring not to a potential but to a *real* source of fragmentation within black migrant labor as a working class fraction, and this too must be recognized in any detailed analysis of political consciousness and action."[50]

When faced with North American race relations, Marxist scholars have encountered similar difficulties in developing a convincing interpretation. During the high point of capitalist contradictions, the Great Depression of the 1930s, American communists pronounced themselves in favor of the creation of separate black states, a nationalist rather than a socialist solution to the race problem. This was based more on tactical fears of a racial split in the ranks of organized labor than on the logical development of socialist doctrine.

In the early postwar years, the leading theoretical text giving a Marxist diagnosis of American race relations, Cox's *Class, Caste and Race,* was in fact a highly idiosyncratic interpretation of Marxism, employing concepts such as a "political class" in a strikingly non-Marxian manner.[51] Not surprisingly, this work gave little assistance to those wishing to resolve the causal priority of class and racial variables in the United States, and Cox's later studies further confuse rather than clarify these issues.[52]

Some American scholars writing in the Marxist tradition, such as the historian Eugene Genovese, have departed a long way from a crudely materialistic explanation of race relations in the United States

---

49. Ibid., pp. 33–34 (authors' emphasis added).
50. Ibid., p. 231 (emphasis mine).
51. See Robert Miles, "Class, Race and Ethnicity: A Critique of Cox's Theory," *Ethnic and Racial Studies,* vol. 3 (April 1980), pp. 169–87.
52. See John Stone, review of Oliver C. Cox, *Race Relations: Elements and Social Dynamics,* in *Ethnic and Racial Studies* vol. 1 (January 1978), pp. 129–30.

and have roundly condemned other Marxists for falling into this error. In discussing the various interpretations of the nature of slavery in the Americas, Genovese attacks the views of the anthropologist Marvin Harris because, "what Harris' materialism, in contra-distinction to Marxist materialism, fails to realise is that once an ideology arises it alters profoundly the material reality and in fact becomes a partially autonomous feature of that reality."[53] In other words, racial attitudes, ideologies, and structures assume a life of their own and cannot be explained as the simple outcome of economic causes.

To understand the nature of ethnic stratification among Chicanos, radical sociologists in America have been forced to shift away from standard Marxian categories toward more flexible theories that recognize the legacy of colonialism and the impact of racism. Some, such as Marcuse, whom I mentioned earlier, have been so disappointed by the lack of revolutionary consciousness on the part of the white working classes, and their evident racism, that they have completely abandoned the idea of a class struggle led by the classical Marxian proletariat comprising all industrial workers. The exploitation of American society is still seen as a capitalist conspiracy, but one that has been implemented with an enormous number of white working-class collaborators. The record of the labor unions has been one among several factors supporting this revolutionary pessimism.[54]

Such an interpretation also fits in with the split labor market theories proposed by some sociologists and economists to account for large differentials in the price of labor involved in the same occupations in multiracial and multiethnic societies. While developing a theory to explain different levels of ethnic antagonism, Edna Bonacich argues that such hostility often "germinates in a labor market split along ethnic lines."[55] Ethnic and racial differences do not necessarily produce a split labor market if the various groups involved have similar resources and share similar goals when they enter the economic system.

When these conditions do not prevail, however, a divergence between existing higher-paid labor and cheaper labor sought by

53. Eugene D. Genovese, "Materialism and Idealism in the History of Negro Slavery in the Americas," *Journal of Social History*, vol. 4 (1971), p. 340.

54. Stanley Lieberson, *A Piece of the Pie: Blacks and White Immigrants Since 1880* (Berkeley and Los Angeles: University of California Press, 1980), pp. 339–41; 358–59. Problems faced by Cesar Chavez's United Farm Workers movement from the Teamsters Union is another aspect of this issue. See Carlos E. Cortes, "Mexicans," in Stephan Thernstrom, ed., *Harvard Encyclopedia of American Ethnic Groups*, p. 717.

55. Edna Bonacich, "A Theory of Ethnic Antagonism: The Split Labor Market," *American Sociological Review*, vol. 37 (October 1972), p. 549.

employers, either from abroad or from indigenous conquered groups, can lead to one of three basic results: (1) the cheap labor can be substituted for higher-priced labor to the benefit of the capitalists and to the detriment of the formerly higher-paid workers; (2) the cheap labor can be excluded by immigration restrictions; or (3) an industrial caste system can be established and produce the split labor market. The outcome will depend on the power of the higher-paid labor group as compared with that of the employers. The capitalists will prefer the first solution, while the workers will opt for the second or third. If the cheaper labor cannot be excluded, the higher-paid labor will strive to create and maintain a reserved section of better-paid jobs so becoming, in Lenin's famous phrase, an "aristocracy of labor."

Although Bonacich maintains that the split labor market approach is a "class theory" of race and ethnicity, it is certainly a far cry from classical Marxism.[56] However, it is compatible with the "open" Marxist account suggested by Genovese, who argues that, no matter how much minority suppression was linked to the capitalist structure of nineteenth-century America, by the second decade of the twentieth century capitalist organizations no longer required racial discrimination as a tool to maximize their exploitation of the American economy. Once set in motion, racist ideologies and the vested interests in the maintenance of a racial structure took on a reality of their own. As a result, the liberalization of American society along color-blind, universalistic lines has been a long and complex battle, but one that has not primarily been opposed by organized business.

The struggle has been fought at least as much on a racial as on a class basis, with white workers, trade union leaders, grass-roots politicians, and policemen being as opposed to racial and ethnic justice as the captains of industry, if not more so. It would seem, therefore, that to understand the dynamics of ethnic stratification in the United States throughout the twentieth century, a theory is needed that can explain, rather than explain away, these facts. And the necessary modifications to the Marxist model lead to the conclusion that the difference between an "open" Marxism and a standard, neo-Weberian approach to these questions, apart from the political rhetoric, amounts to little more than a minor matter of emphasis.

My own preference when considering these issues is to adopt a more general power analysis of race and ethnic relations that incorporates certain elements of all three models—assimilationism, internal

---

56. Bonacich, "The Past, Present and Future," p. 17.

colonialism, and neo-Marxism—but does not give causal priority to any particular variable. Although this approach recognizes the importance of economic factors, following the Weberian tradition, it regards the mode of production as one of several forces that determine the pattern of ethnic stratification in any given society. Group differences in power based on status (including gender and age),[57] political control, access to administrative machinery, and military force have to be considered in addition to the relationships to the means of production.

Some Policy Implications in Relation to Ethnic Stratification

A good illustration of the need to consider the overall power balance when framing policies designed to create a greater measure of racial and ethnic equality can be seen in the debates about aspects of education policy in both Europe and America. It is essential to recognize not only the strength of central government resolve and the various minority reactions to racial oppression, but also the ability of majorities and dominant minorities to adapt to changed circumstances. Anglo power and Chicano power, like white power and black power, are related dialectically, so that what is won in the battle for school integration may well be lost in the war against ethnic inequality.

A recognition of this dilemma has caused some early advocates of school integration to strongly criticize techniques such as busing as being far too crude to succeed in delicate operations in intergroup relations. Such sociologists now favor various forms of incentives that would, so they argue, produce a greater measure of integration through consent rather than trying to enforce a system of ethnically mixed schools by legal means.[58] Other social scientists regard such proposals as a totally inadequate response to the challenge of ethnic inequality in education, which might also inadvertently serve to

57. Only recently have the gender and age dimensions of ethnic stratification been considered in detail. For the position of the Chicana, see Margarita B. Melville, ed., *Twice A Minority: Mexican American Women* (St. Louis: C.V. Mosby, 1980). On the European situation, see Annie Phizacklea, ed., *One Way Ticket: Migration and Female Labour* (London: Routledge, 1983). In the case of the ethnic elderly, see Rosina M. Becerra, "The Mexican-American: Aging in a Changing Culture," in R. L. McNeeley and John L. Colen, eds., *Aging in Minority Groups* (Beverly Hills, Calif.: Sage Publications, 1983), pp. 108–118.

58. James S. Coleman, "The Role of Incentives in School Desegregation," in Adam Yarmolinsky, Lance Liebman, and Corinne S. Schelling, eds., *Race and Schooling in the City* (Cambridge, Mass.: Harvard University Press, 1981), pp. 182–93.

legitimize ethnic segregation; they argue in support of more stringently enforced, metropolitan approaches to busing and integration.[59]

Busing has played a major part in the debate over American race relations policy, but it was never adopted to any significant extent in Europe. In Great Britain this was partly a result of reluctance to pursue racially explicit policies that were the hallmark of official attitudes toward race relations until the 1970s. Dispersal policies were opposed on the grounds that they were racist, a remarkably different interpretation from that found in the United States. Britain's Race Relations Board, the body responsible for enforcing the law on racial equality at the time, actually took legal action to prevent a local education authority from continuing the practice in 1976. In fact, busing received very little support from any group: "It was attacked from every quarter: liberals advocating community education argued that it militated against parental involvement in schooling and undermined community stability; West Indian and Asian pressure groups, along with sectors of the Left, viewed the policy as discriminatory and a concession to racist sentiment (reinforcing the popular stereotype of Asian and West Indian students as educational "problems," and singling them out, rather than whites, for busing); and neo-fascist groups claimed that it constituted "discrimination in reverse."[60]

Despite these interesting transatlantic contrasts, both Europe and the United States were involved in a broad debate about the nature of the school curriculum, which some would suggest had an effect that was just as significant on the climate of ethnic relations and on the levels of achievement of minority students as the actual racial and ethnic composition of the school. This controversy has taken a number of forms: in the United States it has centered on the merits and defects associated with bilingual education and ethnic studies programs; in Britain it has been concerned with the measures variously described as "multiethnic," "multicultural," or "multiracial" education.[61]

The arguments concerning all these developments contain a number of interrelated themes. They assume that an education

59. Thomas F. Pettigrew, "The Case for Metropolitan Approaches to Public-School Desegregation," in Yarmolinsky and others, *Race and Schooling*, pp. 163–81.

60. Bruce Carrington, "Schooling an Underclass: The Implications of Ethnic Differences in Attainment," *Durham and Newcastle Research Review*, vol. 9 (Autumn 1981), p. 295.

61. Steven Fenton, "Multi-Something Education," *New Community*, vol. 10 pp. 57–63; and Lewis Killian, "How Much Can be Expected of Multicultural Education?" *New Community*, vol. 10 (Spring 1983), pp. 421–23.

dominated by the majority's central values and world view—and, in a multilingual society, by the dominant language—will tend to undermine the self-esteem of minority students, putting them at an educational disadvantage. It will have the effect of perpetuating negative stereotypes, fail to make the majority sensitive to the cultural traditions and historical experience of minorities, and create learning and assessment problems for students whose native language differs from the language of classroom instruction. Critics of these schemes see a number of disadvantages in any attempt to offer fundamentally different types of education to minority students, for these can easily degenerate into inferior substitutes for quality education, or can even be interpreted as cynical forms of manipulation by the dominant group in society—a type of educational tokenism.[62]

Few would dispute the importance of removing explicit and implicit racist references from textbooks and teaching materials or the need to avoid the use of negative stereotypes and to correct the ethnocentric biases often found in traditional history courses. The value of bilingual education and the adoption of ethnic studies programs, however, are more complex issues. With language it is by no means obvious who actually requires linguistic assistance and in what form it is best provided. In the British case the educational authorities have been more sensitive to the problems faced by Asian children than to the problems confronting West Indians. The need to provide supplementary language instruction to those whose native language is Urdu or Gujerati is more apparent than the difficulties faced by schoolchildren of West Indian origin using a dialect or patois form of English.[63] This may be one factor accounting for the different levels of academic achievement often found in studies comparing West Indian and Asian students. The issue of fully bilingual education in Britain has only arisen in Wales, where it has been closely associated with the demands of the nationalist movement.[64]

In the United States the question of the medium of instruction in schools has been a much more central issue. The influential 1974 Supreme Court ruling in the case of *Lau* vs. *Nichols* concerned the failure of the San Francisco public school district to provide adequate

62. Brian Bullivant, *The Pluralist Dilemma in Education* (London: George Allen & Unwin, 1981); Maureen Stone, *The Education of the Black Child in Britain* (London: Fontana, 1981).

63. Alan Little and Richard Willey, *Multi-ethnic Education: The Way Forward*, Schools Council Report 18 (1981), pp. 17–20.

64. Colin J. Thomas and Colin H. Williams, "Language and Nationalism in Wales" *Ethnic and Racial Studies*, vol. 1 (April 1978), pp. 235–58.

special educational assistance to non-English-speaking Chinese students. The Court declared: "There is no equality of treatment merely by providing students with the same facilities, textbooks, teachers and curriculum . . . for students who do not understand English are effectively foreclosed from any meaningful education . . . [which makes] a mockery of public education."[65] The Court did not specify the particular means by which these disabilities were to be overcome, whether by supplementary English instruction, or by tutoring in the student's home language, or by some combination of the two.

Subsequent federal government policy, developed by the Office of Civil Rights and the Department of Education, has tended to encourage bilingualism, but the wisdom of this strategy has been challenged on several grounds.[66] Critics usually accept the claim that children from linguistic minorities may need special educational assistance, although the type of aid that would be of most use is more debatable. The difficulties faced by these children may not be attributable to their dependence on a language other than English— they may be more skilled in English than in their nature language— but to a deficiency in *both* languages.

Recent studies suggest that class background and associated levels of poverty may account for much of the low achievement previously attributed to language problems, so that attempts to improve linguistic skills are at best only a partial solution.[67] The effectiveness of bilingual education in purely academic terms is therefore questionable, as are the ability of school districts to provide qualified bilingual teachers and the lack of reliable tests to assess children's language proficiency.

For many advocates of bilingualism, however, the policy is not just aimed at promoting educational attainment and a positive self-image, it also provides job protection for minority teachers and acts as "an important weapon in strengthening the power of their own ethnic group."[68] Chicano pressure groups have drawn up plans to segregate Hispanic schoolchildren in schools with bilingual programs, producing a reversal of previous tactics in the battle against ethnic disadvantage. As Cohen points out, "Segregation was no longer seen only in terms of a ploy by middle-class Anglos to maintain the low

---

65. Keith A. Baker and Adriana A. de Kanter, *Bilingual Education: A Reappraisal of Federal Policy* (Lexington, Mass.: D.C. Heath, 1983), pp. ix–xxi.

66. Noel Epstein, *Language, Ethnicity, and the Schools: Policy Alternatives for Bilingual Education* (Washington, D.C.: George Washington University Institute for Educational Leadership, 1977).

67. Baker and de Kanter, *Bilingual Education*, pp. 33–86.

68. Gaynor Cohen, "Alliance and Conflict among Mexican Americans," *Ethnic and Racial Studies*, vol. 5 (April 1982), p. 179.

social status of minority groups, but as 'the only way to preserve the ethnic culture of the barrio.' "[69]

This strategy is based on a rationale similar to that of many of the ethnic studies programs, and the dangers are obvious. Isolation from the majority can result in an erosion of financial support, so although the "gilded ghetto" approach may appeal to community leaders and ethnic activists and theoretically offer an opportunity for greater ethnic autonomy, in reality it can soon degenerate into educational apartheid. People with qualifications in "ethnic studies" or fluency in a minority language may find them of little use in the job market and, in fact, a liability when they are competing against persons with technical or professional qualifications. Programs designed to bolster a minority's self-esteem may well be misjudged when confidence is no longer the basic problem.[70] The very success of the ethnic power movements may have made ethnic studies redundant.

If this diagnosis is correct, then developing instrumental skills, demanding a fair share of educational resources (if necessary, by means of quotas), and removing posteducation discriminatory barriers in employment become the important priorities. It may be of greater value to direct multicultural studies toward students of majority background rather than toward ethnic minorities, where such initiatives can become a substitute for basic education. Contemplating one's ethnic navel can be an expensive luxury in the hard world of group competition.

Critics of multiculturalism as it is practiced in Britain, the United States, Canada, and Australia,[71] may be overstating the case when they dismiss it as trendy rhetoric, or even as a more sinister strategy to entrench "ethnic hegemony." It is certainly valid, however, to stress the limitations of the educational system, confined as it is within the general power structure of society. As Bullivant notes: "The school system and its associated teacher education cannot achieve anywhere near the degree of social change required through the curriculum.

---

69. Ibid., p. 180.
70. Delroy Louden, "A Comparative Study of Self-Concepts among Minority and Majority Group Adolescents in English Multi-Racial Schools," *Ethnic and Racial Studies*, vol. 4 (April 1981), pp. 153–74. For a comparison between the self-concepts of Chicano, black, and white adolescents in Los Angeles, see Jennifer Hurstfield, " 'Internal' Colonialism: White, Black and Chicano Self-Conceptions," *Ethnic and Racial Studies*, vol. 1 (January 1978), pp. 60–79.
71. Brian Bullivant, *The Pluralist Dilemma in Education* (London: George Allen & Unwin, 1981); Kogila Moodley, "Canadian Multi-culturalism as Ideology," *Ethnic and Racial Studies*, vol. 6, (July 1983), pp. 320–31.

This in essence is the pluralist dilemma in education, and it is manifestly not being solved."[72]

My focus on education policy issues is purely illustrative, and I am not implying that these questions are more significant in the development of ethnic stratification, either in the United States or Europe, than employment opportunities or political mobilization.[73] In practice, all these factors are closely interrelated. The connection between different institutions in society is graphically demonstrated, for example, by the impact of "white flight" on the American busing program. Discrimination in the housing market is both a cause and a consequence of ethnic stratification in education. Housing inequality makes the search for greater opportunity in education more difficult and this, in turn, affects the pattern of ethnic disadvantage in employment. No realistic policy aimed at eliminating racial or ethnic disparities can consider one set of institutions in isolation from the others or neglect the complex patterns of causal interconnections between them.

One final lesson emerges from this comparison between two of the major migrations of the postwar period: whatever strategies are adopted to change the existing structures of ethnic stratification, if the outcome means that the haves and the have-nots are still divided along ethnic and racial lines, the prospects for peace and progress in Europe and the United States will be poor indeed.

---

72. Bullivant, *Pluralist Dilemma*, p. 226.

73. The potential power of the Chicano vote, as indeed the wider Hispanic vote, is a matter of considerable contemporary speculation. See, for example, Christopher Thomas, "Traditional Crop Pickers of U.S. Prepare to Pick the President," *Times* (London), August 19, 1983.

CHAPTER FIVE

One of the more evident differences between Mexican-Americans and the preponderant number of other Americans is the immediately adjacent location of the Mexican-Americans' country of ancestry. While this is also true of French-Canadian Americans, the settlement pattern of these people detracted somewhat from the potential significance of the adjacency of Canada. Although the Canadians settled principally in New England (that is to say, not too far from Quebec), they did so in a series of urban pockets that were geographically unconnected to one another and to the Quebec-United States border. By contrast, despite substantial and growing pockets of Mexican-Americans outside the southwestern United States, overall settlement has demonstrated a more geographically uninterrupted pattern from the border northward.

Milton Yinger earlier reminded us of the impact that "transborderdom" is apt to exert upon assimilation (a situation in which "return to homeland [is] easy and frequent" was catalogued as "dissimilative"). And, as Myron Weiner makes evident in the following essay, situations characterized by a transborder people have often proven politically volatile, increasing the porousness of the border, raising issues of primary loyalty, and materially influencing the relations between the bordering states.

Examples of transborder peoples are numerous. The political map of the world has been superimposed upon the ethnic map with cavalier disregard for the distribution of peoples. Nearly everywhere, political land borders and ethnic borders fail to coincide. Peoples find themselves separated from ethnic kin by lines drawn on a political map.

Comparativists desiring to study the phenomenon of transborder peoples are not troubled by a shortage of case studies, therefore. Yet anyone wishing to treat the Mexican-Americans as a transborder people within a comparative framework is confronted by the absence of additional cases involving an immigrant society. As was observed in the first chapter of this volume, extreme caution must be taken when contrasting experiences derived from homeland and nonhomeland environments. Attitudinal and behavioral patterns are likely to diverge sharply between the two situations, causing analogies bridging this division to be faulty. Although he is sensitive to this pitfall, Myron Weiner has established an impressive variety of parallels in the sets of circumstances surrounding the southern borders of the United States and Assamese India. He also examines a number of other cases.

TRANSBORDER PEOPLES

Myron Weiner

$\mathbf{M}$exican-Americans are among dozens, possibly hundreds, of peoples whose traditional homelands are divided by an international border. Indeed, international boundaries rarely neatly separate linguistically and culturally distinct peoples. Even in western Europe, the model of the nationalist ideal of "one country—one people," linguistic groups are not wholly confined within their own national boundaries. And among the newly independent countries of the third world, it is common for postcolonial boundaries to cut across tribal, linguistic, cultural, and religious communities.

There are three types of transborder peoples. In one type or pattern a "people" constitute a majority in each of the countries in which they live, divided, as it were, among several countries. The Arabs, for example, characterize themselves as a single "people" or "nation," living under a variety of different governments. A second pattern is one in which the ethnic group constitutes a majority in one country, but spills across the borders into neighboring countries where it is a minority. The Somali people, for example, constitute a majority in Somalia, but a minority in Kenya, Djibouti, and Ethiopia. Similarly, Turks, Greeks, Chinese, Indians, Bangladeshis, Nepalis, and, of course, Mexicans, live as minorities in neighboring countries. The third pattern is one in which a people constitute a minority in each of the states in which they live and can claim no country of their own. Among the many such transborder peoples are the Baluchis in

For assistance in collecting data for this paper I want to express my gratitude to Tahir Amin and Ahmed Ansur Rehman, both graduate students in the Department of Political Science at the Massachusetts Institute of Technology. My understanding of the Mexican-American perspective has been greatly helped by comments on an early draft of this paper by Gilberto Cardenas of the University of Texas, Carlos Arce of the National Chicano Council on Higher Education, and by my colleague Peter Smith of the Department of Political Science at M.I.T. My understanding of the comparative dimensions has been greatly sharpened by pointed comments made and questions raised by Walker Connor.

Pakistan, Iran and Afghanistan; the Kurds in Iraq and Iran; the Pushtuns of Afghanistan and Pakistan; and the Armenians in Turkey and the Soviet Union—all in western Asia—as well as countless ethnic groups within Africa.

Transborder peoples have many features in common with migrants; indeed many of the transborder peoples may themselves be migrants or of migrant origin. And as a minority they may share the problems of other minorities. But transborder peoples may make claims that are quite different from those made by other minorities. They may assert the right, for example, to freely cross the international borders. They are more likely than other minorities—immigrants for example—to claim the right to maintain their own language and culture. They may assert a special attachment to the region of the country in which they live, on the grounds that it constitutes a portion of their historical homeland. In short, a transborder people may believe they have certain "national" rights, not merely "civil" rights, a claim that often goes beyond those put forth by immigrant minorities.

One distinctive characteristic of transborder peoples is that questions are often raised about their loyalties in either or both of the countries in which they reside. Where they constitute a majority in one country and a minority in the other, the inhabitants of the country in which they are a minority may perceive them as a people whose loyalty and identity lie elsewhere. Indeed, the transborder peoples themselves may be ambivalent as to where their attachments lie. To the extent that they are perceived by some as lacking loyalty and patriotism, they may see themselves as rejected outliers and look to the land in which they constitute a majority as the "motherland" and to its government for support. When the transborder people form a minority in both countries, the governments and majority populations of both countries may question their loyalty, an accusation that may undermine whatever attachment the transborder people might have toward the countries in which they live and their governments.

An irredentist demand is virtually certain to undermine the position of the transborder people in the country in which they are a minority. The government of the country against which territorial demands are made is likely to look upon its transborder minority as potentially disloyal, whether or not the transborder people have indicated their support for the demand.

Similarly, a secessionist movement, even a demand for greater regional autonomy, is likely to arouse the ire of the government and of the majority population. Of course, if the movement is small and it lacks popular support, the government may minimize its importance, but even a small militant group can do much to create a perception of disloyalty.

Few governments feel wholly at ease with their transborder peoples; irredentist, secessionist, and even regionalist aspirations are invariably viewed unsympathetically. Indeed, only to list the names of transborder peoples perceived by their rulers as disloyal is to evoke images of suffering and bestiality: Kurds, Armenians, Macedonians, Somalis, Anatolian Greeks. At best, governments have often sought to deny a distinctive identity to its transborder peoples that might link them to a people across the border. Thus, the Turkish government describes its Kurds as "eastern Turks," and to the Greeks the Macedonians are "Slavophones" or Slavic-speaking Greeks. It is uncommon to find a transborder people who have successfully retained their cultural identity and yet are perceived by the country in which they are a minority as politically loyal and patriotic. Under what conditions transborder people can retain their distinctive ethnic identity without having their loyalty questioned is a key issue for Mexican-Americans.

Mexican-Americans are a transborder people, and they share some of the characteristics of other border peoples. But there are some features of the relationship between the United States and Mexico and some particular characteristics of American society that distinguish Mexican-Americans from other border peoples. This essay discusses the ways they are alike and the ways they differ. To draw out these similarities and differences, I compare the Mexican-Americans with other transborder peoples, looking first and in some detail at the Bengalis in northeastern India, where they constitute a minority, and in neighboring Bangladesh, where they form a majority. The Indian region in which they live, the state of Assam, has been torn by conflict between Bengalis and Assamese, a conflict that took a particularly violent and brutal form in 1983. In many respects this case comes closest to the situation of Mexican-Americans because both India and the United States are democracies, the borders between the two countries have been porous, and the issue of illegal or undocumented migrants has been central in both countries.

I then turn to two cases involving transborder peoples in which the issues of irredentism, secession, or regionalism have been paramount: the Baluchis of Pakistan, who also reside in Iran and Afghanistan; and the Somalis who form a majority in the Somali Republic and a minority elsewhere in the Horn of Africa. In the conclusion to this chapter I return to the issues of ethnic identity, political loyalty, and group conflict involving transborder peoples, especially as these relate to the Mexican-Americans.

The Bangladeshis in Assam

In certain respects the problems raised by the presence of Bangladeshis in the Indian state of Assam come close to those of the Mexicans in the United States. Just as sections of the U.S. Southwest were once under Mexican control, so too were the areas of Assam in which Bangladeshis live once politically controlled by Bengalis. The borders between Bangladesh and Assam are, as a practical matter, open, although in a legal sense they are not and, as in the case of the U.S.-Mexican border, substantial numbers of people migrate from one country to another. Similarly, there is considerable local opposition to what is regarded as an illegal and—for many, at least—an unwanted influx. And finally, both receiving countries, the United States and India, are democratic countries whose policy responses have been framed within an open political framework in which a variety of contending interests are involved.

Before 1947 all the northeastern part of the Indian subcontinent, including what is now Bengladesh, was part of an undivided India. The story of the conflict between Bangalis and Assamese in Assam began more than a hundred and fifty years ago in 1826 when the British conquered Assam, ending some four hundred years of independence.[1] Between 1838 and 1874 and again between 1905 and 1912, the British administered Assam as part of Bengal. Moreover, even when Assam was constituted as a separate province in prepartitioned India, the movement of people from one province to another was unrestricted. The Bengalis saw portions of Assam—Sylhet and Cachar districts—as part of their own homeland and the remainder of Assam as part of the frontier, as freely open to Bengalis as to other Indians.

And a frontier it was. By 1891 an estimated one-fourth of the population of the region that is now Assam was of migrant origin. In fact, by the beginning of the twentieth century, Assamese nationalists were pitted against the Bengalis as well as against the British, both of whom were seen as alien rulers. The largest influx of migrants

---

1. For a history of migrations into Assam analyzed in the context of British colonial rule, see Myron Weiner, *Sons of the Soil: Migration and Ethnic Conflict in India* (Princeton: Princeton University Press, 1978), chap. 3, "When Migrants Succeed and Natives Fail: Assam and Its Migrants." For a detailed bibliography, see pp. 139–43.

took place after 1900, however, when Bengali Muslims moved into Brahmaputra Valley from East Bengal. In the next several decades Muslim migrants changed both the religious and linguistic composition of the state. They also fostered a political climate in which questions of ethnicity and migration became central.

It is interesting to note how the various ethnic groups successively employed the state government as an instrument by which to extend, consolidate, or transform their position in the economy and social system. In the nineteenth and early twentieth centuries the Bengali Hindus used their dominance in the government administration to consolidate their position in the educational system. In the 1930s and 1940s when electoral politics were introduced, the more numerous Bengali Muslims won control over the state government and then attempted to use their position to facilitate further migration of Bengali Muslims from East Bengal as a means of strengthening their political position. As independence approached, they began to press for the incorporation of Assam into the proposed Muslim-majority state of Pakistan. The British rejected this demand but agreed to partition Assam by transferring the Bengali-speaking Muslim-majority district of Sylhet to Pakistan, while making the Bengali-speaking Hindu-majority area part of the Indian state of West Bengal.

As a result of these decisions, the coming of independence in 1947 found the Assamese, particularly the Assamese middle class, in control of the government of the newly formed state of Assam. For the first time in more than a century, the indigenous people of Assam were back in power. In the next few decades they used that control to assert the paramountcy of Assamese cultural identity and to seek economic and social equality in relation to the Bengali Hindu middle classes, who were their rivals for jobs in the administrative services, the professions, and the private sector. Assamese was made the official language of the state. A system of preferences, a kind of affirmative action program, was established for "sons of the soil" (that is, Assamese) in employment in the state administrative services. Assamese were appointed teachers in the schools, and Assamese was made the medium of instruction in the schools, colleges, and universities.

Although the Assamization of the state was bitterly opposed by educated Bengali Hindus, there was remarkably little opposition from Bengali Muslims. For one thing, Bengali Muslims turned to the state government for protection. Many Muslims feared that they might be expelled to East Pakistan. In an effort to dissuade the Assamese from taking this course, Bengali Muslims sided with the Assamese on a number of sensitive issues. For example, they accepted Assamese as the language of instruction in primary and secondary schools, supported the government against Bengali Hindus on the controversial issue of an official language for the state and for the university, voted for the governing Assamese-dominated Congress party, and even declared their mother tongue as Assamese to census takers.

For many years this tractability protected the Bengali Muslims. In the later 1960s and early 1970s there were clashes between Assamese and communities of migrant origin—especially Bengali Hindus and Marwaris. But notably absent was any clash between the Assamese and Bengali Muslims, the largest of the migrant communities, and one with religious ties to neighboring East Pakistan.

In a way it is quite remarkable that the conflict between the two communities did not take place until the late 1970s. Even after the creation of an international border in 1947, migration of Bengali Muslims from East Pakistan into Assam continued. Since the flows were illegal, no reliable numbers exist on how many entered. Bengali Muslims who entered illegally did not, of course, inform the census takers as to their actual place of birth; nor did they report Bengali as their mother tongue. They did, however, report their religion, thereby enabling the census commission to conclude on the basis of an examination of the data on the growth rate of Muslims that nearly a quarter of a million Bengali Muslims had entered the state between 1951 and 1961, almost all illegally from East Pakistan. A similar calculation in the 1971 census led to an estimate that approximately 424,000 more Muslims were in the state than could be accounted for by natural population increase.

How many migrants entered illegally after the 1971 Pakistan civil war and the 1972 war between India and Pakistan, which led to the secession of East Pakistan and the formation of the independent country of Bangladesh, is unknown; but government estimates of the population of Assam in 1981 showed a population increase of 5.3 million, or 36.3 percent, well above the 24.7 percent growth rate for India as a whole. There is some evidence that the natural population increase of Assam was actually lower than that of the rest of India. On the basis of these figures, the immigration into Assam has been estimated at about 1.8 million between 1971 and 1981 (and this in a state with a 1981 population of 19.9 million). How much of this was migration from elsewhere in India and how much from Bangladesh is conjectural, though it is plausible to assume that most of it was illegal migration from Bangladesh.

Most migrants from Bangladesh are engaged in agriculture. Considerable resentment has arisen among Assamese farmers and among some of the indigenous tribal peoples against Bengali Muslim squatters. The desire by Assamese and tribals to take over lands cultivated by Bangladeshi Muslims was an element in the violent clashes of 1983.

Competition for control over land—the rural equivalent of competition for employment in a predominantly urban society—was not, however, what actually precipitated the violent conflict. The changing political framework at the time when the influx was increasing was particularly decisive. The Congress party in Assam was badly defeated in the 1978 state assembly elections. For the first time since independence, the Congress party was out of power. There then followed a succession of coalition governments. A major issue before these governments and the various political parties was the question of what to do about the increasing number of aliens on the electoral rolls. (In India electoral rolls are prepared by the Election Commission, a central government body responsible for all matters related to elections.)

The first non-Congress government in Assam, led by the Janata party, supported a policy of screening voters to ensure that noncitizens were not on the voters' list. A second coalition government, formed in mid-1979, was split; Congress and Communist leaders in the coalition government refused to support efforts to screen the electoral rolls on the grounds that the government might not only exclude illegal Bangladeshis but might also disenfranchise many refugees who were entitled to citizenship although they were unable to prove that they had migrated to India some thirty years earlier.

Also clearly at issue was a political question: Mrs. Gandhi's Congress and the Communists were eager to win the support of the migrants, the long-term Bengali Hindu and Muslim residents and Assamese Muslims sympathetic to their Muslim brethren. By late 1979, when the central government announced that it was calling national parliamentary elections, the state was badly divided. A number of Assamese organizations, particularly the All Assam Students Union, agitated for screening the electoral rolls to exclude aliens. The Assamese demanded that all persons who had entered the state from Bangladesh after 1961 be expelled from the state and their names expunged from the electoral rolls. What particularly alarmed the Assamese was the growth in the number of registered voters from 6.3 million in 1972 to 8.7 million in 1979.

The agitation grew to such proportions that the central government canceled the elections for Assam, the first time in postindependence India that the central government had declared a region so disturbed that it was not possible to hold parliamentary elections.

For several years thereafter indecisive negotiations took place between Mrs. Gandhi's government and the Assamese leadership. The central government agreed to a March 1971 cutoff date to determine de facto citizenship, implicitly agreeing that persons who entered after 1971 should be deported or dispersed to other states. The Assamese, however, continued to press for a 1961 cutoff.[2]

In an effort to break the stalemate, Mrs. Gandhi called state elections for the Assam state legislative assembly and for the unfilled parliamentary seats for February 1983. Since the existing electoral rolls were to be used as the basis for voting, the Assamese were inflamed by a decision that they viewed as extending de facto citizenship to the illegal immigrants. The state was polarized. The Assamese opposed the elections, as did some of the indigenous tribal groups, especially the Lalung, who resented the encroachment of Bengali immigrants into tribal tracts. The elections were supported by the two major Bengali-speaking communities, Bangali Hindus and Bengali Muslims. One group of indigenous tribals known as Boro also supported the elections, since the Boro advocated the creation of an autonomous territory in the Boro-populated region of the state to resist what they viewed as the Assamization policy of the state government.

What thus began as an issue of illegal immigration soon grew to a broader conflict among Assamese, tribals, and Bengalis. The violence began with attacks by Assamese against government offices and even police stations, followed by retaliation from the police. The state administration was virtually paralyzed as state government employees refused to obey government orders and Assamese officials refused to serve as polling agents. In mid-February 1983, Boro tribesmen supporting the poll attacked Assamese villagers, followed by Assamese attacks against the Boros. The worst killings took place in Nellie, a region along the southern banks of the Brahmaputra that contains thousands of Muslim migrants from Bangladesh. Mobs of Lalung tribals, along with some Assamese, attacked several villages, killing thousands of people, mostly women and children, leading some observers to describe the massacre as a quasi-genocidal attempt to prevent the reproduction of Bengalis. Army units arrived to find

---

2. For an account of the antimigrant movement and its negotiations with the government of India written from a pro-Assamese point of view, see Amiya Kumar Das, *Assam's Agony: A Socio-Economic and Political Analysis* (New Delhi: Lancers Publishers, 1982). Political developments within Assam between April 1979 and October 1982 are described by T. S. Murty, *Assam, The Difficult Years* (New Delhi: Himalayan Books, 1983).

bodies everywhere and thousands left homeless. The death toll was estimated at more than 4,000. Another quarter of a million people moved to refugee camps and thousands more fled the state.[3]

The elections were held and Mrs. Gandhi's Congress party easily won a majority of seats, but the boycott was successful in the Assamese-populated constituencies, where turnouts were often well below 20 percent. The boycott successfully prevented the emergence of a popularly elected Congress government that could negotiate with the center on behalf of the Assamese. The new government, supported by the center, has nonetheless taken steps intended to resolve the dispute. The government declared 1971 as the cutoff point, in effect granting amnesty to people who entered India before 1971. The government also announced that it would attempt to seal the borders by reinforcing border patrols and by building a fence to deter immigrants from illegally entering. The fence has been denounced by the Bangladesh government, while the 1971 cutoff has been rejected by the major Assamese organizations, which continue to press for a 1961 cutoff date, and reject, in any event, any proposals from a state government they consider to be illegitimate. The Assamese agitation continues, though somewhat abated, as many of its supporters have grown weary after more than five years of agitation.

Several features of the Bengali-Assamese dispute make finding a resolution difficult. One is the difficulty of distinguishing between people who cross the border illegally, whatever cutoff date is chosen, and those Bengalis who are citizens of India, have been longtime residents of the state, or have entered Assam from the Indian state of West Bengal. This inability of the authorities to distinguish between illegal and legal Bengali settlers is a major element of the problem.

A second difficulty is that whatever cutoff date is chosen, there remains the issue of the legal status of children born in Assam whose parents entered illegally from Bangladesh. If an early cutoff date is chosen, many of these "children" are already adults. Moreover, in the absence of birth certificates or identity cards, large numbers of Bengalis would be unable to verify their status, whatever the cutoff

---

3. For an analysis of the violence and the events leading up to it, see Myron Weiner, "The Political Demography of Assam's Anti-Immigrant Movement," *Population and Development Review*, vol. 9 (June 1983), pp. 279–92. For a Marxist interpretation of the agitation, see the articles by Hiren Gohain in *Economic and Political Weekly* (Bombay), February 23 and May 24, 1980; and see Udayon Misra, "Assam: Trends within the Left," *Economic and Political Weekly*, July 30, 1983. See also Sanjoy Hazarika, "In Assam, The Killings Abate but The Fear Lingers," *New York Times*, March 28, 1983.

date. Should the government threaten deportation, many Bengalis might migrate to West Bengal, where the state government would find it even more difficult than in Assam to sort out legal from illegal migrants. (For the Assamese, of course, an exodus would reduce the problem even if large numbers of illegal Bengalis resettled in West Bengal.) Nor is it easy for the Indian government to adopt a policy that would lead to large-scale forced repatriation. Hundreds of thousands or even several million Bengalis might resist efforts to deport them across the borders.

Nor is it politically expedient for India to take action to expel large numbers of Muslims. The response of its own Muslim population and that of the Islamic world could not easily be ignored. Nor could the government ignore the response of the millions of Bengali voters, both in Assam and in West Bengal. India's democratic political process precludes taking some coercive measures that might more readily be adopted by authoritarian regimes. India's ethnic pluralism further inhibits central government policymakers; the government cannot ignore the impact of its decision in Assam on ethnic groups elsewhere in India, especially Muslims and Bengalis. Finally, there is the practical problem of border control. The borders between Bangladesh and India are long. They cut through dense forests and hills so that no amount of border patrols could effectively seal the borders.

One feature of the Assamese problem that is unusual from an American perspective is the way in which the problem became defined as an issue between the state and the central government, not simply as a national problem. For political reasons the central government chose to perceive the illegal immigrant issue as a matter for negotiation between Assam and the central government, rather than as a problem warranting the attention of a national commission and of parliament. Although a solution to the migration problem might not have proven easier, the issue would have been less likely to have embittered the Assamese toward the central government and to have led, as it did, to the growth of anti-Indian sentiment among young Assamese. The central government assigned an estimated 150,000 police and paramilitary personnel to the state, not to deal with the migrants but to deal with an increasingly embittered local population. The Assamese resented the loss of land to the migrants and feared that their own position as the dominant cultural and political force in their own homeland would be eroded, if not destroyed, by the migrants, adding as they did to the large number of long-term Bengali residents and citizens. Political power, culture, and economic position all appeared to be threatened by the migrants, and when the center failed to show its concern, the Assamese turned their wrath against the migrants, both legal and illegal, and against the central government.

Among the many parallels between the Mexican-American and the Bengali-Assamese situation, the most striking is the demand in both the United States and in India for the deportation of illegal aliens. In both countries there is also strong support for some form of amnesty. In both countries there is uncertainty about whom should be given amnesty (the issue of the cutoff date). In both there is controversy about how one distinguishes between people who came before and after the cutoff point and whether amnesty would "reward" people who crossed illegally and entice others to enter. In both countries there is controversy about what steps, if any, should be taken to prevent further illegal border crossings. Opposition to restrictive barriers comes from the affected ethnic group. In India, not only the Bengalis in Assam and the government of West Bengal are concerned with the fate of Bangladeshis in Assam. The Congress party of Mrs. Gandhi and the various Marxist leftist parties (with their social base strongest among the Bengalis) seek the support of the migrant communities and other Bengalis. Similarly, in the United States both Democratic and Republican party officials are affected by the Mexican-American vote in shaping their views on immigration policies.

Neither country has found a widely acceptable or effective solution for controlling its borders. In India there is support for reinforcing border patrols and building a fence, but opposition from Bangladesh (which denies that there are any illegal crossings) resulted in shootings between border guards in April and May of 1984. The Indian government subsequently decided to suspend further construction of the fence pending high-level discussions among officials of the two countries. In the United States, a proposal to impose sanctions upon employers who hire illegal aliens has encountered strong opposition from some Mexican-American spokesmen, who fear that employers will then discriminate against legal aliens and citizens. Mexican government officials have opposed the proposal as well.

One striking similarity between the two situations is that immigration legislation, once viewed as the exclusive prerogative of a sovereign country, is now seen by foreign governments as a bilateral issue. Thus, both the Mexican and Bangladesh governments insist that policies affecting future migration and the treatment of illegal residents are matters to be negotiated between the two countries, perhaps placed in the broader context of other bilateral issues.

One other similarity comes as a surprise. Many view the vast income disparities between Mexico and the United States as the primary reason for the migration and argue that a reduction in these disparities through an increase in the rate of economic growth and employment in Mexico would substantially reduce the flow. In the case of India and Bangladesh, however, both countries are poor, both have high rates of unemployment, and both have serious pressures on the land. And yet there are large population flows from one country to another. Relatively modest differences in opportunity (somewhat more access to land in Assam than in Bangladesh), strong kinship ties, a history of migratory flows, and the ease with which individuals can cross the borders all help to account for the persistence of the population movement between two very poor countries.

One important difference, however, is that the United States is an immigrant society so that in none of its states is there an indigenous "sons of the soil" population with a sense that this is their homeland from which others should be excluded. Although many people in the Southwest oppose illegal migration, there is no concern over being culturally overwhelmed by "outsiders" as exists in Assam, nor is there a widely shared sense that non-Texans or non-Californians should not be allowed to live in these states. The American notion of the legitimate rights of migrants—a history of discrimination and prejudice notwithstanding—entitles people of migrant origin and migrants who have become citizens to the same political rights as any other inhabitants. In contrast, the Assamese belief in the special claims of "sons of the soil" serves to legitimize a range of policies that give the Assamese people rights and entitlements not given to Bengali inhabitants of the state, regardless of how long they have lived there or from where they come.

Another significant difference is that Bengalis within Assam claim no right for further migration into India from Bangladesh. The borders are accepted by all, based the decision made by the British parliament in the 1947 partitioning of the country. The Bangladesh government denies that illegal migration has occurred, for fear that to say otherwise would legitimize an Indian government's decision to expel large numbers of people, but it does not question the right (in principle) of a closed border. This latter position is also shared by Bengalis living in India. In contrast, some Mexican-Americans consider the border between the United States and Mexico as illegitimate, the consequence of Mexico's military defeat by the United States. If the borders are illegitimate, migration across the border is not illegal. Thus, what to the U.S. government is "illegal" migration is to many Mexican-Americans and to the Mexican government merely a question of "undocumented workers."[4]

The Baluchis of Pakistan

The two transborder peoples to whom I now turn—the Baluchis of Pakistan, Afghanistan, and Iran and the Somalis in the Horn of Africa—traverse borders that they, or at least one of the governments concerned, do not accept as legitimate. In analyzing these two cases and in comparing them with the Mexican-Americans, I explicitly address the consequences for the transborder peoples of disputed boundaries.

One reason Pakistan remains one of the least stable states in the world and is among the states most burdened with ethnic conflict is that every one of its four major ethnic groups is a transborder people. The demographically and politically predominant ethnic group, the Punjabis, are in both India and Pakistan and share a common language. So too do Sindhi speakers live in both countries. But both these groups are divided along religious lines (the Hindus living in India, the Muslims in Pakistan), and with respect to neither group is there any dispute about boundaries.

In the case of Pakistan's Pushtun-speaking population, however, boundaries are at issue. The Durand line, a line negotiated by Sir Mortimer Durand with Amir Abdur Rahman Khan of Afghanistan in 1893, divides the Pushtun-speaking people. When India was partitioned, the British government offered the Pushtuns in its Northwest Frontier Province the choice of joining either Pakistan or India; the government of Afghanistan, however, demanded that Pushtuns living east of the Durand line be offered the alternative of independence. When the British refused, the Kabul government declared that it did not recognize Pakistan's claim to any of the territory between the Durand line and the Indus River. Instead, Kabul called for the establishment of an independent state of Push-tunistan. The demand, which many interpreted as a veiled call for the creation of a Greater Afghanistan, was clearly intended to win

---

4. One small fringe group of Mexican-Americans based in Denver pushes this argument to its logical conclusion, arguing that the entire Southwest constitutes "the occupied territories."

the loyalty of the Pushtuns on both sides of the border. The call resonated deeply among the Pushtuns of Pakistan, some of whom have supported the demand for a Pushtunistan and many of whom have pressed for greater regional autonomy within Pakistan.

Farther to the south are the Baluchis, a people who span three countries—Pakistan, Afghanistan, and Iran. The borders dividing these people are not disputed by the governments concerned, but the Baluchis themselves, or at least many of them, have demanded that the borders be rearranged so as to enable them to create a state of their own.

There are 1.65 million Baluchis, of whom approximately a million live in Pakistan, 600,000 in Iran, and 40,000 in the southern part of Afghanistan.[5] Until recently the Baluchis were an obscure people to those living outside the region, and even today I doubt whether many educated people in the West could identify the Baluchis and where they live. But within many of the world's foreign affairs ministries and intelligence agencies the Baluchis are well known and carefully watched. The main reason is that the Baluchi region of Pakistan separates Soviet troops in Afghanistan from the Arabian Sea, which overlooks the Persian Gulf. If the Soviet occupation of Afghanistan created a major crisis in Soviet-Western relations, a Soviet occupation of Baluchistan would be seen as a significant shift in the world balance of power, since the Soviets, for the first time, would then have direct access to the Indian Ocean.

Baluchistan has been a troublesome area for successive Pakistan governments since independence. There were Baluchi revolts in 1948, 1958, and 1962 and a large-scale insurgency from 1973 to 1977.[6] The problem dates to the colonial era. The British, concerned with border security, paid subsidies to the sardars or Baluchi tribal chiefs to assure their loyalty. The sardari system is highly centralized and hierarchical. At the apex is the sardar, the hereditary chief. Power flows downward to the section chiefs, or waderas, and beyond them to subordinate clan and subclan leaders of the lesser tribal units.

---

5. Population estimates for Kurds, Baluchis, and Turkmen can be found in Eden Naby, "The Iranian Frontier Nationalities: The Kurds, the Assyrians, the Baluchis and the Turkmen," in William O. McCagg, Jr., ed., *Soviet Asian Ethnic Frontiers* (New York: Pergamon Press, 1979).

6. For an account of these conflicts and of the relationship between the Baluchis and the government of Pakistan, see Selig S. Harrison, *In Afghanistan's Shadow: Baluch Nationalism and Soviet Temptations* (New York: Carnegie Endowment for International Peace, 1981). See also Robert G. Wirsing, *The Baluchis and Pathans,* report 48 (London: Minority Rights Group, March 1981) and his "South Asia: The Baluch Frontier Tribes of Pakistan," in Robert G. Wirsing, ed., *Protection of Ethnic Minorities: Comparative Perspectives* (New York: Pergamon Press, 1981).

After independence, the Pakistan government was eager to build loyalties toward the new state while at the same time it sought to extend its own administrative power into the region. The sardars did not want the government to interfere with the nearly unlimited internal autonomy they enjoyed under the British. Some sardars, like the khan of Kalat, actually declared their independence when the Pakistan government demanded they sign an accession document transferring the area under their control to the central government.[7] The Pakistan government used force to quell the revolt, and the stage was set for confrontation between the two loyalties, one to the ethnic group and its traditional tribal system and the other to the new state.

Pakistan's governments have consistently taken a centralist stance toward the various ethnic groups.[8] The governing elite of Pakistan have emphasized the need to build a single nation based on one language, Urdu, and have underestimated the potency of subnational loyalties. In 1955 the Pakistan government created a single unit from the various provinces in West Pakistan, with the result that a number of parties emerged pressing for regional autonomy. The military takeover in 1958 reinforced the centralizing tendencies of the Pakistan government while at the same time it gave a boost to regional sentiments. Despite the official ban on regional parties they continued to grow during the decade of Ayub Khan's rule (1958–68).

Because the military ruled the country and the military was largely dominated by Punjabis, the Baluchis were effectively excluded from the political system. This exclusion extended not only to the traditional sardars but also to the emerging educated middle classes. From 1947 to 1977 only four of the 179 persons named to the central cabinet were Baluchis, and it has been estimated that among the 40,000 civil servants of all ranks within Baluchistan in 1972 only 2,000 (5 percent) were Baluchis, and they generally held low-level positions.[9]

The return to civilian rule under Prime Minister Bhutto did little to improve the position of the Baluchis. Bhutto abolished the sardari system, invested public funds in the region, and opened some twenty-seven college facilities, agricultural extension services, and electrifi-

---

7. For an analysis of the Baluchi tribal system, see Frederik Barth, ed., *Ethnic Groups and Boundaries* (Boston: Little, Brown, 1969), pp. 117–34.

8. For an account of Pakistan's ethnic problems and policies see Howard Wriggins, ed., *Pakistan in Transition* (Islamabad, Pakistan: University of Islamabad Press, 1975).

9. Shaheen Mozaffar, "The Politics of Cabinet Formation in Pakistan: A Study of Recruitment to the Central Cabinets, 1947–77" Ph.D. diss., Miami University, Ohio, 1980.

cation and tube wells. Bhutto's strategy was clear. As he himself said, "I recognize that the Sardari system is a symbol of their identity to many Baluch. . . . You cannot get rid of it overnight without putting something in its place, something substantial in the form of modernization. This is what we have been trying to do and the Sardars realize they are done for if we can do it, if we can get roads in, schools in, hospitals in. That is why they are opposing us. They know that if we destroy the Sardari system, we will destroy Baluch identity, or at least begin the process of destruction."[10]

As it turned out, opposition came not simply from the sardars but also from the educated middle class and especially from the student organizations that advocated independence from Pakistan. A civil war erupted in Baluchistan between 1973 and 1977 in which some 5,000 Baluchis died, and many guerrillas fled to Afghanistan. The civil war was precipitated by the central government's dismissal of the provincial government in 1973 after a decision by the provincial government to replace all non-Baluchi employees with Baluchis for all positions in the provincial bureaucracy.

Many of the Baluchi secessionists became Marxist. Pakistan's Communists, faced with repression from the central government, found it easier to work with the regional movements, while the secessionists found it useful to enlist Communist support from other regions of the country in their struggle against the central government.

Afghanistan, with its long history of antagonistic relations with Pakistan, found it useful to provide support to the Baluchis. After the Marxist coup in Afghanistan in 1978, the leftist-oriented educated middle-class Baluchis actively supported the Marxist regime and saw its emergence as benefiting their demand for autonomy and secession. In the Baluchistan city of Quetta in August 1979, students covered the walls of the city with leftist slogans praising the Marxist regime. Even after the Soviet intervention in Afghanistan, a considerable portion of the Baluchi middle class reportedly continued to support the Babrak Karmal regime. Ironically, the sardars' attitude has shifted. Many fear replication of what took place in Afghanistan. One leading sardar said, "I tell the students that independence is not possible without a terrible price and might not be possible at all. I tell [them] that our location makes others feel it necessary to control us. I ask them would you like to change masters?"[11]

Under the shah, the government of Iran actively supported the

---

10. Harrison, *In Afghanistan's Shadow*, p. 156.
11. Ibid.

efforts of the Pakistan government to quell the insurgency, fearful of how the movement might affect the loyalty of their own Baluchi minority. The Iranian government permanently stationed troops in their Baluchi areas, waged intermittent punitive expeditions against rebellious tribesmen, and coopted influential sardars by channeling development funds through them in return for their loyalty. The shah officially banned the use of the Baluchi language and made it a criminal offense to publish, distribute, or possess any materials in Baluchi. A ban was even imposed on wearing traditional Baluchi attire in schools, offices, and public places. In the schools young Baluchis were informed that they were "pure Iranians," not a separate people. Nonetheless, there is considerable evidence that younger Baluchis, many of whom have lived and worked as migrants in the Persian Gulf sheikdoms, have been exposed to Pakistan Baluchis and to the idea of a "Greater Baluchistan."

The Baluchis in Iran have also received support from Iraq. Baghdad has become a center for intensified radio broadcasting and insurgency activity in Iranian Baluchistan.

Before the Marxist coup in Afghanistan in 1978, the Afghan government neglected the Baluchi areas, but also interfered little in the traditional tribal structure. The Marxist regime adopted a Soviet type of nationalities policy, introduced the Baluchi language in the schools for the first time, and promoted Baluchi cultural activities. But the Afghan government alienated many of the Baluchi tribesmen by circumventing the established tribal leadership. Many fled to the adjacent areas of Iran, and some joined the resistance movement within Afghanistan.

The issue of Baluchi loyalty is now closely linked to the larger international issues raised by the Soviet presence in Afghanistan. An estimated 3 million to 4 million refugees—about 20 percent of the population of Afghanistan—have left, mostly for Pakistan. Unable to prevent insurgents from returning with arms, the Soviets have demanded that Pakistan use its armed forces to close the borders. But the Pakistan government recognizes that to make such a commitment would not only place it in conflict with the refugees, but might very well put Pakistan into armed conflict with its own Baluchi and Pushtun populations, many of whom support the struggle of their ethnic kinsmen. (For this reason the Pakistan government has been particularly wary of the demand by Soviet negotiators at Geneva that a precondition for Soviet military withdrawal is an agreement on the part of the Pakistan government to seal its borders to prevent insurgents from moving into and out of Afghanistan.)

Neither the Soviet nor the Afghan governments recognizes the Durand line, and neither has rejected the call for an independent Pushtunistan or Baluchistan. For the moment Afghanistan's claims upon Pakistan remain quiescent, a "card" that could be played with Soviet support. Thus, the entire issue of transborder peoples on the Afghan-Pakistan border is no longer a matter solely shaped by local sentiment and by the local powers.[12]

These are by no means the only uncertain borders dividing an ethnic group. Examples abound of ethnic groups divided by international boundaries who seek unification, and of governments making irredentist claims upon their neighbors to incorporate their ethnic kinsmen. In central and eastern Europe there is a long history of irredentist claims—German claims upon Poland and Czechoslovakia; Greek claims upon Turkey, Albania, and Yugoslavia; Bulgarian claims upon Yugoslavia; and Italian claims upon Austria and Switzerland (hence the Italian word *irredenta*—unredeemed—from which the term irredentism is derived). In the contemporary third world, one of the best examples of the impact of irredentist politics on the loyalty and well-being of a transborder people can be found in the countries and peoples living in the Horn of Africa.

The Somalis in the Horn of Africa

The predominantly Somali-speaking Muslim peoples are spread over four countries in the Horn of Africa, a region of roughly 750,000 square miles in the northeastern part of the African continent. The largest number live in the Somali Republic, where they constitute a majority. The second-largest number reside in Ethiopia, where they form a significant minority. Another group resides as a minority in Kenya, while in the tiny Republic of Djibouti the Somalis are the majority ethnic group. In each of these countries, with the possible exception of Djibouti, the Somalis have generally been loyal to the Somali Republic.[13]

---

12. The loyalty of the Baluchis may be further complicated by the influx of Pushtuns from Afghanistan and from Pakistan's Northwest Frontier Province into Baluchistan. There are reports of growing resentment by Baluchis at the presence of Pushtuns and other non-Baluchi populations in Baluchistan; indeed, it is reported that the Baluchis are now a plurality, rather than majority, within their historic homeland in Pakistan.

13. For an account of the transborder peoples in the Horn of Africa, see Saadia Touval, *Somali Nationalism, International Politics and the Drive for Unity in the Horn of Africa* (Cambridge, Mass.: Harvard University Press, 1963); Tom J. Farer, *War Clouds*

The Somali Republic has been persistently an irredentist state, seeking to bring under a single flag all the Somali-speaking peoples. This goal is institutionalized both in the constitution and in the symbolism of its flag, a five-pointed star, each point representing one of the five colonially carved Somali regions. (The Somali Republic contains two of these regions: the former Italian Somalia and the former British Somaliland.)

Although it is difficult to assess the loyalty of the Somalis in the various states within the Horn there is reason to believe that the Somalis in Ethiopia are loyal to the Somali Republic. Somali guerrilla organizations operate inside the Somali-inhabited areas of Ethiopia. Migrations of Somalis continue from Ethiopia into the Somali Republic, despite the harsh conditions in the refugee camps inside the republic. Relations between the two major states where most of the Somalis live, the Somali Republic and Ethiopia, have been historically hostile, and they continue to be bad. At times the government of Ethiopia has claimed the entire stretch of the Somali-occupied areas as part of its historical empire—a claim that seems to be largely legendary—while in turn the Somali Republic has claimed the Somali-inhabited regions of Ethiopia.

Socialist ideologies notwithstanding, ethnic favoritism plays a significant role in the Somali Republic and in Ethiopia, both socialist dictatorships. In Ethiopia the ousting of the Amhara monarchy in 1974 and the subsequent emergence of the Galla Mengistu regime did not result in any betterment for the Somalis, despite historical and possible ethnic links between the Galla and Somali peoples. Mengistu, the ruling strongman, is himself a Christian Galla. Religious ties have played an important role in the kinds of political coalitions formed in Ethiopia and in the relations among the various ethnic groups. Successive Ethiopian regimes have pursued an assimilationist policy toward the Somalis. Historically, this meant attempts to convert the Somalis to Coptic Christianity, to linguistically transform the Somalis into Amharic speakers, and even to encourage intermarriage. Since World War II, the Ethiopian government has pursued a linguistic assimilationist policy with great fervor, although less attention has been paid to religious conversion. Educational facilities were

---

on the Horn of Africa (New York: Carnegie Endowment for International Peace, 1979); John Gordon Stewart Drysdale, *The Somali Dispute* (New York: Praeger, 1964); David D. Laitia, *Politics, Language and Thought: The Somali Experience* (Chicago: University of Chicago Press, 1977); Tom J. Farer, "Dilemmas on the Horn," *African Report* (March-April 1977); Irving Kaplan et al., *Area Handbook for Somalia* (Washington, D.C.: U.S. Government Printing Office, 1977).

located in Somali areas to accelerate the Somali acquisition of the Amharic language and to inculcate Ethiopian patriotism. Somalis were employed in local administration, but they were generally excluded from the higher levels of administration. Somali chiefs were included in the Ethiopian parliament as deputies, but the parliament itself had relatively little power under the monarchy.

After the revolution the government declared itself in favor of a more pluralistic approach based on the Soviet nationalities theory. But the cornerstone of the new regime's policy appears to be loyalty to the Ethiopian state, along with a predominant role for the Amharic language. The government maintains a policy to root out by military action any autonomist or secessionist activities. The government has, however, appointed Somalis to serve in the administration of at least one of the Somali-populated areas known as the Harar region. The Ethiopian regime continues, however, to have a deep distrust of Somalis; this attitude is reflected in the reluctance of the central government to employ Somalis in any responsible central government positions.

The borders between Ethiopia and Somali remain porous; this is not the result of deliberate policy by either government to keep the borders open to a divided people, but rather a reflection of the difficulties of controlling exit or entry in a sparsely populated, harsh desert landscape. The flows are largely from Ethiopia into the Somali Republic. As a result of the conflict between the two countries and the insurgency within the Somali regions of Ethiopia, numerous Somali refugees have fled from Ethiopia into the Somali Republic, largely into refugee camps. An estimated 700,000 ethnic Somalis, victims of the protracted war with Ethiopia, now live in refugee camps within Somalia. (Another estimated 637,000 refugees, mostly secessionist Eritreans, have fled Ethiopia into the Sudan.) Economic as well as political conditions for Somalis in Ethiopia have been bad since the early 1970s, first becoming acute during the Ethiopian famine of 1973–74, then worsening when the Somali Republic made its irredentist bid in the wake of the chaotic revolutionary conditions in Ethiopia from 1974 to 1976.

Under French rule the Somalis in Djibouti had considerable opportunity to improve their educational position. In the late 1960s, the Somalis were three times more numerous in the schools than were the other significant ethnic group, the Afars. In 1966 there were 2,257 Somalis in school as compared with 762 Afars. Most of the handful of local students who completed the Djibouti lycee were Somali. As it turned out, however, an independent Djibouti did not choose to merge with the Somali Republic. The dominant Somali community in Djibouti belongs to what is known as the Issa clan, while the politically dominant elite in the Somali Republic belongs to non-Issa clans.

An equally important determinant in the reluctance of Djibouti to merge with the Somali Republic was the emergence of a Marxist regime in the Somali Republic. Indeed, not only is there no tendency for Somalis in Djibouti to seek unification with the Somali Republic, or for people in one country to migrate to the other, but Djibouti has even shown some hesitation to admit refugees from Ethiopia. The attitude of the Djibouti government toward migrants from neighboring countries may be affected by the peculiar demographic and political balance among the two major ethnic groups within Djibouti, the Somalis and the Afars.

The Afars are spread over two countries, Djibouti and Ethiopia, with the larger number in Ethiopia, which until recently contained the seat of the group's traditional sultanate. In contrast, the Afars in Djibouti constitute nearly half of the population of that country. Until recently the Afars were in favor of merging with Ethiopia. The preindependence Djibouti liberation organizations, which were largely dominated by Afars, advocated close ties and even union with Ethiopia. Thus, both the Somalis and Afars in Djibouti before independence advocated merger with a neighboring country—the Afars with Ethiopia, the Somalis with the Somali Republic. Neither had any particular loyalty to an independent Djibouti state.

Just as the emergence of a Marxist regime in the Somali Republic affected the attitude of Djibouti Somalis toward the Somali Republic, political changes within Ethiopia affected the attitude of the Afars toward that regime. The 1974 overthrow of the Haile Selassie regime, which had respected the Afar sultans' virtually complete internal autonomy, and the subsequent emergence of a new Marxist revolutionary regime transformed the attitude of the Afars. The new Marxist regime was seen as anti-Afar and anti-Islamic.

Among the people of the Horn, religion has played an important role in the pattern of political loyalties. The Afar resistance to Ethiopian control has strong religious roots, drawing from the legacy of medieval jihads of combined Afar and Somali Muslim forces against the Christian Ethiopian empire. Faced with non-Muslims, Afar loyalties are generally shaped by religious affinities, but faced with other Muslims, their loyalties are primarily shaped by tribal affinities.

Ethiopia's Marxist regime has sought to win the support of the pastoral Afaris by promising land reforms, including the transfer of the Afar sultans' lands to Afar pastoralists. The Afar pastoralists, however, have resisted the antisultan measures, their commitment to their traditional institutions apparently weighing more heavily in their loyalties than class considerations alone. Moreover, the Afars have not won any political power in Ethiopia, whereas in Djibouti, although their initial political predominance has declined, they remain a significant political force.

Djibouti remains, however, a fragile political system. Refugees from Ethiopia continue to enter the country, swelling the number of unemployed in the capital city and its port. Rail lines between the port of Djibouti and Ethiopia have from time to time been cut by Somali guerrillas. Clashes between Somalis and Afars are not uncommon. As many as ten thousand refugees are estimated to have flooded into Djibouti as a consequence of the conflict between Ethiopia and Somalia. Indeed, were it not for the presence of French troops in the country and some Saudi assistance, it is likely that Djibouti as an independent country would cease to exist, overrun by either Somali Republic or Ethiopian forces.

As is so often the case in ethnic matters, what constitutes a political solution for one group can only be viewed as catastrophic by another. The irredentist goal of the Somalis for a unification of all the Somali people in the Horn could only have been achieved at the political expense of both the Ethiopians and the Afars. Moreover, historic antipathies among the various ethnic groups are now compounded by regime conflicts and international considerations. As with other irredentist claims, each of the contending parties has sought to build an alliance with outside forces that might provide military equipment and political clout. Just as the irredentist powers of the Balkans in the period before World War I and in the interwar period tied themselves to Russia, Germany, France, or Britain, so too have regimes in the Horn tied themselves to the Soviet Union, the United States, or France.

Whatever the legitimacy of the Somali claims for a unification of the Somali peoples, the irredentist demands have worsened the situation of the Somali peoples, certainly those within Ethiopia and Kenya. Hundreds of thousands of Somalis have been forced into refugee status, their loyalty questioned by the countries in which they are a minority.

Loyalty and Conflict

Irredentism, secession, or regional autonomy have not been on the political agenda of Mexican-Americans, and for this reason alone the experiences of the Baluchi, Pushtun, and Somali peoples are different. Only a handful of Mexican-Americans have adopted positions somewhat similar to those of these transborder peoples: that the borders between the two countries are illegal; that the Southwest therefore is occupied territory; that if it is not returned to Mexico, then at least the borders should be de facto open, permitting Mexicans to move back and forth freely; and that Spanish should be made an official language of the region on a par with English. But these positions are not openly advocated by major Mexican-American groups, nor do surveys suggest that these views are widely shared within the community. It would be farfetched, therefore, to speculate what the political consequences would be for American politics, and for the Mexican-Americans themselves, if such claims were widely put forth, but it may be useful to briefly review what the consequences have been elsewhere.

As we have seen, much blood has been shed in this century over the demands by contending states for the territory in which transborder peoples reside, and over the loyalty of the transborder peoples themselves. The Somalis, Baluchis, and Pushtuns are only a few such examples. Nor have these conflicts been confined to the third world. The breakup of the Ottoman and Hapsburg empires was accompanied by numerous conflicts as the newly formed successor states claimed ancient (and conflicting) boundaries and sought to "redeem" the kinsmen from whom they were divided by international boundaries.

The boundaries themselves were often drawn with little regard for the preferences of persons who resided on one side or the other. The Macedonians were divided among the Yugoslavs, Greeks, and Bulgarians. Greeks were scattered like pebbles across the Mediterranean and along its rim. Italians, Hungarians, Germans, and French found themselves not simply living among other peoples—that was hardly new—but living in countries whose governments were often hostile to the country to which they gave their loyalty. Many of Europe's wars—the Franco-Prussian wars, the two Balkan wars preceding World War I, World War I itself, the Greek-Turkish conflicts over Crete and now Cyprus—have their roots in the lack of congruence between ethnic groups and the countries in which particular ethnic groups found themselves unwillingly located.

The list of conflicts over transborder peoples is so long (Armenians, Kurds, Kashmiris, Basques, Palestinians, and so on) that one is tempted to conclude that conflict is inevitable. That, however, is not always the case. There are peoples divided by international boundaries who do not seek to be reunited and whose loyalty to the country in which they live is not in doubt (for example, the French and Italian minorities in Switzerland). Admittedly these are among the exceptions on a continent whose countries have in the main been committed to the principle of a single culture in a single country, the nation-state.

Among the developing countries there are also transborder peoples whose loyalties are not questioned. For example, few people in India doubt the loyalty of the people of West Bengal, although they share a common language, culture, and history (but not religion) with the people of Bangladesh. Similarly, the Turks in Iran and in the Soviet Union are not seeking reunion with Turkey, nor do India's Punjabis want to be reunited with Pakistan, a country with a Punjabi-speaking majority.

What constitutes a single "people," of course, is often the crux of the matter. India's Punjabis and Bengalis are ambivalent about whether they are the same people as those across the border—in language and in some features of culture, they are; but in religion and with respect to sharing a common history with common heros, they are not. Politics and religion can often sever cultural and linguistic identities from national identities.

How fluid these identities can be is illustrated by recent developments in India's Punjab where there is now a sharp cleavage between Punjabi-speaking Sikhs and Punjabi-speaking Hindus. In recent years many Sikhs have claimed that they are a separate "nation" from Punjabi-speaking Hindus and are entitled to a state of their own. In response many Punjabi-speaking Hindus have shifted their linguistic, and hence ethnic identity, to Hindi. Both groups, therefore, are ceasing to be transborder peoples as their links to Pakistan's Punjabis diminish.

In the treatment of its transborder minorities, one strategy of governments is to break the communication links between the minority and the "mother" country. The governments of Turkey, the Soviet Union, and Iran, for example, each sought to sever the ties among their respective Turks. Ataturk began the process by requiring that the Turkish language be written in Roman script, thereby severing the ties of modern Turks to their ancient history and above all to their Islamic heritage. The Soviets pursued a similar policy by requiring that Turkish be written in Cyrillic script, thereby breaking the umbilical ties both to Islam and to the Turks of Iran who continued to employ the Persian script. The Soviets followed a similar policy with other central Asian peoples—Uzbeks and Tajiks, for example—whose languages are also now written in Cyrillic.

The preservation of the culture, religion, and language of a transborder people has not necessarily resulted in a conflict with the dominant ethnic group. Where the country is a multiethnic society that provides a legitimate status to each of its ethnic groups (by recognizing, for example, several "national" languages), there is a greater possibility that the transborder people can be accommodated without cultural assimilation or linguistic change. Note, for example, the difference on this point between Sri Lanka and India. Sri Lanka is predominantly a Sinhalese society and its government has been unitary. In contrast, India is a multiethnic society in which each of the major linguistic groups has a state government of its own within a federal framework. The Indian political structure more readily permits power to be distributed among ethnic groups, while the Sri Lankan system does not—one reason, perhaps, why the Tamil problem has festered so long in postindependence Sri Lanka.

The central issue for transborder peoples has not been their ethnic identity but their political loyalty. The most interesting questions, therefore, are what makes a transborder minority loyal to the country in which it resides, and under what conditions does the dominant ethnic group accept the transborder minority as loyal. Although the cases discussed here are too few to draw firm generalizations, nonetheless it may be useful to suggest some tentative hypotheses, if only to provoke some discussion relevant to the Mexican-American experience.

First, an irredentist demand by one country against another is perhaps the most critical factor in undermining the loyalty of an ethnic minority and in creating in the government and in the majority population doubts about the loyalty of a transborder minority. A transborder minority that persists in viewing the territory in which it resides as belonging in a moral if not juridical sense to a neighboring country will invariably be viewed as disloyal, its political actions circumscribed by government, its leaders distrusted, and its "right" to share power at the national level questioned. The plight of the Somalis in Ethiopia has had its counterparts many times before, most notably in the prewar Balkans, where virtually every state made irredentist demands or was itself the target of such demands.

Mexico does not, of course, make irredentist claims upon the United States, nor for that matter do any significant Mexican-American groups. The experience of transborder minorities in those situations in which irredentist claims have been put forth suggests the following: were significant Mexican-American groups to advocate irredentist-like positions, such as open borders or state-recognized official billingualism, one should expect to see the growth of nativist sentiments on the part of many Americans, who would question the loyalty of Mexican-Americans. Putting normative judgments aside, the experience of other countries suggests that neither governments nor the majority of a country's citizens are particularly tolerant of irredentist or irredentist types of sentiments.

Second, when a country is multiethnic and has a political structure that provides for a system of power sharing among ethnic groups based on a federal arrangement, however, power sharing may provide the transborder minority with a degree of political and cultural autonomy. As noted earlier, India with its federal system based on linguistic groups has been able to retain the loyalty of its major transborder communities—Bengalis, Kashmiris, and, notwithstanding current difficulties, Punjabis. Switzerland, of course, is the classic European example of a multiethnic society with structural arrangements for power sharing at the canton level. In a country in which various other national groups have rights, the demand by a border people for similar national rights is more likely to be viewed as legitimate than in a political system that abjures the notion of group rights, especially along ethnic lines.

Third, authoritarian regimes obviously have more difficulty in power sharing than democratic regimes, but by providing a transborder minority access to the civil or military bureaucracy (that is, by making recruitment more representative), the loyalty of a minority may be strengthened. For example, the entrance of Pushtuns into senior positions in Pakistan's military may have done much to remove Pushtun disaffection. In contrast few Baluchis have joined Pakistan's military and civil service. When Bangladesh was Pakistan's eastern province, few Bengalis held positions either in the cental administrative services or in the military, hence the demand for power sharing through regional autonomy.

In short, the willingness of the dominant ethnic groups to share power appears to be a critical factor affecting the loyalty of a transborder people—the fourth hypothesis suggested by the above discussion. Indeed, power sharing may be a more critical determinant of minority group loyalty than the economic standing of the minority in relation to the majority ethnic group. Affluent minority groups may be as disaffected as economically subordinate minority groups. The comparatively prosperous Malaysian Chinese or Sri Lankan Tamils, for example, are no less disaffected than the comparatively poor Baluchis in Pakistan.

This observation suggests that the sense of integration Mexican-Americans feel may be shaped not simply by an improvement in their education, income, and employment but by an increase in power sharing, especially at the state and local levels.

Fifth, although power sharing may enhance the sense of integration felt by Mexican-Americans, it may also increase tensions between Mexican-Americans and other Americans if power is exercised in ways that are perceived as threatening to what most Americans regard as "central" American values. For this reason, language policies pressed by some Mexican-Americans could become a particularly divisive issue, especially if what is advocated is state-sanctioned, state-supported bilingualism in a country where "American" identity is so closely tied to the English language.

A sixth and final hypothesis is that the porousness of borders has become an increasingly controversial question in countries with transborder peoples. It is true that the porousness of borders has not always been a source of conflict between a transborder minority and its host society. The Pakistan government, for example, has long lived with unadministered borders in its northwest, and for many years the Indian government and even the government of Assam paid minimal attention to the movement of Bengalis from Bangladesh. Similarly, the borders between Nepal and India, Afghanistan and Iran, and countless countries within Africa have been relatively open.

But in recent years a number of regimes have become concerned with their open borders. One concern is with the influx of refugees, often the forced exodus of a transborder minority returning to the homeland in which it is a majority. Another concern is with an influx which substantially increases the size of the minority and results in the dispersal of the ethnic minority into other parts of the country. The Assamese response to the growing influx of Bangladeshis (many of whom have migrated up-country to what were once exclusively Assamese areas) is a case in point. The current concern in Baluchistan with the influx of Pushtuns from Afghanistan is another. And the recent responses in Nepal to an influx of Indians is still another. In each of these cases, the movement is not simply one of temporary sojourners, but of increasingly permanent migrations affecting the demographic balance, competition for land and employment, the cultural and social anxieties of the indigenous majority, and the political power of competing ethnic groups.

The United States is thus not alone in its long history of response to large-scale immigrations. Various forms of nativism, racism, and cultural atavism on the part of long-term inhabitants to recent settlers is, alas, nearly universal and no less pronounced in low-income than in advanced industrial countries. (And if the phenomenon seems more pronounced in the capitalist societies of the United States, the United Kingdom, Australia, Germany, and France than in the socialist societies of East Europe and the Soviet Union, it is only because these last two countries seal their borders to outsiders.) Indeed, antimigrant sentiments notwithstanding, the United States continues to admit more migrants, both legal and illegal, than do most other countries of the world.

How relevant then are the experiences of other transborder peoples to those of Mexican-Americans? In some respects, as I have noted, there are similarities: many migrants from Mexico illegally cross the porous borders; many Mexican-Americans live in an area that was historically Mexican and hence feel a special attachment to what they regard as their homeland within the American borders; and some Mexicans believe they have special "national" rights that were not historically given to immigrants.

In other respects the differences with other transnational peoples are considerable: Mexico makes no irredentist claims upon the United States; as a democratic country the United States provides more opportunities for power sharing—especially at the state and local levels—than is the case in many other countries with transborder peoples; and as an immigrant society the United States has permitted groups to retain their cultural identities and has made ethnic politics legitimate even as it has insisted that a shared public language is required in civic life.

For many Americans the border issue, like the language issue, has become increasingly symbolic.[14] For many the concern over illegal migrants is not simply whether migrants as such displace Americans in employment, use public services, or crowd local schools (although

---

14. Neither issue, it should be noted, has arisen with respect to another transborder people, the French Canadians. Although French Canadians have settled in northern New England, the legitimacy of the borders has not been at issue, nor has there been any demand for bilingual policies. French Canadians are thus viewed as are other immigrant communities, though they retain a strong cultural identity, and many continue to speak French. On the Canadian side of the border, however, bilingualism is an official policy, reminding us how two societies with very different histories may deal with transborder peoples.

for many Americans these are concerns, real or imagined). Rather, the concern is whether the government can control who enters, who can be employed, and who is permitted to remain. These are fundamental (if, to some, old-fashioned) notions of sovereignty. In the same vein, language too is a kind of "boundary" issue, for it opens the question of what defines an American and what characterizes a shared public life in American society.

As the Mexican-American population in the United States grows in the next few decades, one can expect to see enormous social and cultural changes within the community and an increasingly activist political role. It is not clear yet whether Mexican-Americans will view themselves as a transborder people with special claims by virtue of a historical attachment to the lands of the Southwest United States or as an immigrant community, not unlike other immigrant communities in America. In matters of ethnic politics, how a group chooses to define itself often shapes its own loyalties, the political demands it makes, and the attitudes of others toward it.

CHAPTER SIX

In introducing Myron Weiner's essay on transborder peoples, we noted the general lack of coincidence between ethnic and political borders. In recent years, this lack of coincidence has been magnified by massive migrations. In general, these migrations have triggered resentment and hostility on the part of the host populations. The carnage resulting from the Bengali migration into Assam has previously been described. Heinous, too, was the reception often awaiting the "boat people" from Vietnam. In 1979, for example, the Malaysian government ordered its navy to tow hundreds of boatloads of refugees back onto the high seas, threatened to empower the navy to shoot on sight any boat people found within its territorial waters, and likened the refugees to "rubbish" thrown into "a neighbor's gardens." In 1983, the Nigerian government, faced with a recession and an approaching election, went scapegoating and suddenly became aware of more than 2 million illegal immigrants within its borders. To round applause from both Nigeria's communications media and the general public, the illegal aliens were expelled with unconscionable haste. And in Europe, the "guest workers" have encountered disrespect and prejudice from the outset.

Despite the popular self-depiction of the United States as "a nation of immigrants," migration across its southern border became a matter of increasing concern in the United States during the 1980s. The acute permeability of this border was highlighted by the inability of U.S. immigration authorities to adequately estimate the number of people who had recently crossed this border and illegally settled in the United States. Estimates ranged from less than 2 million to more than 12 million. Concern over this inability to gauge, much less control, transborder migration was lent additional urgency by the likelihood that the rate of migration would accelerate rather than abate. The great discrepancy in economic opportunities within third-world Mexico and the first-world United States, particularly when viewed against the backdrop of Mexico's rapidly growing population, portended a more massive trek northward.

Several aspects of the Mexican migration differentiate it from other migrations to the United States. These include its size, the expectation of its indefinite prolongation, the inability of the U.S. government to exert effective control over it, and its high incidence of extra-legal border crossings. But despite these features, Rosemarie Rogers maintains that a better understanding and more balanced perspective of the Mexican migration can be gained by viewing it in the context of overall U.S. immigration policy and experience, as well as within the still wider framework of world migratory patterns.

MIGRATION THEORY AND PRACTICE

Rosemarie Rogers

The scope of migration studies is vast, and to attempt in one paper to analyze how Mexican migration to the United States fits into a comparative framework, if at all, involves the risk of excessive dissection of the question. I have nevertheless attempted such a broad investigation. My discussion is divided into three sections, based upon rather conventional distinctions between major analytical concerns in migration studies: the determinants of migration, the types of migration movements (as defined by the migrants' legal-administrative status in the host country), and the consequences of migration. Discussions of migration policies are interwoven, particularly in the section concerning types of migration movements. I hope the brief concluding remarks will serve to bring a unified perspective to the topic.

Definitions of migration often involve (1) the concepts of distance (is the move from one housing unit to another, within the same community, migration?) (2) intended or actual length of stay in the place of destination (some United Nations statistics, for example, distinguish between "short-term" and "long-term" movements), and (3) the purpose of the move (for example, tourism, business travel, or migration for employment). For the purposes of this paper I have disregarded distance as a defining criterion; rather, it is the crossing of an international boundary that is important here. As to duration of stay, permanent or long-term migrations as well as repeated, short-term migrations are relevant to this study. As to purpose, I exclude tourism, shopping, and business travel, but include migration for employment even in the form of "border commuting," refugee movements, and the movements of family members who accompany or later rejoin a migrant.

161

Determinants of Migration

Migration, internal or international, is generally a response to differentials in opportunities—economic, social, and cultural—between two areas. Such differentials are not a sufficient condition for migration but they come close to being a necessary one. Kingsley Davis stresses in particular the technological gap between sending and receiving communities, many of the earlier movements having taken place from the technologically more advanced countries to the technologically less advanced parts of the world.[1] Concerning internal migration, McNeill notes that although historically the cities of Europe and Asia attracted rural immigrants, these cities also absolutely depended on such in-migration for their survival: contagious diseases repeatedly diminished their populations to such an extent that they needed regular replenishment from the countryside.[2]

Today we are dealing with reversals of these situations. Rural-urban migration, rather than being a necessity for the survival of major cities, may threaten their very ability to remain viable. Most voluntary international migrations occur from economically less developed to economically more developed countries. International population movements to settle empty or nearly empty lands, or to exploit natural resources, have essentially become events of the past. (This is not true, however, of all internal migration; we see such migration in Brazil, for example, and in the United States. We also see some instances of government-stimulated migrations, such as the virgin lands campaigns in the Soviet Union and the "transmigration" in Indonesia.)

Although most migration decisions probably have multiple motivations, including some that may be quite diffuse, I find it useful to characterize migration movements, at the macro level, as broadly economically, socioculturally, or politically motivated.[3] Except for Mexico's revolutionary period in the early part of this century, the majority of the migration from Mexico to the United States has been economically motivated. Thus, in the following brief review of analyses of determinants of migration, I will focus on these types of movements.

---

1. Kingsley Davis, "The Migrations of Human Populations," *Scientific American*, vol. 231, (1974), pp. 94–105.

2. William H. McNeill, "Human Migration: A Historical Overview," in William H. McNeill and Ruth S. Adams, eds., *Human Migration: Patterns and Policies* (Bloomington: Indiana University Press, 1978), pp. 3–19.

3. The fact that in some instances the appropriateness of a particular classification may be disputed (as, for example, in the ongoing controversy about how to classify Haitians seeking political asylum in the United States) does not invalidate this point.

I shall distinguish between three levels of analysis here, two macro levels and one micro level. As Simmons and his colleagues have noted, many macro-level studies emphasize proximate causes of migration, such as income differentials, rather than underlying structural causes, such as different systems of land tenure or the role of population growth.[4]

Most of the *structural factors* identified in the literature on different migration contexts throughout the world have played a role in stimulating Mexican migration, internal as well as international:[5]

1. *General development strategies of countries of out-migration.* Many countries have emphasized industrial over rural development and, within industry, capital-intensive over labor-intensive investments. An example is Turkey in the 1960s.[6] Alba notes that in Mexico the policy of industrialization by import substitution has produced negative consequences, among them, widespread unemployment and underemployment.[7]

2. *Differing patterns of land distribution, land tenure, and agricultural productivity.* Mexican agriculture has a dual nature: (1) the private sector, which includes large landholdings and a disproportionate share of irrigated land, and which benefited disproportionately from the Green Revolution, and (2) the ejido system. Both have been discussed at some length in the literature.[8]

3. *The role of population growth.* When the creation of jobs in a country cannot keep pace with the entry of new workers into the labor market, the pressures for migration do not automatically increase. But such pressures will occur when a tradition of migration is already established, as has been the case between Mexico and the United States since even before the establishment of the present-day

---

4. Alan Simmons, Sergio Diaz-Briquets, and Aprodicio A. Laquian, *Social Change and Internal Migration: A Review of Findings from Africa, Asia, and Latin America* (Ottawa: International Development Centre, 1977).

5. For comparative references, in addition to those cited below, see Simmons, ibid., which deals predominantly with internal migration but refers also to some salient findings concerning the contexts of international migrations.

6. Samuel S. Lieberman and Ali S. Gitmez in Ronald E. Krane, ed., *International Labor Migration in Europe* (New York: Praeger Publishers, 1979), pp. 201–20; and Suzanne Paine, *Exporting Workers: The Turkish Case* (Cambridge, England: Cambridge University Press, 1974).

7. Francisco Alba, "Mexico's International Migration as a Manifestation of Its Development Pattern," *International Migration Review,* vol. 12, (1978), pp. 503–4.

8. See, for example, Harry E. Cross and James A. Sandos, *Across the Border: Rural Development in Mexico and Recent Migration to the United States* (Berkeley: University of California Institute of Governmental Studies, 1981); and Paul R. Ehrlich, Loy Bilderback, and Anne H. Ehrlich, *The Golden Door: International Migration, Mexico, and the United States* (n.p.: Wideview Books, 1981).

borders, but particularly since the 1920s. According to Cross and Sandos, "an average of 800,000 people are expected to enter the [Mexican] labor market annually during the 1980s, an estimate that assumes no further 'feminization' of the labor population. In 1978 and 1979, the numbers of employed increased by about 450,000 annually, leaving a minimum of 200,000 new unemployed per year."[9]

4. *Foreign economic influences.* Scholars have noted such effects specifically with respect to certain Asian countries.[10] Such influences occur with respect to U.S.-Mexican relations on several levels; for example, U.S. trade policies (protectionist measures favoring U.S. agriculture and other economic sectors) and Mexico's Border Industrialization Program (which, although it has created valuable jobs for Mexican citizens, has attracted excessive numbers of Mexicans to the border cities, who become prime candidates for illegal migration when they are unable to obtain jobs on the Mexican side of the border).[11]

Macro-level analyses of determinants of migration that emphasize more proximate causes have been applied primarily to the study of internal migrations, in the form of regression models.[12] When applied to the study of international migrations, the models either assume that migration policies were constant over the analysis period, or they explicitly include changes in policies as one of the independent variables. Lianos found employment opportunities in Germany, rather than levels of unemployment in Greece, to be the major variable explaining the volume of outflows from Greece and of return flows to Greece between 1955 and 1973.[13] When differential flows from

9. Cross and Sandos, *Across the Border,* p. 71.

10. Simmons, Diaz-Briquets, and Laquian, *Social Change and Internal Migration.*

11. Walter Fogel, *Mexican Illegal Workers in the United States,* Institute of Industrial Relations Monograph 20 (Los Angeles: University of California, 1978); Ehrlich, Bilderback, and Ehrlich, *The Golden Door;* and Donald Walter Baerresen, *The Border Industrialization Program of Mexico* (Lexington, Mass.: D.C. Heath and Co., Lexington Books, 1971).

12. Manuel J. Carvajal and David T. Geithman, "An Economic Analysis of Migration in Costa Rica," *Economic Development and Cultural Change,* vol. 23 (1974), pp. 105–22; Mildred B. Levy and Walter J. Wadycki, "What is the Opportunity Cost of Moving? Reconsideration of the Effects of Distance on Migration," *Economic Development and Cultural Change,* vol. 22 (1974) pp. 198–214; Michael J. Greenwood, "The Influence of Family and Friends on Geographic Labor Mobility in a Less Developed Country: The Case of India," *Review of Regional Studies* (1973), pp. 27–36; Michael P. Todaro, "A Model of Labor Migration and Urban Unemployment in Less Developed Countries," *American Economic Review,* vol. 59 (1969), pp. 138–48; and John R. Harris and Michael P. Todaro, "Migration, Unemployment and Development: A Two-Sector Analysis," *American Economic Review,* vol. 60 (1970), pp. 126–42.

13. Theodore P. Lianos, "Flows of Greek Out-Migration and Return Migration," *International Migration,* vol. 13 (1975), pp. 119–33.

Greece to Germany and Belgium were modeled, relative size of earlier migration to each host country joined employment opportunities in the host country as an explanatory variable.[14]

A comparable analysis of illegal migration from Mexico to the United States between 1946 and 1965 (based on apprehension statistics as a proxy for illegal migration, with all the imprecisions that this entails) concluded: "The ebb and flow of illegal Mexican aliens is clearly affected by changes in the relative vigor of agricultural enterprise in the two countries. Wages paid farm workers and agricultural productivity in the U.S. and Mexico, along with Mexican farm prices and American capital investment explain approximately half the variation. It is interesting to note that 'push' factors are of greater import than 'pull' factors."[15]

One should heed Lianos's admonition not to extrapolate beyond the parameters of the data. Frisbie points out that for the period he investigated, it was appropriate to concentrate on the agricultural sector only. This stategy becomes clearly more questionable when one analyzes illegal migration from Mexico in the 1970s and 1980s, much of which has involved employment outside agriculture.[16] Because of the various limitations of Frisbie's analysis, I do not consider that study as a strong test of Piore's hypothesis, argued from a theoretical perspective, that U.S. employment opportunities, rather than "push" factors in the home countries, account for the volume of illegal migration to the United States.[17]

Qualitative analyses add to the understanding of noneconomic factors in migrants' choices of destinations. At the international level, the historical relationships between countries (or subunits of countries) can illuminate migrants' choices (for example, in the Yugoslav labor migration, Serbs went predominantly to France, and Croats to Germany). Often these particular relationships are also reflected in differential treatment accorded certain sending countries by the host

---

14. Lianos cautions, however, against interpretations beyond the limits of the data: if employment opportunities in Greece had shown more variation, that is, if they had been higher—as they were to become in subsequent years—they might well have emerged as an additional significant explanatory variable.

15. Parker Frisbie, "Illegal Migration from Mexico to the United States: A Longitudinal Analysis," *International Migration Review*, vol. 9 (1975), p. 13.

16. This objection can be made to Jenkins's study. See Craig J. Jenkins, "Push/Pull in Recent Mexican Migration to the U.S.," *International Migration Review*, vol. 11 (1977) pp. 178–89, which is largely derived from Frisbie, "Illegal Migration," but includes bracero migration and extends the analysis of illegal flows to 1972.

17. Michael J. Piore, *Birds of Passage: Migrant Labor and Industrial Societies* (Cambridge, England: Cambridge University Press, 1979).

country (for example, the history of Algerian migration to France).[18] Internally, at the level of selection of particular host communities, anthropologists have demonstrated the process of "chain migration."

Micro-level explanations of migration often approach the question of why people migrate by looking at who the migrants are, describing them according to social and demographic characteristics such as age, education, skills, or income levels. In their review of the literature on internal migration in Africa, Asia, and Latin America, Simmons and his colleagues observe that these migrants were overwhelmingly young, with some education and skills, and, if coming from a lower stratum of society, nevertheless not from the very poorest.[19] It is useful to compare the profiles of migrant groups leaving the same area for different destinations. For example, it appears that in Spain and Portugal in the 1960s and early 1970s, rural migrants going to the cities and coastal areas within their own countries reflected the aforementioned demographic characteristics more than did those migrating to West Europe. There were corresponding differences in return orientations.[20]

However, as migrant streams mature and become institutionalized, we often see a change from greater selectivity (the "pioneers") to less selectivity ("mass" migrations). This was observed, for example, in the post-World War II Yugoslav labor migration in Europe, as well as in patterns of internal migration in Mexico.[21] The explanation generally lies in two simultaneously occurring trends: changes in the selectivity of migrating heads of households and a greater proportion of family migration. However, even when we are dealing with a single migration stream—going from one origin to one destination, happening at a single point in time, and involving migrants all having the same legal-administrative status in the host country—we must consider not only commonalities but also the range of variability in

---

18. Since Algeria's independence, that migration has been regulated by a separate series of treaties. See Stephen Adler, *International Migration and Dependence* (Farnborough, England: Saxon House, 1977). The entries of Algerians into France have been outside the jurisdiction of the French National Immigration Office.

19. Simmons, Diaz-Briquets, and Laquian, *Social Change and Internal Migration.*

20. Robert, E. Rhoades, "Intra-European Return Migration and Rural Development: Lessons from the Spanish Case," *Human Organization*, vol. 37 (1978), pp. 137–47; and David D. Gregory and Jose Cazorla Perez, "Intra-European Migration and Regional Development: Spain and Portugal," in Rosemarie Rogers, ed., *Guests Come to Stay: The Effects of European Labor Migration on Sending and Receiving Countries* (Boulder, Colo.: Westview Press, forthcoming).

21. Harley L. Browning and Waltraut Feindt, "Selectivity of Migrants to a Metropolis in a Developing Country: A Mexican Case Study," *Demography*, vol. 6 (1969), pp. 347–57.

the data. When a migrant stream shows substantial heterogeneity, it makes little sense to base one's analysis on averages.[22]

Analyzing macro conditions, describing migrant "profiles," and even asking migrants why they chose to migrate still does not answer the question why, among individuals in the same socioeconomic conditions and with the same migration opportunities open to them, some choose to migrate whereas others choose to remain. A more complete analysis must include sociopsychological and psychological variables as well.[23]

It is often asserted that migration "skims off the cream" of particular population groups, in the sense that it is the most enterprising and ambitious or the most resilient among a population who migrate.[24] In a survey of six Philippine cities Laquian "found that the slum and squatter dwellers, although some have no regular sources of income, appeared to be more progressive than their relatives who stayed behind."[25] In his studies of the economic progress of legal immigrants in the U.S. labor market and in those of other countries, Chiswick found that immigrants start out with an earnings disadvantage, but "[male economic immigrants] catch up to the native born with similar demographic characteristics by the time they have been in the country eleven to sixteen years, and thereafter the immigrants have higher earnings. . . . Although the background and historical experiences of [the] groups [included in the analysis] vary, certain persistent patterns emerge, *apparently* from differences in the international transferability of the skills acquired in the country of origin and from the self-selection of immigrants in favor of those with *more innate ability* and *economic motivation*."[26] Refugees were found to be on the whole less successful, which Chiswick attributes, among other factors, to less selectivity among these groups.

---

22. This point is well illustrated by Hernández Alvarez's study of return migration from the U.S. mainland to Puerto Rico. See José Hernández Alvarez, *Return Migration to Puerto Rico* (Berkeley: Institute of International Studies, University of California Population Monograph 1 (1967); reprinted by Greenwood Press, Westport, Conn. (1976).

23. See for example, the study of internal migration of unemployed British miners by R. C. Taylor, "Migration and Motivation: A Study of Determinants and Types," in J. A. Jackson, ed., *Migration* (Cambridge, England: Cambridge University Press, 1969).

24. See, for example, Taylor's "aspiring" type in ibid.

25. Simmons, Diaz-Briquets, and Laquian, *Social Change and Internal Migration*, p. 56. Emphasis added.

26. Barry R. Chiswick, "The Economic Progress of Immigrants: Some Apparently Universal Patterns," in William Fellner, ed., *Contemporary Economic Problems 1979* (Washington, D.C.: American Enterprise Institute for Public Policy Research, 1979), p. 398. Emphasis added.

Although it makes intuitive sense to point to psychological factors to explain these variances, at this point we have little systematic understanding of the psychological determinants of migration.[27] Do migrants have higher needs for achievement than nonmigrants? Are they more cognitively flexible? Are they more instrumentally rather than sentimentally attached to their own state systems?[28] More is known about the role played by some of these variables in the adjustment process of migrants than in the decision to migrate.

Types of Migration

Migrations are often characterized according to such dichotomies as voluntary versus forced, permanent versus temporary, controlled versus free, or legal versus illegal. I find it more useful for the purposes of this paper to discuss different types of migrations according to the migrants' administrative-legal status in the host countries.

International migration has not always been the tightly controlled phenomenon that it generally is today. Before World War I, "in the United States and western Europe (and therefore in most of the globe which was then still controlled by western European powers), passports and official regulation of migration were regarded as an improper infringement of personal freedom."[29] Today sovereign states consider it their right to decide on how far to open their doors, to whom, and for how long a stay. A few states remain willing to increase their populations by a regular, if limited, influx of settlers. They are all immigrant states historically, and include the United States, Canada, Australia, New Zealand, and a number of South American countries. "Homeland states," using Walker Connor's typology, stand ready to receive their own people—for example, Volksdeutsche from eastern Europe are welcome in the Federal Republic of Germany, as are Jewish settlers in Israel. But neither "homelands," nation-states, nor multinational states consider themselves as immi-

---

27. For example, because of his dependence upon census data, Chiswick (ibid.) cannot push his analyses further than he does.

28. Herbert C. Kelman, "Patterns of Personal Involvement in the National System: A Social-Psychological Analysis of Political Legitimacy," in James N. Rosenau, ed., *International Politics and Foreign Policy: A Reader in Research and Theory* (New York: Free Press, 1969).

29. McNeill, "Human Migration," p. xiii.

grant countries.[30] Among all types of states, however, some will accept economic migrants for limited periods of time, some will host persons seeking asylum, and some will incorporate limited numbers of refugees on a permanent basis.

In discussing different types of migrations, I refer consistently to the migratory movements between Mexico and the United States. However, the breakdown into types of migration does not mean that the different types of migration flows are not closely interwoven. Indeed, many Mexican migrants belong to several of these migration categories at different times.[31]

Any analysis of international migration movements concerns regional concentrations. While the highest level of government normally formulates a country's policies on international migration[32] (and certain statistics on migratory movements may be available only for that aggregate level), migration flows are never evenly distributed over countries of out-migration or countries of in-migration, nor are the impacts of migration evenly distributed. Nearly always some specific regions in a country are particularly affected by migration. For example, much of the Mexican migration to the United States has been from north central Mexico to the southwestern states of the United States.

Immigration

Countries accepting immigrants must decide such policy questions as how many immigrants to admit in a given year and what criteria to use in selecting the immigrants. Legislative reforms in the 1960s and 1970s have led the English-speaking countries that accept immigrants to abandon racial and ethnic barriers to immigration and—with the exception of the United States—to increase their emphasis on manpower needs. This emphasis implies a focus on occupational selection criteria and flexible numerical limits. The United States

---

30. See chapter 1 of this volume. One might recall here also Soviet Armenia's appeal after World War II for Armenians to return to settle in their "homeland." Thousands of Armenians from the United States and France, among other countries, followed this call. Many were disappointed and returned later to the places they had left when it became possible for them to remigrate.

31. This phenomenon is nicely documented in Josh Reichert and Douglas Massey, "History and Trends in U.S. Bound Migration from a Mexican Town," *International Migration Review,* vol. 14 (1980), pp. 475–91.

32. In the United States, for example, the Supreme Court ruled in 1876—only one year after the first immigration law had been passed—that power to legislate on immigration rests exclusively with Congress.

emphasizes family reunification over labor market criteria and operates with a fixed ceiling (with close family members of immigrants and of permanent residents being admitted outside the numerical ceiling). Refugee admissions are treated separately.

Argentina, traditionally a major magnet for immigrants, has in recent years been losing population through emigration. Like Venezuela, it is interested in selective immigration, seeking to attract immigrants with skills that are in particular demand, as well as those willing to settle in the country's underpopulated areas. However, today both of these countries play a greater role as hosts to considerable numbers of illegal migrants from neighboring countries than to legal immigrants.[33]

All countries that accept immigrants also experience emigration, primarily through the return to their own countries of a part of their immigrant populations, but also through emigration of the native-born. Return migration of immigrants has long been a research and policy concern in Australia, especially throughout the 1950s and 1960s, when a considerable proportion of immigration to that continent was "assisted passage" immigration.[34] Thus, for many policy purposes it is more important to look at net rather than at gross immigration figures.

According to a recent United Nations report, net immigration to Canada was 133,000 in 1974–75 and 30,000 in 1978–79, while net immigration to Australia was 51,600 in 1978 and 69,000 in 1979.[35] New Zealand in recent years has aimed at an annual net intake of some 5,000 persons, but has actually experienced negative immigration balances in some years.[36]

Accurate figures on resident alien or citizen emigration from the United States do not exist, although useful estimates are available.[37]

33. See United Nations Department of International Economic and Social Affairs, *International Migration Policies and Programmes: A World Survey,* Population Studies 80 (New York: United Nations, 1982).

34. See, for example, R. T. Appleyard, "The Return Movement of United Kingdom Migrants from Australia," *Population Studies,* vol. 15 (1962), pp. 214–15; and A. Richardson, "A Shipboard Study of Some British Born Immigrants Returning to the U.K. from Australia," *International Migration,* vol. 6 (1968), pp. 221–38.

35. United Nations Department of International Economic and Social Affairs, *World Population Trends and Policies: 1981 Monitoring Report,* Population Studies no. 79, vol. 1 (New York: United Nations, 1982), p. 145.

36. United Nations, *International Migration Policies,* pp. 4–5.

37. Robert Warren, "Alien Emigration from the United States: 1963 to 1974," paper presented at the Annual Meeting of the Population Association of America, Philadelphia, Penn., April 27, 1979; Robert Warren and Jennifer Marks Peck, "Foreign-Born Emigration from the United States: 1960 to 1970," *Demography,* vol. 17 (1980),

The debate on U.S. immigration policy issues is hindered by the virtual absence of recognition given to return migration. It is highly misleading to ignore it, although the macro figures are merely estimates, and the results of micro-level studies are not representative of the total phenomenon.[38]

The history of U.S. immigration can be conveniently divided into four phases: free movement (1790–1874); qualitative screening

---

pp. 71-84; G. Jasso and M. R. Rosenzweig, "Estimating the Emigration Rates of Legal Immigrants Using Administrative and Survey Data: The 1971 Cohort of Immigrants to the United States," *Demography*, August 1982, pp. 279–90; and Ada W. Finifter, "American Emigration," *Society*, vol. 13 (1976), p. 5.

From 1908 through 1957 the Immigration and Naturalization Service collected data on the emigration of aliens, from which it has been estimated that of the 15.7 million immigrants admitted for permanent residence during that period, 4.8 million later remigrated. (See Warren and Peck, "Foreign-Born Emigration," p. 71.) Based on careful manipulation of a variety of data sources, including the decennial census and yearly alien registration statistics, Warren ("Alien Emigration," p. 8) concluded that "the number of emigrants per 100 immigrants during [1963–1974] was about 31, which is nearly identical to the ratio for 1907 to 1957 derived from I&NS [Immigration and Naturalization Services] data. The ratio of emigrants per 100 immigrants is similar for European and Western Hemisphere countries but somewhat lower (14 per 100) for Asian countries." For the 1971 cohort of immigrants, Jasso and Rosenzweig even estimated that "the cumulative net emigration rate for the entire cohort could have been as high as 50 percent [by January 1979]. Canadian emigration was probably between 51 and 55 percent. Emigration rates for legal immigrants from Central America, the Caribbean (excluding Cuba), and South America were at least as high as 50 percent and could have been as high as 70 percent. Emigration rates for Koreans and Chinese could not have exceeded 22 percent over the same period" (Jasso and Rosenzweig, "Estimating the Emigration Rates," p. 279).

38. For example, Reichert and Massey found in their study of a rural mestizo town in Michoacan that 35 percent of the population of the town (which consisted of 2,167 persons) was actively engaged in migration to the United States. See "Patterns of U.S. Migration from a Mexican Sending Community: A Comparison of Legal and Illegal Migrants," *International Migration Review*, vol. 13 (1979), pp. 605–6. Approximately three-fourths of all families and households were affected by this. Furthermore, a majority of the town's households and families contained at least one person legally entitled to U.S. residence: "Of families sending migrants to the United States, 56.7 [percent] send legals (41.7% of all families) and 36.3 percent send illegals (26.7% of all families), while another 7 percent send both (5.2% of all families). These legal migrants can in no way be considered to be residents of the United States in the usual sense. The vast majority of them return home each year after a period of temporary employment in the United States. . . . Since 1910, only 70 residents (11 family units totaling 57 persons, and 13 single individuals) have left Guadalupe permanently to live in the United States" (ibid., p. 606).

The authors further observed that "the average period of time spent away from home by legal migrants each year . . . tended to be *significantly less* than that of illegals" (ibid., p. 599, emphasis added). The authors note that although with respect to the volume of migration Guadalupe is probably an extreme case even for the traditional migrant area in which it is located, "there is no reason to assume that findings relating to the relative size of legal and illegal migrant flows, and the various differences between them, are unrepresentative of broader patterns within much of rural Mexico" (ibid., p. 622).

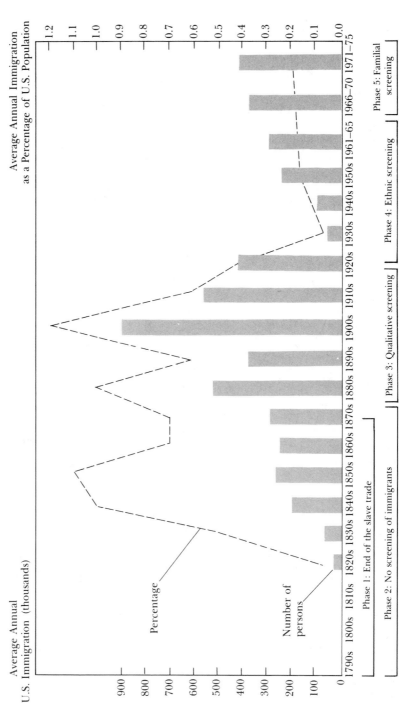

Figure 1. Average Annual Immigration through Five Immigration Policy Phases, 1790–1975, as Numbers and Percentage of U.S. Population at Beginning of Decade

Average Annual
U.S. Immigration (thousands)

Average Annual Immigration
as a Percentage of U.S. Population

Percentage

Number of persons

Phase 1: End of the slave trade

Phase 2: No screening of immigrants

Phase 3: Qualitative screening

Phase 4: Ethnic screening

Phase 5: Familial screening

1790s 1800s 1810s 1820s 1830s 1840s 1850s 1860s 1870s 1880s 1890s 1900s 1910s 1920s 1930s 1940s 1950s 1961–65 1966–70 1971–75

Sources: Immigration averages computed from U.S. Immigration and Naturalization Service, Annual Report, 1975 (Washington, D.C.: U.S. Government Printing Office, 1976), table 1; population data from The World Almanac and Book of Facts (New York: Newspaper Enterprise Association, Inc. 1977), p. 228. Reprinted from David S. North and Allen LeBel, Manpower and Immigration Policies in the United States, Special

(1875–1920); national origins quotas (1921–64); and emphasis on family reunion and labor market needs (1965–present).[39] During the first two periods (until 1920), U.S. immigration policy treated both hemispheres in essentially the same manner; the third period (1921–64) was characterized by radically different policies toward the Eastern and the Western Hemispheres; and the fourth period was characterized by the slow convergence of the two sets of policies, a process that was completed only in 1978.

The United States instituted national origins quotas for the Eastern Hemisphere in order to favor western and northern European immigrants over those from southern and eastern Europe. In 1952 the United States set a ceiling on Eastern Hemisphere immigration (158,561 immigrants per year, with spouses and children of adult U.S. citizens admitted outside the ceiling), and instituted a preference system. Meanwhile immigration from the Western Hemisphere continued to be regulated only by universally applicable criteria of individual exclusion, although these criteria, combined with bureaucratic delays, served quite well to keep the numbers of Western Hemisphere immigrants low in years in which this was desired (for example, during and immediately after the Great Depression).

In 1965 the United States finally abolished its national origins quotas, but different sets of regulations continued to be applied to the two hemispheres. The preference system governing immigration from the Eastern Hemisphere was somewhat revised, and uniform ceilings of 20,000 immigrants per country per year (in addition to close relatives), were applied within an overall hemispheric ceiling of (now) 170,000. In the same year, the United States imposed for the first time an overall yearly ceiling (120,000) on Western Hemisphere immigration, which was to be regulated without separate ceilings per country by a system of labor certification, rather than by the preference system used for the Eastern Hemisphere. In 1976 the Eastern Hemisphere regulations began to be applied to the Western Hemisphere as well, and in 1978 the two ceilings were finally combined into a worldwide ceiling of 290,000.

Figure 1 shows the volume of gross immigration flows to the United States through 1975. For 1976–80 the average flow was

---

39. Charles B. Keely, *U.S. Immigration: A Policy Analysis* (New York: The Population Council, 1979); and David S. North and Allen LeBel, *Manpower and Immigration Policies in the United States,* Special Report of the National Commission for Manpower Policy 20 (Washington, D.C.: n.p., 1978). The history of the exclusion of Orientals, which did not end until 1952, had already begun in the second phase.

TABLE 1
MEXICAN MIGRATION TO THE UNITED STATES, 1925–79
(Thousands)

Fiscal Years	Immigrants	Contract Farm Laborers	Illegal Immigrants Apprehended	Fiscal Years	Immigrants	Contract Farm Laborers	Illegal Immigrants Apprehended
1925–29	238.5	...	25.6	1960		315.8	29.7
1930–34	19.2	...	58.6	1961		291.4	29.8
1935–39	8.7	...	46.3	1962	217.8	195.0	30.3
1940–44	16.5	118.5	49.0	1963		186.9	39.1
1945		120.0	63.6	1964		177.7	43.8
1946		82.0	91.5	1965		20.3	55.3
1947	37.7	55.0	183.0	1966			89.8
1948		35.3	179.4	1967	213.8		108.3
1949		107.0	278.5	1968			151.7
1950		67.5	458.2	1969			201.6
1951		192.0	500.0	1970	44.5	...	265.5
1952	78.7	197.1	543.5	1971	50.3	...	348.2
1953		201.4	865.3	1972	64.2	...	430.2
1954		309.0	1,075.2	1973	70.4	...	576.8
1955		398.7	242.6	1974	71.9	...	710.0
1956		445.2	72.4	1975	62.6	...	680.0
1957	214.7	436.0	44.5	1976	58.4	...	781.0
1958		432.9	37.2	1977	44.6	...	954.8
1959		437.6	30.2	1978	92.7	...	963.0
				1979	52.5	...	976.7

SOURCES: Walter Fogel, *Mexican Illegal Alien Workers in the United States*, Institute of Industrial Relations Monograph 20 (Los Angeles: University of California, 1978), p. 14; Kenneth F. Johnson and Miles W. Williams, *Illegal Aliens in the Western Hemisphere: Political and Economic Factors* (New York: Praeger Publishers, 1981), pp. 88–89; and U.S. Bureau of the Census, *Statistical Abstract of the United States* (Washington, D.C.: U.S. Government Printing Office, 1980).

540,000.[40] This number is higher than any since World War I, but, recent claims to the contrary notwithstanding,[41] the number of legal immigrants in recent years has not equaled that of the first decade of this century (and the number of immigrants as a percentage of the U.S. population has been much lower still).

The mix of countries that have supplied the United States with the largest numbers of immigrants in the nineteenth and twentieth centuries has changed over time. The five leading countries have been furnishing a decreasing proportion of the total volume of immigration, from a high of 94 percent in 1841–50 to a low of 40 percent in 1971–78.[42] Mexico was among the top five source countries in the 1820s (before the present-day borders were drawn), but then not again until 1921–30, when the national-origin quotas went into effect for Eastern Hemisphere immigration. Since then Mexico has been consistently among the five largest suppliers and since the 1960s has ranked at the top. Overall, however, Canada has been the source of far more legal immigrants than Mexico, leading Mexico from the 1830s through the 1950s.

Table 1, which contains selected data on migration from Mexico to the United States between 1925 and 1979, shows that the levels of legal Mexican immigration were relatively low in the 1930s, 1940s, and the first half of the 1950s, despite the absence of country and hemispheric ceilings. The flows have substantially increased since then, to considerably larger numbers than the quota of 20,000 per year now in force.[43] An indication of the volume and distribution of pressures on immigration to the United States from various countries today can be gained from an analysis of the backlog of applications. In 1980, Mexican visa applications registered the largest backlog (274,838), with applications from the Philippines a close second (250,947), whereas the country next in line had fewer than half this number of pending visa applications. The long waits that these

40. Calculated from data in *U.S. Immigration Policy and the National Interest*, report submitted to the Congress and the President of the United States by the Select Commission for Immigration and Refugee Policy (Washington, D.C., March 1, 1981), figure 2, p. 93.

41. See, for example, Michael S. Teitelbaum, "Right versus Right: Immigration and Refugee Policy in the United States," *Foreign Affairs* (Fall 1980), pp. 21–59.

42. See U.S. Select Commission on Immigration and Refugee Policy, *U.S. Immigration and the National Interest* staff report (Washington, D.C.: U.S. Government Printing Office, 1981) table 6, p. 96.

43. The effects of this more restrictive legislation are not yet evident in the table because an exceptional court ruling allowed a temporary increase in the number of yearly entries (the "Silva case").

backlogs represent for prospective immigrants no doubt indicate for some a considerable temptation to migrate illegally.[44]

Year-Round Migration

Year-round migration involves a situation in which migrants are admitted to a country for a limited period of time, either to work or to join family members working there, and can be granted permission to extend their stay without having to return to their home country in the interim. This feature distinguishes year-round migration from seasonal and other forms of administratively enforced circular migration.

Year-round migration has been chosen by some countries that do not welcome immigrants as a solution to their manpower needs. They attempt to "rotate" temporary foreign workers through permanent jobs or to employ foreign workers in certain jobs until indigenous manpower becomes available to fill them. Such employment is also intended to provide employers with flexibility in times of economic downturns. In Europe primarily lower-level jobs have been taken up by foreign workers, whereas in the Arab Middle East, foreign employment has permeated nearly all economic sectors and all levels of the job hierarchy, and foreign workers make up far larger proportions of the host countries' labor forces than they do in Europe.

Year-round migration systems have created problems that are by now quite well known. First, there are tensions built into these situations as host country governments try to keep the migrations temporary by restricting housing, opportunities for family reunification and the schooling of children, a variety of other social services, and virtually all political rights, while despite continual spontaneous returns, some of the migrants nevertheless begin to put down roots (their own initial intentions to stay only briefly notwithstanding), and they, as well as various supportive organizations in the host and sending countries, begin to press for a liberalization of the restrictive policies. Second, some of these "temporary" migrants become in fact

---

44. The majority of the applications from Mexico had been made under the lowest, the "nonpreference" category (173,681), whereas the second-largest group (59,207) constituted applications under the second preference (spouses and unmarried sons and daughters of permanent resident aliens). By contrast, the majority of applications from the Philippines (165,776) fell under the fifth preference (brothers and sisters of U.S. citizens), and most of the remaining applications had been made under the second (32,914) and the third (32,266) preferences (the third being the occupational preference for highly trained and exceptionally able individuals). See Select Commission on Immigration and Refugee Policy, *U.S. Immigration Policy and the National Interest.*

long-term (if not permanent) residents. Third (the point that so far has received the least attention), when host countries attempt to terminate year-round migration systems, they find that the migratory tradition that has been established now acts as a stimulus to other forms of migration that may still be available (for example, seasonal and illegal migration).

European countries have gradually liberalized their policies with respect to the "guest workers" already employed in the host countries, while either "stabilizing" the total numbers (Switzerland, beginning in 1970) or halting the flow of new workers entirely (the other European host countries, around 1973–74) but continuing to permit family reunification. The Swiss policy was clearly a response to public concern about the impacts of these migrations on Swiss society and culture (a concern that manifested itself in the nearly successful referenda on "overforeignization"). The other countries' decisions to halt recruitment were made at the time of the energy crisis and were largely justified in economic terms. However, these decisions too were preceded by internal discussion concerning the "discovery" that the migrants were more than inorganic forces of production—that they made demands on schools and hospitals, occupied housing, and were gradually changing the "face" of the host countries.

The volume of return migration from northern and western Europe has been lower in the 1970s and 1980s than had been expected based on the experience of the 1967–68 recession. Many migrants are now long-term residents and plan to stay. Meanwhile, the hundreds of thousands of foreign children born in the host countries do not automatically acquire citizenship in the host country, nor is naturalization an option easily available to most migrants (except in Sweden). Some host countries (most notably, parts of Germany) have experimented with highly ambiguous policies concerning the education of the second generation (attempts to educate the children simultaneously for "integration" into the host country and for return to their parents' countries). Finally, with unemployment rates high in all host countries except Switzerland, some countries attempted to induce migrants to leave through offers of financial incentives (France established a "return bonus" scheme in 1977, which remained in force for several years, and is now experimenting with a refined version; also Germany recently offered a return bonus).[45]

---

45. See André Lebon, "L'aide au retour des travailleurs étrangers," *Economie et Statistique*, vol. 113 (1979), pp. 37–46; Rosemarie Rogers, "Incentives to Return: Patterns of Policies and Migrants' Responses," in Mary M. Kritz, Charles B. Keely, and Silvano M. Tomasi, eds., *Global Trends in Migration: Theory and Research on*

In the early 1970s, the seven major European host countries (Austria, Belgium, France, West Germany, the Netherlands, Sweden, and Switzerland) had within their borders close to 10 million migrants from six southern European and three North African countries, slightly more than half of them in the labor force. The proportion of *all* foreigners in these countries' labor forces ranged from 3.6 percent in the Netherlands to 23.8 percent in Switzerland. Despite spontaneous returns and no admittance of new economic migrants by most host countries since 1973–74, the total number of migrants from the nine sending countries has remained essentially unchanged because of continued family reunification.[46]

Policymakers in the European host countries did not expect that their countries would come to rival or surpass the classic immigrant countries in their degree of admixture of foreign populations. Actually, the percentage of foreign citizens (year-round migrants, many of whom have by now the right of permanent residence; seasonal workers are not included) in their populations in 1981 was 6.9 percent in France, 7.6 percent in West Germany, and 16.8 percent in Switzerland. This compares with the percentage of foreign-born in the populations of such immigrant countries as the United States, 6.2 percent in 1980; Australia, 21.7 percent in 1981; and Canada, 15.3 percent in 1971.

Ten labor-receiving countries of the Arab region in 1975 had approximately 3.5 million migrants, of whom 2.6 million were Arabs. Slightly more than half of these (1.8 million) were in the labor force, a proportion that was only slightly higher among the non-Arab than among the Arab migrants.[47] The proportion of foreigners in the labor forces of the seven major Arab receiving countries ranged in 1975 from 34 percent in Saudi Arabia to 84.7 percent in the United Arab Emirates.[48] Some of these migrations are de facto seasonal, some are relatively short-term target migrations, and some are long-term migrations pointing to a gradual settling process.[49]

International Population Movements (Staten Island, N.Y.: Center for Migration Studies, 1981); "Bitter Lemons," *Economist*, January 14, 1984, p. 62; and Heinrich Meyer, *SOPEMI 1983: Federal Republic of Germany* (Paris: OECD, 1983).

46. See table 1 in Rosemarie Rogers, "Western Europe Today: The End of Immigration?" paper delivered at the Fourth International Conference of Europeanists, Washington, D.C. October 13–15, 1983.

47. J. S. Birks and C.A. Sinclair, *International Migration and Development in the Arab Region* (Geneva: International Labour Office, 1980), 137–39.

48. Ismail Serageldin, James Socknat, Stace Birks, Bob Li, and Clive Sinclair, *Manpower and International Labor Migration in the Middle East and North Africa* (New York: Oxford University Press, 1983), p. 33.

49. Birks and Sinclair, *International Migration and Development*, pp. 37–63. There is also a good deal of labor migration occurring in West Africa, but the stock data

In the United States today the number of foreigners admitted for temporary work is very small in comparison with those admitted as immigrants and refugees and with the estimated flows and stocks of illegal migrants. In 1977–78 the United States admitted a total of 42,979 temporary workers. This included 16,838 "workers of distinguished merit and ability," 22,832 "other temporary workers," and 3,309 "industrial trainees" (identified respectively as H-1, H-2, and H-3 visa holders under the present U.S. classification system).[50]

The admission of temporary workers under the "H" classification is discussed under year-round migration because these visas are extended for periods of varying length, and some are renewed while the workers remain in the United States. Although this program plays a negligible role in the migration from Mexico to the United States,[51] a consideration of systems of year-round employment of nonimmigrant foreign workers is highly relevant to a discussion of Mexican-U.S. migration. Some such system, on a far larger scale, has repeatedly been proposed, either as part of amnesty provisions for Mexican migrants now in the country illegally, or as an independent policy measure to respond to migration pressures from Mexico.

Circulatory Migration (Including Seasonal Migration)

Here I refer to foreign workers who are bound by contracts to return to their home countries. They may enter into a new contract only after having spent a few months outside the host country. In this way some migrants shuttle between two countries for the better part of their lives. Such contract workers' rights in the host country

---

(based primarily on censuses and surveys) do not allow one to separate out year-round migrants from seasonal migrants, or documented from undocumented workers. According to Zachariah and Conde, "The total number of foreign nationals living in [nine West African] countries was 2.8 million around 1975, about 7 percent of the total population of the nine countries." See K. C. Zachariah and Julien Conde, *Migration in West Africa: Demographic Aspects,* a joint World Bank-OECD Study (New York: Oxford University Press, 1981), p. 5. The four countries with the largest percentages of foreign citizens in their populations were Ivory Coast (21.3 percent), the Gambia (10.6 percent), Senegal (7.1 percent), and Ghana (6.6 percent) (ibid., p. 34). As in Europe and the Middle East, this number includes children born to the foreign residents in these countries.

50. U.S. Department of Justice, Immigration and Naturalization Service, *1978 Statistical Yearbook of the Immigration and Naturalization Service* (Washington, D.C.: U.S. Government Printing Office, 1978), pp. 43–48. Of the 22,832 H-2 workers, 8,306 were farm laborers and farm foremen and 890 were lumbermen, most of them, no doubt, in seasonal jobs; 8,406 were classified as professional, technical, and kindred workers; 18,203 came from North America, including the Caribbean (the two largest groups being 7,072 workers from Jamaica and 4,748 workers from Canada).

51. In 1977–78, Mexico contributed about 5 percent of the participants in the total program: 975 were H-1 workers; 1,189 were H-2; and 107 were H-3.

are highly limited: they are usually tied to one employer, are rarely allowed to bring their families, and sometimes have part of their wages withheld for subsequent payment to them at departure or for remittance to their home country. They cannot remain legally in the host country after their contract has expired, and they have no claim on a new contract in the future.

Employers typically seek to fill jobs with circulatory migrants for one of two reasons. In the case of seasonal jobs, it may be convenient for employers to increase their labor force at particular times through the hiring of foreign short-term workers. This accounts for much of the seasonal employment in France (the only European country besides Switzerland to employ foreign seasonal labor) and for the employment of many H-2 workers in the United States (for example, Caribbean migrants brought in to cut sugar cane in Florida). The second situation is quite different and involves permanent jobs, which, for whatever reason, cannot be filled by domestic workers. The employers wish to hire foreign workers, and the host country governments decide, generally based on sociocultural rather than economic considerations, to use a system of controlled circular migration. The employers may or may not consider such decisions to be in their own interest. Both South Africa and Switzerland use (or misuse) circulatory migration today.

South African employment of black Africans from abroad on a circulatory migration basis is especially prevalent in the mining industry. Employers have benefited from the system by being able to pay comparatively low wages, but many would prefer greater continuity in their work force, as is evident from repeated requests made to the South African government to that effect as well as from the offers of "reemployment bonuses" extended to workers who return to the same jobs.[52]

Switzerland has a proportionately larger year-round foreign population than the other major European host countries and since 1970 has put sociocultural considerations before labor market demands in setting countrywide "ceilings" on the admittance of year-round workers. Switzerland's extremely low unemployment rate[53] has meant that some employers cannot attract sufficient numbers of Swiss

52. F. de Vletter, "Conditions Affecting Black Migrant Workers in South Africa: A Case Study of the Gold Mines," in W. Roger Boehning, ed., *Black Migration to South Africa: A Selection of Policy-Oriented Research* (Geneva: International Labour Office, 1981), p. 97.

53. The unemployment rate in Switzerland was 0.2 percent in 1981, compared with 9.6 percent in Belgium, 7.3 percent in France, 4.6 percent in West Germany, and 2.5 percent in Sweden. See OECD, *Historical Statistics: 1960–1981* (Paris: OECD, 1983), p. 39.

TABLE 2
MIGRANT STOCKS IN FRANCE AND SWITZERLAND, EARLY 1980s
(Thousands unless otherwise specified)

Type of Migrant	France	Switzerland
Foreign population entitled to year-round or permanent residence (1981)		
All foreign migrants		
All foreign residents	4,223.9	909.9
Foreign migrants as a percentage of total population and native population	(7.8)	(14.3)
Foreign migrants in the labor force	1,591.9	515.1
Foreign migrants as a percentage of total labor force and native labor force	(6.9)	(16.8)
From nine Mediterranean recruitment countries		
All foreign residents	3,364.4	631.2
Economically active	1,348.3	369.5
Seasonal migrants (1981)	117.5	157.4
Border commuters (1981)	. . .	109.0
Illegal migrants		
Estimated number (1980; early 1980s)	300–400	25–100
Expulsions (1980)	13.5	. . .
Applications received under regularization program (1981–82)	149.7	. . .

SOURCES: SOPEMI (Continuous Reporting System on Migration), *SOPEMI Report* (Paris: OECD, 1982), pp. 1–2, 11, 32; Organization for Economic Corporation and Development, *Historical Statistics: 1983* (Paris: OECD, 1983), p. 18; Bundesamt für Statistik (Switzerland), ed., *Statistisches Jahrbuch des Schweiz* (Basel: Birkhauser Verlag, 1983), p. 113; Raffaele de Grazia, *Le Travail Clandestin: Situation dans les Pays industrialisés à Économie de Marché* (Geneva: International Labour Office, 1983), p. 16; J. P. Garson and Y. Moulier, "Clandestine Immigrants and Their Regularisation in France: 1981–1982," International Migration for Employment Working Paper 6E (Geneva: International Labour Office, 1982), p. 20; Ministry of Social Affairs and National Solidarity (France), "Les Migrants sans Documents et la Regularisation de leur Statut," Sixth Seminar on Adaptation and Integration of Immigrants, Information Document 23 (Geneva: Intergovernmental Committee for Migration, 1983).

or resident foreign workers and therefore resort to the employment of seasonal workers in year-round jobs. Table 2 compares the number of seasonal migrants in France and Switzerland in 1981 with other types of migrants. In Switzerland, seasonal migrants constituted almost half the number of economically active year-round migrants from the Mediterranean recruitment countries, and almost a third of all economically active foreigners resident in Switzerland year-round. One observer estimated that 70 to 80 percent of the jobs held by seasonal workers in the early 1980s were in fact year-round jobs.[54]

---

54. Aido Messina, "Les migrants sans papiers en Suisse," Sixth Seminar on Adaptation and Integration of Immigrants, Information Document 19 (Geneva: Intergovernmental Committee for Migration, 1983), p. 15.

For some migrants, participation in a system of circular migration seems to be a desired option,[55] but other migrants accept this arrangement only because they have no other choice. In Swaziland labor turnover among internal migrants in mines and forestry companies decreased from 85 percent to 1 percent when family housing units were provided.[56]

There are several problems inherent in systems of enforced circular migration. First, in most cases migrants are forced into living situations that deny them basic rights enjoyed by native workers and longer-term migrants. Second, in situations in which circular migrants are actively involved in two economies, the likelihood of their being paid at noncompetitive wages in the host country becomes especially great.[57] Third, this system makes host and sending countries particularly vulnerable to abrupt changes in supply or demand for labor.[58] However, the sending countries are usually in the weaker bargaining position.[59]

Finally, circulatory migration systems result in considerable pressures for illegal migration. This may be simply because more and more migrants gain experience in working and "getting around" in

55. See Michel Poinard, *Le retour des travailleurs portugais* (Paris: Las Documentation Française, 1979) concerning Portuguese seasonal workers in France.

56. Many of these workers nevertheless maintained rural ties or homesteads, but the continuation of a dual income pattern, that is, of continued personal involvement in agricultural production in the home community, seemed to be chosen only when the conditions for permanence in the modern sector were not available. See F. de Vletter, M. H. Doran, A. R. C. Low, F. D. Prinz, and B. D. Rosen-Prinz, "Labour Migration in Swaziland," in W. Roger Boehning, ed., *Black Migration to South Africa: A Selection of Policy-Oriented Research* (Geneva: International Labour Office, 1981), pp. 69–70.

57. With respect to internal as well as external Swazi circulatory labor migration, de Vletter et al. (ibid., p. 72) concluded "Migration engenders a vicious circle of mutual support between the modern capitalist sector and the traditional rural sector. Rural production is no longer sufficient to meet the changing norms of 'subsistence,' but wages (even following the recent substantial increases) are barely adequate for the maintenance of the family during the period of employment and cannot sustain the migrant and his family after retirement."

58. When Malawi halted the recruitment of its workers by South Africa in 1974, "it took the gold-mining industry at least two years to fill the gap created by the withdrawal of Malawian workers." See C. W. Stahl, "Migrant Labour Supplies, Past, Present and Future: With Special Reference to the Gold-Mining Industry," in W. Roger Boehning, ed., *Black Migration to South Africa: A Selection of Policy-Oriented Research* (Geneva: International Labour Office, 1981), pp. 34–36.

59. See, for example, Garcia y Griego's analysis of Mexico's diminishing influence on specific aspects of the implementation of the bracero program. Manuel Garcia y Griego, "The Importation of Mexican Contract Laborers to the United States, 1942–1964: Antecedents, Operation, and Legacy," in Peter Brown and Henry Shue, eds., *The Border that Joins: Mexican Migrants and U.S. Responsibility* (Totowa, N.J.: Rowman and Littlefield, 1983).

a particular host country and are therefore better able to return to work illegally when this seems more desirable or when the option of circulatory employment is not available. In other cases employers encourage seasonal migrants to stay on to work in what are in fact year-round jobs.

South Africa has reacted to its negative experience of dependence on outside labor supplies (and also to increasing unemployment in the country) by the "internalization" of its mine labor supply (the number of foreign "oscillating" workers was reduced by one-third between 1970 and 1979), accompanied by increased restrictions on family migration.[60] In Switzerland the dividing lines between different types of migrations have been made somewhat more porous: seasonal migrants are permitted year-round resident status after working in the country for a certain number of months during four consecutive seasons.

An important phase in the history of Mexican migration to the United States was the bracero program, a contract labor program to fill agricultural jobs, which existed from 1942 to 1964. Initially established to fill wartime labor needs, it was intended to last until 1947,[61] but was repeatedly extended, and the largest numbers of contract workers were introduced after 1950 (see table 1). Garcia y Griego argues persuasively that the program must be seen in the context of the earlier migrations, legal and illegal, from Mexico to the United States, which were to a large extent seasonal.[62] The program served to institutionalize seasonal labor migration on a large scale (involving more than 4.6 million contracts, almost three-quarters of which were issued in the last ten years of the program).[63] Cross and Sandos stress, in addition, the program's regional effects: more than half of the contracts were allocated to rural residents of Mexico's north central sending states, although these had only about one-quarter of Mexico's rural population.[64]

Garcia y Griego documents the Mexican government's concern, in the early years of the bracero program, about the treatment of its citizens in the United States and the pressures it brought on the U.S. government to penalize employers of illegal workers. At the same time the program certainly contributed to the incidence of illegal migration, by sending workers who never returned home, and by

60. Stahl, "Migrant Labour Supplies," pp. 24–28.
61. Ehrlich, Bilderback, and Ehrlich, *The Golden Door.*
62. Garcia y Griego, "The Importation of Mexican Contract Laborers."
63. See table 1.
64. Cross and Sandos, *Across the Border,* p. 35.

creating expectations for jobs; prospective migrants soon realized that these jobs could sometimes be obtained more quickly (without paperwork or bribes, and even in sectors other than agriculture) by going outside the established channels.[65] The Mexican government's concern for the well-being of its workers—for example, its insistence on fair wages and the negotiated requirement that contracts be issued for a minimum of four months' work—may have contributed to some growers' preference for hiring illegal laborers.[66]

When the United States terminated the bracero program in 1964, partly out of a concern about displacement of U.S. workers, the Mexican labor force that had participated in the program still needed work. Some employers did not turn to U.S. workers, nor did U.S. workers want some of these jobs. Termination of a long-time legal arrangement could hardly be expected to stop the migration flows where the demand for jobs was high and work was available.

Border Commuting

Border commuting has generally received little attention in the analysis of migration flows. Although it is largely irrelevant to certain theoretical and policy concerns (for example, border commuters do not contribute to host country population growth), it is relevant to other concerns (for example, labor market impacts). Border commuting is hardly mentioned in the literature on European migration and goes unreported in the statistical yearbooks of most European countries. Switzerland has substantial numbers of border commuters, but they do not seem to be a significant policy issue. This is understandable since the noneconomic impact of border commuters on host societies is comparatively small and Switzerland has not had to be greatly concerned about the economic impact.[67]

The U.S. situation is unique in permitting only persons who have immigrant status or who are U.S. citizens to be border commuters. These immigrants are permitted to live in Canada or Mexico without losing their "resident alien" status, because the Immigration and Naturalization Service has issued administrative rulings that define working in the United States as fulfilling the requirement of legal

---

65. Ibid., pp. 36–38.
66. Ehrlich, Bilderback, and Ehrlich, *The Golden Door,* p. 213.
67. For an interesting case study of border commuting between Belgium and northern France, see Robert J. Berrier, "The French Textile Industry: Segmented Labor Market," in Rogers, ed., *Guests Come to Stay.*

residence.[68] Estimates of the numbers of legal border commuters from the mid-1960s to the mid-1970s range from about 40,000 to 70,000.[69] An unspecified number of illegal commuters also works regularly in the United States; they enter the country on visitor's cards that are valid for seventy-two hours, but these cards do not entitle them to work.

The numbers of legal commuters may not seem to be particularly high, but they must be interpreted with reference to the size of the labor markets of the communities to which the imigrants are commuting. The U.S. Commission on Civil Rights noted, with reference to the mid-1960s, that "it has been estimated that over 17% of the labor market in El Paso, Texas, are commuters. Further estimates have shown that 5% of the San Diego, California, labor market and 23% of the Brownsville, Texas, labor market are commuters."[70] I discuss the resulting concern about displacement of resident workers in the last section of this paper.

Irregular Status Migration

The term *migrants in an irregular status* was used in the title of a 1983 seminar held by the Intergovernmental Committee on Migration to encompass the broad range of situations of informal, undocumented, clandestine, or illegal migration. In some contexts (for example, sub-Saharan Africa), movements across borders have been

---

68. George C. Kiser and Martha Woody Kiser, eds., *Mexican Workers in the United States: Historical and Political Perspectives* (Albuquerque: University of New Mexico Press, 1979), pp. 215–17.

69. Ibid., p. 215; U.S. Commission on Civil Rights, "The Commuter on the United States-Mexico Border," reprinted in ibid., pp. 217–38; Anna-Stina Ericson, "The Impact of Commuters on the Mexican-American Border Area," reprinted in Kiser and Kiser, *Mexican Workers in the United States*, pp. 238–56. According to Kiser and Kiser (p. 215), "In 1974, daily commuters numbered more than 40,000 while there were over 8,000 seasonal commuters." The Commission on Civil Rights ("The Commuter on the United States-Mexico Border") stated that "one . . . count, taken on January 11, 1966, showed that 42,641 commuters, of which 17,653 were employed in agriculture, entered the United States." Ericson ("The Impact of Commuters"), presumably referring to the late 1960s, begins her article by stating that "approximately 70,000 persons cross the Mexican border daily to work in the United States. Of these, 20,000 are U.S. citizens living in Mexico; about 50,000 are Mexican immigrants who have valid U.S. immigration documents but who, for various reasons, continue to live in Mexico while they work in the United States."

70. United States Commission on Civil Rights. "The Commuter on the United States-Mexico Border," undated staff report, p. 226. Reprinted from U.S. Congress, Senate, *Hearings of the Senate Subcommittee on Migratory Labor of the Committee on Labor and Public Welfare*, 91st Cong., 1st and 2d sess., Part 5-B, *Migrant and Seasonal Farmworker Powerlessness*.

extensions of internal migratory patterns; neither host nor sending countries have as a rule paid much attention to formalizing exits, entries, or length of stay for persons going to neighboring countries, although mechanisms to do so exist. At the opposite end of the policy spectrum are countries (for example, South Africa) with unambiguous positions on the illegality of uncontrolled entries and stays, and having laws and enforcement policies that work together toward strict controls. Many situations fall somewhere between these extremes. They are often characterized by general policy postures favoring controls, and laws to that effect, but with sporadic or relatively ineffective enforcement, pointing perhaps to a need for legal revisions if stricter control is to be achieved.

Illegal or undocumented migration flows occur throughout the world (even under the most restrictive conditions), and they generally accompany patterns of legal flows. Because such flows are difficult to measure, estimates may be based on a variety of sources and methodologies. The available estimates of stocks and flows of illegal migrants traveling from Mexico to the United States illustrate this variety of techniques: surveys of apprehended illegal migrants undertaken on either side of the border;[71] interviews with trusted nonapprehended respondents in the host country;[72] interviews with migrants who have returned to their home communities; household interviews in sending countries that include questions about family members currently abroad in undocumented status;[73] inferences from a combination of data sources, such as home and host country censuses, data on the filing of income tax returns or social security payments, or micro studies of host country labor markets;[74] data on

71. David S. North and Marion F. Houstoun, "The Characteristics and Role of Illegal Aliens in the U.S. Labor Market: An Exploratory Study," report prepared for the Employment and Training Administration, U.S. Department of Labor (Washington, D.C.: Linton and Co., 1976); the National Survey on Emigration to the Northern Border and to the United States undertaken by the National Center of Labor Statistics and Information of the Mexican government's Ministry of Labor and Social Welfare; Jorge A. Bustamante and Geronimo G. Martinez, "Undocumented Immigration from Mexico: Beyond Borders but within Systems," *Journal of International Affairs*, vol. 33, (1979), pp. 265–84.

72. Maurice D. van Arsdol, Jr., et al., *Non-Apprehended and Apprehended Undocumented Residents in the Los Angeles Labor Market: An Exploratory Study*, report for the Employment and Training Administration (Los Angeles: U.S. Department of Labor, 1979).

73. Wayne A. Cornelius, "Illegal Migration to the United States: Recent Research Findings, Policy Implications, and Research Priorities," Monograph C/77–11 (Cambridge: Massachusetts Institute of Technology Center for International Studies, 1977).

74. See citations in Cross and Sandos, *Across the Border;* for the 1920s, see also Manuel Gamio, *Mexican Immigration to the United States: A Study of Human Migration and Adjustment* (New York: Dover, 1971).

apprehensions in the course of attempted entries or on apprehensions of illegal migrants with longer residence in the host country;[75] and information obtained during amnesties.[76]

If the estimated number of refugees in the world ranges from about 8 million to more than 10 million, depending on whether a narrower or a broader definition is used (as is discussed below) the number of undocumented or illegal migrants (sometimes termed *economic refugees*) is also within this range or even greater, depending on which estimates one uses. Countries that have historically ignored undocumented migration have on occasion sharply reversed their policies because of numerous economic or political considerations (for example Ghana abruptly began enforcing its Alien Compliance Act in 1968; and Nigeria recently expelled vast numbers of Ghanian migrant workers). More generally, one observes today in many parts of the world a trend toward greater control of undocumented migration through a more rigorous use of entry visas and residence permits, often accompanied by offers of regularization or amnesty to those already in the countries.[77]

Although the European host countries have an administrative apparatus to monitor entries and stays of migrants, and most countries have also used employer sanctions, illegal migration alongside the inflows of year-round migrants between the mid-1950s and mid-1970s has been generally acknowledged to constitute as much as 10 percent of the foreign labor force.[78] More recent estimates indicate

---

75. The yearly reports of the U.S. Immigration and Naturalization Service.

76. For the French example, see J. P. Garson and Y. Moulier, "Clandestine Immigrants and Their Regularisation in France: 1981–1982," International Migration for Employment Working Paper 6E (Geneva: International Labour Office, 1982); and Ministry of Social Affairs and National Solidarity (France), "Les migrants sans documents et la regularisation de leur statut," Sixth Seminar on Adaptation and Integration of Immigrants, Information Document 23 (Geneva: Intergovernmental Committee for Migration, 1983).

77. Examples include Saudi Arabia, where the number of undocumented migrants has been in the hundreds of thousands; Venezuela, with an estimated 2 million undocumented migrants, about 800,000 of whom are from neighboring Colombia; and Argentina, where estimates of the illegal migrant population range from 600,000 to 2.7 million (See United Nations Department of International Economic and Social Affairs, *International Migration Policies*, pp. 62–63 and 68–81.) Hong Kong has also tightened its policy toward illegal migrants from China. Other substantial movements of illegal migrants in East Asia occur from Malaysia to Singapore, and from Indonesia to Malaysia (where the estimated stock of illegal Indonesian migrants is 100,000 to 300,000). Australia and New Zealand also record illegal migrant populations.

78. This would have brought the number close to 600,000 in the early 1970s. For a relatively "early" discussion of clandestine workers in Europe, see Jaques Houdaille and Alfred Sauvy, "L'immigration clandestine dans le monde." *Population*, vol. 29 (1974), pp. 725–41.

that the stock of illegal migrants in these host countries has increased considerably since the recruitment of new year-round labor migrants was stopped in 1973–74.[79]

Perhaps Europeans could have learned some lessons from the Mexican-American situation. As a result of the earlier year-round migrations, sending and receiving countries in Europe now have a complex network of relationships. The network operates at governmental levels, between nongovernment institutions in the various countries and, most important, between migrants who have settled abroad and their families and friends at home. When the host countries halted the further recruitment of labor migrants by simple administrative decisions, it was impossible to simply return to the "baseline" of twenty years earlier. Information about employment opportunities and living conditions is Europe had in the meantime become widespread in the sending countries; expectations concerning future migrations had been created among segments of the sending country populations, including persons who had already had migration experience; and there were now migrant communities in the host countries that could receive family members, friends, and compatriots, shelter them, and help them find employment. Moreover, some employers clearly remained ready to employ (now-illegal) migrants. The presence of illegal migrants attests to the importance of the family as an agent in migration and, more generally, to the autonomous character of mature migration streams. Unlike a faucet, migration streams cannot simply be turned off at will.

Migration from Mexico to the United States has a far longer history than these particular European migration flows, and it has been institutionalized for a far longer time, both in form of immigration and the twenty-two year contract labor program. In addition, it takes place in the context of ethnic communities that predate even the current borders, across a land border that is one of the longest in the world, and from an economic system that is heavily oriented toward that of the host country, in its historical migration flows, trade flows, and investment patterns. Twice in the past, after ignoring undocumented migration from Mexico for some time, the United States suddenly clamped down on it. In the 1930s this policy resulted in strong pressures for return and actual deportations (including a

---

79. Raffaele de Grazia (*Le travail clandestin: Situation dans les pays industrialisés à économie de marché* [Geneva: International Labour Office, 1983], p. 16) reports these estimates for the following countries: West Germany (1976), 200,000 to 300,000; France (1980), 300,000 to 400,000; Switzerland (1980s), 25,000 to 100,000; Italy— traditionally a sending country—(1978), 300,000 to 400,000; (1981), 600,000 to 700,000.

number of legal residents and citizens). The second time, in the mid-1950s, even larger numbers were affected by "operation wetback."[80] Concerns about illegal migration have again been voiced since the early 1970s.

Illegal migrants from all over the world live in the United States today. Prominent among them are migrants from less-developed Asian countries, from Central America and the Caribbean, and (by most estimates, about 60 percent of the total) from Mexico. Estimates of stocks have ranged widely, but the consensus seems to be in the range of 3 million to 6 million persons.[81] Using the 60 percent figure, the number of undocumented Mexican migrants in the United States may range from 1.8 million to 3.6 million. By comparison, Garcia y Griego, on the basis of apprehension data provided by the Immigration and Naturalization Service, estimated the stock of Mexican migrants (of all characteristics) exposed to the risk of being expelled in 1977 to have ranged from 480,000 to 1.2 million.[82] He interprets the results of the National Survey on Emigration to the Northern Border and to the United States as suggesting that "the total number of Mexican workers in the United States in early 1979 [was] 519,300 [absent persons irrespective of their status in the United States] plus 480,000 [returned workers] minus those persons habitually residing in Mexico who register with the Immigration and Naturalization Service, plus those undocumented Mexican workers who habitually reside in the United States."[83] Finally, Heer has estimated that between 1969 and 1977 the net additions to the stock of undocumented Mexican migrants residing permanently in the United States averaged 115,900 persons annually.[84] (No estimate of the total stock was attempted.)

All such estimates are problematic: analysts using data on border

---

80. Juan Ramon Garcia, *Operation Wetback: The Mass Deportation of Mexican Undocumented Workers in 1954 (Westport, Conn.: Greenwood Press, 1980).*

81. See Clarise Lancaster and Frederick J. Scheuren, "Counting the Uncountable Illegals: Some Statistical Speculations Employing Capture-Recapture Techniques," *1977 Proceedings of the Annual Meeting of the American Statistical Association* (Washington, D.C.: 1978) as cited in Cross and Sandos, *Across the Border;* Ehrlich, Bilderback, and Ehrlich, *The Golden Door,* p. 188; Fogel, *Mexican Illegal Alien Workers,* p. 25; Select Commission on Immigration and Refugee Policy, *U.S. Immigration Policy.*

82. Manuel Garcia y Griego, "El Volumen de la Migración de Mexicanos no Documentados a los Estados Unidos (Nuevas Hipotesis)," cited in Manuel Garcia y Griego, "Comments on Bustamante and Sanderson Papers and on Research Project ENEFNEU," in Clark W. Reynolds and Carlos Tello, eds., *U.S.-Mexico Relations: Economic and Social Aspects* (Stanford: Stanford University Press, 1983), pp. 299–314.

83. Ibid., p. 312.

84. In van Arsdol et al., *Non-Apprehended and Apprehended Undocumented Residents.*

apprehensions must make assumptions about the ratio of attempted entrants who get through to those apprehended; analysts conducting household surveys in Mexico cannot obtain information on entire families who have settled illegally in the United States; and analysts whose data are gathered from apprehended migrants or from spontaneous returnees to Mexico following their stay in the United States assume that these respondents are representative of the total undocumented Mexican population (rather than constituting the less experienced and less settled group, in the case of the apprehended, and the most return-oriented in the case of the returnees). The divergent estimates of stock and flow are reflected in the disagreement about the illegal migrant population's effects on U.S. labor markets and on U.S. society, a topic that is addressed below.

Refugee Movements

The *World Refugee Survey 1983* estimates that in mid-1982 there were 7,816,200 refugees in need of "permanent solutions."[85] Adding internally displaced persons (for whom there are far less complete estimates) to this number could push the total above 10 million. Some of these people have a realistic hope of eventually returning to their home countries or regions; others have the opportunity to become integrated into the country of first asylum; but for some, especially for most refugees in Southeast Asia, resettlement in a third country seems to be the only long-term solution. The three countries accepting the largest numbers of immigrants—the United States, Canada, and Australia—lead also in the admission of refugees for resettlement; they are followed by France, the United Kingdom, and West Germany.

The Refugee Act of 1980 introduced important changes in U.S. refugee policy, most notably a revision of the definition of a refugee (to accord with the United Nations definition), a mechanism for the U.S. president and Congress to set yearly quotas for refugee admissions and changes in the domestic structures for refugee resettlement. But even as late as 1980 the United States still perceived itself as almost exclusively a country of refugee resettlement (along the post–World War II European model), rather than as a country of first asylum. On matters relating to refugees, as in immigration policy, the perception that the major pressures for entry would come from parts of the world other than the Western Hemiphere, died hard.

---

85. U.S. Committee for Refugees, *World Refugee Survey 1983* (New York: American Council for Nationalities Service, 1983), p. 61.

Mexico today is itself a country of asylum. In 1983 the Mexican state of Chiapas held an estimated 100,000 Guatemalans who had left their country and were afraid to return because they feared for their lives.[86] Mexican authorities have classified few of these people as seekers of asylum or refugees; most are called "frontier visitors" or "displaced persons"—a decision that seems to arise out of foreign policy as well as domestic economic concerns.[87] Only in May 1984 did the Mexican government decide to relocate close to 50,000 of these exiles to refugee centers farther inside the country.[88]

Free Movement of Labor

Where free movement exists today between countries, it is not the result of laissez-faire policies, but of negotiations that have led to the establishment of supranational communities—for example, the European Economic Community or the Nordic Common Labor Market. Within these communities, citizens of member countries are entitled to take up available jobs almost immediately after these have been advertised to the country's own citizens (whereas the self-employed do not have free movement). The communities have been formed with due deliberation, and the economic differentials between member countries are generally small enough so that no country needs to fear being "overrun" by migrants from another.

Within the Nordic Common Labor Market the primary movement is that of Finns to Sweden. Among the original six EEC member countries, the only country with substantial out-migration was Italy; however, one of the major destinations of Italian migrants was a country outside the EEC: Switzerland. The slow pace and the difficulties encountered in bringing about the "southern enlargement" of the EEC that was sought by several applicant countries reflect in part individual governments' concerns about the potential effects of the free movement of labor. In the case of Greece (admitted in 1981), the EEC mandated a seven-year transition period for selected agri-

---

86. Daniel Conde, "Guatemalan Refugees in Mexico." *Cultural Survival Quarterly,* vol. 7 (1983), p. 50.

87. Given Mexico's own population pressures, it is not surprising that there should be concern not to arouse in these displaced people hopes of long-term stays and of integration into the region. It is worth adding that Guatemalans have traditionally played an economic role in this part of Mexico: before 1980, about 60,000 seasonal workers from Guatemala had worked on the yearly harvest in the region. See Deirdre Kelly, "Guatemala's Refugees: Victims and Shapers of Government Policies." *Fletcher Forum,* vol. 7, (1983), p. 338.

88. "Mexico Will Move Guatemala Exiles," *New York Times,* May 3, 1984.

cultural issues and for migration.[89] The negotiations for EEC membership with Spain and Portugal are proceeding slowly, manpower migrations being one of the important issues in the discussions; and Turkey seems to have little prospect for attaining full membership in the community in this century because some of the member countries, especially Germany, are concerned about the impact that the provision for free movement of labor would have on them.

Although there are no real prospects for a "North American Free Labor Market" at this time, current proposals for new U.S. immigration legislation have recognized the existence of a special relationship between this country and its neighbors to the north and south. The 1984 draft of the Simpson-Mazzoli bill contained a provision for higher immigration quotas for Canada and Mexico (40,000 rather than 20,000); and since immigration from Canada has been below the 20,000 limit in recent years, a second provision that would allow the unused portion of the Canadian quota to be applied to Mexico is no less important than the assigning of the quotas themselves.[90]

The Effects of Migration

An analysis of the effects of migratory movements must distinguish among effects on the migrants and their families, effects on the receiving countries, and effects on the sending countries. With respect to the receiving and sending countries, there are again several levels to consider: the impacts on the communities from which the migrants come and to which they move, regional impacts, and effects on the countries as a whole. The effects are also likely to vary according to the migrants' legal status in the host countries and according to whether the decision to migrate was taken by the migrants

---

89. This was done despite the fact that around 1973–74, when the recruitment of new labor was halted by most European countries, Greece, along with Italy, already had the lowest rate of out-migration among the traditional Mediterranean sending countries. Both countries also had considerably higher rates of return migration throughout the 1970s than other sending countries, such as Portugal or Turkey.

90. The current patterns of movement between Canada and the United States probably correspond to most movements within the EEC. Taylor analyzed the recent population exchanges between the two countries according to detailed occupational classifications and found that in most classifications the *net* gains or losses experienced by the two countries are quite low. See Christoper E. Taylor, "Occupational Exchanges of Immigrants between Canada and the United States: 1973–1979," paper delivered at the Tenth World Congress of the International Sociological Association, Mexico City, August 16–21, 1982.

themselves or by family members whom they are following. These variables are in turn associated with migrant selectivity and may influence return orientations and patterns of migrants' integration into the host societies.

Effects on Migrants and Their Families

A large body of theoretical literature deals with the integration and assimilation of international migrants into host countries, in the context of immigrant states as well as in the recent year-round European labor migrations.[91] The variables used in these studies are primarily sociological and sociopsychological. I do not discuss these processes here because a separate paper in this volume by J. Milton Yinger is devoted to this topic.

Another group of studies throws light on the "economic progress" of immigrants. Chiswick asks how, other things being equal, immigrants compare in terms of economic success with native-born workers (as measured by yearly earnings).[92] His general findings concerning differences in earnings among successive immigrant generations within the same ethnic groups have already been noted. This generally observed pattern is found also with Mexican-Americans: over time, Mexican-American male immigrants catch up to U.S.-born males of Mexican origin, and a crossover occurs after about fifteen years (that is, the immigrants' earnings surpass those of the U.S.-born). The sons of Mexican immigrants have a clear earnings advantage over the sons of U.S.-born parents of Mexican origin, holding other variables constant. As noted earlier, Chiswick's explanation for this concerns the process of self-selection in migration.

---

91. See, for example, Milton Gordon, *Assimilation in American Life* (New York: Oxford University Press, 1964); Ronald Taft, *From Stranger to Citizen: A Survey of Studies of Immigrant Assimilation in Western Australia* (London: Tavistock Publications, 1966); Anthony H. Richmond, "Aspects of the Absorption and Adaptation of Immigrants," Canadian Immigration and Population Study (Ottawa: Information Canada, 1974); J. Ex, *Adjustment after Migration* (The Hague: Martinus Nijhoff, 1966); and S. N. Eisenstadt, *The Absorption of Immigrants* (London: Routledge and Kegan Paul, 1954). On year-round migrations, see Hartmut Esser, Eduard Gaugler, Karl-Heinz Neumann et al., *Arbeitsmigration und Integration: Sozialwissenschaftliche Grundlagen* (Königstein/Taunus, West Germany: Peter Hanstein Verlag, 1979); Hans-Joachim Hoffmann-Nowotny, *Soziologie des Fremdarbeiterproblems: Eine theoretische und empirische Analyse am Beispiel der Schweiz* (Stuttgart: Ferdinand Enke Verlag, 1973); and other citations in Rosemarie Rogers, "On the Process of International Migrants' Integration into Host Societies: A Hypothesis and Comments," Monograph C/78-16 (Cambridge, Mass.: Massachusetts Institute of Technology Center for International Studies, 1978).

92. Chiswick, "The Economic Progress of Immigrants."

However, compared with other ethnic groups in the United States, Mexican-Americans report very low average earnings. (In 1970 the figures for U.S.-born Mexican-Americans were barely higher than those for the U.S.-born black Americans, and average earnings for foreign-born Mexican-Americans were lower than those for foreign-born blacks.) Even with schooling, age, labor market experience, and other variables held constant, the earnings disadvantages with respect to other groups do not disappear: "Other things the same, first-, second-, and later-generation Mexican-Americans earn about 15 to 25 percent less than Anglos, and the difference does not appear to diminish between successive generations."[93]

Far less information is available on illegal migrants. For migrants with strong return orientations, their basis for evaluating their economic well-being lies in comparison with their standard of living in their home country, and it is the substantial wage differences between the two countries that attracted them in the first place. Some evidence concerning wages paid to illegal migrants will be noted in the discussion of their perceived labor market effects. What must also be recognized and studied are the psychic costs to illegal migrants of living in insecurity and sometimes in substandard conditions, and the costs to them and to their families of long separations.

Effects on Host Countries

Host countries admit immigrants in order to increase their populations and accelerate economic growth. In doing so they wish to avoid negative social, cultural, or political consequences of these migrations. They admit year-round workers, contract workers, and border commuters in order to benefit from migrants' economic contributions without increasing the domestic population in the long run. The potential fallacy of this expectation in some migration contexts has already been noted: the migrants become structural components of the economy in the host country; they cannot easily be dispensed with, and they can be periodically "exchanged" for other migrants only at the cost of considerable limitations to the migrants' personal freedom. When year-round migrants become long-term or permanent residents, questions of social, cultural, and political consequences come to the fore, as they do with immigrants.

The immigrants' contributions to a host country's population growth are often disproportionate to their numbers for two reasons. First, migrants tend to have higher fertility rates than the host

93. Ibid., p. 379.

populations.[94] Second, migrant groups tend to be disproportionately young. Thus, their contributions to population growth are likely to be disproportionate to their overall numbers, even when fertility rates are the same.

Concerning economic performance, immigrants with comparable training and skills have been found by Chiswick to compete well with native populations. Simon has analyzed the current immigrant population in the United States to determine whether, taken as a group, immigrants give more to the public coffers than they take from them.[95] His conclusion is that the public coffers gain because of the age composition of the migrant group. Although most countries receiving immigrants have recently tried to control more closely the skill composition of the immigrants they admit, the United States has not. It is almost unique today in its lack of emphasis on occupational criteria in immigrant selection. Approximately 80 percent of U.S. immigrants are selected without reference to occupational or skill criteria; nevertheless, two years after their arrival more than half of all immigrants have entered the labor market.

When migrants are only poorly or partially integrated into the host country economies (as, for example, when they have little employment security, are outside the trade union structures, or have little or no access to social services), their potential negative consequences for domestic labor markets are especially likely to be realized. One way to analyze the contribution of migrants to the labor force is to ask if they complement the domestic labor force or substitute for it. Substitution occurs when migrants work alongside domestic workers because there are not enough domestic workers to fill the jobs. This is the case in many economic sectors in the receiving countries in the Arab Middle East today, and it was the rationale for much of the labor migration within Europe. Complementarity refers to situations in which certain jobs are overwhelmingly filled by migrants. This is true, for example, of the majority of the construction industry in several oil-rich Arab countries. It has also been observed in certain industries in Europe and in the United States.[96]

Piore has offered a theoretical explanation for his observations on the dual or segmented labor markets in the United States.[97] The

---

94. See, for example, the data on Mexican immigrant women in the 1970 census in Ehrlich, Bilderback, and Ehrlich, *The Golden Door*, p. 326.
95. Julian L. Simon, "What Immigrants Take from, and Give to, the Public Coffers," unpublished document (University of Illinois at Champaign-Urbana, 1976).
96. On Europe, see Berrier, "The French Textile Industry."
97. Piore, *Birds of Passage*.

dual labor market hypothesis states that there are jobs waiting to be filled that domestic workers do not want to take because they are low paying, often unpleasant, and basically dead-end jobs. Piore argues that in the United States these jobs have been filled by wave after wave of migrants, internal as well as external, as the migrants' children or, at the latest, their grandchildren reject these jobs. Others reject this hypothesis by arguing that certain types of migrants are simply willing to work for very low wages because of the insecurity of their positions in the host countries and because their standards of reference are still conditions in their home countries, whether or not they will actually return there. In this scenario, the migrant workers depress wages and finally displace domestic workers who find it no longer worthwhile to take such low-paying jobs. Much of the current discussion in the United States concerning the economic consequences of illegal migrants, border commuters, and H-2 workers, as well as of proposals to expand the H-2 program or to institute other temporary worker programs, revolves around this issue.

The evidence brought to bear on the question is of three kinds. The first consists of comparisons of cities or counties or regions in which the proportion of foreign migrants in the local populations varies inversely with current wage rates or directly with rates of unemployment.[98]

A second kind of evidence is provided by illegal migrants' own reports on their employment experiences, including the wages they were paid (which on average seem to be higher than the federal minimum in the case of non-Mexican illegals, but "near the federal minimum" in the case of apprehended Mexican illegals).[99] The problem with these surveys is that we do not know how representative any group of respondents is of the total undocumented population.

A third form of evidence consists of case studies from which conclusions are drawn. For example, when the Immigration and Naturalization Service has raided a work place and apprehended illegal workers, what happens to the jobs that become available?[100] If

---

98. See Sidney Weintraub and Stanley R. Ross, *The Illegal Alien from Mexico: Policy Choices for an Intractable Issue*, Mexico-United States Border Research Program (Austin: University of Texas, 1980), pp. 18 and 26–28 for a review of a number of studies on Mexican illegals; see also, U.S. Commission on Civil Rights, "The Commuter on the United States-Mexico Border," pp. 226–31; Ericson, "The Impact of Commuters," pp. 240–45; Fogel, *Mexican Illegal Alien Workers*, pp. 119–30; and Cross and Sandos, *Across the Border*, pp. 84–92.

99. Fogel, *Mexican Illegal Alien Workers*, pp. 89–92.

100. A recent example of such an analysis, which made headlines in the *New York Times*, is Donald L. Huddle, "Illegal Immigrant Workers: Benefits and Costs to the Host Country in the Context of the Immigration and Naturalization Service Raids—

the jobs are offered again at the same wages and working conditions and domestic workers refuse to take them, we still do not know whether they would have taken them had the jobs been upgraded. In addition, the length of such investigations tends to be short. If the jobs are in fact filled by domestic workers after the raid, will the turnover in the following months be greater than with illegal workers, leading the employers to *prefer* illegal help?

The evidence suggests, not surprisingly, that migrant labor both complements the domestic labor force and substitutes for it. Migrants fill secondary jobs that domestic workers are not interested in, and some job displacement occurs. The major problem lies in determining the particular mix of these two processes, and it seems that no one knows.

Another economic question concerns how much illegal migrants cost the public coffers. Cross and Sandos have brought together evidence from a variety of studies that shows a considerable range in the incidence of taxes deducted, income tax reports filed, receipt of welfare and unemployment benefits, and use of health and educational facilities.[101] The wide range of data depends on the particular "samples." Apprehended illegal migrants tend to have made relatively little use of social services and not to have claimed tax refunds; but some community impact studies are probably biased toward long-term illegal residents and overstate the average use of services. On the whole it is probable that the direct effects are fairly small, but the argument really must be brought back to the question of job displacement. If considerable job displacement occurs, the cost of illegal migrants may be greater, because their taxes and social security contributions would probably not make up for unemployment compensation and other payments made to the displaced domestic workers.

The question of the migrants' social, cultural, and political effects on the host countries arises primarily as a settling-in process takes place, regardless of the migrants' legal status. Many studies on the adjustment of migrants suggest that structural integration into the economy and society of the host country usually precedes cultural integration. Where cultural integration occurs, it may vary from more pluralistic to more assimilationist integration, depending on host country conditions and on the migrants themselves. Contract workers

---

Project Jobs," unpublished manuscript (Houston, Texas: William Marsh Rice University, December 28, 1982).

101. Cross and Sandos, *Across the Border*, pp. 96–106.

and year-round workers with limited personal freedom in the host country are not likely to enter much into the host countries' cultures.

Politically, migrants have been of interest to certain parties in the host countries that hoped to gain votes from their incorporation into the polity. In several European countries, West Germany and Austria prominent among them, debates over the past two decades concerning the status of year-round workers have taken shape to a considerable extent along party lines, the social democratic parties leaning more toward full incorporation of the foreign populations into their countries than have the conservative parties. Sweden offers an interesting example of what can be expected to happen when foreigners are incorporated into a polity. Foreigners fulfilling certain residence requirements have been permitted to vote in local and provincial elections. Although the foreign voters registered a slightly greater preference for the socialist parties than did the Swedish population as a whole, these differences were smaller than those between social classes (paralleling the findings on the Swedish voters); there were also some differences by nationality.[102]

Another consequence to the host countries arises from the fact that some migrants "bring their home country politics with them." This has been a factor to reckon with in recent European history. There have been several confrontations among migrants belonging to different political factions in their home country politics (notably Turks in Germany).

One of the most striking effects of migration is, of course, the establishment, and maintenance, of ethnic communities in the host countries. In this respect the situation of Mexican-Americans in the United States in unique in a number of ways. One unique consideration is the fact that a part of that community is descended from a conquered people, some of the communities predating the current borders; and it is to this same region that the largest proportion of newly arriving Mexicans still migrates. Moreover, the migrants' home country is next door to the United States. Finally, there is the presence of a Spanish-speaking continent next door—one of the important factors contributing to this ethnic group's prospects for language maintenance.

Effects on Sending Countries

The effects of out-migration on the sending countries can be treated under three headings: the immediate effects, such as reduction

---

102. Tomas Hammar, "Citizenship, Aliens' Political Rights, and Politicians' Concern for Migrants: The Case of Sweden," in Rogers, ed., *Guests Come to Stay.*

of unemployment and loss of skilled manpower; the effects of remittances; and the effects of return migration. These subjects have received increasing research attention in recent years, so that there is now a large body of findings. Nevertheless, we still know far too little even in a descriptive sense about these effects, let alone being able to account for the differences from context to context. Much of the literature is anecdotal or focuses on small communities, so that it is impossible to generalize from the findings. Few of the analyses go beyond a listing of simple, direct effects to an investigation of more complex, indirect ones. And finally, there is often a judgmental tone to the analyses; the returnees, for example, are expected to perform superhuman feats in "developing" their community or region, and when this does not happen they are judged as falling short of—what? the analyst's expectations?

Manpower. In a masterly analysis of the effects of Turkish labor migration on the sending country, Ebiri showed that out-migration from the mid-1960s to mid-1970s had a measurable effect on the volume of surplus labor in Turkey, reducing it by one-quarter. He also found that participation in the labor force markedly decreased in the same period. After rejecting several other explanations, he attributed this as an indirect effect to labor migration (that is, persons in certain households apparently did not seek work because they were supported by migrants' remittances).[103] The out-migration from Turkey included substantial numbers of skilled workers. One might assume this meant enormous losses to the sending country, but again Ebiri suggests a more complex analysis. He argues that in order to understand the real consequences of the out-migration of skilled workers, it is necessary to examine (1) the composition of skills and their relative scarcity, (2) the changes in organization of production that are stimulated by the loss of skilled workers, and (3) the real value of these workers' skills to the economy. By this type of analysis he established that although one sector, the Turkish manufacturing industry, was indeed negatively affected by the loss of skills, other sectors with proportionately even greater out-migration did not suffer.

Bustamante and Martinez report results from the second survey by the National Center of Labor Statistics and Information on undocumented Mexican migrants expelled from the United States, which show these migrants to have a higher educational level than the Mexican national average.[104] The researchers suggest that even

---

103. Kutlay Ebiri, "Impact of Labor Migration on the Turkish Economy," in Rogers, ed., *Guests Come to Stay.*

104. Bustamente and Martinez, "Undocumented Immigration from Mexico," pp. 282–83.

though these migrants return to Mexico, this is "a drain of human capital and a kind of subsidy [to the host country] that has not been yet conceptualized in the balance of payments between the two countries." I question whether any conclusions on costs and benefits can be drawn from such data by themselves.

It has been noted in several migration contexts (for example, in parts of Yugoslavia and Spain in the 1960s and 1970s) that rural areas of out-migration experience considerable population drain, that the majority of young men leave, and that the dependency ratios increase. Again one must ask further questions. To what extent do women and older men take over the work satisfactorily? And, even more important, is it perhaps true that agriculture was becoming less profitable for these villagers, and migration is a *consequence* of this fact, rather than a direct cause?

Another "skill" drain sometimes noted in the literature, usually in a type of counterfactual analysis, refers to migration as a "safety valve." The argument runs that if there had been no out-migration and there had been so many more unemployed workers in the country, the people would have revolted; or, that migration "syphons off" some of the people who would be the best motivated to bring about social change. These hypotheses certainly deserve further research. The safety-valve hypothesis is not infrequently encountered in the literature on Mexico.[105]

Remittances. Remittances and otherwise repatriated savings are very important to the subsistence of the migrant families left behind. Studies of Mexican migration to the United States contain various estimates of how many hundreds of thousands or millions of individuals in the home country depend (or depended) on support from the earnings of braceros, illegal migrants, and border commuters.[106]

In many European countries one important use of remittances— and an explicit target for many migrants—has been the building of a house or the improvement of an existing one. Remittances are used to buy various consumer items and to pay for the education of children. Sometimes they are used to buy agricultural machinery or more land, or they are an important basis for obtaining additional credits for a project from home country banks. Until recently the

---

105. Cross and Sandos, for example, argue it with specific reference to the north central region. Cross and Sandos, *Across the Border*, pp. 41–43.

106. Ibid., pp. 114–115; Wayne A. Cornelius, "Mexican Migration to the United States: Causes, Consequences, and U.S. Responses," Monograph C/78–9 (Cambridge: Massachusetts Institute of Technology Center for International Studies, 1978); Kiser and Kiser, *Mexican Workers in the United States*, p. 215.

European literature has criticized the migrants and their families for not using remittances more "productively," a criticism that suffers from inadequate analysis. In some contexts remittances pay for goods that governments would otherwise attempt to provide (for example, subsidized housing in Algeria), thereby freeing government funds for other uses; they are also used for job creation, but again little is known about the frequency of these efforts. Another negative effect of remittances that is often mentioned is their inflationary impact. The argument appears to be logical but it is usually made without supporting data.

Remittances make a contribution at the macroeconomic level to the sending countries' balances of payments. Of course, the countries remain vulnerable to the possibility of sharp fluctuations in remittances, whether as a result of changes in economic conditions in the host countries, or of migrants' responses to fluctuations in exchange rates that may influence them to use black market channels instead. In the case of many sending countries, the influx of foreign exchange through migrant remittances exceeds that from tourism. For Mexico, Cornelius estimated remittances from illegal migrants to be "probably in excess of $2 billion per year";[107] the United Nations cites an estimate by North and Houstoun of $1.5 billion annually but notes that "studies undertaken by the Mexican Government have placed the amount at nearer to $300 million."[108]

Return migration and employment creation. Within the overall subject of the impact of migration on sending countries, return migration is probably the area in which knowledge is weakest. Many researchers suggest that the returnees are negatively selected from among the total migrant population. But a study of Puerto Rican return migration, based on census data as well as on a comprehensive survey, shows there can be among a returning population many different streams, including a group of highly selected migrants.[109] These migrants were the least likely to return to the rural areas of Puerto Rico; they tended rather to settle in the capital or in other prospering cities. This is not an isolated pattern, yet many studies that discuss the "conservative" nature of return migrants are based on data collected solely in rural areas.[110]

107. Cornelius, "Mexican Migration to the United States," p. 46.
108. United Nations Department of International Economic and Social Affairs, *International Migration Policies,* p. 65.
109. Hernandez Alvarez, *Return Migration to Puerto Rico.*
110. See the discussion in Rosemarie Rogers, "Return Migration in Comparative Perspective," in Daniel Kubat, ed., *The Politics of Return* (Rome: Center for Migration Studies, 1984), pp. 277–99.

Discussions of employment creation by returning migrants suffer especially from sampling problems. What is lacking (and what is admittedly costly to undertake) are broadly designed surveys that study the incidence of different types of returns. With regard to Mexico, one often-cited example of successful employment creation is that of a small textile industry established in a part of Jalisco, which was observed by Diez-Cañedo.[111] Cross and Sandos supply examples from Michoacan.[112]

Several European sending countries have seen attempts at creating new industrial employment by groups of returning migrants or of migrant "investors" still in the host countries, usually in collaboration with banks or government authorities in the sending countries.[113] In my study in Yugoslavia I found considerable variation, from project to project, in the sociodemographic backgrounds of the participating migrants; the most highly skilled returnees, however, were more likely to become self-employed than to participate in these projects.[114]

Finally, there is little systematic evidence on changes in social and political attitudes among migrants who have returned and on the impact that such changes *exert* on the patterns of their reinsertion into the host countries. The effects of migration on fertility levels of returning migrants are also an underresearched topic.

Conclusions

The foregoing discussion has identified a number of parallels between Mexican migration and other migratory flows. It has shown that Mexico is certainly not unusual with respect to determinants of its out-migration. Moreover, there are several parallels to be drawn about the impact that migration exerts upon the sending country: certain areas in the sending country become highly dependent on remittances, and international migration becomes an alternative to internal migration. And when Mexican documented immigration is placed within the framework of the entire experience of the United

---

111. Juan Diez-Cañedo, "Mexican Migration to the United States," paper prepared for the Workshop on Comparative Labor Movements, Harvard University Center for European Studies, Cambridge, Mass., October 14–16, 1977.

112. Cross and Sandos, *Across the Border*, p. 45.

113. Most of these efforts are reviewed in Rogers, "Incentives to Return"; for Greece, see Ross Fakiolas, "Problems and Opportunities of the Greek Migrants Returning from Western Europe," unpublished paper (Athens: Centre of Planning and Economic Research, 1980).

114. Rosemarie Rogers, "Social Sector Employment Creation in Yugoslavia: the Migrants' Contributions through Investments and Return," in Rosemarie Rogers and Klaus Unger, eds., *Return Migration to the Mediterranean Littoral: Strategies and Their Implementations* (in preparation).

States, it appears that Mexico did not begin to play a numerically important role until the 1920s (when the pattern of relative preponderance of only a few migration streams was already less marked than it had been in the preceding century).

In other ways migration from Mexico to the United States is an atypical or even a unique phenomenon. Certain uncommon geographical and historical conditions suggest that the movement of people between the two countries should itself have some special features. The geographical condition is of course the border of 2,000 miles that separates two countries with substantially different standards of living. The division of language and national groups by international borders is hardly unique to the Mexican-U.S. case; but this situation, combined with a border separating two countries that are quite unequal in population pressures and standards of living, probably is.

The historical condition lies in the fact that the American Southwest was once part of Mexico, so that the people living there who are descended from the Spanish settlers can indeed say, "We did not migrate to the United States—the United States came to us." As a result, there was throughout the latter half of the nineteenth century and into this century a good deal of informal movement across the border, especially short-term, circular migration. This migration had the flavor of an internal movement more than of an international one. Some cases that might suggest parallels, however weak, turn out not to provide them: the substantial Italian migration to Switzerland since World War II, for example, does not seem to have been particularly aided or otherwise influenced by the fact that there exists an Italian-Swiss "charter group," nor has the Croatian minority in Austria played a role in receiving the labor migrants who came from Croatia in the 1960s and 1970s. Still another unique feature of the Mexican migration pattern is the incidence of Mexican migrants who have had a variety of different migratory statuses.

Even today much migration from Mexico to the United States is circular migration. This is particularly important with respect to Mexican migrants who are in fact legal immigrants.[115] Although circular migration is not unique to Mexicans, the frequency with which it occurs probably is. The bracero experience, on the other hand, is unequaled in the history of migration to the United States, and memory of that experience affects current discussions of large-scale contract labor systems as a policy option. It fitted the pattern of circular migration, which at the beginning of the bracero program

---

115. Reichert and Massey, "History and Trends."

was already established as a pattern of primarily undocumented migration. And the bracero experience itself served as an additional stimulus to undocumented migration.

Many Mexicans now have a "culture of migration"—that is, an acceptance of migration as a way of life, and the motivation to migrate in whatever status (legal or illegal) is available to the individual. Reichert and Massey found in a Michoacan town (where they divided former braceros into five cohorts according to the date of their first trip to the United States) that from 50 to 83 percent of former braceros in the different cohorts eventually obtained U.S. resident visas while 11 to 25 percent of these former braceros were now migrating illegally.[116] Moreover, some migrants who had first migrated illegally later obtained U.S. resident visas.

Some Mexican migrants, of course, settle in the United States, and this group includes not only legal but also undocumented migrants. In their choice of destinations they still favor the Southwest, as do the migrants who shuttle back and forth between Mexico and the United States. Heer's careful estimate of the yearly net flow of illegal migrants from Mexico far exceeds the current yearly quota of 20,000 legal immigrant admissions (except for close family members who are admitted outside the numerical limits).[117]

The U.S. experience in the 1920s with respect to migration from the Eastern Hemisphere and the European experience of the 1970s have shown that the incidence of spontaneous returns decreases when more restrictive legislation is enacted or existing legislation is more strictly enforced. This prospect may pose something of a dilemma to host country policymakers who want to exercise stricter controls on immigration. Might it not better serve their goals to simply maintain the status quo? Or, in the case of Mexican-U.S. migration, can a new equilibrium perhaps be found through the provision of a larger yearly quota for legal immigration—as proposed, for example, in 1984 in the Simpson-Mazzoli bill? The enactment of such migration legislation would constitute a transition step from a unique informal relationship between two countries—in light of the memory of periodic deportations of undocumented migrants and of the bracero experience—to a situation in which Mexico, along with Canada, would occupy an officially recognized and legally sanctioned special position as a migrant-sending country on the North American continent.

116. Ibid., p. 481. The illegal migrants were found only in the three more recent bracero cohorts, that is, among those who had migrated for the first time in 1950 or later.
117. In van Arsdol et al., *Non-Apprehended and Apprehended Undocumented Residents.*

CHAPTER SEVEN

In a paraphrase of the New Testament's injunction, Kwame Nkrumah, a former head of Ghana, once advised his disciples: "Seek ye first the political kingdom, and all these things shall be added unto you." In multinational societies, politics conventionally takes on an ethnic cast and, in extreme cases such as Sri Lanka, Uganda, and Zimbabwe, it could be described, not too hyperbolically, as the continuation of ethnic warfare by other means. On the outcome of the political struggle may depend such issues as whose language is to be the official language, the language of school instruction, and the language of examinations for university admissions and civil service positions. More important is the question of which ethnic groups will dominate the military, the constabulary, and the secret police?

The immigrant society has certainly not been free of ethnic politics. Throughout much of U.S. history, even foreign observers considered the country to be ruled by an Anglo-Saxon elite, as witness the 1921 statement of the British prime minister: "The people who govern America are our people. They are our kith and kin. The other breeds are not on top. It is the men of our race who govern in America. I do not know whether they are in the minority or not, but in the main they are on top." Despite the prime minister's complacency, the ethnonational mix within the United States was changing rapidly. Americans of non-English descent were increasingly filling positions of political influence, and, within four decades of the prime minister's statement, a person of Irish ancestry was to occupy the country's highest and most powerful office.

A key factor in bringing about this change had been the mobilization of ethnic groups for political action. Regard for "the ethnic vote" became reflected in both the policies and lists of candidates of the major political parties. In the short run, political mobilization proved an effective brake upon ethnic discrimination and, in the longer run, an important step in the Americanization process. But what of Mexican-Americans? In the following essay, Nathan Glazer stresses that the attitudes of the larger community

205

will materially affect the capacity of Mexican-Americans to become politically effective. Using a comparative perspective, he notes several structural factors that might cause the experience of the Mexican-Americans to diverge from the path followed by earlier immigrant groups. But he also notes powerful countervailing forces pressing for integration.

THE POLITICAL DISTINCTIVENESS OF THE MEXICAN-AMERICANS

Nathan Glazer

Comparative ethnic studies might encompass comparisons of ethnic situations throughout the world. But one can more narrowly, and more fruitfully, compare the experience of previous immigrants to the United States with current immigrant groups in this country. Even this more limited comparison raises problems, although it does not compel us to deal with the bewildering array of forms of political community around the world. The United States, despite the enormous changes that have affected it since previous waves of immigrants were subjects of public concern, remains in many ways the same country today as yesterday. Its Constitution (though variously interpreted over the years), its federalism (and its variation from state to state), its advanced economic structure (which has undergone enormous and increasingly rapid change), and its social character as a multiethnic, multiracial, immigrant state, (to use the term that Walker Connor has so usefully defined) remain as constants.

We might well have limited our comparative studies to other immigrant states because the ethnic situation in immigrant states is so different from that in nation-states or multinational states. Thus our points of comparison might have been Argentina and Brazil, Australia and Canada. Indeed, we might have further limited our comparisons to immigrant states of Anglo-Saxon origin—Australia and, in measure, Canada. However, even our neighbor Canada has a very different social situation as a binational state and even the portion of Canada of Anglo-Saxon origin takes an approach to ethnicity rather different from the approach found in the United States. I have therefore chosen to compare our present immigration situation with our own past as an immigrant state.[1]

1. Mexico is a multiethnic state, not an immigrant state, but it does not view itself as a multiethnic state. I suspect in this conference dealing with a comparative view of the Mexican-American situation, hardly anyone will draw examples or lessons from

In analyzing political mobilization, this is certainly the most useful scope of comparison. We only have to consider political mobilization occurring within an American framework structured by the Constitution, federal and state law, formal and informal political structures, and a unified history—specifically, the memories as to what political behavior is appropriate for immigrant and ethnic groups. A cumulative memory, altered by nostalgia, willed distortion, and simple lack of information, deeply affects the response of other Americans to the political behavior of Mexican-Americans. Laws fashioned in other times for other groups in response to other needs affect what Mexican-Americans can do. Political structures, state and local, determine their capacity to become politically effective.

Scope of the Problem: The Role of History

It is within the context of our own past that the Mexican-American "problem" must be analyzed. Do we expect Mexican-Americans to follow the path of previous immigrant groups? (Referring to *one* path is an idealization, but it is basically an accurate formulation.) Or do we expect something different? If we expect something different, is this something that is dangerous to the degree of unity that we have come to expect—not great compared with what other countries expect—in American society, in American politics, in the projection of American ideals and interests to the world? This is the question underlying the surface concerns of most Americans about Mexican-Americans. It was expressed in Senator S.I. Hayakawa's proposed constitutional amendment, now taken up by the organization "U.S. English," to make English the national language of the United States and in the efforts of FAIR (Federation for Immigration Reform) to restrict immigration. But the concern, often not directly expressed, is far more widespread than the influence of these two groups.

What *is* the common expectation concerning the political path of immigrant ethnic groups in the United States? The existing model is for *large* groups; it is predicated on studies of the Irish, Jews, and

---

Mexico as a multiethnic state. Is this because it is at a different stage of economic development? Or is it because Mexico has successfully obscured this aspect of its social structure, projecting instead a unified Mexico, in which the Indian element is ideologically paramount even if this element actually has only limited power and influence? Tourists are told that there is no statue of Cortes in Mexico City. The murals make it quite clear that the Spanish invaders are to be considered aggressors rather than participants in the creation of a unified Mexican society.

Italians, as well as of Germans of an earlier period. Some smaller groups, such as the Greeks, have had remarkable political success. Massachusetts, where there are few Greeks, has a Greek-origin governor and a Greek-origin senator. We have had a Greek-origin vice president of the United States. But the general focus of our studies and our concerns is understandably on large groups, for they can swing some weight. But what is large? If we take the Jews as the smallest of the large groups I have mentioned we are talking about groups of at least 5 or 6 million people. Such groups may have both national influence and local influence in different parts of the country.

Americans generally expect large ethnic groups to become acculturated to American politics, organizing around a combination of interests that affect all people in a given economic or occupational situation, as well as around interests specific to the group itself. The Irish—by far the most successful ethnic group in U.S. politics—reflected this mix of interests. Originally poor and uneducated urban laborers, they had to be concerned about their economic situation. Entering politics in the mid- and later-nineteenth century, when public social policy did not exist, they expressed their general interest by attempting to control the jobs that the local political machine could give out. More specifically, the Irish opposed Protestant control of schools, supported Ireland's struggle for independence against England, opposed England in general, and opposed Prohibition.

This mix of the general and the ethnic, or the class- and interest-based and the value- and emotion-based issues, is characteristic for all ethnic groups. Later, when government was becoming involved in protecting the interests of workers, Irish political leaders such as Al Smith were among the leaders in social reform. Speaker of the House Thomas P. ("Tip") O'Neill still represents this tradition and this mix—although by now most of the Irish have moved to the suburbs and few are poor and uneducated workers (except in the Boston area, which has continuously attracted Irish immigrants).

Longer settled groups have always feared that new immigrant groups might prove disloyal. Thus we have a long history of efforts to suppress schools where the teaching is in foreign languages, and parochial schools, efforts that reached peaks in the later 1880s and in the 1920s. The fear of disloyalty was so pronounced that German-Americans as a distinct and self-assertive ethnic group more or less went underground in World War I. By World War II, few people worried that German-Americans (or Italian-Americans, more recent immigrants) might be disloyal. But Japanese-Americans were made to suffer far more than had the Germans in World War I.

One element, then, in our perceived history is that although new immigrant groups may be viewed with suspicion, in time they become good Americans—acculturated, assimilated, participating fully in American politics, and eschewing undue interest in the affairs of their home countries. Most Americans benignly accept the fact that an immigrant group's interests in politics reflect its class, occupation, and region, plus the distinctive interests that arise from its ethnic status and specifically its relationship to a homeland. Thus the American public accepts the hostility of Greek-Americans to military aid to Turkey. This stance outrages American military and strategic planners who think that Turkey is much more important than Greece in maintaining the line of defense against the Soviet Union (because it shares a common border) and is far more dependable as an ally against the Soviet Union. But the political influence of Greek-Americans (there are few Turks in the United States) means that military aid to both countries must remain equal.[2]

This commonly accepted history of assimilation, in which the interest of immigrant groups in homeland and ethnic issues declines and interests based on class and occupational characteristics rise, is of course not the true history for all groups. Nevertheless, it is what we generally *expect* in this country.

However, a group's involvement with a homeland interest may raise questions of dual loyalty ("hyphenated Americans," as Theodore Roosevelt called it in World War I) and therefore of potential conflict between loyalty to the United States and loyalty to a homeland when the interests of the two countries diverge.[3] America's Jewish population is now in this position. Jews have had great economic and occupational success and are represented in Congress in substantially greater number than their proportion of the American population. (Their overrepresentation is less marked if we take into account the group's high average age and vigorous participation as voters and contributors to political campaigns.) Because of their economic success, Jewish political figures have few important domestic interests

2. There are 959,856 Greeks versus a mere 64,691 Turks in the United States (*Ancestry of the Population by State: 1980, Census of Population, Supplementary Report*, PC80-S1-10). But numbers alone are no index to influence—there are only 76,170 Greeks in Massachusetts. Wealth, education, and organization are also important to political influence. For many ethnically identified persons in politics, the ethnic connection plays little role in attainment of influence or in definition of their political position. But this is not generally the case with persons from new immigrant groups who attain elective office.

3. For an important study of ethnic group involvement in foreign policy, see Louis L. Gerson, *The Hyphenate in Recent American Politics and Diplomacy* (Lawrence: University of Kansas Press, 1964).

that they must pursue for their own group. The only Jewish issue that most Jewish elected officials pursue is that of the security of Israel. When the issue of anti-Semitism was raised in the 1984 Democratic primary campaign, it was in connection with Jesse Jackson's remarks indicating annoyance at Jews for opposing him because of his positions on the Middle East conflict. (This is very far from the anti-Semitism of the past, in which Jews were attacked as Jews because of their role in the United States—in supporting Bolshevism, or undermining morals, or opposing Christianity.)

Because of the Israeli situation, we find Jews diverging from the common expectation that elected officials from a long-settled and successful ethnic group will represent their district or their party rather than championing special causes of that group. We expect elected representatives of groups that are recent immigrants, poor, or recently emerged from exclusion from politics (for example, Hispanic-Americans and black Americans) to be wrapped up in the problems of their group. Indeed, both Hispanic and black members of Congress represent their respective groups very directly because almost all are elected from districts in which their group constitutes a substantial majority.

The Jewish members of Congress once also almost exclusively represented districts with a majority of Jews. In recent years, although the number of Jewish-dominated districts has declined the number of Jewish representatives has risen. Few now run for office as Jews; instead they run as Democrats, liberals, business leaders, lawyers, or less commonly, as Republicans. The same is true of members of Congress of Irish origin and of German origin. As ethnic minorities become integrated into the common political culture, elected officials of a given ethnic origin have less need to support specific ethnic issues. Thus German-Americans in Congress do not particularly represent German-American interests.

The long period that has elapsed since their mass emigration to this country tends to reduce the identity of an ethnic group. But groups who perceive their homeland as being in peril may delay this attenuation of specific ethnic interests over time. Thus elected officials of Irish descent have had as long a history in this country as Germans, but to a much greater extent the Irish become involved in homeland issues. American political figures of Irish descent—Senator Edward Kennedy, Senator Daniel P. Moynihan, Congressman Thomas P. ("Tip") O'Neill, former New York governor Hugh Carey, and others— whatever the attenuation of their ties to Ireland, are forced to take stands on the conflict in Northern Ireland because it is *there*.

The Jewish situation is unique in that their "homeland" is not really a homeland in the usual sense. Few American Jews come from Israel (the Bureau of the Census publication *Ancestry of the Population* reports 53,000 Israelis although other estimates of Israelis in the United States run to over 300,000). But as a created homeland surrounded by enemies since its creation in 1948, Israel arouses more commitment from American Jews than do their actual homelands (as defined by the Census Bureau). For example, most Jews are indifferent to the fate of Poland, the census-definition homeland of perhaps half of all American Jews, but a country which is now nearly devoid of Jews. Similarly, the Jews' principal interest in the Soviet Union concerns whether and how Russian Jews can leave it.

American Jews thus raise for us the question of the circumstances under which loyalty to another state—ever the underlying concern of Americans to immigration—may rise to the surface. Jewish loyalty to the United States has not been questioned because there are so few Arabs here to raise it and because Israel is an ally of the United States (but then, perhaps Israel is an ally because 6 million American Jews have influenced American politics in this direction).

Structural Features and Their Effects on Acculturation and Assimilation

One raises the question of loyalty because it is the basic and final issue, not because it is an obvious issue. Mexican-Americans seem to have no great interest in homeland issues, and they seem to have no great interest—no more than that of other Americans—in Latin American issues.[4] This makes sense. Many Mexican-Americans come from rural settings, in which the sense of Mexico as a nation may be weak. Others have long been settled in this country. Moreover, Mexico does not appeal to U.S. citizens of Mexican origin to support Mexico's interests in this country; these interests extend to trade, investment, and emigration, but Mexican-Americans are not specially involved in these issues, except for immigration, and Mexican-American attitudes there are not determined by a concern for Mexico.

---

4. See the excellent treatment of the loyalty question in Walker Connor's paper, earlier in this volume, chapter 1, and to references therein. The evidence in a number of Rodolfo de la Garza's papers is convincing. See his "Chicanos and U.S. Foreign Policy: The Future of Chicano-Mexican Relations," *Western Political Quarterly*, vol. 33 (1980), pp. 571–582; and "Chicano-Mexican Relations: A Framework for Research," *Social Science Quarterly*, vol. 63 (1982), pp. 115–30.

One suspects this situation is similar to that of Italian immigrants of the late nineteenth and early twentieth centuries to this country, who had no strong sense of Italy as a nation, and who, it has been suggested, "became" Italian (rather than Apulians or Sicilians or Calabrians) in this country, where they became aware of their larger identity. Perhaps this is true of Mexican-Americans as well. After all, it is not the leaders of Mexican society and politics, business leaders and political figures, or the inhabitants of Mexico City who emigrate to the United States. Nevertheless, despite Mexican-Americans' very low degree of political identification with Mexico today, its possibility remains a concern for many Americans.

Statements by some Chicano intellectuals, during the rise of the Chicano movement in the 1970s, might have aroused fears as to their loyalty to the United States. (The same fears could have been aroused then, of course, and perhaps even more so, by some extremist black intellectuals and political leaders.) We quite properly see that period as one of extreme views espoused by a minority for only a short period of time. Even the term *Chicano*, now enshrined in the names of research and teaching centers that have become more moderate over time, was never the preferred term of more than a small minority of Mexican-Americans.

Current concerns of Mexican-Americans are such matters as employment, inflation, police protection, and better education—concerns related to the economic and social position of Mexican-Americans, rather than to any involvement with Mexico. "When asked what were the principal issues facing the Chicano community, over sixty Hispanic political appointees in Washington. D.C., and legislators in Texas responded by identifying [issues such as police brutality, housing, employment, and education]. Not one mentioned immigration or any other international issue."[5] The result would undoubtedly be different today, but even now, concern with immigration is predicated on the assumed interests of the Mexican-American and Hispanic communities, not on any Mexican national interest. Mexican-American leaders have come to oppose immigration control because they see it as a possible mechanism to increase discrimination against Hispanic-Americans, not because Mexico needs emigration to control population and unemployment and to bring in foreign exchange.

The Mexican-American rank and file probably would have a list of concerns different from the concerns of their leaders. Although a comparable survey for leaders was not available, a recent survey of

---

5. De la Garza, "Chicanos and U.S. Foreign Policy," p. 580.

Mexican-Americans in San Antonio and Los Angeles showed that most considered inflation (45 percent of the respondents) and unemployment (28 percent) to be the main problems facing the country—responses not particularly different at that time from those of other Americans. As an issue, immigration was not evident among the responses.

Although the heated rhetoric of the early 1970s has now generally abated,[7] the future political development of a population group that is in the midst of such rapid change in a country that is itself changing rapidly cannot be forecast with any certainty. The political orientations of Mexican-Americans have already changed in the past fifteen or twenty years. For example, in the 1950s and 1960s Mexican-American political groups and leaders were prominent in the demand for control of illegal immigration; they saw illegal immigration as a threat to the position of resident Mexican-Americans, creating competition for jobs and driving down wages. The debate of 1984 makes it clear there has been a great shift among Mexican-Americans against effective immigration control. One cynic (but a very well-informed one) writes:

> In the 1940's and 1950's Mexican-American organizations, like the American G.I. Forum and the League of United Latin American Citizens, were conspicuous leaders in demanding wetback control. Today many such leaders have gone "Chicano". . . . The *mojado* is no longer seen as a threat, but as a racial and political reinforcement. And the Chicano liberationists find they no longer need or want the jobs taken by the newcomers. . . . Political climates have been so changed by ethnic populism that immigration-enforcement officials. . .have been reduced to pleading their case, like any other client group in the Great Society.[8]

---

6. Rodolfo de la Garza and Robert R. Brischetto, with the assistance of David Vaughan, *The Mexican American Electorate: Information Sources and Policy Orientations,* Mexican American Electorate Series, Occasional Paper no. 2, Southwest Voter Registration Project, San Antonio, Texas, and the Hispanic Population Studies Program of the Center for Mexican American Studies, University of Texas, Austin, 1983, p. 8.

7. The heated rhetoric has not completely abated. See, for example, the Declaration of Albuquerque of 1979 and the Bill of Rights for the Undocumented Worker adopted at a conference in Mexico City in 1980, and other statements in Antonio Rios-Bustamente, *Mexican Immigrant Workers in the U.S.,* Anthology no. 2 (University of California, Los Angeles, Chicano Studies Research Center Publications, 1981), pp. xiv, 177–78. These and other statements (in this publication and elsewhere) assume that the United States has no right to control immigration from Mexico or to distinguish between the rights of U.S. citizens of Mexican origin and noncitizens of Mexican origin. These extreme claims are somewhat legitimated by the special relationship between Mexico and the United States. Of course, they can also be dismissed as mere rhetoric or as extreme demands that no one expects to be adopted.

8. Arthur F. Corwin, *Immigrants . . . And Immigrants: Perspectives in Mexican Labor Migration to the United States* (Westport, Conn.: Greenwood Press, 1978), p. 73.

Or, consider the picture of Mexican-American political effectiveness in the classic 1970 work by Leo Grebler, Joan W. Moore, and Ralph Guzman, *The Mexican American People:*

> The political effectiveness of the Mexican-American minority in the Southwest has been handicapped by internal disunity, by external restraints imposed through voting laws and procedures, by the gerrymandering of election districts. In addition, many urban Mexican Americans are relatively recent migrants from rural areas and have probably maintained the limited view of their own potential role in political life that was derived from their experience in small towns and in the countryside. The low naturalization rate of the Mexican aliens has been an important factor in keeping the political effectiveness of the whole group below its potential.[9]

This, as the authors themselves later point out, may have been overstating the case of Mexican-American passivity even then, but certainly we have seen two substantial changes that these authors probably never foresaw: (1) strong laws passed in 1975 and 1982 protecting the political rights of Mexican-Americans and (2) a greater degree of political mobilization among Mexican-Americans. We should not, however, draw any simple conclusions from the degree of political participation among Mexican-Americans. By "simple" conclusions I mean the deduction that Mexican-Americans are less "American" because they don't become citizens, register, and vote in high proportions, or that they are more "American" because they do.

Increased involvement in the American political process will not necessarily forestall potential conflict and divisiveness in the future. Certainly German-Americans were deeply involved in American politics; yet World War I led to a huge attack on their loyalty, resulting in the virtual disappearance of German-Americans as a distinctive ethnic element in the United States.[10] Similarly, Jewish-Americans are active participants in the American political process. But the future fate of Israel, its internal politics, external problems, and relations with the United States have the potential of introducing enormous strains on American Jews.

Other unexpected changes in the Mexican-American situation have come about in the past twenty years. One is an enormous increase in Mexican-American immigration, and a surprising—in view of our past history of immigration control—inability to come to a national consensus on the matter. Once again, it is striking to see what well-informed observers fifteen years ago believed:

9. Leo Grebler, Joan W. Moore, and Ralph Guzman, *The Mexican-American People* (Stanford, Calif.: Stanford University Press, 1970), p. 569.

10. John Hawgood, *The Tragedy of German America* (Evanston, Ill.: R.S. Barnes, 1940).

It is clear from the job certification procedure of 1963 and the end of the *bracero* program in 1964 that immigration policy has entered a new, more restrictive era. This is a remarkable change. Until recently, employers have been able to convince policy makers of the desirability of an ample supply of workers from Mexico; the opposition of labor and civic organizations was of no avail. Now business interests are counterbalanced by considerations of levels of domestic employment, protection of wages and labor standards, and the implications of immigration for antipoverty programs. Under these circumstances, the volume of immigration will unquestionably depend far more on United States policy than on Mexican migration potential.[11]

This was what the authors of *The Mexican American People* believed in 1970. Yet for the past fifteen years immigrants have flowed at an unparalleled rate over the southern border. Whether the authors will be proved right fifteen years hence we do not yet know, but it appears doubtful.

What future scenarios can we envision? Suppose moderate immigration controls fail. Suppose there is an enormous public demand to tighten controls—to create a wall across the border. What would be the Mexican response? The Mexican-American response? One presumes this will never happen, that economic relations across the border are too extensive, that movements of workers, shoppers, and tourists are too great for effective control. Perhaps this is true.

My point, however, is that the course of future development for a population group undergoing rapid expansion and change as a result of mass migration is ambiguous. The unique features that set the Mexican-American immigration apart from other immigration streams suggest possibilities that may affect political responses to the Mexican-American population and its growth—and suggest responses in turn from Mexican-Americans. It would be naive to ignore these possible influences on future political developments.

What are these distinctive differences? (1) Mexico is adjacent to the United States; (2) the territory in which most Mexican-Americans live was once Mexican, taken from Mexico in war; (3) Mexico's economic level is far below that of the United States; there are inevitable issues of conflict on this score alone, such as Mexico's interest in emigration to relive its economic problems; (4) the concentration of Mexican-Americans in cities and sections of the country near the Mexican border makes them the single dominant ethnic group in a substantial part of the Southwest, and this may hamper their assimilation; (5) the conditions in the United States that facilitate assimilation—legal, political, and cultural—appear to be less effica-

---

11. Grebler, Moore, and Guzman, *The Mexican-American People*, p. 75.

cious today than they were during the previous period of mass immigration into this country, which ended in the 1920s.

I consider these distinctions as "structural" features. They in no way contradict the concrete empirical evidence that Mexican-Americans are following the general course of acculturation and assimilation that has characterized, at varying rates, past immigrant groups to this country. The structural realities nevertheless exist, and it is worth expanding on each in turn.

The Common Border

Mexico and Canada are both major sources of American immigration and both have a long land frontier immediately adjacent to the United States. Many French Canadians, in particular, have settled close to the Canadian-U.S. border, just as many Mexican immigrants have settled near the Mexican-U.S. border. There are, however, substantial differences between Canada and Mexico as sources of immigration. English-speaking Canadians become almost instant Americans if they so wish. A common language, culture and ethnic roots make this possible. Most of the French Canadian immigrants came to the United States long ago, and they are by now acculturated and assimilated. They do not reflect the political ferment that now enwraps their homeland, Quebec.

Conquered Territories

As Walker Connor points out, no significant faction, even among the most extreme fringe elements of the Mexican-American community, demands secession and reunification of the Southwest with Mexico.[12] Reference to this nineteenth-century conquest may therefore seem spurious. But the unraveling of the nineteenth-century occupation of most of the world by economically and militarily advanced peoples proceeds apace. Territorial claims are being heard which hope to set back decisions even older than that of the Treaty of Guadalupe Hidalgo. That the American Southwest was once a part of Mexico is a reality in the listing of structural features, even if it has no present consequence.

---

12. See chapter 1 of this volume.

Economic Differences

This is a unique situation. No other highly developed country—not Germany, France, the United Kingdom, Switzerland, Belgium, the Netherlands, the Scandinavian countries, or Japan—shares a long land frontier, or indeed any land frontier at all, with a developing country. Mexico is large, rapidly growing, and progressing economically at a rate that does not give much hope of soon closing the enormous economic gap that separates it from its developed neighbor, the United States. This is the overwhelming factor (along with the common frontier) that raises such apparently insuperable problems in controlling immigration. Illegal immigration to European countries is much less serious because of their geographical situation; illegal immigration to Japan is nonexistent.

The immigration issue is now the most serious issue raised by this difference in economic level. But other issues involving trade and investment or involving the identification of Mexico with a developing world often critical of American foreign policy may come to the fore. These are not now significant issues for Mexican-Americans. Public opinion polls report their views on immigration are similar to those of other Americans.[13] But as long as the great difference in economic levels exists, the potential conflicts of interest between Mexico and the United States exist. Whether this will affect the political assimilation of Mexican-Americans is another question. It probably will not, yet one cannot ignore these potential strains.

Concentration of Mexican-Americans

American cities in the past have had heavy concentrations of immigrant and ethnic groups. Generally, however, these concentrations have consisted of a number of groups, often in some degree of conflict with each other. The largest American ethnic groups have

---

13. "Stronger Policies on Aliens Favored," *New York Times*, November 15, 1983: "Seventy-five percent of the respondents of Hispanic descent in the most recent [Gallup] survey expressed approval of the restrictions on hiring illegal aliens, the same percentage that supported the idea of requiring identification cards." For the whole sample, 79 percent favored restrictions on employers, and 66 percent favored identification cards. Thus persons of Hispanic descent favored identification cards more than other Americans did. But when these issues become extensively debated, as in the presidential campaign and the House debate on immigration in the spring of 1984, views on these issues can change rapidly.

come in tandem—Germans and Irish from the 1840s on, Italians and Jews from the 1880s on. Present-day immigration too is balanced between Hispanic-Americans, primarily Mexican-Americans, and a number of Asian groups. But Mexican-Americans are overwhelmingly the largest single immigrant group today. Because of the size of this group and its concentration in the Southwest, it may dominate some cities and regions the way the Irish dominated Boston for generations.

One consequence of this concentration might be delayed assimilation. More than half of Los Angeles schoolchildren are now of Spanish-language background, and most attend schools where Hispanic-American students are in the vast majority. This concentration means that the process of language learning from English-speaking classmates is diminished. Efforts to distribute schoolchildren by race and ethnic group under laws or constitutional interpretations that prohibit segregation have faltered. Such efforts have run into too much opposition from white, non-Hispanic parents, and have received too little support from Hispanic parents. Whatever the future of desegregation efforts affecting black children (it is not bright), we are unlikely to see any major effort to desegregate Mexican-American schoolchildren.

Although concentration in the schools inhibits acculturation and assimilation to some degree, in other respects concentration may facilitiate it. Concentration offers the opportunity for political representation and political power. Political participation has an enormous potential for education because it requires cooperation with other groups. Indeed, politics facilitates a degree of coming together of different groups that almost no other institution (neighborhood, church, school, or work place) seems capable of generating. Concentration has in the past only rarely inspired minority political movements; usually it inspires participation, even in some idiosyncratic way, in the national two-party system.

But political education as encouragement to assimilation has its limits. If Mexican-Americans come to dominate the politics of major cities (San Antonio today, Los Angeles tomorrow), they may find only scattered opposition from the established Anglo groups and small Asian immigrant groups. These groups are likely, if past experience is any guide, to concentrate their efforts in education, business, and the professions. We could well have a situation similar to that of the dominant Irish in Boston, where politics is seen as the principal route to advancement, and education and business are neglected. Indeed, in part because their numbers do not permit dominance in politics, smaller groups (such as the Asian groups, Greeks, and Armenians) often place their energies in education, business, and the professions, creating a more secure base for later political advancement.

The implications of concentration and dominance will, of course, depend on other concurrent developments.

Conditions Facilitating Assimilation

Finally, we come to the most distinctive structural feature that may affect the acculturation and assimilation of Mexican-Americans in comparison with immigrant and ethnic groups of the great European immigration. These are the revolutionary changes in law and constitutional interpretation of the 1960s and 1970s designed to eliminate discrimination based on race and ethnic origin. These changes limit the actions, public and private, that may be taken to encourage or force acculturation and assimilation, or to penalize those who do not change language, customs, loyalty, and identity.

National legislation—principally the Civil Rights Act of 1964, and its expansion in 1972, and the Voting rights Act of 1965, and its expansion in 1975 and 1982—has radically changed the situation in this country compared with the period of the last mass immigration. Most important for the economic future of immigrant and ethnic groups is the prohibition of education and employment discrimination; most important for their political future is the protection of political rights of persons who do not speak English and the elimination of all "tests and devices," including literacy tests, that may be used to prevent registering and voting.[14] These acts have been supplemented by regulations and legal interpretations, as well as by an executive order requiring affirmative action in recruitment, employment, and promotion by government contractors. Major regulatory agencies—the Equal Employment Opportunity Commission, subdivisions of the Department of Justice and the Office of Federal Contract Compliance Programs—are enforcing these acts and orders. Major changes in the employment practices of employers, public and private, and of political jurisdictions have resulted from these laws.

Debate continues over the degree to which these laws and regulations are enforced and the extensiveness of changes they have

---

14. A good survey of the Voting Rights Act and its consequences may be found in *The Voting Rights Act: Unfulfilled Goals,* United States Commission on Civil Rights, September 1981.

wrought. Undoubtedly they were more strongly enforced under the Democratic administration of President Carter than they are under the Republican administration of President Reagan. Nevertheless, despite changes of attitude and enforcement strategy from one administration to another, the hard skeleton of law, regulation, and executive order persists unchanged. Indeed, the Voting Rights Act was renewed in 1982 (during the Reagan administration), and legislation to strengthen antidiscrimination laws is now moving through Congress as a result of the Supreme Court decision in the Grove City College case.[15]

From the point of view of political mobilization, the key importance of these major legal changes of the 1960s and subsequently their enforcement by federal agencies and courts has been to place a legal brake on efforts to encourage a more rapid acquisition of English and more rapid shedding of immigrant identity. One can now speak Spanish and participate fully in the political process. No "test or device," such as the requirement to speak English, can be used to limit voting. Indeed, the anomaly of the present situation is that knowledge of English is still required to become a citizen but is not required to exercise political rights as a citizen. This complex of law also to some extent encourages maintenance of distinctive ethnic identity. An employer may want to hire or promote an employee of Hispanic background in order to fulfill affirmative action requirements. Similarly, applicants to selective educational programs may benefit by being of Hispanic background.

Obviously the changes that have lessened pressures to acculturate

---

15. Attitudes have changed radically in the past thirty-five years. Consider this excerpt from a 1950 Senate report defending national quotas for immigration quoted by David Reimers, "Recent Immigration Policy: An Analysis," in Barry R. Chiswick, ed., *The Gateway: U.S. Immigration Issues and Policies* (Washington, D.C.: American Enterprise Institute, 1982) p. 25:

Without giving credence to any theory of Nordic superiority, the subcommittee believes that adoption of the national origins formula was a rational and logical method of numerically restricting immigration in such a manner as to best preserve the sociological and cultural balance in the population of the United States. . . . The people who had made the greatest contribution to the development of this country were fully justified in determining that the country was no longer a field for further colonization, and henceforth . . . immigration would . . . be . . . directed to admit immigrants considered to be more readily assimilable because of the similarity of their cultural background to those of the principal components of our population.

Can anyone imagine such sentiments being expressed in 1984?

and assimilate are not simply changes in law. They also reflect changes in popular attitudes. Although the major change has been a desire to eliminate discrimination on grounds of race and ethnic origin, popular opinion also now questions the legitimacy and desirability of forcefully imposing a common identity on immigrants and members of minority groups.

A change in thinking has occurred among immigrants and minority groups too. In the past, most voluntarily embraced Americanization and shed old identities. The advocates of group and language maintenance were usually minorities given little weight in their own ethnic groups. These advocates are now, in part because of changes that have taken place in America as a receiving society, more influential. "Cultural pluralism" was advocated by a few writers during World War I and the 1920s who championed diversity and by critics of enforced Americanization who pleaded for the right to maintain differences. Since the 1960s, proponents of cultural pluralism are no longer pleading; they are demanding and their demands are backed by a huge expansion of law.

This last feature of structural change—conditions facilitating assimilation—leaves us in the same ambiguous position as the discussion of earlier features did. Although the structural change is real, up to now its consequences appear to have been minor. The powerful forces that acculturate and assimilate immigrants to the United States, that again and again have prevented immigrants from becoming "nations within nations," and have prevented the United States from becoming a "nation of nations" (despite the atttactiveness of that definition to many immigrant and minority advocates in the past), continue unabated.

American Popular Culture, Politics, and Public Schools

Despite the substantial changes in law and attitudes, other forces in American society seem to maintain their strength. Two in particular, although weakened, serve to give the forces of acculturation and assimilation precedence over those that maintain differences in language, identity, and loyalty. One such force is simply American popular culture, a popular culture once expressed primarily through press, movies and radio, and now expressed most powerfully through television. There is a strong minority presence in the mass media; and even television, expensive as it is, provides stations in Spanish beamed to the growing Mexican-American population. One suspects their content is similar to that of the foreign-language press, which both provided the chief means of communication within immigrant communities in the first three decades of the century and supplied an education in Americanization, modulated by the specific needs and characteristics of the group. I would be surprised if the Spanish-language television stations paid more attention to what is happening in Mexico than in San Antonio and Los Angeles, or paid more attention to a Mexican election than to an American election.

The second major continuing force of acculturation and assimilation is American politics. No immigrant or minority group, regardless of its size or influence in any city or state, has found it worthwhile to operate outside the American two-party system. By operating within it, powerful assimilating forces are brought into play, even while one is engaged in the process of advancing the interests of the group. One sees these forces at work as Mexican-Americans who represent Mexican-American districts try to formulate a position on immigration. Their position seems to represent the interests of their constituents in getting ahead in America much more than it does any interest, concrete or ideological, that competes with what we may conceive of as an American national interest.

A third powerful assimilating force of the past is, I believe, considerably weakened. This is the American public school. It has lost a good deal of its self-confidence as judges and minority advocates have been able again and again to overrule school administrators, local elected leaders, and public opinion in the search for desegregation. It has lost more self-confidence as civil libertarians have limited the disciplinary powers of teachers, principals, and administrators. Complex and ambiguous requirements for bilingual education have been imposed on it, and it has been buffeted by demands for recognition of the culture of the new immigrants. Advocates of these changes complain that too little has been done. They may have a point, but if little has been done positively, enough has been done negatively to undermine the sense of the public schools that they have a mission to reshape children of different cultures and languages into a common format, a conviction that dominated the public schools until twenty years ago.

To tote up the balance today with any confidence is still rather premature. Mexican immigration still flows heavily, and we can only guess its outcome. It is like trying to guess in 1910 how the massive flow of immigrants from eastern Europe and Italy would affect American society. Any effort to discern the future today may be as far off as a similar effort would have been then. Until now, the particiption of Mexican-Americans in the American political process seems remarkably similar to that of earlier ethnic and immigrant groups. It is affected by the same forces. Poorer education, less income, modest participation in the key professions from which political leaders are drawn—all have limited the political weight of Mexican-Americans, as was true of other immigrant and ethnic groups in the past. Growing numbers increase their significance, and, assisted to some extent by the new legislation, their participation in the political process continues to grow.

I believe the structural features that may make a difference for Mexican-Americans are real and significant. Until now their effect has been less than the powerful cultural, economic, and political assimilative forces of American life. That is the way, I believe, most Americans would want it. It is now the way most Mexican-Americans want it. But as long as the distinctive structural forces I have enumerated are evident, the American public will continue to observe Mexican-American developments with considerable uneasiness.

CHAPTER EIGHT

Analyses of the relative strengths and weaknesses of states conventionally assume that the loyalty of national minorities is suspect. The foreign policies of states also reflect a perception of national minorities as Trojan horses grazing within another state's borders. Pressure is often indirectly exerted upon another government by propagandistic appeals of a separatist nature aimed at minorities. Such appeals have been a staple of the cross-border campaign conducted by China and the Soviet Union whenever their relations became acrimonious. More recently, as a means of applying pressure on Iran's Khomeini regime, Moscow's propaganda directed to that country has adopted the theme that the Azerbaijani of northwestern Iran desire political unification with their kin on the Soviet side of the border.

The behavior of minorities over the years would certainly appear to justify a presumption that the loyalty felt to a state by a national minority is substantially less than that of the politically dominant group(s). The successful independence movements of the Greeks, Serbs, Bulgars, Norse, Hungarians, Czechs, and Irish all testify to this. During World War I, some thirteen different national minorities took advantage of the Russian Revolution to secede, although all but the Finns have been reincorporated into the Soviet state. Nazi appeals to state disloyalty found at least some favorable response among the Bretons of France, the Flemings of Belgium, the Croats of Yugoslavia, and the Slovaks of Czechoslovakia; and the Nazis were also originally greeted as liberators by the Ukrainians of the Soviet Union. More recently, Bengalis seceded from the state of Pakistan, and the Ibos nearly succeeded in doing so from Nigeria. Today, secessionist elements can be found among such diverse peoples as the Basques of Spain, Shans of Burma, Turks of Cyprus, Tigre of Ethiopia, Lithuanians of the Soviet Union, Kurds of Turkey, Quebecois of Canada, Ovambos of Angola, Quechuans of Peru, and Corsicans of France.

The histories of immigrant communities in the United States are devoid of illustrations of noteworthy levels of disloyalty. But this has not prevented members of the dominant group from

225

imputing infidelity. Imputations of disloyalty have been a mainstay of the nativist movements that have pockmarked U.S. history in response to major spurts in immigration. World War I was a period of unusually frank accusations concerning the loyalty of what were often called "hyphenated Americans." (Instructively, the literature regularly refers to German-, Irish-, Jewish-, or Polish-Americans, but never to English-Americans.) To former President Theodore Roosevelt, "adherence to the politico-racial hyphen [was] is the badge and sign of moral treason to the Republic." For his part, President Woodrow Wilson was equally prepared to charge hyphenates who disagreed with his decidedly anti-German, pro-English foreign policy as being "disloyal Americans." In effect, America's most influential leaders interpreted the hyphen as a subtraction sign from 100 percent Americanism.

Perceiving disloyalty where there was no evidence of its existence did not end with World War I. During World War II, under an executive order, more than 100,000 Japanese, two-thirds of whom were citizens, were removed from their homes near the West Coast and relocated in camps in the interior. Without evidence of disloyalty, they were declared "dangerous persons." To Earl Warren, the attorney general of California and later the chief justice of the United States Supreme Court, the lack of evidence was itself evidence of disloyalty. Before a congressional committee in early 1942, he testified: "Many . . . are of the opinion that because we have had no sabotage . . . none [has] been planned for us. But I take the view that that is the most ominous sign in the whole situation."

Myron Weiner and Nathan Glazer have both raised the issue of loyalty. It is essential to stress, however, that they did so not within the context of questioning Mexican-American loyalty but within the context of perceptions of disloyalty often entertained by the dominant community. Rodolfo de la Garza here addresses the issue directly.

AS AMERICAN AS TAMALE PIE

Mexican-American Political Mobilization and the Loyalty Question

Rodolfo de la Garza

Rather than address Mexican-American political mobilization from a comparative perspective in this paper, I intend to try to clarify some key conceptual, empirical, and political issues related to the political world of the Mexican-origin population. I have taken this approach because even well-intentioned policymakers and scholars who are now examining how the Mexican-origin population has affected and will affect American society are viewing the issue from perspectives that distort historical and contemporary reality. I hope this effort will contribute to developing a consensus regarding the fundamental characteristics of the Mexican-American political world. Without some agreement on this question, little can be gained from viewing Mexican-American political life in a comparative perspective.

The dramatic increase in the size of the Mexican-origin population in the United States between 1970 and 1980 has fueled the continuing debate on national immigration policy. Central to the debate is the concern regarding the impact of legal and undocumented Mexican immigration on American society at large. People advocating a new and more restrictive policy initially charged that the presence of Mexican immigrants lowered American wage scales and displaced American workers.[1] Over the past few years these arguments have been repudiated by numerous studies that show that Mexican immigrants are a net economic asset to the United States.[2] Although

---

1. See, for example, Vernon M. Brigg, "Illegal Aliens: The Need for a More Restrictive Border Policy," *Social Science Quarterly*, vol. 56 (Dec. 1975), pp. 477–84; Sidney Weintraub and Stanley Ross, *The Illegal Alien from Mexico: Policy Choices for an Intractable Issue* (Austin: Mexico-United States Border Research Program, University of Texas at Austin, 1980).

2. See, for example, Thomas Muller, *The Fourth Wave: California's Newest Immigrants: A Summary* (Washington, D.C.: The Urban Institute, 1984); and Sidney Weintraub and Gilberto Cardenas, *The Use of Public Services by Undocumented Aliens in Texas* (Austin: LBJ School of Public Affairs, Policy Research Project Report no. 60, 1984).

some politicians continue to charge that Mexican immigration drains this country's economy, the contrary findings have been so widely circulated that people who raise such claims find themselves immediately on the defensive.[3]

Advocates of more restrictive immigration policy also suggest that the presence of large numbers of Mexican immigrants poses a serious political threat to the United States. According to this view, the continued and expanded presence of Mexican immigrants is one of the major factors impeding the integration of Mexican-Americans into mainstream American sociopolitical life. To support their assertion they cite the reluctance of Mexican-Americans to become monolingual English speakers and the widespread support Mexican-Americans give to bilingual education.[4] Furthermore, the maintenance of these cultural traditions is interpreted as potentially leading to the balkanization of the United States, to irredentism in the Southwest, or to the development of political ties between the Mexican government and the Mexican-origin population that may threaten U.S. interests.[5]

These views have little evidence to support them. Instead, like the charges that Mexican immigrants drain the economy, these assertions are based on untested hypotheses, confused conceptualizations, and a flawed understanding of the sociopolitical history of the Mexican-origin population in the United States. This paper suggests an alternative perspective regarding the impact that the Mexican-origin population is likely to have on American sociopolitical life.

Specifically, in this paper I address the following issues: first, the political implications of the size of the Mexican-origin population from several perspectives, second, the possible consequences of Mexican-American political participation and mobilization, and finally, the validity of the claims regarding the threat that a politically mobilized Mexican-origin citizenry poses to the national interest.

3. "Hance Data on Immigration Challenged," Southwest Voter Registration Education Project Report, May 10, 1984 (San Antonio, Texas).

4. For a review of these arguments, see Richard Rodriguez, *Hunger of Memory: The Education of Richard Rodriguez* (Boston: David R. Godine, 1982); and Guadalupe San Miguel, "Conflict and Controversy in the Evolution of Bilingual Education Policy in the United States—An Interpretation," *Social Science Quarterly*, vol. 65 (June 1984), pp. 504–17.

5. These arguments are reviewed in Rodolfo O. de la Garza, "Chicanos and U.S. Foreign Policy: The Future of Chicano-Mexican Relations," *Western Political Quarterly*, vol. 33 (Dec. 1980), pp. 571–82; and Rodolfo de la Garza, "Chicano-Mexican Relations: A Framework for Research," *Social Science Quarterly*, vol. 63 (March 1982), pp. 115–30.

The Mexican-Origin Population: Numbers Do Not Count

Two characteristics of the Mexican-origin population significantly influence the concern over the political impact this group might have on American politics: first, this group increased by more than 90 percent between 1970 and 1980 and now numbers 8.7 million, and second, approximately 80 percent of these people live in the Southwest, and of these, more than three-quarters live in Texas and California.[6] These numbers and concentrations suggest that this population has the potential to influence decisively all aspects of public life in the region.

Although a population of this size obviously influences a region's sociopolitical reality merely by its presence, the characteristics of this group are such that its political impact is far less than its numbers imply. It includes more than 2 million legal and undocumented aliens and approximately 2 million individuals under age eighteen.[7] Thus, only approximately 4.7 million of the 8.7 million are eligible to participate in the electoral process.[8]

Clearly, there is much more to politics than elections; thus it is possible that noncitizen Mexican-origin residents could become active in nonelectoral political activities. To date, however, there is no evidence that they have done so. Moreover, two compelling arguments indicate that they are unlikely to do so for the foreseeable future. First, most Mexican immigrants arrive in this country as adults or young adults,[9] so it seems likely that their "political self" was developed prior to their arrival in this country.[10] This means that, like most Mexicans, particularly those from the lower classes, they will manifest "high levels of negativism about politics, politicians, and the functioning of political institutions," will have low levels of political efficacy, and will have almost no experience with attempting to influence public policy through autonomous citizen-directed efforts.[11]

---

6. U.S. Bureau of the Census, *Conditions of Hispanics in America Today* (Washington, D.C.: 1984), pp. 4–7.

7. Ibid.

8. As reported in *New York Times*, May 4, 1984.

9. Frank Bean, Allan King, and Jeffrey Pasgel, "The Number of Illegal Migrants of Mexican Origin in the United States: Sex Ratio-Based Estimates for 1980," *Demography*, vol. 20 (February 1979), pp. 99–109; and U.S. Department of Justice, *1979 Statistical Yearbook of the Immigration and Naturalization Service* (Washington, D.C.: U.S. Government Printing Office, 1979).

10. Richard E. Dawson and Kenneth Prewitt, *Political Socialization* (Boston: Little, Brown and Co., 1969).

11. Ann Craig and Wayne A. Cornelius, "Political Culture in Mexico: Continuities

Second, the socioeconomic characteristics of these noncitizens also suggest that they have a low probability of political involvement. Political participation of all types correlates positively with income and education.[12] Numerous studies have found that Mexican immigrants score low on both these measures.[13] Given these characteristics, it is not surprising that this group generally manifests little awareness about contemporary policy concerns in this country and has little information about Mexican political life.[14]

This group also has very low levels of participation in voluntary associations. A survey in San Antonio and East Los Angeles found that 75 percent of noncitizens belonged to no organization of any type, 2 percent were union members, and none reported memberships in either political or civic organizations. The only affiliations of any size were with church groups, in which 17 percent reported membership, and parent-teacher associations, with 6 percent.[15]

Prior socialization and socioeconomic factors thus combine to reduce the probability that the noncitizen segment of the Mexican-origin population will soon become politically active. Moreover, Garcia and de la Garza found that the consequences of prior socialization appear to have a strong independent effect on the participatory characteristics of this population. Thus, even if their socioeconomic conditions improve, the noncitizen population is still likely to resist efforts to mobilize it politically. For these reasons Garcia and de la Garza conclude that this group is not "a political resource readily available to enhance the political fortunes of the Mexican American

and Revisionist Interpretations," in Gabriel Almond and Sidney Verba, eds., *The Civic Culture Revisited* (Boston: Little, Brown and Co., 1980), pp. 325–93.

12. Sidney Verba and Norman H. Nie, *Participation in America* (New York: Harper and Row, 1972).

13. Marta Tiena, "Familism and Structural Assimilation of Mexican Immigrants in the United States," paper prepared for the Center for Demography and Ecology, Working Paper no. 79–11 (Madison: University of Wisconsin, 1979); Harry E. Cross and James A. Sundos, *Across the Border: Rural Development in Mexico and Recent Migration to the United States* (Berkeley: Institute of Governmental Research, University of California, 1981); and Douglas S. Massey, "Patterns and Effects of Hispanic Immigration to the United States: A Report to the National Commission for Employment Policy," March 1982.

14. Data regarding views on U.S. policy are from unpublished results of surveys conducted by the Southwest Voter Registration Education Project in East Los Angeles and San Antonio in 1982; Mexico-related findings are from Rodrigo Martinez-Sandoval, Rosa Elisa Rodriguea-Huerta, and Mario M. Carrillo Huerta, "Social Background and Political Participation of Mexican Migrants to Los Angeles County, CA," paper prepared for delivery at the Annual Meeting of the Society for Applied Anthropology, San Diego, California, March 1983.

15. John Garcia and Rodolfo de la Garza, "Organization Behavior of the Mexican Origin Population," unpublished paper, 1984.

community" and that "there is little reason to conclude that Mexican immigrants will for the foreseeable future involve themselves either in Mexican American issues or in American politics more generally."[16]

Even if noncitizens were more politically active, it would be incorrect to assume that they would become part of a cohesive Mexican-American political movement. Recent studies reveal important differences between Mexican-origin citizens and noncitizens. Romo, for example, found important differences in citizen and noncitizen evaluations of educational programs. Noncitizens evaluated educational programs much more positively than did citizens, and they were much more willing to accept existing school policies than were citizens.[17] This suggests that Mexican-American citizens will have difficulty persuading noncitizens to join them in efforts to change the educational system, an issue that concerns the citizens greatly.[18]

Nunez and Rodriguez found equally important social differences between the two groups. In both social and work settings, citizens and noncitizens each preferred to function independently of the other. Rodriguez and Nunez concluded that relations between the two groups would be affected at least as much by differences in class interests as by shared cultural characteristics.[19] There are, of course, issues on which both groups could join forces. However, it should not be assumed that the noncitizen population will automatically and immediately become part of Mexican-American political efforts.

Politically, then, the Mexican-origin population is much weaker than its numbers imply. Not only is its strength diminished by the presence of more than 2 million noncitizens, it also includes more than 2 million who are too young to vote. Moreover, there are few indicators and thus little reason to conclude that noncitizens are likely to become politically mobilized, or if they do, that they will become part of a cohesive Mexican-origin political group. Any attempt to

16. Garcia and de la Garza, "Organization Behavior of the Mexican Origin Population."

17. Harriet Romo, "Chicano, Transitional and Undocumented Mexican Families: Perceptions of the Schooling of their Children," *Social Science Quarterly*, vol. 65, (June 1984), pp. 634–49.

18. F. Chris Garcia and Rodolfo de la Garza, *The Chicano Political Experience: Three Perspectives* (North Scituate, Mass., 1977); and Susan A. MacManus and Carol Cassell, "Mexican Americans in City Politics: Participation, Representation and Policy Preferences," *Urban Interest*, vol. 4 (7), 1982), pp. 57–69.

19. Rogelio Nunez and Nestor Rodriguez, "An Exploration of Chicano-Undocumentado Relations," paper presented at the Conference on the Effects of Mexican Immigration on Mexican Americans, University of Texas at Austin, October 1982.

assess the future implications of Mexican-origin political behavior, therefore, must reflect an understanding of these sociopolitical and demographic realities.

The Consequences of Mexican-American Political Mobilization

Any effort to predict the consequences of Mexican-American mobilization, that is, the consequences of the increased political participation of Mexican-origin citizens, must begin with an understanding of the history of the political life of this population. From shortly after the signing of the Treaty of Guadalupe Hidalgo in 1848 through the early 1970s, political processes throughout the Southwest (outside of New Mexico) were specifically and deliberately designed to disenfranchise the Mexican-American citizen.[20] This disenfranchisement was part of a larger process that led to the economic, social, and political subjugation of Mexican-origin communities.[21]

During the nineteenth century, Mexican-Americans opposed this process in several ways, including armed resistance.[22] In the twentieth century, various segments of the population initiated efforts to gain access to the political process. The League of United Latin American Citizens advocated an assimilative strategy designed to convince the Anglo community that citizens of Mexican origin could be "good Americans."[23] The American G.I. Forum tried to develop into a lobby for the interests of Mexican-American veterans and the general community as well.[24] Other groups, such as the Mexican American Political Association, attempted to develop organizations that would work within the existing political structure to ensure that political parties and public officials would become responsive to Mexican-American concerns.[25] Although each of these efforts contributed to

---

20. See David J. Weber, ed., *Foreigners in their Native Land: Historical Roots of the Mexican Americans* (Albuquerque: University of New Mexico Press, 1973); Leonard Pitt, *The Decline of the Californios: A Social History of the Spanish-Speaking Californios, 1846–1890* (Berkeley: University of California Press, 1971); and Rodolfo Acuna, *Occupied America: A History of Chicanos* (New York: Harper and Row, 1981, second edition).

21. Acuna, *Occupied America.*

22. Robert J. Rosenbaum, *Mexican Resistance in the Southwest: The Sacred Right of Self Preservation* (Austin: University of Texas Press, 1981); and Acuna, *Occupied America.*

23. Garcia and de la Garza, *Chicano Political Experience*, pp. 27–29.

24. Carl Allsup, *The American G.I. Forum: Origins and Evolution* (Austin: Center for Mexican American Studies, University of Texas, 1982).

25. Garcia and de la Garza, *Chicano Political Experience*, p. 31.

improving some aspect of the Mexican-American condition, if only symbolically and temporarily, overall they did not in any measurable way change the structures that prevented Mexican-Americans from becoming autonomous and effective political actors. Thus, by 1970 Mexican-Americans were as effectively denied access to all aspects of the political process as they had been in the nineteenth century.[26]

The Chicano protests of the 1970s awakened national political leaders to the reality of the Mexican-American political condition. In 1975, Congress renewed the 1965 Voting Rights Act and brought the Southwest under its jurisdiction. This act prohibited the use of literacy tests in any elections, required that election materials in languages other than English be made available, and required federal approval of any changes in rules and regulations related to the elections process. In 1982, the act was renewed again, and its coverage was broadened to prohibit electoral practices that resulted in denying or abridging a citizen's right to vote because of race, color, or language status. Prior to 1982, such practices were illegal only if it could be proved that they had been instituted with the intent of disenfranchising minority voters.[27] The 1982 law thus provided Mexican-Americans the mechanism for immediately challenging the use of at-large elections in local, school board, and county elections, and they have done so with great success.[28]

Not until the mid-1970s, then, did national political leaders become fully aware of the extent to which Mexican-American political rights had been abridged. With the extension of the Voting Rights Act to the Southwest, Congress and the president acknowledged that access to the political process had been denied as effectively to Mexican-Americans in the Southwest as it had been to black Americans

---

26. Lee Grebler, Joan Moore, and Ralph C. Guzman, *The Mexican American People: The Nation's Second Largest Minority* (New York: Free Press), p. 561; Charles Cotrell, *A Report on the Participation of Mexican Americans, Blacks, and Females in the Political Institutions and Process in Texas, 1968–1978*, vol. 1 (Washington, D.C.: Texas Advisory Committee, United States Commission on Civil Rights, U.S. Government Printing Office, 1980), pp. 15–116; Garcia and de la Garza, *Chicano Political Experience*, pp. 106–13.

27. For a discussion of the 1975 Voting Rights Act, see Cotrell, *A Report on the Participation of Mexican Americans*, pp. 148–52; see Lawyers' Committee for Civil Rights Under Law, Section 2 Litigation Manual (Washington, D.C.: Voting Rights Project, 1982), pp. 1–89, for a review of the changes in the 1982 Voting Rights Act.

28. For a discussion of the changes that the Voting Rights Act has had on southwestern politics, see Rodolfo O. de la Garza, "Democratizing the Borderlands: The Changing Role of Mexican Americans in Politics of the American Southwest," in Stanley Ross, coordinator, *New Views Across the Border* (Albuquerque: University of New Mexico Press, forthcoming).

TABLE 1
MEXICAN-AMERICAN REGISTRATION AND VOTING RATES, 1976–80

	Registered Mexican-American Voters			Actual Mexican-American Voters		
	1976	*1980*	*Percentage Change*	*1976*	*1980*	*Percentage Change*
Arizona	92,500	105,200	14	58,300	72,588	25
California	915,600	988,131	38	522,400	643,285	23
Colorado	81,000	114,201	41	60,000	83,366	39
New Mexico	135,000	170,900	27	97,300	116,212	19
Texas	488,000	798,563	64	278,200	415,253	49

SOURCE: Choco Gonzalez Mesa, "The Latino Vote in the 1980 Presidential Election," Southwest Voter Registration Education Project, San Antonio, Texas, 1981, p. 16.

in the South. With the 1975 and 1982 extensions, they prohibited the continued use of those electoral mechanisms that had functionally disenfranchised the Mexican-American electorate throughout the twentieth century.

The political structures that existed prior to 1975 are one of the reasons that Mexican-Americans have had such low voter registration and voter turnout rates.[29] Even with the removal of these impediments to electoral involvement, Mexican-Americans continue to participate at rates significantly lower than Anglos. In the 1982 election in Texas, for example, almost 50 percent of all registered voters turned out, compared with only 38 percent of Mexican-Americans.[30] Although these low rates of participation may reflect the lingering effects of pre-1975 socialization, it is more likely that they are now primarily a function of socioeconomic factors.[31]

Although Mexican-American electoral participation rates remain relatively low, both registration and voting have increased dramatically since 1975 (see table 1). These increases may be attributable to the changes effected by the Voting Rights Act extensions and to the extensive voter registration campaigns conducted by Mexican-American organizations. The Southwest Voter Registration and Education Project, for example, completed more than 600 voter registration drives in the Southwest between 1975 and 1984.[32]

Most Mexican-Americans, then, are relatively new to the political process. Their ability to influence local, state, and national decision making will depend in large part on their ability to increase rates of electoral involvement. In 1980, fewer than 1.5 million of 4 million eligible voters actually voted.[33] Although it seems likely a larger proportion will participate in 1984, that will not necessarily affect the outcome of state and national elections in the Southwest. In highly competitive contests, such as the 1960 presidential and 1982 Texas gubernatorial elections, Mexican-Americans can play a decisive role if they turn out in high numbers and vote as a bloc. But unless both these conditions are met, the Mexican-American vote may be marginal

---

29. Garcia and de la Garza, *Chicano Political Experience*, pp. 94–96.

30. Robert R. Brischetto, Annette A. Avila, and Yolanda Doerfler, *Mexican American Voting in the 1982 Texas General Election* (San Antonio: Southwest Voter Education Registration Project, 1982), p. 1.

31. Raymond E. Wolfinger and Steven J. Rosenstone, *Who Votes?* (New Haven: Yale University Press, 1980), pp. 91–93.

32. Interview with Robert Brischetto, research director, Southwest Voter Registration Education Project, San Antonio, Texas, May 10, 1984.

33. *New York Times*, May 4, 1984, p. 9.

to electoral outcomes. (In 1984 the Mexican-American turnout was again lower than the Anglo turnout, and, although Mexican-Americans cast approximately 68 percent of their votes for the democratic party, they had little impact on the outcome of the election because of the landslide republican victory.)[10] Their ability to influence local elections is much greater, however, because Mexican-Americans are highly concentrated in specific jurisdictions throughout the Southwest.

Another factor that will influence the effect of Mexican-American participation on the political process is the nature of the demands Mexican-Americans make. If their demands differ radically from those of the general public, an increased Mexican-American presence could destabilize regional and national political processes. Results from a San Antonio survey indicate, however, that although Anglos and Mexican-Americans differ in a few important areas, overall they do not constitute distinct electorates. They differ primarily in their views of government spending on minority-related issues; somewhat with regard to spending on education, environment, space, and welfare; and not at all in their evaluation of spending on crime, drug addiction, defense, foreign aid, and urban problems.[34]

These results suggest that the impact Mexican-American mobilization will have on the political process will vary from one type of jurisdiction to another. In local areas with high concentrations of Mexican-Americans, such as San Antonio or Crystal City, Texas, their presence will radically alter the composition of local political elites and the content of public policy.[35] Local jurisdictions with smaller Mexican-American populations, such as Houston, Texas, will be much less affected.[36] At the state and national levels, their impact will depend on the competitiveness of the elections and the cohesiveness of their vote; but even with high levels of involvement, Mexican-American participation is unlikely to alter greatly the existing political process or the government's public policy priorities.

---

34. Rodolfo de la Garza and Janet Weaver, "Mexican Americans and Anglos in San Antonio: A City Divided?" Paper presented at the American Political Science Association Annual Meeting, September 1983.

35. See, for example, John Booth, "The Impact of the Voting Rights Act in San Antonio, Texas," in Robert Brischetto, ed., *Bilingual Elections at Work in the Southwest* (San Francisco: Mexican American Legal Defense and Education Fund, 1982), pp. 111–78; and John Staples Shockley, *Chicano Revolt in a Texas Town* (Notre Dame, Ind.: University of Notre Dame Press, 1974).

36. Luis Fraga, "The Impact of the 1975 Extension of the Voting Rights Act on Houston's Hispanic Community," unpublished paper, n.d.

Mexican-American Political Mobilization and the Loyalty Question

Perhaps the most troublesome issue raised about the consequences of Mexican-American political mobilization concerns loyalty. This is, according to Nathan Glazer, "the basic and final issue," one that "remains a concern for many Americans" (see chapter 7 of this volume). Those who raise this concern suggest that Mexican-American political mobilization will threaten national interests either because Mexican-Americans have refused to follow the path of other immigrants and assimilate into American society, or because of the ties that Mexican-Americans have or will develop with the Mexican state.[37]

Again, a response to this issue requires an understanding of Mexican-American political history. People who raise this concern are implicitly arguing that Mexican-Americans have refused to participate in the mainstream of American life, and thus cannot be trusted to join the body politic if they mobilize in the future. Such a view ignores the historical realities within which the Mexican-American community has evolved.

As described previously, shortly after the end of the U.S.-Mexican war in 1846–47, political systems in the southwestern states functionally disenfranchised the Mexican-origin population. Despite repeated efforts, Mexican-Americans were prevented from obtaining full access to the political process from the mid-ninteenth century until the passage of the 1975 and 1982 Voting Rights Acts. Mexican-Americans thus remained outside the political process because the political process kept them out. As the obstacles to participation have been removed, Mexican-American participation has increased. Today, when demographic factors are held constant, "Chicanos are 3 percent more likely to vote than the rest of the population."[38] In terms of political involvement, then, there is no basis for arguing that Mexican-Americans have remained aloof from mainstream American life. Instead, the political process was closed to them for over a century.

Mexican-Americans were similarly barred from fully participating in other aspects of American society. Across the Southwest, they encountered de jure and de facto residential segregation.[39] They

---

37. Nathan Glazer, chapter 7 of this volume.
38. Wolfinger and Rosenstone, *Who Votes?* p. 92.
39. Ricardo Romo, *East Los Angeles: History of a Barrio* (Austin: University of Texas Press, 1983), pp. 61–88; Douglas E. Foley et al., *From Peones to Politicos: Ethnic Relations*

were often discouraged from attending school, and those that did enroll were placed in "Mexican" schools or in segregated programs within integrated schools.[40] The labor market was similarly segregated. Mexican-Americans were relegated to the lowest-paying, least-desirable jobs, and when they held the same type of jobs that Anglos held, they earned less than Anglos did.[41] Because of these practices Mexican-Americans could not have become integrated into mainstream society even if they had desired. Instead of encouraging Mexican-Americans to integrate, American social, educational, and economic institutions erected barriers that contributed greatly to the maintenance and expansion of ethnically distinct Mexican-origin communities.

In view of these barriers, it is impossible to determine to what extent the Mexican-origin population would have integrated into mainstream society if it had been allowed to do so. Furthermore, since Mexican-Americans were prevented from "Americanizing," it is no wonder they still speak Spanish and continue to exist as an identifiable cultural community. There is no justification for charging that they have been unwilling to integrate into mainstream society and therefore pose a threat to the country's social fabric.

Furthermore, and perhaps more important, there is no evidence that the retention of Mexican cultural practices has in itself prevented Mexican-Americans from identifying with the American political system. Prior to 1975, for example, Spanish monolinguals had difficulty participating in the electoral process because election materials were all in English. Since Spanish-language materials became available, Spanish monolinguals have registered and voted at impressively high rates.[42]

Similarly, Mexican-American support for bilingual education does not necessarily indicate separatist inclinations. More likely, Mexican-Americans support bilingual programs largely because they

in a South Texas Town, 1900–1977 (Austin: Center for Mexican American Studies, 1977), pp. 32–69.

40. Foley et al., Peones to Politicos, pp. 38–40; Mario Garcia, Desert Immigrants: The Mexicans of El Paso, 1880–1920 (New Haven, Conn.: Yale University Press, 1981), pp. 110–26.

41. Mario Barrera, Race and Class in the Southwest (Notre Dame, Ind.: Notre Dame University Press, 1979).

42. Robert Brischetto, "The Availability and Use of Bilingual Election Services," in Brischetto, Bilingual Elections, pp. 84–110; Robert Brischetto and Rodolfo de la Garza, The Mexican American Electorate: Political Participation and Ideology, Occasional Paper no. 3, The Mexican American Electorate Series (Joint publication of the Southwest Voter Registration Education Project, San Antonio, and the Center for Mexican American Studies, University of Texas at Austin, 1983).

think such programs will more effectively educate their children and thus aid the process of becoming integrated into the societal mainstream. One of the major objectives of these programs, after all, is to help Spanish-speaking children stay in school rather than drop out. Historically, across the Southwest, schools have punished and discriminated against them for the mere fact that they are Spanish-speaking and of Mexican origin.

Bilingual programs also have great symbolic significance to Mexican-Americans. For over a century, the Mexican-origin population has seen Mexican values and language ridiculed and suppressed. The existence of bilingual programs reverses that trend and signals an official recognition of the intrinsic worth of Mexican culture.

Mexican-Americans may be as concerned with having society acknowledge that Mexican culture is deserving of respect and recognition as they are with actively maintaining it. Except for their concern about retaining Spanish, Mexican-Americans in Los Angeles and San Antonio in the late 1960s were relatively unconcerned about retaining any specific Mexican cultural trait.[43]

Mexican-American support for Spanish-language retention does not imply support for Spanish monolingualism. Leaders in the Mexican-American community do not advocate Spanish monolingualism. Furthermore, the number of Spanish monolinguals has decreased in recent years. Whereas about 55 percent of Mexican-Americans in Los Angeles and San Antonio were bilingual in the late 1960s, 89 percent were bilingual in 1982. Moreover, 22 percent of those over age sixty-five spoke only Spanish, compared with 6 percent of those age eighteen to twenty-five.[44]

Finally, there is no evidence that Mexican-Americans have any political attachments to the Mexican state or to Mexican political processes. In the mid-1960s, fewer than 2 percent of Mexican-Americans in Los Angeles and San Antonio expressed a desire for retaining a sense of Mexican patriotism.[45] In the 1980s, when asked to identify their principal concerns, Mexican-Americans almost never

---

43. Grebler, Moore, and Guzman, *Mexican American People*, pp. 383–85.

44. Rodolfo O. de la Garza and Robert R. Brischetto, *The Mexican American Electorate: A Demographic Profile.* Occasional Paper no. 1, The Mexican American Electorate Series (Joint publication of the Southwest Voter Registration Education Project, San Antonio, and the Center for Mexican American Studies, University of Texas at Austin, 1983).

45. Grebler, Moore, and Guzman, *Mexican American People*, p. 384.

mention U.S.-Mexican relations or any issues related to domestic Mexican politics. Indeed, only in South Texas does immigration appear as an identifiable concern, and there only 11 percent raise it as an issue.[46]

Mexican-Americans are unlikely to develop into an ethnic lobby supporting Mexican interests for several reasons.[47] First, Mexican-Americans are unconcerned about the issues of greatest interest to Mexico, and the Mexican elite has no interest in the primary concerns of Mexican-Americans. Second, after briefly considering developing this kind of relationship with Mexican-Americans, Mexican officials have "discarded [this idea] from the panorama of objectives of the relations between the government of Mexico and Chicanos."[48] Considering that Mexican-Americans have a long history of attempting to participate in U.S. sociopolitical life, manifest no political attachments to Mexico, are unconcerned about Mexican political issues, and are unlikely to become actively involved as an ethnic lobby supporting Mexican interests, one wonders why any questions about Mexican-American loyalty would even be raised. This is particularly curious since other ethnic groups such as Greek-Americans and Jewish-Americans actively engage in issues related to policy toward Greece and Israel respectively without having their loyalty questioned.

How the noncitizen segment, particularly those most recently arrived, will behave vis-à-vis Mexico is unknown. But presumably they will act as Mexican immigrants have in the past. Moreover, now that the Mexican-origin population is less discriminated against than it was in the past, recent immigrants may develop a political allegiance to this country even more rapidly than did immigrants in prior generations.

---

46. Rodolfo de la Garza and Robert Brischetto, with the assistance of David Vaughn, *The Mexican American Electorate: Information Sources and Policy Orientations*, (San Antonio: Southwest Voter Registration Education Project and the Center for Mexican American Studies of the University of Texas at Austin, 1983), pp. 7–9; Rodolfo de la Garza, *Public Policy Priorities of Chicano Political Elites*, U.S.-Mexico Project Series Working Paper 7 (Washington, D.C.: Overseas Development Council, 1982); and Lawrence W. Miller, Jerry L. Polinard, and Robert Wrinkle, "Attitudes toward Undocumented Workers: The Mexican American Perspective," *Social Science Quarterly*, vol. 65 (June 1984), p. 484.

47. Rodolfo de la Garza, "Chicanos and U.S. Foreign Policy: The Future of Chicano-Mexican Relations," *Western Political Quarterly*, vol. 33 (Dec. 1980), pp. 571–82; and Rodolfo de la Garza, "Chicano-Mexican Relations: A Framework for Research," *Social Science Quarterly*, vol. 63 (March 1982), pp. 115–30.

48. Jorge Bustamante, "Relacíon Cultural con los Chicano," *Uno Más Uno*, Oct. 11, 1982, p. 2.

Conclusion

At various times in the history of the United States, American officials and the general public have been concerned about how continued immigration will affect the country's social and political fabric. In view of the continued and expanded presence of Mexican immigrants, it is not surprising that this question is now being asked again.

The tone in which the question has been raised, however, is troublesome. Policymakers and scholars seem to assume that Mexican immigrants will have a primarily, if not exclusively, negative effect on this country. In the debate on the economic impact of Mexican immigration, charges that Mexican workers caused unemployment and were a drain on social services were given credence in the debate over national immigration reform, even though the claims could not be substantiated. Numerous studies have now shown that such assertions were either unfounded or greatly exaggerated. Nonetheless, the belief that Mexican immigrants are weakening the economy persists, although it is less pervasive than it once was.

The debate over the sociopolitical consequences of Mexican immigration seems to be following the same pattern. Opponents of this immigration argue explicitly or by implication that the presence of large numbers of Mexican immigrants poses a serious threat to the future of this country. To support their views, they claim that the Mexican-origin population has refused to "Americanize" in the way that Italians, Jews, and other immigrants have. Therefore, they argue, if this minority becomes politically active, because of its size, regional concentration, and lack of commitment to American values and institutions, the Mexican-origin population has the potential to threaten the political stability and national security of the nation.

I have attempted to show that such fears are groundless for several reasons. First, they are based on a very distorted understanding of the history of the Mexican-origin population in the United States. The Mexican-origin population has, since 1848, been denied equal and meaningful access to societal institutions. Although various European groups also encountered discrimination when they began to settle in the United States, none encountered obstacles as pervasive or enduring as has the Mexican-origin population. In the political realm, the impediments to political participation were so severe that national legislation had to be enacted as recently as 1982 in order to ensure that Mexican-Americans would have equal access to the political process.

Second, these fears are based on a blurring of the distinction between citizen and noncitizen segments of the Mexican-origin population. Despite important cultural similarities between the two, there are also important class, cultural, and political differences between them. The two do not exist as a unified political community, nor will they necessarily develop into one in the foreseeable future. Furthermore, the noncitizen segment of this population is politically inactive and likely to remain so. Population totals that combine citizens and noncitizens distort the real political clout of the Mexican-origin population and fuel unsubstantiated concerns regarding the consequences of Mexican-American mobilization.

Finally, concern about their political loyalties presumes the existence of Mexican-American political allegiance to Mexico, although there is no evidence of such an attitude. This concern mistakenly equates cultural affinities for political commitments and ignores the fact that Mexican-Americans are unconcerned about the major issues that concern Mexico and the Mexican public. The loyalty question also assumes that programs such as bilingual education will impede the political integration of the Mexican-origin population, and that Mexican-Americans' support for such programs indicates their unwillingness to identify with basic American values. As I have argued here, bilingualism has not been shown to impede political participation. Indeed, one of the principal reasons that Mexican-Americans support bilingual education is that it facilitates the education of Spanish-speaking children and thus better prepares them to participate fully in all aspects of mainstream society.

In conclusion, I have suggested that although Mexican-American political mobilization may disrupt the political status quo of the Southwest, it surely poses no threat to the body politic. To the contrary, increased participation by Mexican-origin citizens will contribute to the continued democratization of the Southwest. Historically, Mexican-American concerns have been irrelevant to policymakers. Now that they have access to the political process, Mexican-Americans should be able to influence changes in government. There is no reason, however, to think that their involvment in any way threatens core American political values.

Ironically, then, only those groups that have historically profited from denying the Mexican-origin population its political rights should be threatened by its political mobilization. Those of us who are committed to American political principles should welcome the increased involvement of Mexican-Americans, for it will signal the continuation of the democratic process that is the cornerstone of the American political system.

CHAPTER NINE

Nathan Glazer and Rodolfo de la Garza have each stressed the role of political mobilization in the integration process. Admittedly, such mobilization is not absolutely essential to "making it" in a purely economic sense. Ethnic minorities have economically outperformed the dominant groups in many societies, while remaining political pariahs. But if a community wishes to guarantee itself full and continuing access to the entire complement of rights and privileges enjoyed by other members of the society, political mobilization of the community is sound strategy.

The well-known political history of black Americans is instructive in this regard. Although blacks were technically granted the right to vote by constitutional amendment following the Civil War, a series of policies and stratagems effectively kept blacks, then concentrated in the South, outside the body politic for nearly another century. Effectively disenfranchised blacks suffered severe discrimination without effective recourse. Only after a significant portion of blacks moved to the North and became enfranchised was the issue taken out of the closet. Today voter registration drives, the Congressional Black Caucus, and Jesse Jackson's 1984 presidential bid are among many bits of evidence that the black community has learned the strategic value of mobilizing for political action. Japanese-Americans have also learned that political mobilization is the best guard against discrimination. Today, members of that relatively small community (substantially less than 1 million) vote proportionately well above the country's average, are the most dominant ethnic force within Hawaii, and are well represented in the U.S. Congress. By contrast, it is no coincidence that the statistically most deprived group in the United States, the American Indians, are also the most poorly mobilized and represented.

In the following essay, Harry P. Pachon evaluates the political mobilization efforts of Mexican-Americans to date. In measuring these efforts against the record of other groups, he alludes to a number of factors that exert the same baneful effects upon the political behavior of Mexican-Americans that they had upon others, although the degree of influence may vary. For example, he notes that the low voting rate among young adults throughout the entire society exerts a particularly negative effect upon the voting turnout of a group, such as the Mexican-Americans, who have an unusually large percentage in this age category. Pachon also stresses some important distinctions that set the Mexican-American experience apart. In particular, he draws attention to the danger, when contrasting group experiences from different time-frames, of overlooking intervening structural changes, such as the demise of machine politics. He concludes that political mobilization is growing among Mexican-Americans, although important problems remain to be overcome.

POLITICAL MOBILIZATION IN THE MEXICAN-AMERICAN COMMUNITY

Harry P. Pachon

Mexican-American political mobilization in the United States carries two contradictory images. One image is that of a community with growing political force and vast political potential. Another, contradictory, image holds that Mexican-Americans participate less in the political process than other groups in American society. Politicians, journalists, and academic researchers all have speculated on why Mexican-Americans do not participate to their full potential and why Mexican-Americans do not vote.[1]

This paper first looks at factors affecting Mexican-American political mobilization[2] and then examines why two such contradictory images have developed.

With the doubling in the number of Mexican-American congressmen in the 1982 elections (from four to eight), with close to 90 Mexican-American state legislators holding office, and with the election of Mexican-Americans to mayorships in such southwestern cities as San Antonio and Denver, many analysts are now examining the political mobilization potential of Mexican-Americans. These political gains have occurred despite several factors that currently limit the electoral impact of the Mexican-American community commensurate to its numbers.

---

1. See Edgar Litt, *Ethnic Problems in America* (Glenview, Ill.: Scott, Foresman, 1970); Ray Gonzales, "The Myth of the Chicano Sleeping Giant," *California Journal* (February, 1979) pp. 46–47; Keith Melville, "Moving into the Political Mainstream" (New York: Public Agenda Foundation, 1984), pp. 12–14.

2. As used in this paper the term *political mobilization* will encompass two meanings: (1) the use of ethnicity as the primary standard on which individuals base their political choices; and (2) political behavior congruent with, and supportive of, ethnic political values.

Factors Affecting Political Participation

The first of these factors is that the spectacular growth of the Mexican-American population is still regional, primarily confined to the Southwest and to a few key states outside of the Southwest. Furthermore, even within these states, the growth is geographically concentrated. In California, for example, 50 percent of the state's Hispanic (mostly Mexican-American) population is found in thirteen congressional districts in Southern California (out of a total of forty-five). In Texas, five congressional districts in the southern part of the state contain 50 percent of the Mexican-American population. This concentration means that many elected representatives at the local, state, and federal levels in the nation (and even in the Southwest) have few Mexican-American voters to contend with in their districts. This concentration in turn has affected the national political visibility of Mexican-Americans. Traditionally low national visibility, especially on the East Coast, helps explain why, before the 1970s, the national media, labor unions, various liberal groups, and the large charitable foundations did not champion Mexican-American causes as seriously as those of black Americans.[3]

Geographic concentration has also meant that there are very few (six at present) congressional districts in which the majority of the population is Mexican-American.[4] Significantly, half of the Mexican-American members of Congress come from these six districts. The importance of ethnic constituencies in electing ethnic candidates is suggested by the fact that sixteen of the twenty-one black representatives in the House of Representatives come from congressional districts with populations that are more than 40 percent black. Similarly, most Mexican-American political gains have been made in areas where Mexican-Americans are a majority. In California three of the six state legislators who are of Mexican-American background represent areas within the Twenty-fifth Congressional District, where Hispanics constitute 64 percent of the population. In South Texas, an area in which Mexican-Americans constitute a majority of the population, Mexican-Americans have also seen gains in political representation.

---

3. Harry Pachon, "Politics in the Mexican American Community," in Joan Moore with Harry Pachon, eds., *Mexican Americans*, 2d ed. (Englewood Cliffs, N.J.: Prentice Hall, 1976).

4. See also "An Overview of Hispanic Elected Officials," in the *National Roster of Hispanic Elected Officials* (Washington, D.C.: NALEO Education Fund, 1984).

TABLE 1
HISPANIC VOTER REGISTRATION, SELECTED YEARS, 1974–82
Millions unless Otherwise Specified

Year	All Hispanics of Voting Age	Registered Voters		Not Registered to Vote	Ineligible to Vote Because of Non-citizenship	Registered Voters among Those Eligible to Vote (percent)
		Number	Percent			
1974	6.1	2.1	34.9	4.0	1.6	47.1
1976	6.6	2.5	37.8	4.1	1.7	50.6
1978	6.8	2.2	32.9	4.6	2.1	48.0
1980	8.2	3.0	36.3	5.2	2.6	53.6
1982	8.8	3.1	35.0	5.7	2.8	51.0

SOURCE: U.S. Bureau of the Census, "Voting and Registration in the Election of November 1974," *Current Population Reports,* Series P-20 (Washington, D.C.: U.S. Government Printing Office, 1975, and reports from this series for other election years shown in the table.

Not only is the majority of the Mexican-American population geographically concentrated, but the demographic characteristics of the community have political significance. The Hispanic population is younger than the American population as a whole; in 1980 nearly 40 percent of the Mexican-American community was below voting age and close to 50 percent was below twenty-four years of age, according to the census. The age group from eighteen to twenty-four is least likely to vote or to be involved in politics. But obviously a substantial number of potential new voters will be coming of age every year, thereby increasing Mexican-American electoral strength throughout the 1980s. Furthermore, as the population ages, it will tend to participate more in the electoral process.

Another factor that influences Mexican-American voting participation is the high proportion of foreign-born or recent immigrants, most of whom are not U.S. citizens. Curiously, the large number of noncitizens is often overlooked in studies of Hispanic political participation. For example, it appears in table 1 that Hispanic political participation (of which Mexican-Americans constitute a majority) is much lower than either Anglo or black electoral participation. But if one controls for citizenship, Hispanic political participation is comparable to that of the black population.

Not taking citizenship into account is a major error that consistently plagues most analyses of Mexican-American political behavior. In all likelihood it contributes to the idea that Mexican-Americans do not vote as readily as do other ethnic groups. Any in-depth study of the Mexican-American community, however, confirms that a high percentage of persons cannot vote because they are not citizens. A few examples illustrate this. A study conducted among Mexican-Americans in Houston found that "the population figures used in districting, which include non-citizens, overstate the real electoral potential of this ethnic group."[5] In Chicago, a study of Chicano, Puerto Rican, and Cuban political behavior found that "about 70 percent of Mexican Americans and Cubans in Chicago are foreign citizens."[6] The 1970 census showed that 33 percent of the residents in East Los Angeles were Mexican citizens.[7]

The presence of large numbers of immigrants in a community also affects its political behavior. Most new immigrants are not immediately integrated into their new environment.[8] Factors delaying the integration of immigrants into social and political institutions are often overlooked. Mexican immigrants familiar with the Mexican political system, for example, may have difficulty in adjusting to the supposedly "nonpartisan" politics of California.

Another relevant aspect of the immigration experience is the phenomenon of relative deprivation. The ethnic political mobilization that has already occurred in the Mexican-American community may depend on a world view that sees Mexican-Americans as different and disadvantaged from the rest of society. Newly arrived immigrants may not feel relatively deprived vis-à-vis American society and may tend to view the political world of the United States quite differently from the way it is seen by a Mexican-American political activist born and reared in the barrio and whose family has lived there for generations.

Yet it is a mistake to view Mexican-American political mobilization entirely from the context of newly arrived immigrants. Other external factors are equally relevant to the Mexican-American experience, such as the history of the Mexican-American interaction with the larger society after the Anglo-American conquest. This factor was overlooked by a previous generation of scholars. It is said that "history is written by the victors," and certainly this is true with respect to

---

5. Susan MacManus and Carol Cassek, "Representing America's Mexican Americans: The Districting Difficulties," paper presented at the 1980 Annual Meeting of the American Political Science Association, Washington, D.C., August 1980.

6. Luis Salces and Peter Colby, "Mañana Will Be Better: Spanish American Politics in Chicago," paper prepared for publication in *Illinois Issues*, 1980.

7. Harry Pachon, "Politics."

8. See Joan Nelson, "The Urban Poor: Disruption or Political Integration in Third World Countries," *World Politics* (April 1970) pp. 393–415: Wayne A. Cornelius, Jr., "Urbanization as an Agent in Latin American Political Instability: The Case of Mexico," *American Political Science Review*, vol. 63 (September 1969), pp. 833–57.

Mexican-American history in the Southwest. Social banditry and rebellions swept the native Mexican-American population in the 1850s and later. The Cortina uprising in Texas, the Salt War in 1877, and the formation of Las Gorras Blancas may well have been politically motivated.

Another oversight has been the failure to notice the institutionalized obstacles to Mexican-American political activity in the Southwest. The discriminatory poll tax, the White Man's Union in Texas (which existed until 1944), gerrymandering to dilute Mexican-American political power, and overt suppression by threats, economic sanctions, subterfuge, and violence all hampered Mexican-American participation.[9] Further obstacles existed in the form of English literacy tests that disenfranchised Mexican-Americans after the 1890s in all southwestern states, except New Mexico. (Residency requirements for voters still disenfranchise significant segments of Mexican-American migrant laborers.)

The Relevance of European Immigrant and Black American Models

One reason for these historical and institutional oversights may be that scholars tended to use inapplicable models of Anglo-American political organizations when studying Mexican-American communities. One researcher notes that political organizations in Chicano communities were not visible because outside observers failed to understand that many of their political groups were multifunctional and undifferentiated. He notes that during the early part of this century the Mexican-American would "establish undifferentiated multipurpose organizations which not only served his political needs but also his economic, social and cultural ones as well."[10] This multifunctional organization is illustrated by the Alianza Hispano Americana, which, for more than sixty years, provided services ranging from insurance benefits for burial to civil rights advocacy (in the 1950s). Because of the "invisibility" of such groups, the political obstacles they encountered were generally overlooked.

Another reason for such oversights is that Mexican-American political mobilization has been traditionally compared with models of

---

9. Joan Moore and Harry Pachon, *Hispanics in the United States* (Englewood Cliffs, N.J.: Prentice Hall, forthcoming).

10. Miguel David Tirado, "Mexican American Political Organization," *Aztlán*, vol. 1 (Spring 1970), pp. 53–78.

black American politics or of ethnic immigrant politics of the late nineteenth and early twentieth centuries. The comparison is inappropriate because both analogies are misleading. Mexican-Americans arrived at a time and in a place different from the time and place of either black or European arrivals—an important consideration. Perhaps most important, European ethnic immigrants were not discriminated against because of racial distinctiveness.[11] Nor were they associated with a traditionally subordinate and conquered population (as are the American Indians).

Moreover, because European immigrants tended to settle in the East, they immediately encountered institutions favoring political participation. The political machines of urban America in the 1800s and early 1900s depended heavily upon successive waves of new European immigrants.[12] The political machine gave the new immigrants both physical and psychic rewards in return for their votes. The machine politicized the immigrants. It established avenues for upward political movement, from precinct worker to precinct captain and eventually to elected office. Most of the urban centers of the Southwest do not have comparable political machines to assist Spanish-speaking immigrants. (In some states, notably California, political institutions were "reformed" by the progressives to eliminate political machine rule based on mass partisan voting.) The importance of political structure is illustrated by the fact that where machine-type politics do exist, such as in parts of Texas and New Mexico, Mexican-Americans realized political gains at earlier dates.

Nor is it reasonable to compare Hispanic political activity with that of black Americans. Both groups are racially distinctive, of course, but Hispanics are much less so. As a result Hispanics experience more upward mobility and assimilation than do blacks. The residence patterns of the Los Angeles area bear this out, as do those of other cities. Mexican-Americans living in Los Angeles have spread far out into such East Los Angeles County cities as Montebello, Pico Rivera, Whittier, and La Habra, as well as into many areas in Orange

---

11. For a flavor of the discrimination toward Mexican-Americans in Texas, see Ronnie Dugger, "Gonzalez of San Antonio: Conversations with a Congressman," *Texas Observer* (April 11, 1980), pp. 8–10, 20–22; see also Paul S. Taylor, *An American Mexican Frontier: Nueces County, Texas* (Chapel Hill: University of North Carolina Press, 1934).

12. See Oscar Handlin, *The Uprooted* (Boston: Little, Brown & Company, 1952); Elmer Cornwell, "Bosses, Machines and Ethnic Politics," in Harry A. Bailey, Jr., and Ellis Katz, *Ethnic Group Politics* (Columbus, Ohio: Charles E. Merrill Publishing Company, 1969). For the effect of machine rule in South Texas, see V.O. Key, *Southern Politics* (New York: Vintage Books, 1949); also Robert Caro, *The Path to Power* (New York: Vintage Books, 1981).

County. The fact that some Mexican-Americans can "pass" or "escape" from Anglo-American color consciousness has affected the development of political solidarity.[13] Mexican-Americans are not inextricably bound to being Mexican-American.

The Roots of Mexican-American Political Mobilization

Despite the inapplicability of either model (blacks or European immigrants), before the 1960s outside observers generally concurred that Mexican-Americans were apparently following the idealized model of American ethnic group politics. In 1964 there were four Mexican-American members of Congress; Mexican-Americans had been elected as state legislators in most southwestern states and to a myriad of local offices. By the middle of the 1960s Mexican-American electoral power was evident and Mexican-Americans could expect to be symbolically courted by presidential candidates as a matter of course. With some notable exceptions, such as the period immediately following the Mexican-American War (1846–47), the repatriation of the 1930s, and overt discriminatory actions enhanced by the Zoot Suit Riots of the 1940s and Operation Wetback of the 1950s, Mexican-Americans were generally perceived to be following a path similar to that of European ethnic groups in the political process.

Yet in the early 1960s the traditional route by which ethnic minorities gained clout in American politics was no longer as rewarding as before. At the local level where European immigrants had the most impact, local government agencies had been largely removed from political control by a new set of bureaucracies, usually under the control of the civil service. Thus fewer patronage positions were available. This was a serious matter for a community with problems embedded in such institutions as the schools, police, and various forms of social service. Many of these public service jobs had come under state and federal jurisdictions. In short, political equality was no longer enough reward for a political victory. The deep problems of Mexican-American communities required an awareness of the new structure of government. A growing awareness of this complexity is the new and most important aspect of Mexican-American political mobilization.

---

13. Harry P. Pachon and Joan W. Moore, "Mexican Americans," *The Annals of the American Academy of Political and Social Science* (March 1981) pp. 111–24.

This political mobilization has been aided by several developments affecting the Mexican-American community. First, the Twenty-fourth Amendment to the Constitution eliminated poll taxes in 1964. Poll taxes had been widely used, especially in Texas, to discriminate by selectively enforcing deadlines for payment or by not announcing locations for payment. Then the Voting Rights Act was passed in 1965. It was designed to protect the civil rights of black Americans, but it also helped Chicano communities in the Southwest. Because many Mexican-Americans were poorly educated, the literacy examination further discouraged voter registration. The elimination of this test by the Voting Rights Act effectively enfranchised many Mexican-American citizens. In California the legal case of *Castro* vs. *California* (1966) went a step further to eliminate literacy tests based solely on the English language. These legal changes tended to create a much larger Mexican-American voting population.

Also in the 1960s, two important Mexican-American organizations were formed—the Mexican American Legal Defense and Education Fund (MALDEF) and the Southwest Voter Registration Project. These organizations engaged in voter registration, litigation to support voter registration, "get out the vote" activities, and legal advocacy on behalf of Mexican-Americans. These activities directly supported ethnic political mobilization.

Then both Democrats and Republicans began to see Mexican-American barrios as a "swing vote" that could affect elections.[14] For example, the Mexican-American vote in 1968 allowed Hubert Humphrey to carry Texas by 39,000 votes, an edge made possible by his winning 90 percent of the vote in Mexican-American districts. Third-party efforts, such as those of La Raza Unida, also demonstrated the possible impact of a bloc vote in close elections in Texas and California. As a consequence, both major political parties showed increasing support for Mexican-American candidates after the mid-1960s. As shown in table 2, the number of Hispanic state legislators in the Southwest jumped abruptly after 1965—and continues to grow. Even a relatively small number of state legislators (as in Colorado and California) can have a significant effect by articulating ethnic interests. Mexican-American legislators in Colorado, for example, firmly ad-

---

14. For recent elections, see Neal Pierce and Jerry Hagstrom, "Democratic Primaries in California and Texas May Hinge on Chicano Vote," *National Journal* (April 26, 1980), pp. 681–84; Phil Gailey, "Courting Hispanic Voters Now a Reagan Priority," *New York Times*, May 19, 1983; and Dick Kirschten, "The Hispanic Vote—Parties Can't Gamble That the Sleeping Giant Won't Waken," *National Journal* (November 19, 1983), pp. 2410–16.

TABLE 2
MEXICAN-AMERICAN STATE LEGISLATORS IN FIVE SOUTHWESTERN STATES
Selected Years, 1950–84

State	1950	1960	1965	1974[a]	1984[b]
Arizona	0	4	6	11	12
California	0	0	0	8	7
Colorado	0	1	1	6	6
New Mexico	20	20	22	33	35
Texas	0	7	6	15	21
Total	20	32	35	73	81

SOURCES: Data for 1950, 1960, and 1965 were derived from the *Book of the States,* Supplement I, *State Elected Officials and the Legislatures* (Chicago: Council of State Governments, 1950, 1960, 1965). Figures for these years are approximate and are based on the author's determination of Spanish-surnamed legislators.
  a. Data for 1974 provided by the Southwest Voter Registration Project, San Antonio, Texas.
  b. National Association of Latino Elected and Appointed Officials (NALEO) Education Fund, *A Preliminary Listing of Hispanic State Legislators* (Washington, D.C.: NALEO, 1983).

vocate bilingual education. And in California, the Chicano caucus in the state legislature is deeply involved in addressing such issues as increasing Mexican-American representation in the government bureaucracy, farmworker problems, and bilingual education.

National political parties have increasingly courted the Mexican-American vote in Texas and California because of the peculiarities of the electoral college vote. California and Texas together account for approximately one-quarter of the electoral votes needed for a presidential victory and thus become pivotal states. In a close election the victory edge might be only one or two percentage points in these states. Table 3 shows that every 8 percent of the Mexican-American vote drawn by a presidential candidate in Texas in 1980 accounted for a 1 percent difference in the general election. Although a majority of the Chicano population traditionally votes Democratic (because of the New Deal, Kennedy, the Great Society, and the social liberalism associated with the Democrats), another segment of the community reponds to the Republican appeal to conservatism, its emphasis on family moral values and self-reliance. This variability makes the Mexican-American community one of the true "swing" votes in America today. Democratic candidates are not satisfied to capture a simple majority of the Mexican-American votes because every couple of percentage points that the Democratic presidential or statewide candidate gains above 50 percent may crucially alter the election. Conversely, Republican candidates benefit even from a minority of Mexican-American votes.

TABLE 3
1980 PRESIDENTIAL ELECTIONS AND MEXICAN-AMERICAN/HISPANIC VOTES

State	Statewide Presidential Vote	Hispanic Vote	Number of Hispanic Votes Needed to Produce a 1 Percent Shift in Election (Percent of Voters in Parentheses)	Number of Electoral Votes
Arizona	853,483	77,704	8,535 (11)	7
California	8,348,319	586,978	83,483 (14)	47
Colorado	1,150,906	65,043	11,509 (18)	8
Illinois	4,686,261	120,483	46,862 (39)	24
New Mexico	448,064	165,687	4,480 (3)	5
Texas	4,503,465	557,291	45,034 (8)	29

SOURCES: Statewide presidential vote from "Official 1980 Presidential Election Results," *Congressional Quarterly Almanac*, 96th Cong. 2d sess., vol. 36 (1981), appendix B, p. 6-B; Hispanic vote from U.S. Bureau of the Census, "Voting and Registration in the Election of November 1980," Series P-20 (Washington, D.C.: U.S. Government Printing Office, April 1982).

This crucial edge of victory leads to what some observers call "fiesta politics." Every four years presidential candidates start making overtures to the Hispanic and Mexican-American community. It was no coincidence that the first national commission on Mexican-American affairs was set up in 1967, one year before a presidential election. The Watergate hearings substantiated the efforts of the Nixon administration in 1971 in its "responsiveness" and "incumbency" programs to court the Mexican-American vote in 1972. In 1979, one year before his reelection bid, President Jimmy Carter began a series of town hall meetings to publicize the efforts of his administration to help Mexican-Americans. In 1983, again just before an election year, President Ronald Reagan appointed a Mexican-American from Texas to a job in the White House and made a series of highly publicized visits to Hispanic groups in Texas. Research remains to be done on how these overt ethnic political appeals by actors in the larger political system have reinforced political mobilization in the Hispanic community.

By the 1980s Mexican-Americans had won governorships in Arizona and New Mexico, and there were a host of Mexican-American elected officials at all levels of government. Yet much dissatisfaction remains as to the responsiveness of the political system to Mexican-

American concerns, a dissatisfaction that will continue to serve as the fuel for political mobilization.[15]

Several concerns are reflected in this general dissatisfaction. First, Mexican-Americans have unique problems that cannot be remedied by government programs aimed exclusively at other traditional minorities, such as black Americans. Bilingual education and bilingualism in general are prime examples of unique Mexican-American and Hispanic problems not shared by the black community. Furthermore, the lack of concern for Mexican-American problems shown by federal civil rights agencies such as the Equal Employment Opportunity Commission (EEOC), reinforces the perception that Mexican-Americans and Hispanics are not automatically helped by programs serving other minority groups.[16]

Second, the underrepresentation of Mexican-Americans in political and government positions is acute. For example, a civil rights report of November 1983 noted that although Los Angeles has the largest Mexican-American population in the United States, that city has not elected a Mexican-American city council member since the early 1960s.[17] Although in time the Mexican-Americans will, in all likelihood, duplicate the political gains of other ethnic groups in terms of elected representatives, bureaucratic representation in government agencies may be more problematic. Mexican-American representation in government lags far behind that of other groups. Underrepresentation in government bureaucracies will continue to be a salient issue as public policy issues become more complex and technical. A growing body of literature argues that national and state bureaucracies are becoming important factors in the development and implementation of public policy.[18]

---

15. Survey data can assess attitudes toward ethnic political mobilization, as well as leadership and organization statements. See Biliana C. S. Ambrecht and Harry P. Pachon, "Ethnic Political Mobilization in a Mexican American Community: An Exploratory Study of East Los Angeles, 1965–1972," *The Western Political Quarterly*, vol. 27 (September 1974), pp. 500–19.

16. Equal Employment Opportunity Commission's Task Force, "Equal Employment Opportunity Commission and Hispanics," (photocopy), December 2, 1983.

17. California Advisory Committee to the U.S. Committee on Civil Rights, "Los Angeles Reapportionment: Unfinished Business," November 1983, unpublished report. However, impressive political gains by Mexican-Americans have been made in the suburban cities of Los Angeles County, especially in the San Gabriel Valley area such as El Monte, Montebello, and Pico Rivera.

18. For more detail see Harry Pachon, "Hispanic Underrepresentation in the Federal Bureaucracy: The Missing Link in the Policy Process," in Armando Valdez, Albert Camarillo, and Tomas Almaguer, *The State of Chicano Research on Family, Labor*

Representation in Public Bureaucracies

A common result of underrepresentation is that Mexican-American organizations and elected officials are forced to "react" to complex public policy options without being involved in the development of policy options. Despite pressure and activism on this issue, the rate of increase of Mexican-Americans in the federal bureaucracy is so slow that Mexican-Americans and Hispanics will not be able to achieve proportional representation until the year 2025. Mexican-American and Hispanic political activity will continue to focus on this problem.

Third, continuing perceptions of discrimination by the larger society against Mexican-Americans provoke a collective ethnic response. The Mexican-American community perceives "English only" ordinances and referenda, for example, as being directly aimed against the use of Spanish in the community. Arguments imputing "separatism" to Spanish language use are particularly disturbing to a community that takes pride in its sacrifices and long-standing presence in this country.

In summary, Mexican-Americans constitute the largest minority group in most of the southwestern states. As a major part of this country's Hispanic population, Mexican-Americans will constitute the largest ethnic minority in the United States by the turn of this century. They represent a varied group that presents a challenge to American society. Issues of biculturalism, bilingualism, and political representation will be in the forefront.

Mexican-Americans have established themselves in the American political system as a significant group, but the shape and direction of future ethnic political mobilization will, in large part, depend on the reaction of the American society to this community.

---

and Migration (Stanford, California: Stanford Center for Chicano Research, 1983), pp. 209–19. See also U.S. Congress, House, Subcommittee on Appropriations, *Equal Employment Opportunity for Hispanics within the Federal Government*, 92d Cong., 2d session, November 3, 1982.

CHAPTER TEN

Policies that appear to favor one language over another usually evoke great emotion because of the interwoven relationship popularly perceived between group identity and a particular language. The close association is customarily reflected in the sharing of the same eponym by a people and its language. Thus, a somewhat tautological definition of the Swedish nation might be the people whose native language is Swedish; a similar terminological relationship between people and language can be observed in the case of the Catalans, Corsicans, Croats, Czechs, Finns, French, Germans, Japanese, and a host of other peoples. As a result of this close association, spokesmen for a people who perceive a threat to the native language will tend to equate its survival with the survival of the group as a distinct entity. The Irish, for example, waged their liberation struggle of the late nineteenth and early twentieth centuries under the banner of the need to reverse anglicization, preserve Gaelic, and thus preserve the Irish as a people. Similarly, the Ukrainians, Letts, and other peoples of the Soviet Union today carry on the struggle against russification largely in terms of preserving the language against Russian inroads.

Governments have also tended to perceive a close linkage between language on the one hand and identity and patriotism on the other. Franco's Spain was not atypical in outlawing the use of non-Castilian tongues as part of a strategy to transform Basques, Catalans, and Galicians into Spaniards. It will be recalled that, as Myron Weiner in chapter 5 of this volume pointed out, both Ethiopia and Iran have traditionally tried to eradicate the native language and thereby the separate sense of identity of, respectively, their Somali and Baluchi minority. And in the Soviet Union, where prevalent theory holds that people who change their language are well on their way to changing their national identity, the authorities have perceived the fostering of the Russian language as a key step toward the elimination of national diversity.

Despite such assumptions concerning a direct relationship between language and identity, comparative analysis confirms that

257

loss of language need not entail a corresponding loss of group consciousness. Most Basques, Bretons, Irish, Scots, and Welsh lost command of their ancestral tongues without losing national consciousness. Conversely, peoples such as the Quebecois have developed a separate sense of identity while continuing to speak the parent tongue. It would appear that language is far more important to group formation than to group maintenance. Thus, the Basques might be described as the people whose ancestors spoke Basque, the Scots as those whose ancestors spoke Scottish, and so on. In this context, it is perhaps worth remembering that Spanish is no more the "native" language of the Indian peoples of and from Mexico than English is of the Mohawks or Navahos. Both languages are hemispheric imports.

As captured in the witticism that "a language is a dialect with an army," all countries exert great impact upon the fate of languages. Even if made in an ad hoc decentralized manner, decisions concerning the language(s) to be used in schools, in government (including the bureaucracy, military, and the courts), in official documents, in the media, and in the public utterances of leaders will materially affect the vitality of languages. Not surprisingly, therefore, the issue of an appropriate language policy toward Mexican-Americans has been a heated one. In the following essay, Shirley Brice Heath examines the issue from the perspective of the history of language policies in both Mexico and the United States, and describes the hurdles hampering the design and adoption of a policy that would respond to the needs and attitudes of newly arrived members of the Mexican-American community. She stresses the need for community-based research.

LANGUAGE POLICIES
Patterns of Retention and Maintenance

Shirley Brice Heath

For centuries, the mystery of why some people keep their native tongue while others give it up to learn another language has intrigued poets, philosophers, politicians, and pedagogues. Actually, throughout most of the world, the established pattern of language learning is an additive one—individuals keep their native tongue while learning a second language, or even several other languages. Countries with an Anglo-Saxon heritage, however, tend toward a replacement pattern—that is, individuals give up their mother tongue when they learn English.

Cultural and societal forces in the United Kingdom and the United States, in particular, have pushed nonnative English speakers who have come to these countries as immigrants, refugees, or migrant workers to learn English so that they might move into the work force and achieve acceptance in the society beyond their own communities. In modern times, no official national-level policies mandate English; the status of English has been achieved in these countries without official declaration or the help of an official language academy. For speakers of other languages, the primary mandate for English has come from societal forces working on an individual's desire to secure education and employment, move into English-speaking social circles, and negotiate daily interactions with the bureaucratic and commercial mainstream.[1]

---

1. The legal background of language policies in the United States is explored by Arnold Leibowitz in *Educational Policy and Political Acceptance: The Imposition of English as the Language of Instruction in American Schools* (Arlington, Va.: Center for Applied Linguistics, 1971); and "Language and the Law: The Exercise of Power through Official Designation of Language," in William M. O'Barr and Jean F. O'Barr, eds., *Language and Politics* (The Hague: Mouton, 1976). For a discussion of recent bilingual education legislation in the context of U.S. legal history on language-related matters, see Shirley Brice Heath and Frederick Mandabach, "Language Status Decisions and the Law in the United States," in Juan Cobarrubias and Joshua A. Fishman, eds., *Progress in Language Planning: International Perspectives* (The Hague: Mouton, 1983).

The United States today is an extremely complex laboratory in which to examine language policies—whether at the national, state, or local level. Truisms often used to describe the path of upward mobility and assimilation for past non-English-speaking groups in the United States have little support from careful historical examinations of immigrant groups in the United States. Moreover, social scientists studying the current context find that they can no longer speak of socioeconomic opportunities for immigrant groups only in the context of rapid industrialization in urban regions and other broad patterns of national economic growth.

Social scientists can no longer consider national economies as isolates; as part of the global economy, they are interdependent, and the economic conditions of one country affect another. Because of the nature of the single world economic system, development and underdevelopment of countries are not autonomous processes but two parts of the same whole. Within the United States (or any other highly industrialized country), migrants and other unskilled workers are part of the whole that includes skilled workers and executive management. Substantial changes in one sector of this work force can have ramifications not only locally but throughout the country and the world economy.

In the past two decades the role of U.S. manufacturing, agribusiness, and industry in the world economic system has greatly altered traditional patterns of cultural and linguistic adjustment for non-English-speaking immigrants or migrants. Generalizations across all nonnative English speakers remain as laden with myths as they have always been, and "conclusions" about language policy for any unit of analysis above the community level are likely to be untestable and subject to charges that they fail to represent the dynamic and diverse natures of these groups. Quantitative attempts to measure national or regional trends can be seriously questioned by qualitative research at the local level. Such research attempts to describe change over time in the context of local economic and social circumstances responding to international and national economic trends. Not only is rapid geographic mobility a reality for many individual families of nonnative English-speaking groups, but also the geographic movement of agribusiness and manufacturing groups has increased in an era of changing state tax laws and improved circumstances in regions of the United States that are not unionized.

In addition, variation across and within immigrant groups with respect to prior education, social class backgrounds, and familiarity with urban industrialized life is complicated by the fact that this variation occurs not only across language groups, as has been the case in the past, but within language groups as well. Among Spanish speakers, the differences are vast. Puerto Ricans, Cubans, Mexican-Americans, and newcomers from South America and Central America have extremely diverse attitudes toward their own language and the role of language in their adaptation to life within the United States.

This chapter focuses on immigrants and migrants who have come to the United States from Mexico since the 1960s and considers the contexts of their linguistic and cultural adaptation. These contexts are (1) the national language policies of Mexico and the United States toward people who do not speak the majority language, (2) the socioeconomic conditions of migration and initial settlement in the United States, and (3) the community and family situations that prevail for these newcomers.

In this paper, I maintain that research examining the responses of these migrants to U.S. language policies will benefit from a distinction between *language maintenance* and *language retention*. The former term refers to federal or state *policies toward a language-minority group* that are aimed at helping the group retain its own language. The latter term refers to those *conditions, behaviors, and values within a language group* that enable it to retain its own language. Language retention may evolve in response to local socioeconomic circumstances and may be largely beyond the awareness of minority speakers; nevertheless, some portions of language-minority communities may consciously promote opportunities, institutions, and ideological supports for retaining the minority language. Because language retention takes place at the community level, research that examines how, when, why, to what extent, and in what forms minority-language groups retain their mother tongues must also be community- and family-based. I conclude with suggestions for such research and sketch the types of findings that may be expected.

A Comparison of Language Policies in Mexico and the United States

The term *language policies* usually refers to the decisions of an authority regarding the appropriate language(s) for carrying out the political, economic, legal, and educational affairs of a country as a whole or of regions within the country. The people who formulate such policies seek to achieve other goals: national unification; modernization; mass education; or reduction of institutional disruption

in courts, markets, and military services. Policymakers usually designate the people who are to implement policies as well as those who
are to carry out the language research and preparation of materials
necessary for the policies to be put into effect.

Throughout world history, institutions such as nation-states,
churches, and schools have formed and implemented language
policies. Ancient literature describes decisions made by military
conquerors to preserve and cultivate some languages while con-
demning other forms of a language or entire languages as "barbaric."
Since human social groups began, the practice by those in power of
restraining, prohibiting, or ignoring one or more languages or forms
of language while cultivating, spreading, and promoting others has
served the dual purposes of separating and unifying peoples.

In the modern world, most nation-states establish language policy
through their constitutions and implement their plans for language
change through their educational systems. A country may declare
one language or language variety to be the official one in which laws
are published and affairs of the government are conducted. A country
may select one language or language variety for secondary or higher
education, while another language or languages are mandated for
use in the lower schools. A state may ignore all languages other than
the official choice, or give other languages ceremonial or symbolic
recognition, or support the use of other languages for certain
functions or specific populations. Until the nineteenth century, imperial powers generally issued language policies in the name of
religious conversion or the building of an empire. The leadership of
nation-states of the nineteenth and twentieth centuries proclaimed
language policies to strengthen national unity or to reconcile internal
dissent among rival language groups.

In the cases just described, most of the language groups have
remained relatively stable geographically, and conquerors or new
national boundaries have brought new language policies. The twentieth century has, however, brought to international attention the
timeless pattern of populations migrating in search of a new homeland,
improved economic opportunities, or freedom from religious or
political persecution. Since World War II, many such migrants have
been workers moving from developing countries to highly industrialized countries in search of wage labor. Thus the imbalance of industrial
development among countries has produced groups around the
world who have become migrant workers or "guestworkers" in other
countries, sometimes through contractual arrangements between the
countries and sometimes without formal international agreements.

Policymakers have had to consider language policies for these groups. Educational decisions, as well as rulings on citizenship, work permits, and property ownership, have included language choice.

Whereas in earlier decades of the twentieth century, host countries seemed to assume these migrants would learn the language of the society in which they worked, some countries in the 1970s and 1980s began to consider it in their best interest to promote maintenance of the guestworkers' native tongues. Ethnic revivalism and reexaminations of human rights have also helped push politicians and educators to consider the responsibilities of the state for *language maintenance,* policy-backed efforts to enable a group to keep its own language.

Different groups have, however, had very different goals for these maintenance efforts. Some language minorities have judged state tolerance—and even promotion—of their native tongue an asset and have increased the number of their ethnic language schools and other ethnic institutions. Especially in periods of declining national economic productivity, language maintenance has also been a way to encourage guestworkers or migrants to keep their identity tied to their homelands. Countries wishing to cut back on social welfare to segments of their population have wanted to support conditions that might facilitate the return of migrant workers to their countries of origin.

In short, authorities, more often than not, have generated language policies to direct changes within the population. Thus language is inevitably an instrument of control to bring about religious, political, or socioeconomic shifts for individuals and groups. Some countries formalize their national language policies. Other countries have brought about changes in language without national-level policies, through alterations in socioeconomic conditions, ideological pressures, and policies related to immigration, naturalization, and employment. Mexico and the United States provide contrasting approaches to language policies; the colonial and early national assumptions about language differed greatly, as have twentieth-century economic conditions and programs of social change for language minorities.

Mexican Language Policies

Mexico is a country with a legacy of a linguistically diverse indigenous population. Throughout much of its colonial history, the majority of people in Mexico spoke one or more of nearly 240 different Indian languages. By the nineteenth century, Spanish was dominant in some areas, but the size of the country and the multitude of indigenous languages presented special problems. The subsequent history of the country has been heavily shaped by the legacy of colonial language policies. Today, though the majority of citizens speak Spanish, many small indigenous groups retain their mother tongues. For four centuries, Mexico has been a testing ground for a struggle between the indigenous and the Castilian or Hispanic languages.[2]

Colonial members of religious orders in Mexico saw Castilian as the common tongue that would provide an effective bond of communication between Indians and the clergy and at the same time expedite the conversion of the Indians. The Spanish crown maintained that Christianization meant Castilianization and counted on religion as the national symbol behind which the citizens of New Spain would rally. In the seventeenth century, when King Charles II attempted to unify the citizens of New Spain behind shared cultural values that extended beyond religion, he raised the Spanish language to a position of highest priority in a massive program of Hispanization. He also promoted an increasing amount of social and cultural contact between Spaniards and Indians. Following independence and throughout the nineteenth century, Mexican political leaders embraced the idea of a new society in Mexico that would be dependent on the "Mexican" point of view. Embedded in the definition of the Mexican individual and the Mexican nation was the desire to unify dissimilar peoples into a new nation.

The crisis of the Mexican Revolution in the early twentieth century stimulated a renewal of interest in indigenism in Mexico's history. The unity of revolutionary Mexico depended on taking the best of the Indian past and incorporating it in the Mexican identity. Increasingly during the twentieth century, however, *indigenismo* has been a tension-ridden movement. In the first years after the revolution, political leaders feared the struggle between the nationalistic and the particularistic in Mexico's culture would create isolated enclaves of Indian-tongue speakers locked away from socioeconomic and political participation in the society as a whole. Officials promoted Spanish instruction in rural schools and other means of incorporating the indigenous populations into the national culture.

---

2. The history of language policies in Mexico is given in Shirley Brice Heath, *Telling Tongues: Language Policy in Mexico, Colony to Nation* (New York: Teachers College Press, 1972).

What has followed—as industrial and urban expansion has attracted more and more rural migrants, including Indians, to Mexico City—has been a commercial focus on the cultural habits and group identification of indigenous groups. Indian craft centers have become modern-day sweatshops of tourist-focused commercial interests. For many, Castilianization has meant movement to the periphery of economic opportunities; many of the indigenous have left their self-sustaining agricultural and market activities to become incorporated only at the bottom rungs of the Mexican national labor force. Individuals and organizations sensitive to indigenous interests continue to face a dilemma. Should they promote assimilation of all groups through the adoption of Spanish as the single Mexican linguistic standard and Hispanic as the national cultural norm, or should they work to maintain indigenous linguistic and cultural values for Indian groups so the latter can retain both a secure sense of control over their own identity and links with their historical roots?

In recent decades, the Mexican government has seen promotion of the indigenous languages as a way to keep Indians involved in productivity, often agricultural, in their own regions. Migration to the cities of Mexico since the late 1960s has become a major problem, as industrialization and urbanization have not brought socioeconomic equality. As the government has sought to increase agricultural productivity and the distribution of manufacturing outside the major cities, some maintenance of indigenous languages is seen as facilitating these goals.

Language policies for the indigenous vary greatly from region to region in Mexico today. In areas such as Chiapas, the indigenous languages are used through the secondary level of public schools; in other areas, such as the Yucatan and Oaxaca, indigenous languages are used only when necessary as a transition to learning to read, write, and speak Spanish. Beyond language differences, the Indian groups have different cultural systems, patterns of language socialization, and attitudes toward their languages. Yet many Mexicans, especially those in the north of Mexico and in the major urban areas, are relatively unaware of the remaining Indian languages and cultures.

The country's indigenous heritage is most evident in its massive archeological riches and its colonial church buildings, which are a synthesis of Castilian and Indian art forms. Many Mexicans do not know that in regions such as Oaxaca and the Yucatan, their fellow citizens must make a choice of one language over another or learn at least one other language to participate as merchants in regional markets. Despite a past in which policymakers, colonial and national, devoted considerable attention to language policies, the majority of Mexicans today view Spanish as the only national language of Mexico and know little of regional and community-level decisions regarding other languages.

U.S. Language Policies

This "linguacentric" notion that the language in widespread use is the only language of the country is shared by Mexico's northern neighbor, the United States. Following the Anglo-Saxon tradition of considering language choice the responsibility of the individual, the United States has maintained the English legal custom of not regulating language officially or of denying personal liberties in language through federal policies. In spite of several efforts in the colonial and early national periods to establish an academy of language to formulate policies and standards of language use, the United States consistently turned down such proposals from both political officials and citizens. Since the nineteenth century some states and local communities have tried to promote a monolingual tradition and to emphasize standard English as the mark of reason, ethics, and aesthetics, but the federal government has formulated no official language policy.

American society has in large part regarded the public school as the institution to create a unified conforming citizenry. Throughout U.S. educational history, training institutions, publishing houses, and professional organizations have supported the public schools' efforts to organize the linguistic and cultural knowledge and behavior of America's young. Standard English as the "right" language has become both a fundamental instrument and a required symbol of knowledge and character.[3]

---

3. Attempts to establish a national language academy are traced in Shirley Brice Heath, "A National Language Academy: Debate in the New Nation," *International Journal of the Sociology of Language,* vol. 11 (1976), pp. 9–44. Reviews of the role of standard English in the shaping of Americans' self-identification may be found in Harvey A. Daniels, *Famous Last Words: The American Language Crisis Reconsidered* (Carbondale: Southern Illinois University Press, 1983); and Shirley Brice Heath, "Standard English: Biography of a Symbol," in Timothy Shopen and Joseph Williams, eds., *Standards and Dialects in English* (Cambridge, Mass.: Winthrop Publishers, Inc., 1972). An historical review of American attitudes toward language is given by Edward Finegan, *Attitudes toward English Usage: The History of a War of Words* (New York: Teachers College Press, 1980). Charles A. Ferguson, "National Attitudes toward Language Planning," in James E. Alatis and G. Richard Tucker, eds., *Georgetown University Round Table on Languages and Linguistics* (Washington, D.C.: Georgetown University Press, 1979), describes language attitudes of Americans in contrast to those of other countries which engage in direct language planning. Heinz Kloss, *The American*

With the Bilingual Education Act of 1968, federal legislators recognized the educational role of languages other than English for language-minority groups. The act promoted the use of the mother tongue of language-minority students in the early elementary years to facilitate the transition of these students to improved academic performance in English. By acquiring early cognitive development for academic skills in the mother tongue, students were expected to be able to move on to higher-order skills in English.

In the 1970–74 *Lau* vs. *Nichols* case, Chinese-speaking students in San Francisco argued that they did not receive an equal educational opportunity in schools where they could not understand the language of instruction. The Supreme Court ruled that under state-imposed standards that required school attendance, mandated use of the English language, and required fluency in English as a prerequisite to high school graduation, the Chinese students were not receiving equal treatment under Title VI of the 1964 Civil Rights Act. The *Lau* regulations that followed this decision greatly affected educational policies for all language minorities, but especially for Spanish speakers.

In California, in other southwestern states, in Florida, and in New York, Hispanics challenged the use of bilingual education as a transitional aid to enable students to replace Spanish with English. These Hispanic groups urged involvement by the federal government in helping language-minority communities maintain their language. The decade from 1974 to 1984 was marked by struggles between those who saw the government's role as simply promoting Spanish sufficiently to instill early academic skills and those urging extended uses of Spanish for higher levels of schooling and for a wider range of economic opportunities outside the immediate Spanish-speaking neighborhood. The latter groups increasingly have called for language policies that would establish bilingual education not as a path of transition to English for native Spanish speakers, but as a program to help Spanish speakers maintain and spread their language by increasing opportunities for its use in work places, the courts, and social services agencies.[4]

Bilingual Tradition (Rowley, Mass.: Newbury House, 1977) sets the language attitude of Americans in historical perspective and suggests that in earlier eras local conditions favored a "bilingual tradition."

4. Susan Schneider, *Revolution, Reaction or Reform: The 1974 Bilingual Education Act* (New York: Las Americas Publishing Co., 1977) provides the history of lobbying efforts and legislative debates surrounding bilingual education between 1966 and 1974. Gary Keller and Joshua A. Fishman, eds., *Bilingual Education for American Hispanics* (New York: Teachers College Press, 1981) fill in some details of the subsequent history of bilingual education. Articles in *Aztlán* and the *Bilingual Review* during the

Such policies would constitute a sharp break in the historical pattern of U.S. language policies. Observers of American society since de Tocqueville have noted the tendency of its citizens toward conformity; traditionally, people who have taken advantage of opportunities for either geographic or socioeconomic mobility have asked in their new surroundings, "What is expected of us?" Institutions of education, work, and leisure have in the past answered that the language that is expected is English. Despite the lack of a federal policy, local and state institutions have created practices limiting access to higher-level jobs to those who speak standard English.

One observer has assessed the U.S. failure to enact a specific language policy as "one of history's little ironies" and has suggested that "no polyglot empire of the old world has dared to be as ruthless in imposing a single language upon its whole population as was the liberal republic dedicated to the proposition that all men are created equal." Throughout U.S. history, in the absence of federal compulsion, socioeconomic forces have created an indirect compulsion, both on a community and individual level, for learning English. However, close examination of current socioeconomic conditions and community and family responses by Mexican-Americans suggests that migrants may increasingly be retaining Spanish while capturing at least some of the economic gains that motivated their migrations north. This community-level retention can, however, proceed without any maintenance efforts from the federal polity.[5]

The Choice of Language among Mexican-Americans

Since their earliest experiences in territory that is now the United States, people of Mexican origin have responded in a variety of ways to choice of language. They have been in what is now the United States longer than any group besides the American Indians, and they have thus faced numerous types of challenges—military, economic, social, and legal. As individuals and as groups, they have met extremely

late 1970s and throughout the 1980s provide further evidence of the trend toward maintenance arguments by Hispanics, as do the documentary records of organizations such as the Center for Hispanic Leadership in Boulder, Colorado.

5. Gerald Johnson in *Our English Heritage* (Philadelphia: J. B. Lippincott, 1949), pp. 118–19, noted the irony of the absence of language policy in the United States. Einar Haugen, *Language Conflict and Language Planning: The Case of Modern Norwegian* (Cambridge, Mass.: Harvard University Press, 1966), identified the focus on the individual as a key factor in U.S. attitudes toward language policies for immigrant groups.

varied circumstances in which to consider the role of the Spanish language as an essential part of the way they identify themselves.

The Indians of the American Southwest had their first contact with European culture from Spanish speakers; early waves of settlers from Mexico spread Spanish in the Southwest before the arrival of English. Until well into the nineteenth century, California and the American Southwest were the Spanish borderlands, but in the late 1800s the Hispanic presence in these areas dropped considerably. In the 1900s, however, economic conditions motivated Mexican immigration. Drawn both to the rapid development of the Southwest after World War I and to agricultural opportunities, especially in Texas and California, in the post-World War II period, Mexican-Americans settled first in the West and Southwest; but, since the 1960s, they have found homes in every state of the Union and a wide variety of occupations.[6]

Language and Socioeconomic Opportunities

Conditions for employment and community building for migrants from Mexico in recent decades differ greatly from those of earlier immigrants from Mexico as well as differing from those of other immigrant groups. In the American Southwest before the latter half of the nineteenth century, many of the settlers from Mexico became landowners. They created economic niches for themselves, and in New Mexico, families of Mexican origin were able to influence state politics and to create legislation that recognized the Hispanic presence in the region.

Later Mexican immigrants turned to mining, sheep herding, and agriculture. In the first half of the twentieth century, they were the backbone of migrant work forces in cotton, fruit, and vegetable production. Unlike many other immigrants prior to the mid-twentieth century who came initially to urban ghettos, most Mexicans prior to the 1960s moved to the cities only after experience in rural life within the United States.

Some European immigrants rapidly learned English, while others remained in transitional immigrant enclaves in which they could continue to use their mother tongues in much of their daily world. In American cities, immigrants in the late nineteenth and early

---

6. A useful brief history of "colonial Spanish," that brought by the earliest Spanish immigrants to the Southwest, is given by Jerry R. Craddock, "New World Spanish," in Charles A. Ferguson and Shirley Brice Heath, eds., *Language in the USA* (Cambridge, England: Cambridge University Press, 1981).

twentieth centuries settled in ghettos from which young and middle-aged men went daily to find factory work. The women and the elderly remained behind to establish small neighborhood businesses and to build family and community bonds; on the whole, the latter continued to use their mother tongues. In cities such as Cleveland, New York, and San Francisco, the children of immigrants attended bilingual schools; in other cities where the immigrant groups were not so large, the children went to schools where only English was used and learned to aspire to economic and social niches that depended upon the primary use of English.

Although the foreign-language presses and radio stations, community religious organizations, and even private schools that offered instruction in the mother tongue kept languages other than English alive for some families, most members of the younger generation set aside their mother tongues in favor of English. Work outside their own community demanded English, and the earning power gained outside those communities made subsequent generations want better housing, improved schools, and more distance between them and the lower-status groups that took their places in the ghetto. As second- and third-generation immigrants moved to the suburbs, they often brought only English with them for use within their families as well as in their leisure and work activities.[7]

The socioeconomic contexts into which migrants of Mexican origin have come since the 1960s stand in sharp contrast to those of earlier European immigrants whose labor was needed in the rapid industrialization of the late nineteenth and early twentieth centuries and in the manufacturing booms surrounding World War I and

---

7. The classic treatment of language among immigrant groups in the United States is Joshua A. Fishman, *Language Loyalty in the United States* (The Hague: Mouton, 1966); this volume contains individual chapters detailing the patterns of language retention of the major immigrant groups. Several chapters in Margaret A. Lourie and Nancy Faires Conklin, eds., *A Pluralistic Nation: The Language Issue in the United States* (Rowley, Mass.: Newbury House, 1978) provide useful updates on those groups covered by Fishman a decade earlier. Other updated information for some of these groups is in Charles A. Ferguson and Shirley Brice Heath, eds., *Language in the USA* (Cambridge, England: Cambridge University Press, 1981). Bilingual schools are discussed in Shirley Brice Heath, "English in our Language Heritage," in Charles A. Ferguson and Shirley Brice Heath, eds., *Language in the USA* and in *The American Bilingual Tradition*. The role of language-related ethnic community schools, as well as other non-English language resources such as the immigrant press and radio, is examined in Joshua A. Fishman, *Non-English Language Resources of the United States* (Final Report to Research Section, International Studies Branch, Department of Education, 1982). Structural and occupational adaptive patterns of European immigrant groups since 1880 are detailed in Stanley Lieberson, *A Piece of the Pie: Blacks and White Immigrants Since 1880* (Berkeley: University of California Press, 1980).

World War II. Although the popular media still frequently identify them as being primarily concentrated in agricultural labor, Mexican-Americans have rapidly moved out of agriculture into other occupations. In 1978, less than 7 percent of the documented Mexican-origin population worked in farm-related occupations, and only 19 percent lived in rural areas.

In recent decades, Mexican-Americans have participated heavily in rural-to-urban migration as agricultural labor markets have contracted and urban areas have offered increased opportunities for employment. The extraordinarily rapid growth of agribusiness, light industry, and the garment industry in the 1960s and 1970s, and of the electronics industry and service occupations (especially in hotels and fast-food establishments) in the 1980s, has provided wage-earning positions in and around cities across the United States. In many work places, the foremen or bosses speak Spanish, and the majority of production line workers can communicate with both co-workers and middle management in Spanish.[8]

For some workers, early experience in manufacturing was acquired in Spanish. Mexico's export-processing zone, located in northern Mexico and devoted primarily to garment and electronics manufacturing, in the 1970s provided initial wage labor experience to many unskilled workers who subsequently migrated across the border to similar jobs in the United States. These industries in Mexico and in the United States pay low wages and heavily discourage any attempts at organization by workers for higher wages or improved conditions. Approximately 90 percent of the laborers have been women, whose low socioeconomic position has been supported by an infrastructure within Mexico linked to multinational business interests within the United States.[9]

Once settled in the United States, recent migrants of Mexican origin have established large communities of Spanish speakers—communities large enough to support small businesses of sufficient variety to meet a majority of the needs of community members.

---

8. The movement by Mexican-Americans out of the migrant stream in the United States and the rapid recent movement away from agricultural labor by this group is detailed by M. Wells, "Emigrants from the Migrant Stream: Environments and Incentives in Relocation," *Aztlán,* vol. 7 (1982), pp. 165–90.

9. Researchers at the Center for Mexican American Studies, University of California, San Diego, have described the export-processing zone phenomenon and have linked its existence to international economic forces. See M. P. Fernandez-Kelly, *For We Are Sold, I and My People: Women and Industry in Mexico's Frontier* (Albany: State University of New York, 1983).

Merchants and service personnel in these community businesses find their native language a business asset.[10]

Language in Community and Family Life

For Mexican migrants, these relatively recently established communities are often the first buffers for adjustment to life in a new homeland. As long as ensuing waves of newcomers were compatible in class, educational background, and regional allegiances, established migrants have taken in the newly arrived migrants, often taking risks to protect undocumented workers. For the most part, however, the recent waves of Mexican migrants have not been able to depend on those of Mexican origin who came in past centuries and earlier decades of the twentieth century to take them in. The earlier immigrants have been so long established that they have left the communities of their first arrival and settled in mixed communities or in suburban neighborhoods away from opportunities for low-income work. Thus in the steady flow of migrants since the 1960s, the people who have been there to assist the new arrivals have been relative newcomers themselves.[11]

---

10. Trends of employment patterns in Southern California are detailed in reports (1982–84) of the Center for Mexican American Studies, University of California, San Diego. For a discussion of the role of small businesses on another recent immigrant group, see Edna Bonacich, Ivan Light, and Charles Coy Wong, "Small Business among Koreans in Los Angeles," in Emma Gee, ed., *Counterpoint: Perspectives on Asian America* (Los Angeles: University of California Asian American Studies Center, 1976). Sympathetic and graphic portrayals of daily life in Mexican-American communities in the Southwest in the 1960s appear in Stanley Steiner, *La Raza: The Mexican Americans* (New York: Harper & Row, 1970), especially chap. 11.

11. A comparison of kinship ties in the support networks of Mexican-Americans and Anglo-Americans is given in S. E. Keefe, "Personal Communities in the City: Support Networks among Mexican Americans and Anglo Americans," *Urban Anthropology*, vol. 9, pp. 51–74; and S. E. Keefe, Amado Padilla, and M. L. Carlos, "The Mexican-American Extended Family as an Emotional Support System," *Human Organization*, vol. 38, pp. 144–52. Compare these reports with that of J. Sena-Rivera, "Extended Kinship in the United States: Competing Models and the Case of La Familia Chicana," *Journal of Marriage and the Family*, vol. 41, pp. 121–29. The pattern in the United States of using personal networks in the adjustment to life in a new area is consistent with patterns described within Mexico as well. Both D. L. Kincaid, "Community Networks: Locus of Control among Migrants in the Periphery of Mexico City," Ph.D. dissertation, Michigan State University, 1972; and F. J. Morrett-Lopez, "Community Networks among Marginals in Mexico City," Ph.D. dissertation, Stanford University, 1979, describe communication networks among recent migrants to Mexico City. In both studies, newcomers depend on personal links to achieve stability. Morrett-Lopez reports the unexpected result, however, that the most stable links are those which are reciprocal and spatially proximate; actual kinship ties are negatively related to the stability of these networks.

Within a community in which the majority of members are still trying to find their way in schools and work places beyond the neighborhood while others have settled into retailing within the community, the key support institution for newcomers is the extended family household, which may be a residential unit or a nonresidential support network. The family itself is a tight nexus of emotional support and primary identification, even under strong influences from acculturating forces. Mexican-Americans maintain relatively large local kinship networks with high rates of reciprocity. Kinship ties of the extended family contribute both to the relative geographic stability of Mexican-American families and to the tendency of those families who do move to consider kinship ties in selecting new locations.

Community-Level Research Agenda

Social science researchers and policymakers know very little about patterns of language use in the homes, communities, and work places of these recent Mexican migrants. The avalanche of sociological, economic, and political writings on Mexican-Americans since World War II contains few examinations of cultural habits and ways of using language in local communities. Information is needed regarding shifts in language and culture patterns when early twentieth-century Mexican immigrants moved from rural to urban environments and changed from agricultural to industrial work settings. For comparison, scholars need detailed descriptions of language use in those communities that have accommodated the repeated waves of migrants since the 1960s.

To be sure, one cannot easily generalize patterns of behavior or expressions of attitudes by people of Mexican origin in one region to any other region or determine whether trends reflected at a given time represent a temporary change or long-term patterns. The relatively few studies that focus on language suggest that the only generalization that accurately encompasses language and culture patterns for this population is that one cannot generalize. Families and communities reflect wide diversities of cultural habits, language acquisition patterns, and values related to language uses. Much of this diversity existed in Mexico, and within the United States it has been both accentuated and leveled by the regional, economic, and socioreligious conditions into which the diverse migrants came.

Within studies of language use among Mexican-origin populations, the major topics are language attitudes, school testing and teaching patterns, and code switching (the alternating use of two languages in a single discourse). Almost no research treats language change in coordination with socioeconomic change for specific communities over time. We do not know (1) the extent to which communication networks remain stable linguistically over time or (2) the values members of such networks hold toward the retention of Mexican Spanish (as contrasted with a variety of Spanish which includes many anglicisms), or their beliefs about the correlation between learning English and adopting other behaviors viewed as alien to those of the local community.[12]

Both bilingual education and efforts since the late 1960s to accommodate more Spanish speakers in public services, medical centers, and law courts have prompted some studies of community attitudes. However, these studies have not systematically analyzed the correlation of behavior patterns with particular attitudes. Existing research is thus insufficient for determining predictable patterns of response to school language policies. Some groups strongly favor using Spanish in the elementary grades and involving parents exten-

---

12. A historical survey of Spanish language and educational policy in California that suggests the types of diversities current communities may present with respect to language decisions is provided by Alexander Sapiens, "Spanish in California: A Historical Perspective," *Journal of Communication*, vol. 29 (Spring 1979), pp. 72–83. A survey of research on Mexican-Americans' language attitudes is given by Miguel A. Carranza, "Attitudinal Research on Hispanic Language Varieties," in Ellen Bouchard Ryan and Howard Giles, eds., *Attitudes towards Language Variation: Social and Applied Contexts* (London: Edward Arnold, 1982). See Fernando Penalosa, *Introduction to the Sociology of Language* (Rowley, Mass.: Newbury House, 1981), for a general discussion of the social and economic factors affecting attitude formation among Spanish speakers in the United States. A recent study of the repertoire of Mexican-Americans' language varieties is reported in Lucia Elias-Oliveras, "Language in a Chicano Community," *Working Papers in Sociolinguistics*, no. 30 (Austin, Texas: Southwest Educational Development Laboratory). A collection of essays on regional varieties of Spanish, with some discussion of their acceptance by educators, is Eduardo Hernandez-Chavez, Andrew D. Cohen, and Anthony F. Beltramo, eds., *El Lenguaje de los Chicanos: Regional and Social Characteristics of Language Used by Mexican Americans* (Washington, D.C.: Center for Applied Linguistics, 1975). Studies of code switching as well as school testing and teaching trends are discussed by authors included in R. P. Duran, ed., *Latino Language and Communicative Behavior* (Norwood, N.J.: Ablex, 1981). For an early analysis of patterns of teacher interactions with Mexican-American students, see U.S. Commission on Civil Rights, *Teachers and Students: Differences in Teacher Interaction with Mexican American and Anglo Students*, Report 5, Mexican American Education Study (Washington, D.C.: Government Printing Office, 1973). David Lopez, in "Chicano Language Loyalty in an Urban Setting," *Sociology and Social Research*, vol. 62 (1978), pp. 267–78, warns against overgeneralizing studies done in one region to populations of Mexican-Americans in other areas.

sively in school activities; others would leave to the schools the choice of language policies; still others are apathetic and believe it would be inappropriate or impractical for them to play a role in making decisions about language use in school. Neither socioeconomic level nor length of residence in the United States correlates consistently with any of the most frequent community responses noted above. Clearly, factors that account for these differences in community links to the schools with respect to language have yet to be identified and compared across communities.[13]

Patterns of valuation of Spanish by institutions closely linked to communities and families, such as the church, are also almost completely unresearched. The relatively few studies available suggest that Mexican-Americans have faced "decades of isolation" from positions of leadership in the Catholic church. Only during the 1960s did volunteer organizations run by Mexican-Americans in Spanish for the benefit of Spanish speakers develop, and as these groups have been taken over by the institutional church, the trend has been to increase the use of English and to reinstate traditional structural patterns of Anglo dominance.

Traditional mutual aid and civic societies, ranging from the relatively conservative Sociedad Progresista Mexicana to the League of United Latin American Citizens (LULAC), have rarely held language policies to be centrally important in their business operations. Providing ballots and government publications in Spanish has helped special-interest groups and local political figures bring some Spanish-only speakers into political participation. Yet political leaders from Mexican-American communities who reach regional, state, or federal offices do not take up language issues as a central concern; instead, they bring language into debate under broader concerns, such as improved education, protection of jobs for Spanish speakers, and

---

13. Guadalupe Valdes, a longtime researcher in the courts of New Mexico, reports her findings and recommendations for future research in "Language Needs of Hispanic Minorities in the Criminal Justice System: A Research Agenda," unpublished report, July 1982. Cynthia Prince, "The Use of Spanish in a San Jose Medical Clinic," Ph.D. dissertation, Stanford University, 1984, describes interpreting services in a clinic that serves a largely Spanish-speaking population. Two Puerto Rican neighborhoods and their interactions with bilingual schools are described by Alicia Pousada, "Community Participation in Bilingual Education: The Puerto Rican Community of East Harlem," Ph.D. dissertation, University of Pennsylvania, 1984. Pousada also summarizes the literature on Hispanic communities' participation in bilingual education programs since the late 1960s. She finds in the two communities of her study that the overwhelming majority of residents maintain at least passive skills in Spanish and that community members carry "a strong conviction that bilingual programs are one of the best ways to foster bilingualism among the youth of the community" (p. 345).

adherence to federal funding guidelines in public agencies. Protestant groups, such as Jehovah's Witnesses, have been strongly influential in some communities of Mexican origin, and their members have encouraged the learning of English and the practice of reading and writing skills by parents and children.[14]

The language practices and policies of labor unions and specific work settings managed by Mexican-Americans have been described relatively infrequently. Here again, generalization is difficult because practices differ from region to region, as well as from group to group. The United Farm Workers, organized by Cesar Chavez in the 1960s, initially used primarily Spanish, but by the 1980s, its leaders used Spanish or English, according to the audience they were addressing. The Aliancia por Pueblo in California has generally carried out its business in English. Some branches of the Mexican-American Political Association (MAPA)—such as that in San Jose, California, which was led in the 1980s by Fernando Chavez (son of Cesar Chavez)—handled many of their affairs in Spanish, while other branches preferred English. COPE, a branch of the AFL-CIO in San Jose, has primarily used English in its activities and published materials.

One description of nondocumented kitchen workers done in the early 1980s in a restaurant with Mexican-American (English-dominant) waitresses and Anglo clientele indicated ways in which the Mexican-American waitresses helped kitchen workers acquire English on the job. It also documented reasons these workers gave for viewing English as necessary for their move up to becoming waiters. The study suggests that these workers will "enter an indefinite period of varying forms of coordinate and compound bilingualism."[15]

Community-level research on patterns of language retention and responses to language maintenance policies by language-minority communities around the world repeatedly stresses the importance of the links between these communities and the larger society. For communities of Mexicans who recently arrived in the United States,

---

14. Most accounts of Chicano life in the Catholic church are either highly journalistic or strongly biased in their presentation of facts. A. Soto, "The Chicano and the Church in Northern California," Ph.D. dissertation, University of California, Berkeley, 1978, provides a thorough study of the leadership opportunities offered Chicanos in one region.

15. For a description of labor and political groups in the 1960s, see Steiner, *La Raza: The Mexican Americans*, chap. 14. The author characterizes one branch of MAPA as "middle-class," and calls attention to the diverse ways different branches represent themselves. Jose Limon, in "Language, Mexican Immigration, and the 'Human Connection': A Perspective from the Ethnography of Communication" working paper, 1982, gives one of the few detailed descriptions of Mexican-Americans' language use in a work setting and predictions for future trends (p. 17).

only the most tentative suggestions concerning the nature of these links can be offered. Links to mainstream institutions such as the school, the work place, and government bureaucracies apparently depend on individual family initiatives or small groups of significant friends.

Despite the availability of Spanish-language newspapers, sources of mainstream institutional information remain primarily oral and family-based. They are therefore so short-lived as to limit possibilities of building habitual cultural patterns of initial contact, clarification of job demands, and follow-up with appropriate paperwork. Spanish remains for many of the adults in these families the primary language, although their children may use English at school, among their peers, and sometimes with their parents. However, institutional links to English, aside from the schools, seem to be minimal even for young people; they have few opportunities to hear or use the formal, standard English required for school success and job placement above the bottom socioeconomic level.[16]

Almost the only economic niche above this lowest socioeconomic level which has been identified primarily with Mexican-Americans in the past two decades is the business of bilingual education. Many immigrants from past decades who have risen in class status and become local elites have moved into positions of influence in education following the Bilingual Education Act of 1968. Their increased number and their influence in education have depended on the continuation of bilingual education. Calls for language maintenance and more supports for language retention from within communities have come largely from this relatively new middle class of educators. Many of these educators have left their old communities and may find it difficult to accept the eagerness of new arrivals who want to learn English and to become "American." Mexican-American educators may unwittingly promote bilingual education for their own institutional and professional goals as well as for the practical needs and personal goals of recent arrivals.[17]

16. Ralph Fasold, "Language Maintenance and Shift," in R. Fasold, ed., *Sociolinguistics and Society*, forthcoming, describes the role of links between immigrant communities and mainstream institutions in bringing about a language shift.

17. R. Romo, *East Los Angeles: History of a Barrio* (Austin: University of Texas Press, 1983), portrays the desires of different waves of residents to become "American." See also H. Romo, "Sra. Mercedes: A Mexican Immigrant Parent," in *Working Papers in Sociolinguistics*, no. 86 (Austin, Texas: Southwest Educational Development Laboratory, 1981). R. Stavenhagen, *Sociologia y Subdesarollo* (Mexico City: Ed. Nuestro Tiempo, 1971); and Pablo Gonzalez Casanova, *Sociologia de la Exploitacion* (Mexico: Siglo XXI, 1969), describe the tendency of formerly exploited groups to develop a

Conscious language retention efforts by the recent Mexican migrants themselves have not been documented; thus they cannot be compared with the methods and goals of their middle-class spokesmen. Some recent migrants seem to see English as the determinant not of their own future but of their children's future in a different community and a different set of jobs. Many migrants who speak minimal English, however, achieve entry into unskilled jobs that provide relatively steady hourly wages. No matter how ruthlessly they are exploited in industry and agriculture by U.S. standards, the wages and social service benefits, combined with the educational opportunities for their children, are a considerable gain over their economic chances in Mexico. The crisis of the Mexican economy after 1981 accentuated this view among migrants who increasingly traveled back and forth to visit family members in Mexico and sometimes bought land there to help family and friends and to give themselves and their children a tangible tie to the homeland.

Aside from a focus on groups, such as the church and labor unions, which directly serve Mexican-American communities and on conditions that help determine self-identification, researchers interested in language retention must also look carefully at patterns of language socialization within families. How do families of recent migrants use Spanish or English at home, and do these uses prepare the young to handle school tasks and communication with the wider society? Some recent research studying mothers' habits of socializing their children to language use details methods of telling stories, asking for clarification, giving directions, and scolding or praising. This research shows that these parents do not provide extended explanations to children, nor do they give direct instructions and model clarification questions. Instead, much verbal instruction is indirect and children are expected to learn through observation and modeling. Several discourse forms that are critical to academic success and skilled jobs (such as sustained accounts on a single topic, punctuated by mention of secondary authorities or reference to written sources) are rare.

---

stratified hierarchy that brings to the top people who become exploiters of those of their own group left below them in the social structure. B. B. Khleif, "Ethnicity and Language in Understanding the New Nationalism: The North Atlantic Region," *International Journal of Comparative Sociology*, vol. 23 (1980), pp. 114–21, compares ethnic revival movements and suggests their interdependence with changes in the world economy in the 1970s. See also E. Allardt, *Implications of the Ethnic Revival in Modern, Industrialized Society, Commentationes Scientiarum Socialium* (Helsinki: Societas Scientiarum Fennica, 1979), on the role of language in new self-identification of ethnic groups.

Although children and adults may read and write at home, their uses of literacy skills are primarily practical (writing letters and completing forms) or confirmational (reading religious materials or preparing for rites of passage, such as the fifteenth birthday). Numerous types of skills that schools require, such as responding to requests for labels of items and events and literate-based information about these, are not called for in language uses at home or in the community.[18]

For the migrants of the past two decades, families represent their only "tightly coupled" institutions. Other institutions, such as the church, voluntary associations, the school, and the work place, appear to be only "loosely coupled" and to offer almost no occasions to supplement the language socialization of the home. Thus, many children of migrants do not become familiar with or have occasions to practice language uses such as focused questioning, sustained oral and written discussion, and extended descriptions of sequential actions. The family remains the primary source of opportunities to use oral and written language, as well as the major source of future self-identification.

Individuals who wish to improve their language skills have to look beyond the family. However, there appear to be no cultural or linguistic institutions ready to help in this regard. Those who do try to extend themselves beyond the family may find few daily interactive learning situations in which they can practice formal discourse and

---

18. For a review of the literature on patterns of language acquisition among children in Mexican-American families, see Davida Desmond, "Language in a Mexican American Community," Ph.D. dissertation, Stanford University, forthcoming. Desmond also provides an ethnography of communication in an immigrant community, which is in the same research tradition as the work of John Attinasi, P. Pedraza, S. Poplack, and A. Pousada, *Intergenerational Perspectives on Bilingualism: From Community to Classroom* (New York: Language Policy Task Force, Center for Puerto Rican Studies, 1982). Luis Laosa has identified several mainstream oral language patterns, such as questioning, verbally explicating directions, and offering repeated praise, which are not used in Mexican-American families; instead these families stress modeling, visual cues, and directives; see "Maternal Teaching Strategies and Cognitive Styles in Chicano Families," *Journal of Educational Psychology*, vol. 72 (1980), pp. 45–54. For further evidence of differences in general discourse forms, see C. Briggs, "Communicative Hegemony in Fieldwork," *Semiotics*, forthcoming. Further evidence of the strong links between home language use and performance in outside institutions such as the school is given by David P. Dolson, "The Influence of Various Home Bilingual Environments on the Academic Achievement, Language Development, and Psychosocial Adjustment of Fifth and Sixth Grade Hispanic Students," Ph.D. dissertation, University of San Francisco, 1984. In this study, students from families who have retained Spanish as the dominant home language outperformed students from homes where a switch to English has occurred on five of ten scholastic measures.

acquire language styles necessary for ensuring job opportunities in semiskilled or skilled domains. In short, the language forms that can translate into capital in moderately skilled or highly skilled jobs are often unavailable for recent migrants in settings other than the school. Opportunities to practice there are insufficient to enable children to acquire a firm footing in standard English skills, particularly when children start school without basic English-language socialization patterns.[19]

Conclusions

The majority of the American populace seems to believe that the United States still holds out the American dream to newcomers from Mexico. Yet the continuing movement back and forth across the border, the purposeful isolation of some of these communities, and the maintenance of intangible and tangible links to Mexico indicate that in recent decades not all people of Mexican origin have adopted this dream as their goal. Most Americans believe that the driving force behind language shift is individual enterprise, and that the society at large need not take much responsibility for facilitating or easing this shift. They believe that people who seek upward social mobility, profitable participation in a labor market, and steady work in modern factories will choose English and that schools will help them make that choice.

Economic conditions in the 1980s, however, have altered this pattern in many regions of the country. Certain sectors of the work force in industrial production and manufacturing and in service occupations for restaurants, hotels, and office buildings may achieve relatively high wages, but remain cut off from the upward mobility that would integrate them with English-only speakers. In some industries, the increased use of computers is making available more jobs at the lowest levels, while creating a greater gap between these unskilled workers and the semiskilled workers above them.

In the mid-1980s, many people of Mexican origin are able to retain their own language because of the supportive nature of their

---

19. The terms "loosely coupled" and "tightly coupled" are drawn from the research on organizational systems of K. E. Weick, "Educational Organizations as Loosely Coupled Systems," *Administrative Science Quarterly*, vol. 21 (1976), pp. 1–19. The characteristic patterns of reading and writing in bureaucratic institutions and the ways in which these control clients' access to goods and services are described in Roger Fowler, Bob Hodge, Gunther Kress, and Tony Trew, *Language and Control* (London: Routledge & Kegan Paul, 1979).

extended family in both the United States and Mexico, their divided sense of community between their residence in the United States and their "home" in Mexico, and the current availability of economic opportunities that do not demand English. Spokesmen for bilingual education may find it useful to consider these conditions for language retention as evidence that the educational policies of the federal government and other public service organizations could support the immigrants' maintenance of Spanish by facilitating its spread. (Language spread is the increase over time in the proportion of a communication network that adopts a given language or language variety for a given communicative function.) Federal or state government sponsorship of rules requiring Spanish in social services, legal affairs, medical establishments, and other institutions serving the general public would increase the communicative functions of Spanish beyond those of face-to-face interactions among intimates within their own homes and friendships or retail networks. People advocating such spread want to make Spanish, along with English, a language that links the mainstream institutions and the Mexican-American communities.[20]

---

20. David E. Lopez, *Language Maintenance and Shift in the United States Today: The Basic Patterns and their Social Implications. Vol. III: Hispanics and Portuguese* (Los Alamitos, Calif.: National Center for Bilingual Research, 1982), points out that, according to national data collected in 1976, Mexican-Americans have "considerable intergenerational maintenance" and there is "a strong indication that Mexican Americans are more language retentive than other groups" (p. 50). National statistics show that approximately 30 percent of all U.S.-born Mexican-Americans retain Spanish as the language of the home; yet, Lopez cautions that considerable differences exist across regions of the United States as well as among Mexican-American communities, and that "our knowledge of the variation . . . is still very crude," p. 50. It is ironic that in 1947–48, George Barker, in *Social Functions of Language in a Mexican-American Community,* Anthropological Papers of the University of Arizona, no. 22 (Tucson: University of Arizona Press, 1972: first published in 1947), reported a study that could be a basic model of the kind of community-level research currently called for on language retention among Mexican-Americans; yet other scholars have not followed and expanded this pioneer study. In Tucson, Arizona, Barker, an anthropologist, studied the uses of Spanish and English among Mexican-Americans and concluded: "In a bilingual minority group in process of cultural change the functions originally performed by the ancestral language are divided between two or more languages, with the result that each language comes to be identified with certain specific fields of interpersonal relations. Thus for each individual, language takes on symbolic values which vary according to the individual's social experience. The character of this experience, in turn, depends on, first, the position of the minority group in the general community; second, the relation of the individual to the bilingual group; and, third, the relation of the individual to the general community," p. 45. Barker studied the uses of Spanish and English in the home and community, as well as in the social and work relations of members of a small Mexican-American community in Tucson in the mid-1940s. He concluded his study by calling for further research examining the

The diverse conditions of persons of Mexican origin who have come to the United States in recent decades and the variation in their subsequent path of adaptation to American life limit the value of generalizations across communities and regions. Community-based research is needed to answer some key questions regarding language retention and maintenance. What are the conditions—social, economic, cultural, and religious—that support language as an instrument of change? Do internal group factors lead groups to retain their language in spite of strong historical and broad societal forces which promote English? Are federal, state, or local policy pressures toward language shift more likely to succeed with some groups of migrants or immigrants than with other groups? A series of carefully conducted community studies in different regions of the United States could provide answers to these questions and help develop a theory accounting for ways in which language uses and the values associated with language held by local groups are connected with socioeconomic conditions brought into play by the global and national economies.

---

retention and spread of Spanish at the community level, and he suggested (p. 47) that the study of language in use could provide "the basis for a new and widely applicable method of sociological analysis." Robert Cooper, ed., *Language Spread: Studies in Diffusion and Social Change* (Bloomington: Indiana University Press, 1982) provides case studies of the spread of languages to new speakers or new functions and a theoretical statement about conditions that facilitate either type of spread.

CHAPTER ELEVEN

The vivid contrast between the present linguistic situation in the United States and the situation contemptuously depicted in a 1909 issue of the *New York Herald Tribune* highlights the immensity of the victory that American English has scored over the non-English tongues of former immigrants:

> Tammany Hall is going after the votes in twenty different languages this year. If the Democratic organization does not get its share of the great cosmopolitan vote it won't be because it didn't try. Spellbinders have been engaged to disseminate doctrine in Yiddish, Hungarian, Bohemian, Greek, Italian, Polish, Russian, Swedish, Norwegian, Chinese, Danish, French, German, Armenian, and Boweryese, among other tongues. There is no reason why any man, no matter his nationality, should be without a mass meeting. He can have it for the asking. The international oratorical brigade has been rehearsing. When they all get together it sounds like a flock of crows being run through a sausage machine.

In addition to the multilevel government policies that have favored English, another key factor in the abandonment of non-English tongues has been the awareness that English is the language of success. Social mobility has presupposed fluency in English. Evidence that the mandated use of English in the public schools cannot in itself explain the disappearance of other immigrant languages can be found in the fact that in the mid-nineteenth century a number of communities in the United States permitted the use of a language other than English as the language of instruction in the public schools. But the demand for such schools dissipated in the face of increasing parental desire for their children to have the same opportunities as did those graduating from English-language schools. More recently, parental concern has resulted in a sharp decrease in the demand for French-language parochial schools among Americans of French-Canadian background.

Both Donald L. Horowitz in chapter 3 and Shirley Brice Heath in chapter 10 have noted the significance of all this for the Mexican-Americans. For members of that community also, the data suggest a correlation between their ability in English and their status and income. Are Mexican-Americans therefore apt to follow the path of linguistic assimilation trod by earlier waves of immigrants? Reynaldo Macías, after reviewing the available statistical data on language ability and use by Mexican-Americans, offers several reasons why he believes that predictions of the demise of the Spanish language within the United States may prove premature.

NATIONAL LANGUAGE PROFILE OF THE MEXICAN-ORIGIN POPULATION IN THE UNITED STATES[1]

Reynaldo F. Macías

Debates about language issues often include competing predictions for the future of the country. Advocates of bilingualism often appeal to a culturally pluralistic world with increased international interaction whereas opponents of bilingualism (that is, advocates of monolingualism) raise the specter of a balkanized country struggling with geolinguistic groups who want to secede from the union. An occasional researcher will analyze survey data to determine whether Spanish (or other non-English languages) is being transmitted intergenerationally or whether we are becoming a country of *monolingual* English speakers (that is, without retaining Spanish).[2] A few researchers even dare to statistically project the size of various language groups into the near future.[3] With the exception of these projections, the survey analyses almost invariably predict a loss of Spanish or a shift from Spanish to English for Chicanos and other Latinos in the United States.[4] In many of these studies the complexity of language use and the processes of language maintenance and shift are ignored. Because many of the studies cite one another, however, their findings become "consistent with the literature."

---

1. The terms *Mexican-origin* and *Chicano* are used in this paper to refer to all persons of Mexican ancestry within the United States regardless of place of birth, citizenship, or immigration status.
2. Calvin Veltman, "The Retention of Minority Languages in the U.S.," in A. Pedone, ed., *The Retention of Minority Languages in the U.S.* (Washington, D.C.: National Center for Education Statistics, 1981).
3. R. Oxford et al., *Contractor Report: Projections on Non-English Language Background and Limited English Proficient Persons in the U.S. to the Year 2000*, 4 vols. (Washington, D.C.: National Center for Education Statistics, 1980, 1981). See also R. Oxford et al., "Projections of Non-English Language Background and Limited English Proficient Persons in the U.S. to the Year 2000: Educational Planning in the Demographic Context," *NABE Journal*, vol. 5 (Spring 1981), pp. 1–30.
4. The terms *Latino* and *Spanish-origin* refer to all persons of Latin-American, Spanish-speaking Caribbean, or Spanish ancestry within the United States.

This paper describes the language ability of Latinos in relation to other sociodemographic characteristics of the population. The general pattern of language change found in the literature on this topic is a three-generation model of English-language assimilation among immigrants. This assimilation is in only one direction (from non-English to English acquisition), and retention of non-English language or cultural attributes is seen as exceptional and sometimes as dysfunctional.

The 1966 study of Fishman and colleagues is a classic in this regard, although they allow for compression or extension of the time period for the three generations of language assimilation.[5] The focus of the study was principally European language groups within the United States. Spanish was also studied because of the size of the group. The authors exempted Spanish-speaking peoples, particularly Mexicans, from some of their conclusions. Yet the examination of Chicanos, "on their own terms," as it were, comes slowly.

Spanish speakers make up the major non-English language group in the United States, and they are growing in numbers (see table 1). With regard to language maintenance and shift, the study by Fishman and colleagues found the "drift has been consistently toward Anglification and has become accelerated in recent years."[6] The growth in the number of Spanish speakers over the years seems particularly important in light of this conclusion made almost twenty years ago. If this growth is to be reconciled with the trend toward anglicization, an alternative source of Spanish speakers (other than through inter-generational transmission of Spanish) must be accepted. In-migration of Spanish speakers is important to this growth but insufficient to fully explain it. The policy implications of this growth in number of Spanish speakers in the United States are only recently, and super-ficially, being explored and considered.

Few book-length works focus on macrosociolinguistic descriptions of Spanish in the United States. For a number of years, Gaarder's 1977 essay was the only one directly concerned with the Spanish language and its maintenance and shift.[7] It also specifically explored the congruence of language and ethnic group (Chicanos). However, it lacked supportive descriptive data, something unavailable on a

---

5. Joshua Fishman et al., *Language Loyalty in the United States—The Maintenance and Perpetuation of Non-English Mother Tongues by American Ethnic and Religious Groups* (The Hague: Mouton, 1966).

6. Ibid., p. 395.

7. A. Bruce Gaarder, *Bilingual Schooling and the Survival of Spanish in the United States* (Rowley, Mass.: Newbury House, 1977).

TABLE 1
GROSS GROWTH OF SPANISH-SPEAKING POPULATION IN THE UNITED STATES,
1850–1976, WITH PROJECTIONS TO 2000

Year	Number of Spanish Speakers in Mainland United States	Population of Puerto Rico	Total Number of Spanish Speakers
1850	118,000	. . .	118,000
1860	170,000	. . .	170,000
1870	234,000	. . .	234,000
1880	333,000	. . .	333,000
1890	423,000	. . .	423,000
1900	562,000	953,200	1,515,200
1910	448,200	1,118,000	1,566,200
1920	850,800	1,299,800	2,150,600
1940	1,861,400	1,869,300	3,730,700
1960	3,336,000	2,349,500	5,685,500
1970	7,823,600	2,712,000	10,535,600
1976	10,608,900	3,217,000	13,825,900
1980	11,745,400	3,187,600	14,933,000
1985	13,191,300	3,390,700	16,582,000
1990	14,778,900	3,593,800	18,372,700
1995	16,436,600	3,796,900	20,233,500
2000	18,145,200	4,000,000	22,145,200

SOURCE: R. F. Macías, "Language Diversity among U.S. Hispanics: Some Background Considerations for Schooling and Non-Biased Assessment," in J. Speilberg, ed., *Proceedings—Invitational Symposium on Hispanic American Diversity* (East Lansing, Mich.: Michigan State University and Michigan State Department of Education, 1982), pp. 110–36.

national scale until recently. Several other monographs have since been published that contribute to or provide a national view of Mexican-origin language abilities. Peñalosa provides a needed synthesis of the extant sociolinguistic work up to 1978.[8] Veltman offers a synthesis of his various analyses of the 1976 Survey of Income and Education data, which still does not report ethnic and language categories.[9] López provides a refreshing, systematic comparative analysis of the Survey of Income and Education data for various language-minority ethnic groups by monolingual and bilingual categories.[10]

---

8. Fernando Peñalosa, *Chicano Sociolinguistics* (Rowley, Mass.: Newbury House, 1980).

9. Calvin Veltman, *Language Shift in the United States* (Berlin: Mouton, 1983).

10. David López, *Language Maintenance and Shift in the U.S. Today: The Basic Patterns and Their Social Implications*, 4 vols. (Los Alamitos, Calif.: National Center for Bilingual Research, 1983).

These analyses have their strengths and weaknesses. Researchers have needed the statistical profiles of various language and ethnic characteristics these studies provide. Because they have been principally concerned with language shift, however, they should be seen as only partial contributions to the data and analyses that are necessary to adequately explore the twin issues of language maintenance and language shift.

Research needs are threefold: (1) an adequate countrywide description of the numbers and characteristics of Spanish speakers; (2) more information on the congruence between Spanish speakers and the various Spanish-speaking national origin populations (for example, Mexican, Puerto Rican, and Cuban); and (3) an analysis, based on adequate descriptive data, of the variables identified in the literature on language contact and bilingualism as they affect the Mexican-origin and other Spanish-speaking populations in the United States. The aim of this paper is to contribute to the first and second of these needs.

Speech and Language Characteristics of the Mexican-Origin Population

Language abilities and their distribution among the national Mexican-origin population have only recently been explored in several national surveys. Local and community descriptions are available in the anthropological and sociological literature as well. Analysis of the 1976 Survey of Income and Education, which is the most comprehensive recent national survey and includes fifteen language and language-related questions, provides the following profile of the Mexican-origin population.[11]

Language Abilities

The process of acquiring one or more languages is a relatively new area of systematic study. Large-scale survey data have not contributed much to this area, in part because they have not focused on language "traits" but have been "gross" surveys. Also, it is difficult

---

11. U.S. Bureau of the Census, *Survey of Income and Education* (Questionnaire), Form SIE-1 (Washington, D.C.: U.S. Government Printing Office, Spring 1976).

TABLE 2
USUAL LANGUAGE AND HOUSEHOLD LANGUAGE CHARACTERISTICS OF THE
MEXICAN-ORIGIN POPULATION IN THE UNITED STATES, SPRING 1976
(Numbers in Thousands)

Language Characteristics	Total		Total U.S.-Born Population		Total Foreign-Born Population	
	Number	*Percent*	*Number*	*Percent*	*Number*	*Percent*
Total population	6,797[a]	100.0	5,366	78.9	1,432	21.1
English-language backgrounds	960	14.1	945	98.4	*	...
Spanish-language backgrounds	5,763	84.8	4,380	76.0	1,413	24.5
English-only households	279	4.1	235	84.2	44	15.8
Spanish-language households	5,505[b]	81.0	4,143	75.3	1,361	24.7
English as usual language	2,548	37.5	2,266	88.9	281	11.0
Spanish as usual language	2,107	31.0	1,055	50.1	1,052	49.9

SOURCE: National Center for Education Statistics, *Bulletin,* October 20, 1978, p. 5, table 2. Percentages may not add due to rounding.
* Fewer than 15,000 persons.
a. Includes an estimated 32,000 persons with language backgrounds other than Spanish and English. Percentages in the next column are based on the total Mexican-origin population (6,797,000).
b. Includes an estimated 554,000 children aged three and younger for whom information on individual languages was not obtained and an estimated 294,000 persons whose individual languages were not reported.

to view process from data collected at one point in time.[12] Another reason that survey data have not contributed much to language acquisition studies is that the administration of survey instruments is usually aimed at an adult member of a respondent unit (usually a household), who then reports on others in the unit.

Questions about a respondent's mother tongue usually concern only the head of the household or—as in the Survey of Income and Education—are asked only of persons over fourteen years of age. In the United States such questions seldom are used to identify the

12. But see Erica McClure, "Aspects of Code Switching in the Discourse of Bilingual Mexican American Children," in Saville-Troike, ed., *GURT 1977—Anthropology and Linguistics* (Washington, D.C.: Georgetown University Press, 1977), pp. 93–116; and Erica McClure, *Aspects of Code Switching in Discourse of Bilingual Mexican American Children,* Technical Report 44, Center for the Study of Reading (Urbana: University of Illinois, April 1977). This author, like other variationists, age-grades the data and imputes acquisitional ordering.

language *acquired* by the child. I am not concerned here with actual acquisition of language or traits of language as much as the socio-linguistic household setting for children.

The interaction between reported usual language abilities and household languages is shown in table 2 for the entire Mexican-origin population of the United States. Only 14.1 percent of the Mexican-origin population was of English-language background (that is, lived in an exclusively English-speaking household and, if over fourteen years of age, had English as their mother tongue). This does not reveal anything about the speech networks of the Mexican-origin population,[13] but it is important in indicating one of their primary socializing contexts. Almost all these persons with English-language backgrounds were born in the United States.

The majority of U.S. Mexicans, then, come into contact with Spanish in one way or another—either as a mother tongue, even if they live in English-only households (4.1 percent), or by living in a household in which Spanish is spoken, whether their own usual language is Spanish (31.0 percent) or English (37.5 percent). In any case, these household data confirm that the Mexican-origin population in the United States is a bilingual community.

Looking at the data more closely, one finds that English was reported slightly more often than Spanish as a usual language, whereas Spanish was reported more often than English as a second language (table 3). Slightly more than 75 percent of those surveyed reported Spanish as their mother tongue (but remember this is the language spoken in the *household* of the adult—age fourteen and older—when that adult was a child, not necessarily the language the adult actually spoke as a child).

It is tempting to impute a language shift in the population on the basis of the percentage reporting Spanish as their mother tongue and the percentage of persons using Spanish as their current language (table 4), but the mother-tongue data as household data are better compared to the current *household* language data. This comparison shows no shift away from Spanish but indicates that Spanish-language households were still very evident.

Language abilities for persons age fourteen and over can also be seen in table 4. A total of 417,000 persons (9.6 percent) reportedly spoke only English; 1,543,000 (35.7 percent) spoke English as their

---

13. Dell Hymes, "Models of the Interaction of Language and Social Life," in J. Gumperz and D. Hymes, eds., *Directions in Sociolinguistics—The Ethnography of Communication* (New York: Holt, Rinehart, and Winston, 1972), p. 55.

TABLE 3
MOTHER-TONGUE, USUAL, AND OFTEN-SPOKEN LANGUAGE
CHARACTERISTICS OF THE MEXICAN-ORIGIN POPULATION, SPRING 1976[a]
(Numbers in Thousands)

Second Language	Mother Tongue		Usual Language		Often-Spoken Language	
	Number	Percent	Number	Percent	Number	Percent
Spanish	3,244	75.0	2,130	35.0	2,174	35.7
English	1,016	23.5	2,857	47.0	1,303	21.4
Unknown or no response	59	1.4	1,101	18.1[b]	2,611	42.9[c]
Total	4,319	100.0	6,088	100.0	6,088	100.0

SOURCE: U.S. Bureau of the Census, *Survey of Income and Education* (1977 Extract). Percentages may not add due to rounding.
a. For persons aged fourteen and older.
b. Includes an estimated 786,000 persons for which there was no response, 311,000 persons for which a "not available" response was given, and 4,000 persons for which another language was listed.
c. Includes an estimated 1,807,000 persons who did not speak a second language, 786,000 persons for whom there was no response, 11,000 for which a "not available" response was given, and 7,000 for which another language was listed.

usual language and Spanish as their second language; 771,000 (17.9 percent) spoke only Spanish; 951,000 (22 percent) spoke Spanish as their usual language and English as their second language; and 637,000 (14.7 percent) were not classifiable. Given possible confusion in the survey's distinction between "usual" and "often-spoken second language," one can still confidently characterize 57.7 percent of the Mexican-origin population as bilingual.

Other research on language abilities indicates that receptive skills are more widespread than productive skills in both languages, and verbal skills are more widespread than literate skills. These differences, however, are not very great, especially considering the small number of persons in the samples used in the studies.

A 1974 study reported this pattern for the Spanish-origin community in South Bend, Indiana (table 5). The proportion of people who self-reported good English skills ranged from 69.5 percent (comprehension skills) to 53 percent (writing skills), while for Spanish language skills the range was from 89.6 percent to 57 percent, respectively. The results are somewhat skewed because more people report they can speak some English (31.8 percent) or Spanish (11.9 percent) than report they can understand some English (25.2 percent) or Spanish (9.6 percent). A greater number had no literacy skills in

TABLE 4

MOTHER TONGUE, BY THE LANGUAGE ABILITIES OF THE MEXICAN-
AMERICAN POPULATION, SPRING 1976[a]

(Numbers in Thousands)

Language Ability	English	Spanish	Unknown or No Response[b]	Total
English monolingual				
Number	146	246	7	399
Percent	34.9	63.3	1.7	100.0
English-Spanish bilingual[c]				
Number	279	1,248	16	1,543
Percent	18.1	80.9	1.0	100.0
Spanish monolingual				
Number	1	768	3	772
Percent	0.1	99.5	0.3	100.0
Spanish-English bilingual[c]				
Number	10	939	2	951
Percent	1.0	98.9	0.2	100.0
Unknown or no response				
Number	580	25	31	636
Percent	91.2	4.0	4.9	100.0

SOURCE: Same as table 3. Percentages may not add due to rounding.

a. For persons aged fourteen and older.

b. This category will generally not be reported. For the group age four and over, it is estimated at 1,118,000 persons (18.4 percent). For the group aged fourteen and over, it is estimated at 637,000 persons (14.7 percent).

c. The two categories, English-Spanish bilingual and Spanish-English bilingual, were constructed from several questions in the Survey of Income and Education: "What language does . . . usually speak? Does . . . speak any other language often? What other language does . . . speak?" If respondents spoke English as their usual language, answered yes to the second question, and Spanish to the third question, they were classified by the author as English-Spanish bilingual. If their responses were Spanish and then English, they were classified as Spanish-English bilingual. These classifications make no claim beyond the reported answers as to the respondent's relative language profiency or language dominance, whether based on ability, frequency of use, functional allocation of language use, or any other construct of language dominance.

Spanish (20.7 percent, no reading; and 25.2 percent, no writing skills) than had no literacy skills in English (12.9 percent, no reading; and 21.2 percent, no writing skills).

These data were self-reported for the respondent only from 135 households randomly selected from an address list compiled from various official and community sources. The population was self-identified as being 91.6 percent Mexican origin, 3.1 percent Puerto

TABLE 5
ENGLISH- AND SPANISH-LANGUAGE ABILITIES OF THE SPANISH-ORIGIN
RESPONDENTS IN SOUTH BEND, INDIANA, 1974

Language Skill	"None"		"Some"		"Good"		Total	
	Number	Percent	Number	Percent	Number	Percent	Number	Percent
Understand								
English	7	5.3	33	25.2	91	69.5	131	100.0
Spanish	1	0.7	13	9.6	121	89.6	135	100.0
Speak								
English	7	5.3	42	31.8	83	62.9	132	100.0
Spanish	1	0.7	16	11.9	118	87.4	135	100.0
Read								
English	17	12.9	37	28.0	78	59.1	132	100.0
Spanish	28	20.7	28	20.7	79	58.5	135	100.0
Write								
English	28	21.2	34	25.8	70	53.0	132	100.0
Spanish	34	25.2	24	17.8	77	57.0	135	100.0

SOURCE: Centro de Estudios Chicanos e Investigaciones Sociales, Inc., *Social and Economic Conditions of the Spanish Origin Population in South Bend, Indiana*, Report 1 (University of Notre Dame, August 1974), p. 72, tables 53 and 54. Percentages may not add due to rounding.

Rican origin, and the remainder of other Latino origin; 25.4 percent of the respondents were born in the United States. The sample represented approximately 22 percent of the constructed universe. At least thirty interviews (22.2 percent) were conducted in Spanish.

An earlier and preliminary study of self-reported opinions about bilingual schooling and curriculum among 199 Chicano-community parents having children in Head Start programs in East Los Angeles revealed similar patterns in language ability. A greater number reported more facility in verbal than literacy skills (table 6). The survey results also indicated that more people could speak or read Spanish than actually did so. This distinction between language ability and actual use is more important, I think, for bilingual and multi-lingual populations than for monolingual ones (although a parallel can be drawn with different varieties of a language).

The same survey included a series of questions asking if the respondents spoke or read literature or newspapers in either language at home. Fewer than half, 44.2 percent, indicated they had speaking ability in both languages, whereas only 32.2 percent reported using both languages. This group of parents was also highly literate; only

TABLE 6
SPANISH- AND ENGLISH-LANGUAGE ABILITIES AND USAGE OF CHICANO-
COMMUNITY PARENTS, EAST LOS ANGELES, 1973

Language Skill	"Yes"		"No"		No Data	
	Number	Percent	Number	Percent	Number	Percent
Spanish						
Can speak	176	88.4	23	11.6	. . .	. . .
Do speak	162	81.4	36	18.1	1	0.5
Can read	156	78.4	37	18.6	6	3.0
Do read	135	67.8	58	29.1	6	3.0
Can write	147	73.9	48	24.1	4	2.0
English						
Can speak	111	55.8	83	41.7	5	2.5
Do speak	97	48.7	90	45.2	12	6.0
Can read	107	53.8	84	42.2	8	4.0
Do read	110	55.3	81	40.7	8	4.0
Can write	92	46.2	86	43.2	21	10.6

SOURCE: From Reynaldo Macías, "Parent Bilingual Education Opinion and Goals
Study," unpublished data, 1973. For a description of the study, see R. F. Macías,
"Opinions of Chicano Community Parents on Bilingual Preschool Education," in Albert
Verdoodt and Rolf Kjolseth, eds., *Language in Sociology* (Louvain, Belgium: Institüt de
Linguistique, 1976), pp. 135–66.

2 percent were unable to read in either language. Persons who were
literate in both languages accounted for 34.7 percent of the respondents, whereas 16.6 percent were able to read only English and 39.7
percent were able to read only Spanish. In practice, those surveyed
tended to use slightly more English than Spanish, although among
those who *did* read, 29.1 percent were biliterates, 35.2 percent were
Spanish-only readers, and 25.6 percent were English-only readers.

These respondents followed the same pattern in writing skills.
One-fourth (25.1 percent) reported they were able to write in both
languages, whereas 40.7 percent reported they could write only in
Spanish and 21.1 percent could write only in English.

Those surveyed identified themselves principally as being of
Mexican origin (85.9 percent), with 7.0 percent identifying themselves
as white, Americans, or Anglo. The majority were born in Mexico
(53.3 percent), whereas only one-third (36.2 percent) were born in
the United States (which helps to explain the Spanish literacy skills).
Those Head Start parents who were surveyed generally were poor,
and most (76.4 percent) were women. Of those who gave their age
(70.4 percent), about half were under age thirty.

TABLE 7
LANGUAGE ABILITIES OF THE MEXICAN-ORIGIN POPULATION, BY SEX,
SPRING 1976[a]
(Numbers in Thousands)

	Male			Female		
Language Ability	*Number*	*Percent*	*Proportion of Total*	*Number*	*Percent*	*Proportion of Total*
English monolingual	359	11.8	52.6	323	10.6	47.4
English-Spanish bilingual[b]	1,055	34.7	48.7	1,109	36.4	51.3
Spanish monolingual	371	12.1	44.6	460	15.1	55.4
Spanish-English bilingual[b]	700	23.0	54.1	593	19.5	45.9
Unknown or no response	560	18.4	50.0	559	18.4	50.0

SOURCE: Same as table 3.
a. For persons aged four and older.
b. See table 4, note c.

Language Distribution

It is important to understand how language abilities correlate with place of birth, sex, age, and other selected characteristics. Differences in the language abilities of individuals within the Mexican-origin community may be explained by looking at these variables.

A person's language abilities do not seem to be greatly influenced either by sex or age (tables 7, 8, and 9). Among an equal number of males and females included in the Survey of Income and Education, a little more than a third of each sex (34.7 percent for males and 36.4 percent for females) were English-Spanish bilinguals. The next largest language subgroups were Spanish-English bilinguals (23.0 percent for males and 19.5 percent for females).

The Mexicans in the United States are relatively young, and their median age is 20.3 years compared with 28.9 years for the total U.S. population.[14] Spanish monolinguals do not have as high a proportion of younger speakers as the other language subgroups, especially English monolinguals (6.3 percent of Spanish monolinguals are aged four to nine as compared with 22.6 percent of English monolinguals).

---

14. U.S. Bureau of the Census, *Current Population Reports,* series P-20, no. 310, "Persons of Spanish Origin in the United States, March 1976" (Washington, D.C.: U.S. Government Printing Office, 1977), p. 3.

TABLE 8
AGE DISTRIBUTION OF SPANISH-LANGUAGE AND OF TOTAL LANGUAGE
MINORITY PERSONS IN THE UNITED STATES, 1976
(Numbers in Thousands)

Non-English Language Background	Total	Age 5 and Under	Ages 6–18	Ages 19 and Over
Total number of persons	27,985	2,224	5,032	20,730
Percent	100.0	8.1	18.0	74.1
Proportion of total (percent)	100.0	100.0	100.0	100.0
U.S.-born	18,529	2,028	4,051	12,450
Percent	100.0	11.1	21.9	67.2
Proportion of total (percent)	66.2	91.2	80.5	60.1
Foreign-born	9,454	196	981	8,278
Percent	100.0	2.1	10.4	87.6
Proportion of total (percent)	33.8	8.8	19.5	39.9
Spanish persons	10,609	1,384	3,022	6,203
Percent	100.0	13.1	28.5	58.5
Proportion of total (percent)	100.0	100.0	100.0	100.0
U.S.-born	7,663	1,304	2,515	3,845
Percent	100.0	17.0	32.8	50.2
Proportion of total (percent)	72.2	94.2	83.2	62.0
Foreign-born	2,944	*	507	2,357
Percent	100.0	. . .	17.2	80.1
Proportion of total (percent)	27.8	. . .	16.8	38.0

SOURCE: Data from National Center for Education Statistics, "Geographic Distribution, Nativity, and Age Distribution of Language Minorities in the U.S., Spring 1976," 78B-5, *Bulletin* (Washington, D.C.: August 22, 1978), tables 1a, 1b, and 1c. Percentages are rounded.
*Fewer than 15,000 persons.

This is the case for the group aged fourteen to seventeen. Conversely, Spanish monolinguals tended to be older than English monolinguals: 14.6 percent of Spanish monolinguals were age sixty-five or older, as opposed to 1.9 percent of English monolinguals. Persons over age twenty-five were more likely to speak only Spanish than only English. Within all age groups, bilingual speakers predominated, except among persons sixty-five and older, of whom 48.9 percent were Spanish monolinguals.

TABLE 9

LANGUAGE ABILITIES OF THE MEXICAN-ORIGIN POPULATION, BY AGE, SPRING 1976

(Numbers in Thousands)

Language Ability	Ages 4–9	Ages 10–13	Ages 14–17	Ages 18–19	Ages 20–24	Ages 25–34	Ages 35–44	Ages 45–64	Ages 65–99
English monolingual									
Number of persons	154	111	104	25	73	100	45	56	13
Percent	14.7	15.4	15.7	10.3	11.0	9.4	6.8	7.3	5.3
Proportion of total (percent)	22.6	16.3	15.3	3.7	10.7	14.7	6.6	8.2	1.9
English-Spanish bilingual[a]									
Number of persons	351	271	275	95	246	386	233	262	46
Percent	33.4	37.7	41.5	39.1	36.9	36.0	35.6	34.0	18.7
Proportion of total (percent)	16.2	12.5	12.7	4.4	11.4	17.8	10.8	12.1	2.1
Spanish monolingual									
Number of persons	53	6	28	21	76	188	138	199	122
Percent	5.0	0.8	4.3	8.8	11.3	17.5	21.0	25.8	48.9
Proportion of total (percent)	6.3	0.7	3.4	2.6	9.1	22.6	16.6	24.0	14.6
Spanish-English bilingual[a]									
Number of persons	222	120	106	41	138	239	179	193	57
Percent	21.1	16.7	16.0	16.7	20.7	22.2	27.2	24.9	23.1
Proportion of total (percent)	17.2	9.3	8.2	3.1	10.7	18.4	13.8	14.9	4.4
Unknown or no response									
Number of persons	271	211	149	61	134	160	61	62	10
Percent	25.8	29.4	22.5	25.0	20.1	14.9	9.3	8.0	4.0
Proportion of total (percent)	24.2	18.9	13.3	5.4	12.0	14.3	5.5	5.5	0.9

SOURCE: Same as table 3.

a. See table 4, note c.

It is unclear whether this is a stable pattern that reflects dominance of different institutions among various age groups (for example, schools for children aged four to nineteen versus family for persons aged sixty-five and older) or whether the pattern reflects sociolinguistic changes (social structure changes affecting language use, such as evolution of a larger middle class with a higher proportion of English use), or an overall language shift toward English. The increasing middle class and the language shift toward English among immigrant groups have often gone hand in hand, but these factors have not been satisfactorily explored for Mexicans in the United States. I therefore leave the question open by enumerating the options.

Not only do Mexicans live in almost all fifty states, but Latinos constituted the largest racial minority in sixteen states in 1976. Although more than three-fourths of the Mexican-origin population lived in only two states—California (40.6 percent) and Texas (36.4 percent)—they nevertheless constituted a sizable proportion of the population in several other states (for example, New Mexico, where they accounted for nearly 40 percent of the population).

A study of the language abilities of Mexican-Americans in California showed that about one-third (34.7 percent) are English-Spanish bilinguals, with the remainder of respondents about equally divided among the other language-ability groups—English monolingual, Spanish monolingual, and Spanish-English bilingual (table 10). In Texas, however, more than two-thirds were bilingual (English-Spanish, 37.3 percent; Spanish-English, 31.8 percent) with 15 percent being Spanish monolinguals and only 7.4 percent English monolinguals among the 'Mexican-origin population. The Mexican-origin populations in New Mexico and Arizona had language ability patterns similar to the pattern in Texas with regard to bilinguals except that the English-Spanish bilinguals tend to be a much greater proportion of the populations. Texas and Arizona have the greatest proportion of bilinguals (69.0 percent), but Arizona's were reportedly more than two to one English-Spanish (47 percent compared to 22.6 percent Spanish-English bilinguals). The largest percentage speaking only Spanish was found in Illinois (21.9 percent) whereas the largest percentage speaking only English was in Colorado (22.5 percent).

More than three out of four (76.8 percent) persons of Mexican heritage were born in the United States (table 11). As might be expected, most of the Mexicans in the United States with English-language facility were U.S.-born—93.5 percent of the English monolinguals, 86.5 percent of the English-Spanish bilinguals, and 66.7 percent of the Spanish-English bilinguals. Only about 4 percent of

TABLE 10

LANGUAGE ABILITIES OF THE MEXICAN-AMERICAN POPULATION, BY SELECTED STATES, DISTRIBUTION, SPRING 1976[a]

(Numbers in Thousands)

Language Ability	California	Texas	Arizona	New Mexico	Illinois	Colorado
English monolingual						
Number of persons	312	165	36	27	18	41
Percent	12.6	7.4	12.6	13.8	9.2	22.5
English-Spanish bilingual						
Number of persons	860	826	133	73	59	59
Percent	34.7	37.3	47.0	37.5	30.1	32.2
Spanish monolingual						
Number of persons	390	332	17	16	43	*
Percent	15.8	15.0	6.2	8.4	21.9	...
Spanish-English bilingual						
Number of persons	353	706	64	52	33	*
Percent	14.3	31.8	22.6	26.8	16.7	...
Unknown or no response						
Number of persons	560	189	33	26	43	70
Percent	22.6	8.5	11.6	13.6	22.0	37.8

SOURCE: Same as table 3.

* Estimate is fewer than 15,000 people.

a. For persons aged four and older. Because the standard error for estimates is 15,000 ± 9,000, the entries for numbers of persons should not be taken as reliable indicators of population size.

TABLE 11
LANGUAGE ABILITIES OF THE MEXICAN-ORIGIN POPULATION,
BY BIRTHPLACE, SPRING 1976[a]
(Numbers in Thousands)

Language Ability	Persons Born in the United States	Persons Born in Mexico
English monolingual		
Number of persons	638	31
Percent	13.6	2.3
Proportion of total (percent)	93.5	4.6
English-Spanish bilingual		
Number of persons	1,872	282
Percent	40.0	20.5
Proportion of total (percent)	86.5	13.0
Spanish monolingual		
Number of persons	197	627
Percent	4.2	45.6
Proportion of total (percent)	23.8	75.5
Spanish-English bilingual		
Number of persons	863	427
Percent	18.4	31.0
Proportion of total (percent)	66.7	33.0
Unknown or no response		
Number of persons	1,108	8
Percent	23.7	0.5
Proportion of total (percent)	99.1	0.7

SOURCE: Same as table 3. Percentages may not add due to rounding.
    a. For persons aged four and older.

the Mexican-origin population born in the United States was Spanish monolingual (about one out of every four Spanish monolinguals). Even among persons born in Mexico, fewer than half (45.6 percent) speak only Spanish.

Among persons born in Mexico, more than half (53.8 percent) learned some English (31 percent were reported as Spanish-English bilinguals, 20.5 percent as English-Spanish bilinguals, and 2.3 percent as English monolinguals). Of those persons born in the United States, 62.6 percent learned some Spanish (40 percent were reported as English-Spanish bilinguals, 18.4 percent as Spanish-English bilinguals, and 4.2 percent as Spanish monolinguals). However, the language abilities of almost a quarter (23.7 percent) of the U.S.-born respondents were categorized as "unknown."

The survey data allow a greater exploration of language subgroups

TABLE 12

LANGUAGE ABILITIES OF THE MEXICAN-ORIGIN POPULATION, BY HIGHEST
SCHOOL GRADE ATTENDED AND TOTAL PERSONAL INCOME, SPRING 1976[a]

Language Ability	Highest School Grade Attended (Mean, in years)	Total Personal Income (Mean, in dollars)	Total Number of Persons (in thousands)
English monolingual	12.0	4,601	417
English-Spanish bilingual	11.8	4,860	1,543
Spanish monolingual	5.6	2,946	771
Spanish-English bilingual	9.4	4,174	951
Unknown or no response	12.3	4,372	637

SOURCE: Same as table 3. Figures are rounded.
    a. For persons aged fourteen and older.

based on years of schooling than on participation in the labor force
or economic status. Greater proficiency in English seems to be
associated with higher levels of schooling (table 12). Whether this
reflects a causal relationship is unclear. In the general absence of
non-English-language school programs for persons without English-
language abilities, there is little profit in English-medium schools.
This finding is also consistent with the lower levels of grade attainment
by Spanish monolinguals and Spanish-English bilinguals. It must be
remembered, however, that more "older" persons are Spanish monolinguals, an age group having less schooling in all ethnic groups.

The median years of schooling for the adult U.S. population
(those aged twenty-five and older) first reached twelve years in 1970.[15]
The median years of schooling completed by the Mexican-origin
population in 1976 was 9.8 years; fewer than one-third (32.8 percent)
were high school graduates.[16] The National Center for Education
Statistics (NCES) also found that "persons with Spanish-language
backgrounds enrolled in grades 5–12 were about twice as likely to be
two or more grades below the grade levels expected for their ages as
were those with English-language backgrounds."[17] The center also
found that "compared with that of persons with English-language

    15. See the National Center for Education Statistics, *Digest of Educational Statistics,
1976 Edition* (Washington, D.C.: U.S. Government Printing Office, 1977).
    16. U.S. Bureau of the Census, *Current Population Reports*, p. 25.
    17. National Center for Education Statistics, *Bulletin*, "The Educational Disadvan-
tage of Language Minority Persons in the U.S., Spring 1976" (Department of Health,
Education and Welfare, July 26, 1978), p. 1.

backgrounds, the drop-out rate was 4.5 times as high for Hispanics (45 percent) who usually speak Spanish and three times as high (30 percent) for those of other language backgrounds who usually speak their native languages."[18] The NCES cautions, however, not to draw causal inferences from the data: "In particular, *these data* are not intended to prove in any sense that the use of the non-English language is the main cause of relatively low academic progress or dropping out of school. Also, *these data* do not imply that the use of English by language-minority persons 'causes' them to progress through school at nearly the same rate as native English-speaking children do."[19]

The occupational distribution of language resources has only recently become a focus of scholarly concern with respect to language maintenance and shift.[20] Class-income correlations with language use generally show the use of less Spanish and more English on the part of higher-income Chicanos. In 1976 a considerable income differential existed according to a person's language abilities (table 12), with Spanish monolinguals having the lowest average personal income ($2,946) and English-Spanish bilinguals the highest ($4,860). Recent anecdotal evidence suggests this may be a transitional phase—as middle-income Mexicans reach even higher income levels they begin to look for, create, and support part-time or full-time schools to develop and retain Spanish among their children.

Veltman has indicated that language and schooling play major roles in determining earned income for persons with a Spanish-language background.[21] In California and New Mexico he found stronger income or labor market incentives, however, to abandon Spanish (even as a second language) than in Texas and Arizona, where he found a liability associated with abandoning Spanish altogether. The favored income position in the latter two states was for bilinguals having English as the dominant and Spanish the subordinate language.

An NCES study also shows a differential in labor force participation and unemployment rates by language and ethnic group (table

---

18. Ibid., p. 3.

19. Ibid.

20. David López, "The Social Consequences of Chicano Home/School Bilingualism," *Social Problems*, vol. 24 (December 1976), pp. 234–46.

21. Calvin Veltman, "The Returns from Learning English and Language Shift for Language Minorities in the United States—The Educational, Occupational and Earning Achievements of Non-English Language Adults," report completed under contract to the National Center for Education Statistics (State University of New York, Plattsburgh, 1979).

TABLE 13
LABOR FORCE PARTICIPATION AND UNEMPLOYMENT RATES IN THE UNITED
STATES FOR THE TOTAL POPULATION AND THE SPANISH-ORIGIN
POPULATION, BY LANGUAGE CHARACTERISTICS, JULY 1975
(Percent)

Characteristic	Labor Force Participation Rate		Unemployment Rate	
	Total persons	Persons of Spanish Origin	Total persons	Persons of Spanish Origin
Total population aged 14 and older	61.2	60.1	8.9	13.4
English as the usual language	61.7	65.0	8.8	13.7
Another household language	59.8	64.4	10.2	13.8
English as the usual individual language	60.7	65.9	10.1	13.3
Non-English as the usual individual language	42.9	51.6	12.4	19.8
Non-English as the usual household language	54.7	55.6	11.6	13.7
English as the usual individual language	63.4	61.7	11.2	15.1
Non-English as the usual individual language	52.8	54.6	11.7	13.5

SOURCE: Data from National Center for Education Statistics, "Data Utilization Planning Conference on the SIE," February 23–25, 1977, Washington, D.C., table 1.

13). Spanish-origin workers (all Latinos) had about the same rate of participation in the labor force as the general population, but a much higher unemployment rate (13.4 percent as compared with the 1975 rate of 8.9 percent for the total U.S. population age fourteen and older). For the Mexican-origin population, the unemployment rate was 10.9 percent, compared with 7.9 percent for the total population in 1976.[22]

The lowest participation and highest unemployment rates were found among persons whose "usual" language was other than English

22. U.S. Bureau of the Census, *Current Population Reports*, p. 27.

and who lived in an English-dominant bilingual household. The next lowest participation rates were for persons who usually did not speak English and who lived in a household where the usual language was not English. Unemployment was next greatest among persons whose usual language was English but who lived in a household where English was not the usual language. This pattern held for all Latinos as well as the total population.

A smaller proportion of persons of Spanish origin spoke a language other than English in the active labor force than of persons who spoke English, regardless of household language. Among Spanish-origin persons in the labor force, the household language apparently did not affect unemployment rates (13.7 percent for persons for which a language other than English was the usual household language). A larger difference in unemployment was found among persons whose usual language was not English (19.8 percent for those in English-bilingual households). Again, these patterns were similar to those for the total population.

In analyzing unweighted data from the Survey of Income and Education for California, Texas, Arizona, New Mexico, and Colorado, García suggests that Spanish monolinguals "were disproportionately employed in mining, agriculture, and construction, while bilinguals (English) predominated in the wholesale/retail industries."[23] English-Spanish bilinguals tended to predominate in white-collar occupations while Spanish-English bilinguals predominated in blue-collar occupations. García also concluded that "the lack of higher occupational status among monolingual English-speaking Chicanos may suggest exclusionary policies and continual discrimination against Chicanos despite the absence of limited English-speaking ability."[24]

In his discussion of the "economic" value of various language resources, López suggests that not knowing Spanish limits a Chicano's available job-information network:

> Why does it help to be bilingual? In part it might be the simple capacity to communicate with Spanish as well as English speakers. But Chicano bilingualism, in both its Spanish and English style, is a badge of ethnic ingroupness, not just a stigma to outsiders. It is very much a bond that strengthens the ties of Chicano to Chicano. Indeed, Chicanos often test each other (not necessarily consciously) on lingual criteria, especially if the other is in some ways marginal in other aspects of ethnicity. I suggest, then, that (home/school) bilingualism provides positive direct effects because it is a sociometric resource, giving better access to an ethnic job network in which knowing Spanish widens and strengthens one's network of contact, without

---

23. García, "Language Use, Occupational Status and Wage Earnings," p. 16.
24. Ibid., p. 17.

reducing the flow of help or information from other sources transmitted through English.[25]

López adds that the direct positive effect goes to increase income rather than alter occupational level.[26] It would be interesting to explore the question for Spanish monolinguals who have little or no access to English language resources and to examine the role other bilinguals play in this regard. It seems that Spanish monolinguals are viewed, and perhaps treated, differently from English monolinguals in these ethnic job networks and in the labor force.

The foregoing exploration of the language data from the Survey of Income and Education indicates several sociolinguistic characteristics of the Mexican-origin population. The greater part of the group was bilingual, with only 11.2 percent English monolinguals and 13.6 percent Spanish monolinguals. Spanish monolinguals tended to be older, whereas English monolinguals tended to be younger. Whether this is reflective of language shift is unclear. It may be a reporting discrepancy. We know that there is a difference between reported language ability and actual language use (at least in the home).[27] The principal contribution of this survey data has been its comprehensiveness rather than the detail of its sociolinguistic behavioral data.

One should be cautious in the interpretation of some of these data. Since regional differences in the distribution of language abilities and use have been noted,[28] the foregoing countrywide description of the Mexican-origin population should be taken as a necessary stopgap description against which local analyses can be compared or measured.[29]

Conclusion and Discussion

This paper presents a language profile of Mexicans in the United States, using recent survey data. In relating these kinds of descriptions

---

25. López, "The Social Consequences of Chicano Home/School Bilingualism," p. 243.
26. Ibid.
27. Reynaldo Macías, "Parent Bilingual Education Opinion and Goals Study;" see table 6 above.
28. See, for example, Veltman, *Language Shift;* Veltman, "Retention of Minority Languages," p. 160; and John García, "Language Use, Occupational Status and Wage Earnings—Chicanos in Southwestern Labor Markets," paper presented at the National Symposium on Hispanic Business and Economy in the United States, Arizona State University, Sept. 1978.
29. See L. F. Estrada, "A Demographic Comparison of the Mexican Origin Population in the Midwest and Southwest," *Aztlán—International Journal of Chicano Studies Research,* vol. 7 (Summer 1976), for a similar macro-level comparison which the author undertook for the same reason.

to the future of the Spanish language in the United States, one should keep in mind their limitations. We should also keep in mind those characteristics that make the Spanish language different from the European immigrant languages. More than twenty countries with predominantly Spanish-speaking populations are now points of origin for persons coming into the United States (especially Central Americans). Official U.S. language policies affecting persons from Mexico and Puerto Rico, as well as the previous history of the Spanish language in North America, are other factors to keep in mind when predicting the future of Spanish. Moreover, acquisition of English among this population need not entail a concurrent loss of Spanish (although since 1900 a growing number of Mexicans and Latinos in the United States have become English monolinguals). These data suggest the need to be aware of forces encouraging bilingualism as well as monolingualism within this population and elsewhere.

The 1966 study by Fishman and his colleagues showed that during the first half of the twentieth century, most European immigrant groups did not pass on their native languages intergenerationally. The increased number of Spanish speakers is a notable exception to this general trend. Among the non-English languages with large numbers of speakers, Spanish alone made significant gains, especially between 1940 and 1960: "In 1940 the numerically strongest mother tongues in the United States were German, Italian, Polish, Spanish, Yiddish, and French, in that order. Each of these languages was claimed by approximately a million and a half or more individuals. In 1960 these same languages remained the "big six" although their order had changed to Italian, Spanish, German, Polish, French, and Yiddish. Among them, only Spanish registered gains (and substantial gains at that) in this 20-year interval."[30] Between 1960 and 1970 there was an increase of 134 percent among Americans who claimed Spanish as their mother tongue, and an additional 35.6 percent increase from 1970 to 1976.

The substantial increase of Spanish speakers—whatever variables are classified (mother tongue, language background, and so on)—is difficult to ignore. Several authors have attempted to identify factors affecting language shift and language spread,[31] but only Gaarder and

30. Fishman et al., *Language Loyalty*, p. 45.
31. See, for example, ibid.; Heinz Kloss, "German American Language Maintenance Efforts," in ibid.; Gaarder, *Bilingual Schooling;* Uriel Weinrich, *Bilingualism in Contact—Findings and Problems* (The Hague: Mouton, 1953); Einar Haugen, *Bilingualism in the Americas—A Bibliography and Research Guide*, American Dialect Society, Publication 26 (Tuscaloosa: University of Alabama Press, 1956); William Mackey, "The Description of Bilingualism," *Canadian Journal of Linguistics*, vol. 7 (1962), pp. 51–85; and Stanley

López have done so systematically for Spanish and Chicanos in the United States.[32]

Gaarder presents nine variables, or characteristics, of Spanish speakers that he feels will support Spanish-language maintenance in the United States: (1) the length of time Spanish speakers, as indigenous groups, have been in the United States prior to Anglos and other Euro-Americans, (2) the large size of the Spanish-speaking population, (3) the relative homogeneity of the Spanish speakers, (4) constant in-migration of other Spanish speakers to reinforce the domestic population, (5) cultural access to and renewal from the hinterland (Mexico, Puerto Rico, Latin America), (6) intergenerational stability of the extended family of Spanish speakers, (7) religiosocietal isolation among Spanish speakers, (8) present-day tolerance of cultural diversity in the United States, and (9) the relative isolation and hence linguistic solidarity of the Spanish-speaking group.

Gaarder argues from the previous experiences of language groups in the United States and elsewhere, but others suggest that some of the variables he has identified as supporting language maintenance actually have not done so. For example, Kloss, in his discussion of German in the United States, classifies the large size of a language group, in and of itself, as an ambivalent (rather than supporting) factor for language maintenance.[33]

One way of exploring this question is to compare Spanish speakers with other language groups in the United States in order to identify similarities and differences. The configuration or simultaneous occurrences of variables also may be important. In addition to the factors just listed, I suggest the following for consideration:

First, Spanish speakers in the United States are the northernmost segment of more than 200 million Spanish speakers in Latin America. This is an additional factor in the historical contiguity between the domestic Spanish speakers and their "country of origin."

Second, unlike the situation among turn-of-the-century immigrants, the linguistic diversity among present-day immigrants is low. As the number of persons from Spanish-speaking countries increases and they swell the barrios of U.S.-born Spanish speakers, the linguistic diversity continues to be low but the numbers of bilingual and monolingual Spanish speakers are increasing.

Lieberson and Timothy Curry, "Language Shift in the United States—Some Demographic Clues," *International Migration Review*, vol. 5 (1971), pp. 125–37.

32. Gaarder, *Bilingual Schooling*, and López, *Language Maintenance and Shift.*
33. Kloss, "German American Language Maintenance."

Third, the historical continuity of Spanish speakers in their primary settlement areas continues (the southwestern United States and Puerto Rico), but their spread or migration to other parts of the United States has given the Spanish-speaking population a national character.

Fourth, there is an intergenerational commingling, partly from the continuing in-migration and partly from internal migration.

Fifth, the development of an institutional language infrastructure has continued. For example, in the schools, bilingual schooling has increased and Spanish continues to be the most popular "foreign language" in high schools and colleges. Language issues have forced the strict enforcement of voting rights and judicial due process (court interpreters are now required) for persons who speak little or no English. The Spanish-language mass media—particularly broadcast media—continue to grow; they have been characterized as the "fifth network." Chicano literature is experiencing a resurgence in Spanish.

Relevant developments on the world scene include (1) the increasing importance of Latin America, (2) the parallel loss of prestige of the United States, and (3) the increasing focus on human (including cultural and linguistic) rights in the international community.

We will soon be able to explore these areas much more empirically and systematically. Thanks to a dramatic increase in national language survey data (for example, the 1978 Children's English Services Study, the 1980 census, and the 1982 English Language Proficiency Study), as well as local studies of Spanish and English among Chicanos and Puerto Ricans.[34] All these resources should help us to compile language, speech, and literacy profiles of Mexicans, Puerto Ricans, and other Latinos in the United States at the national, regional, and community levels. What remains is a broader, more comprehensive integration of these sociolinguistic and nonlanguage variables to enable us to better understand the dynamic interworkings of the group and language.

---

34. See J. Amastae and L. Elias-Olivares, *Spanish in the U.S.* (Cambridge, England: Cambridge University Press, 1982); J. Ornstein-Galicia, *Form and Function in Chicano English* (Rowley, Mass.: Newbury House, 1984); and Language Policy Task Force, *Intergenerational Perspectives on Bilingualism: From Community to Classroom* (New York: Center for Puerto Rican Studies, Hunter College, City University of New York, 1982).

CHAPTER TWELVE

During the late 1960s and early 1970s, a preoccupation with pre-American roots appeared to grip the United States. It seemingly surfaced first in the "consciousness-raising" movement among blacks. By 1970 a broad array of leaders and organizations were vying for the support of the black community. In goals and methods, they ranged from the peaceful, integrationist stance of the National Association for the Advancement of Colored People to the militant, political separatist stance of the Republic of New Africa and the Nation of Islam. Opinion polls establish that the more extreme leaders never enjoyed much popular support, and their organizations subsequently either moderated their goals and methods (as did the Nation of Islam) or withered. But the common thread of the entire movement—a new emphasis upon black pride in black identity—appeared to influence other groups. Among peoples of European ancestry, the new pride of heritage could be seen in such disparate manifestations as the surge of interest in ethnic studies or in bumper stickers reading "Thank God I'm Italian" or, more humorously, "Kiss me, I'm Polish."

Mexican-Americans were also involved. The Chicano movement, with its substitution of "brown power" for "black power," particularly demonstrated the influence that the black movement had exerted. Several colleges and universities initiated programs in Chicano studies, and there was an outpouring of books and articles aimed at chronicling the uniqueness of the Mexican-American heritage and fostering a single Mexican-American identity.

Much of the literature that attempted to explain this countrywide interest in pre-American heritage maintained that the movement proved the characterization of the United States as a "melting pot" was faulty and that the power of acculturation and assimilation exercised by mainstream society in the United States had proven to be grossly exaggerated. As the title of one popular book *The Rise of the Unmeltable Ethnics* suggests, some writers concluded that little change had occurred, or was likely to occur, in the identity patterns of ethnic groups. Yet, even while this movement was flourishing, substantial data indicated that the processes of assimilation were accelerating. As the data presented by Milton Yinger attest, the 1960s and 1970s were a period of increasing intermarriage and acculturation.

What then are we to make of this period of ethnic flourishing? Joshua Fishman here offers his interpretation of "the ethnic revival" and its implications for Mexican-Americans.

THE ETHNIC REVIVAL IN THE UNITED STATES

Implications for the Mexican-American Community

Joshua Fishman

$\mathbf{A}$ vast amount of evidence points to the conclusion that an "ethnic revival" of sorts occurred in the United States between the mid-1960s and the mid-1970s and that it had substantially declined by the late 1970s. The evidence for the revival consists of "across the board" increases in (1) the number of Americans claiming a mother tongue other than English;[1] (2) the number of ethnic periodicals published in other languages;[2] (3) the number of ethnic schools in which languages other than English predominated;[3] (4) the number of local religious units using languages other than English;[4] (5) the number of radio stations and television channels broadcasting in languages other than English;[5] (6) the number of ethnic studies (courses and departments) at American colleges and universities;[6] (7) the amount of ethnic awareness on the part of minority leaders and community members;[7] (8) the number of ethnic pageants and

---

A revised and expanded version of "The Rise and Fall of the Ethnic Revival in the USA" (The Hague: Mouton, 1985), which will appear in the author's forthcoming volume by the same name.

1. This was true even for mother tongues experiencing neither immigrational nor natural increases. See Joshua Fishman, "Mother Tongues Claiming in the United States Since 1960," in Joshua Fishman et al., *The Rise and Fall of the Ethnic Revival: Language and Ethnicity in Sociolinguistic Perspective* (Berlin: Mouton, 1984), chap. 6.

2. Michael H. Gertner, Joshua A. Fishman, Esther G. Lowy, and William G. Milán, "Language and Ethnicity in the Periodical Publications of Four American Ethnic Groups," in Fishman et al., *The Rise and Fall*, chapter 9; and S. Ofelia García, Joshua A. Fishman, Silvia Burunat, and Michael H. Gertner, "The Hispanic Press in the United States: Contents and Prospects," in Fishman et al., *The Rise and Fall*, chap. 10.

3. Fishman et al., *The Rise and Fall*.

4. Ibid.

5. Ibid.

6. Richard Gambino, "A Guide to Ethnic Studies Programs in American Colleges, Universities and Schools," unpublished manuscript (New York: Rockefeller Foundation, 1976).

7. Esther G. Lowy et al., "Ethnic Activists View the Ethnic Revial and Its Language Consequences," in Fishman et al., *The Rise and Fall*, chapter 8.

festivities;[8] (9) the coverage of ethnic concerns in the mainstream press and other mass media; and (10) the evidence of ethnic "sensitivity" on the part of the mainstream political parties.

The federal government passed an Ethnic Heritage Act and the Census Bureau asked an ethnic heritage question in 1979. Within this period of ten to twelve years, "sidestream" ethnicity became a more publicly visible and openly presentable aspect of local and national life, whether in advertising, entertainment, or education. By the late 1970s and early 1980s, however, the "ethnic boom" seemed to have subsided considerably, although ethnicity continued to be of more concern than it had been in the early 1960s. Other items on the public agenda took prominence (the recession and economic inflation, the nuclear arms race, and oil shortages, oil gluts, and energy problems more generally), and several of the aforementioned indicators of an ethnic revival showed a downturn.[9] Mexican-Americans have participated in both the rise and the fall of the recent ethnic revival in the United States—and their involvement is illuminated by and contributes to an understanding of the larger picture.

Ethnic revivals similar to that in the United States between the mid-1960s and the mid-1970s occurred at the same time in many other parts of the capitalist world.[10] Although most of the other occurrences involved indigenous minorities (Welsh, Irish, Scots, Bretons, Alsatians, Frisians, Catalans, Basques, and so on), several immigrant settings also revealed a quickening of minority ethnocultural effort (for example, among *gastarbeiter* immigrants in western and northern Europe, "nonfounding" minorities in Canada, and Euro-immigrants in Australia). Any theory concerning the ethnic revival in the United States must address, therefore, its concurrence with both indigenous and immigrant revivals in many and quite separate parts of the Western world—that is, any meaningful theory must enlighten the specific case as well as be based on more generalized theory.

Recall for a moment what the mid- to late-1960s were like in the United States. The Vietnam War was intensifying and eliciting increased opposition among liberals and the young. The civil rights

---

8. Marjorie R. Esman, "Festivals, Change and Unity: The Celebration of Ethnic Identity among Louisiana Cajuns," *Anthropological Quarterly,* vol. 55 (1982), pp. 199–210; and Penny van Esterik, "Celebrating Ethnicity: Ethnic Flavor in an Urban Festival," *Ethnic Groups,* vol. 4 (1982), pp. 207–28.

9. Fishman, "Mother Tongues Claiming."

10. See Erik Allardt, *Implications of the Ethnic Revival in Modern Industrialized Society* (Helsinki: Societas Scientiarum Fennica, 1979).

movement had ground to a halt even before the assassination of Martin Luther King in 1968, adding to general disenchantment of blacks with the Anglo establishment and to their conviction that black (and black alone) was beautiful. The rising tide of black pride should not be ignored as a stimulant for the white ethnic revival, but neither should it be overstressed. The two movements overlap only in part and have essentially their own dynamics and their own course, intensity, focus, and time frame.[11]

The "flower children" and the hippies of this period expressed disenchantment with big business, big labor, big government, and with the society's fixation on material or financial success. Most striking, however, was the fact that these young people were not the only ones gripped by a counterculture. "Do it yourself," "small is beautiful," and concern for the protection of air, water, and nature against the inroads of a rampant profit motive were widely acceptable and widely implemented indications of alienation among old and young from previously unquestioned mainstream practices and values.

It was an affluent period. Unemployment was low, inflation minor. Funds were apparently available for any and all ventures. The space program was in high gear, as were center-city efforts in education and urban renewal. Yet, with all the verve that the times revealed, there were deep and abiding disaffectation, questioning, and even rejection of mainstream values, priorities, and processes. Indeed, the young that were most disaffected were from comfortably middle-class, Anglo-Saxon or third-generation-immigrant backgrounds.[12] Even before sociologists began to reexamine and question the promise of mere abundance, ordinary citizens had begun to do so.[13] They began to champion causes related to people who had long been slighted by the mainstream: women, homosexuals, blacks, and followers of various alternative life-styles and new departures in music, art, and culture more generally. An attempt to liberate and dignify ethnic minorities was another aspect of this movement.

Campaigns for local cultural autonomy in Europe were paralleled by ethnic study programs and invocation of ethnic dress, food, hairdos,

---

11. See Lowy et al., "Ethnic Activists."

12. Eugene I. Bender and George Kagiwada, "Hansen's Law of 'Third Generation Return' and the Study of American Religio-Ethnic Groups," *Phylon*, vol. 29 (1968), pp. 360–70.

13. For example, Edward Shils, "Dreams of Plenitude, Nightmares of Scarcity," in S. M. Lipset and P. Altbach, eds., *Students in Revolt* (Boston: Houghton Mifflin, 1969) pp. 1–35; and David Reisman, "The Dream of Abundance Reconsidered," *Public Opinion Quarterly*, vol. 45 (1981), pp. 285–302.

song, dance, and music in the United States. Both were "anticentral" expressions, rejective of the power and the ethos, the values and priorities, the rewards and the blandishments of mainstream cultures and their constituted arbiters and authorities.[14] However, the American version was, if anything, more anarchic than the European version; it generally lacked political program or sophistication, whether among Mexican-Americans or among other ethnics. It was often incoherent rather than merely inchoate. It covered the gamut from revolutionary activism to principled activism to principled inactivism and from "weathermen" to "flower children," with greater overall interest in sexual gratification and drugs than in political platforms, programs, or analyses. Anyone older than age thirty was suspect, and the number of years under thirty were extremely finite and fleeting.

The ethnic revival in America was an integral part of this counterculture movement, and, like that movement, it was an expression of alienation rather than a serious analysis of mainstream evils or a serious intent to force or manipulate the mainstream into a new accommodation with sidestream ethnicity. It was not a youth rebellion or even a youth movement in the classic sense in which such phenomena have been described and analyzed previously in the sociological literature.[15] The ethnic revival in America both failed and succeeded to a far greater extent than its protagonists themselves ever imagined; it influenced the mainstream more than an outright rebellion would have, but it was co-opted more fully and more quickly than would have been possible if a full-blown breach had occurred.

The ethnic revival in the United States brought sidestream ethnicity out of the family and the neighborhood closet and made it chic.[16] One's ethnic heritage could be revealed (and even flaunted) in college and in church, in public places as well as private ones. Ethnicity could present itself as being in the general good (for example, in the case of bilingual education). Ethnic communities' personal networks, restaurants, theaters, churches, radio and television programs, neighborhood clubs, and schoolhouses came to be viewed as the spice of life without which all would be Anglo-bland,

---

14. See Richard G. Fox, Charlotte H. Aull, and Louis F. Cimino, "Ethnic Nationalism and the Welfare State," in Charles F. Keyes, ed., *Ethnic Change* (Seattle: University of Washington Press, 1981), pp. 198–245.

15. S. N. Eisenstadt, "Sociological Analysis and Youth Rebellion," in S. N. Eisenstadt, *From Generation to Generation* (New York: Free Press, 1971), pp. vi–xlix.

16. Jerre Mangione, *Mount Allegro: A Memoir of Italian American Life* (New York: Columbia University Press, 1981).

tasteless, and inert.[17] The ethnic revival, as part of the total counter-culture experience of the times, represented an expansion, in both the public and the private spheres of life, of the sidestream ethnicity repertoire. At the same time, its compartmentalization and ideolog-ization remained as weak as it had been. Although third generations can never really return to the life-style of the first,[18] the ethnic revival did not even attempt to do so.

The ethnic revival spilled over into everything, but it remained low in intensity and nonspecific in goals, very much like the counter-culture movement of which it was a part. Both dissipated, leaving a vague but recognizable imprint on the general tone and tenor of American life to the effect that there was no "one-model" American.[19]

Both the revival and its subsequent decline deserve considerable attention, not only because they had their counterparts throughout the Western capitalist democracies, but because they point to a major blind spot in the modern social sciences: the nature of ethnicity and the factors influencing it as a dependent variable.[20] The ethnic revival of the mid-1960s was almost totally unanticipated, both as to time and place, by the very disciplines presumably best equipped to anticipate it. To social theoreticians, open, postindustrial societies seemed to be the most unlikely ones in which sidestream ethnic revivals would occur.[21] Generally favorable economic trends seemed equally contraindicative of "reversions" to ethnicity. The established sociological imagination was focused (and it largely still is) on social class and economic factors as the prime forces (and the only legitimate, "rational" bases of aggregation) in modern society.[22] Thus it could

---

17. See Claude S. Fischer, *To Dwell Among Friends: Personal Networks in Town and City* (Chicago: University of Chicago Press, 1982); and Andrew M. Greeley, "The Ethnic Miracle," in Andrew Greeley, *Neighborhood* (New York: Seabury, 1977).

18. Bender and Kagiwada, "Hansen's Law"; John M. Goering, "The Emergence of Ethnic Interests: A Case of Serendipity," *Social Forces*, vol. 49 (1971), pp. 379–84; and Vladimir Nahirny and Joshua A. Fishman, "American Ethnic Groups: Ethnic Identification and the Problem of Generations," *Sociological Review*, vol. 13 (1965), pp. 311–26.

19. Thomas R. Lopez and Albert W. Vogel, eds., *No One-Model American* (Toledo, Ohio: University of Toledo College of Education, 1979).

20. See Philip Rosen, *The Neglected Dimension* (Notre Dame, Ind.: University of Notre Dame Press, 1980).

21. William R. Beer, *The Unexpected Rebellion: Ethnic Activism in Contemporary France* (New York: New York University Press, 1980).

22. See, for example, Orlando Patterson, *Ethnic Chauvinism: The Reactionary Impulse* (Briarcliff Manor, N.Y.: Stein and Day, 1977); Orlando Patterson, "Context and Choice in Ethnic Allegiance: A Theoretical Framework and Caribbean Case Study," in Nathan Glazer and Daniel P. Moynihan, eds., *Ethnicity: Theory and Experience* (Cambridge, Mass.: Harvard University Press, 1974), pp. 305–49; and Stephen Steinberg, *The Ethnic Myth* (New York: Atheneum, 1981).

not envision ethnicity as either a constructive or an effective force in modern American society.[23] Having neither predicted nor understood the ethnic revival, sociologists remain similarly unenlightened with respect to its renewed relative quiescence. The underlying problem is their failure to understand ethnicity as such, as a social process. Its rise and fall could not be grasped in the absence of understanding ethnicity itself. The major role of immigrant minorities in the language-related ethnic revival in the United States poses an additional complexity that certainly should not be overlooked.[24]

Two misconceptions have monopolized the theories pertaining to the ethnic revival. One misconception dismisses it as "nothing more than nostalgia"; the other misinterprets it as "nationalism" or, what is worse, "chauvinist tribalism." Neither of these explains either the rise or decline of ethnicity because they both *explain away* the matters that should interest us. Not only have these theories failed to account for when and where the ethnic revival occurred, they have not even addressed such related issues as the simultaneous revival of ethnicity throughout the Western capitalist democracies, the likelihood of its recurrence, possible differences between indigenous and immigrant ethnic minorities, and politico-cultural and other possible goals of the revivals. Despite these inadequacies, many insights scattered throughout the general literature can help us understand the new and the evolving Mexican-American ethnolinguistic movement in the United States.

The Ethnic Revival: An Exercise in Nostalgia?

The put-down of the ethnic revival as "mere nostalgia," although infrequently applied to the Mexican-American phenomenon, deserves a few words of serious criticism. To begin, nostalgia is obviously not a technical social science concept. The term implies an orientation toward the past—that is, it is a state of being out of touch with current realities and of triviality. It also connotes a hopelessly ineffectual intellectual or practical posture, a confusion of substance and shadow,

23. Uri Ra'anan, *Ethnic Resurgence in Modern Democratic States* (Elmsford, N.Y.: Pergamon Publishing Co., 1980).

24. Victor Gilbert, "Current Bibliography on Immigrants and Minorities: Monographs, Periodical Articles and Theses, 1971–80: USA," *Immigrants and Minorities*, vol. 1 (1982), pp. 89–141 and 200–32.

and a fascination with things that should be forgotten rather than remembered, respected, activated, or celebrated.[25]

It is interesting that, in his *Human All Too Human,* Friedrich Nietzsche cites an aphorism that not only pertains to nostalgia but does so in the context of minority ethnicity as well. It would be difficult, I think, to find a better example of the nostalgia point of view with respect to the ethnic revival: "We call to mind that Greek city in southern Italy, which once a year still celebrates its Greek feasts, amid tears and mourning that foreign barbarism triumphs ever more and more over the customs its people brought with them into the land; and nowhere has Hellenism been so much appreciated, nowhere has this golden nectar been drunk with so much delight, as amongst these fast-disappearing Hellenes."

The nostalgia view of the ethnic revial—a view commonly encountered at academic cocktail parties but never in the technical literature—begins with the premise that American ethnolinguistic minorities are fast disappearing and inevitably doomed.[26] It further assumes that these nearly extinguished aggregates were engaged in a final and futile gasp of self-recognition and self-assertion in the mid-1960s.[27] Without any research to guide the conclusion and without any theory to structure it, even this purported last gasp is viewed as doomed to be unproductive, self-indulgent, and passing, rather than as part of a process with long-term implications.

Nietzsche's discussion is in terms of "the afterglow of art." The nostalgia view of the ethnic revival considers what occurred from the mid-1960s to the mid-1970s to be the afterglow of ethnicity—a pale shadow, a memory (perhaps even a figment) of "the real thing." Indeed, one school of thought even questions whether "the real thing" exists or *should* exist. It despises ethnicity and, even more so, any implied nostalgia for that phenomenon. This view constitutes the liberal counterpart to racist "myths of the blood." It is itself a myth propagated by people who usually debunk myths, particularly myths that depend on suprarational notions such as intuition and spontaneous longing.

The nostalgia view has no empirical basis whatsoever. It is a case of fighting romanticism with romanticism. Why should ethnic nostalgia exist at all and, more specifically, why should it have arisen in

---

25. John H. Plumb, *The Death of the Past* (Boston: Houghton Mifflin, 1970).

26. The prevalence of this view is documented by L. Paul Metzger, "American Sociology and Black Assimilation," *American Journal of Sociology,* vol. 76 (1971), pp. 627–47.

27. Steinberg, *Ethnic Myth.*

the mid-1960s in the particular places and populations where it was manifest? Has it occurred before? Will it recur or is it strictly a one-time affair? Was it stronger in some ethnolinguistic groups than in others? Was it generationally patterned? Was it related to social class, and if so, how? We look in vain for research on ethnic nostalgia. The nostalgia explanation leaves us just as unenlightened in the end as it found us at the beginning. It is a nonexplanation, an evasion of intellectual responsibility. To call the ethnic revival "an exercise in nostalgia" is to be judgmental without evidence. Those who use the term need no evidence, for they know "intuitively" that the ethnic revival cannot and should not endure. They lack both the objectivity and the discipline necessary to convert their private wisdom into publicly confirmable evidence and theories.

That Mexican-American ethnicity has been spared from the nostalgia designation surely indicates that it is too substantial and vibrant to be shrugged off in this fashion. In a survey of Mexican-American ethnolinguistic activists, almost all (95.4 percent) agreed that an ethnic revival had occurred in their midst during the past two decades.[28] They cited such indicators of a revival as "renewed observance of customs" (95.4 percent), "improved attitudes toward the Spanish language" (90.9 percent), and "increased use of Spanish within Mexican-American communities" (81.3 percent). U.S.-born activists tended to be even more positively disposed to the proliferation of Spanish than were foreign-born activists. Both subgroups agreed that the "black is beautiful" sentiment and other manifestations of black pride and self-confidence were important stimuli vis-à-vis the Mexican-American ethnic revival but, once again, more U.S.-born activists (92.9 percent) than foreign-born (87.5 percent) cited this. Obviously, changes did occur in many Mexican-American communities during the past two decades and neither the members of these communities nor careful outside observers of them find nostalgia to be an appropriate way of characterizing these changes.

The Ethnic Revival from the Perspective of Nationalism

If nostalgia provides an unresearched, judgmental, and anti-intellectual perspective on the ethnic revival, the perspective derived from inquiries into nationalism provides an embarrassment of riches.

---

28. Lowy et al., "Ethnic Activists."

The latter perspective has produced a rich harvest of historical, sociological, and political science treatises, empirical and theoretical, quantitative and qualitative, by scholars around the world. (Indeed, the exhaustive bibliographies of such studies commonly list more research than any one person can possibly follow.)[29] Thus, our problem is how best to be parsimonious and yet locate the most relevant works that can give us maximum insight into what nationalism might contribute to an understanding of the ethnic revival.

Early Research on Nationalism

The continental divide separating early from modern studies of nationalism is probably Karl Deutsch's *Nationalism and Social Communication,* first published in 1953.[30] Before that time, most publications stressed either the ideas of noteworthy nationalist spokesmen and intellectuals, on the one hand, or the differences between separate (but simultaneous) ideological, chronological, and geographic occurrences, on the other hand. A distinction was frequently drawn between the "good nationalism" (rational, voluntarist, contractual) of western Europe and the "bad nationalism" (irrational, "organic," "aggressive") of most other parts of Europe. Whereas the former derived from the libertarian traditions of the French Revolution and from the free association of citizens in order to accomplish popular participation in national sovereignty, the latter derived from German and Italian experiences initially and from eastern Europe subsequently, each with its legacy of totalitarianism, extremism, and abandonment of democratic freedoms.

This latter brand of nationalism represents the total nationalistic phenomenon in the eyes of many modern liberal and Marxist critics of the ethnic revival.[31] The leap from Frisian demands for use of

---

29. See, for example, G. Carter Bentley, *Ethnicity and Nationality: A Bibliographic Guide* (Seattle: University of Washington Press, 1982); the annual bibliographic supplement of the *Canadian Journal of Studies in Nationalism;* and the topical bibliographies of language and nationalism per se, in Joshua A. Fishman, *Language and Nationalism: Two Integrative Essays* (Rowley, Mass.: Newbury House, 1972); and Joshua A. Fishman, "Studies of Language as an Aspect of Ethnicity and Nationalism (A Bibliographic Introduction)," *Sociolinguistic Newsletter,* vol. 14 (1984), pp. 1–6. See also the magisterial general survey by H. Seton-Watson, *Nations and States* (London: Methuen, 1977).

30. Karl Deutsch, *National and Social Communication* (Cambridge, Mass.: MIT Press, 1953, revised 1966).

31. For a critique of this view, see Joseph Rothschild, *Ethnopolitics: A Conceptual Framework* (New York: Columbia University Press, 1981).

their own language in local administrative jurisdictions, or from
Chicano mobilization on behalf of bilingual education, to charges or
suspicions of "racism," "chauvinism," or "Nazism" is quickly and
unjustifiably made,[32] perhaps because of the common romantic stress
on inherited ethnic identity, responsibility, and continuity in each of
these instances.

Although the modern origins of "organicist" nationalism are
commonly found in Herderian imagery, the combination of stress on
innate authenticity, on the desirability of discontinuity between one
ethnocultural aggregate and another, and on the imperatives of such
discontinuity is much older than Herder or his immediate intellectual
progenitors.[33] Indeed, the combination is older than the medieval
snippets that have usually been adduced for it,[34] and even older than
the early eastern Christian accommodations to Balto-Slavic realities.[35]
Its earliest sophisticated Euro-Mediterranean attestations are Greek[36]
and Hebrew,[37] and probably reflect the sanctification of small-scale
econotechnical and sociocultural establishments.

Since such establishments were originally the rule throughout
the world, they were undoubtedly sanctified and stabilized elsewhere
as well, but research on ancient Southeast Asia, sub-Saharan Africa,
and the Americas is lacking in this connection. Our Eurocentrism—
both in building theories of ethnicity and in offering critiques of
those that have been advanced by others—leads us to overstress our
own intellectual, ideological, and sociopolitical origins in these respects
(as well as in many others). Similarly, the notion of a rationalist
compact (and, therefore, of rationalist reethnization in the direction
of greatest mutual advantage) does not really originate in revolution-

---

32. For a critique of this view, see Pierre van den Berghe, *The Ethnic Phenomenon*
(New York: Elsevier-North Holland, 1981).

33. See Joshua A. Fishman, "The Lively Life of a 'Dead' Language, or 'Everyone
Knows Yiddish Died Long Ago,' " *Judaica Book News*, vol. 13 (1982), pp. 7–11.

34. This has been amply demonstrated by Ernst H. Kantorowicz, "Pro Patria
Mori in Medieval Political Thought," *American Historical Review*, vol. 56 (1950–51), pp.
472–92; and John A. Armstrong, *Nations Before Nationalism* (Chapel Hill: University
of North Carolina Press, 1982).

35. Roman Jakobson, "The Beginnings of National Self-Determination in Europe,"
Review of Politics, vol. 7 (1945), pp. 29–42.

36. See Joshua A. Fishman, "Language, Ethnicity and Racism," *Georgetown University Roundtable on Languages and Linguistics* (1977), pp. 297–309; J. Jüther, *Hellenen
und Barbaren* (Leipzig: Neve Floge VIII, 1923); and Goldsworthy Dickinson, *The Greek
View of Life* (London: Methuen, 1896).

37. David E. Fishman, Rena Mayerfeld, and Joshua A. Fishman, "Am and Goy
as Designations for Ethnicity in Selected Books of the Old Testament," in Fishman et
al., *The Rise and Fall*, chapter 2.

ary France. It has definite Alexandrian,[38] Roman (*civis romanus sum*), western Christian,[39] and triumphant Islamic precursors as well.[40]

Modern Western students of nationalism have only recently recognized the extremely varied and heterogeneous forms that it can take. Organic and political; rational and irrational; contractual and inherited; left and right; democratic and authoritarian; secular and religious; stable and changeable; conflictual, competitive, and cooperative—these are all possibilities within the nationalist mix. To relate the "ethnicity boom" of the mid-1960s to mid-1970s (and the Mexican-American segment thereof) to this area of discourse is, therefore, merely to relate it to a *particular* stress on ethnicity rather than to necessarily similar goals or levels of intensity.

The Objective Reality of Nationalism, Nationality, and Nations

Most of the commonly attributed characteristics of nationalism posited in the early studies of this phenomenon can now be recognized as merely pertaining to a restricted subset of its possible (and at times incidental) sociofunctional "colorations." Like all other social categories and processes, nationalism has more situational characteristics than fixed ones. Americans' familiarity with their two major political parties and their constantly shifting ideological grounds for accomplishing practical ends should have made American students of ethnicity more attuned to this aspect of nationalism than it evidently did. And do not social scientists realize that religious systems are highly changeable and contextual in their beliefs and emphases and that they are, in essence, much more invented and created than discovered or received?

Is this not even more true of social class as a force in American political life? Instead of expecting one class or another to maintain forever a certain interest or a certain level of awareness, we now generally recognize that class is just one of several crosscutting allegiances and that it cannot be expected to be predictably on one side or another of issues that arise. Certainly, the distinction between class and class consciousness is universally made, and the lack of correspondence between the two is not taken to imply that one or

---

38. Arnold Toynbee, *The Greeks and Their Heritages* (New York: Oxford University Press, 1981).

39. See Galatians 3:28 in the Bible; and Raymond F. McNair, "A Universal Language," *The Plain Truth*, Jan. 7–9, 1982.

40. Fuad Baali and Ali Wardi, *Ibn Khalden and Islamic Thought-Styles: A Social Perspective* (Boston: G.K. Hall, 1981).

the other is false or useless or base; "Although few abstract concepts have more strongly influenced modern social theory and ideology than the notion of class, in advanced countries the theoretical concept is rarely transformed into an actual consciousness of class solidarity strong enough to overcome the effects of other attachments, more primordial and often more parochial, formed out of the experiences of daily life."[41]

However, the fact that class does not have the power in American life that some people wish (or that some have predicted it would have) not only has failed to invalidate the concept, but also has led to more refined understandings of its situationality.

Yet in connection with nationalism-related phenomena, their situationality and subjectivity not only came as a great surprise but, for some, have seemed to bring into question the very tenability of the concept. Kedourie concludes that "nationalism is a doctrine invented in Europe at the beginning of the 19th century."[42] Turner claims that "nations are not so much discovered as created by the labours of the intelligentsia."[43] Similar statements can be cited from most other major syntheses, commentaries, and critiques of earlier work on nationalism, including my own.[44] Nevertheless, the subjective and situational nature of nationalism, however much it has come to be accepted and understood within the field of nationalism research itself,[45] still exacts a high price of opprobrium when it is rediscovered in connection with American ethnicity phenomena.

Seemingly, the authenticity claim, on the one hand, and ongoing ideological, artifactual, and behavioral innovation and syncretism, on the other hand, make not only odd but difficult bedfellows. It is as if critics were saying: "A movement that advocates 'authenticity' is nothing more than a hoax if it is other than authentic." The unauthenticity of pro-authenticity movements then becomes an intensifier of the nostalgia charge. The ethnic revival is charged not only with pining for a past that is over, done with, and irretrievably

---

41. Robert A. Dahl, *Dilemmas of Pluralist Democracy: Autonomy vs. Control* (New Haven: Yale University Press, 1982), p. 64.

42. Elie Kedourie, *Nationalism* (London: Hutchinson, 1961), p. 20.

43. B. S. Turner, *Marx and the End of Orientalism* (London: Allen and Unwin, 1978), p. 55.

44. Fishman, *Language and Nationalism*.

45. See, for example, E. J. Hobsbaum, "Inventing Traditions in Nineteenth Century Europe," in E. J. Hobsbaum, ed., *The Invention of Tradition in Past and Present Society* (Cambridge, England: Cambridge University Press, 1977), pp. 1–24; and Michael Moerman, "Ethnic Identification in a Complex Civilization: Who are the Lue?" *American Anthropologist*, vol. 67 (1965), pp. 1215–30.

lost, but (which is worse) of pining for the past that never even was. However, aside from the fact that the creation of self-fulfilling prophecies and the formulation of usable pasts are part and parcel of all social movements and social institutions,[46] what should concern us is not so much that this activity also typifies authenticity quests as much as that such quests occur and recur and require satisfaction. Furthermore, manufactured authenticity may be as moving, as stirring, and as commanding as "the real thing." This situation testifies to the symbolic needs and symbolic capacities of the human species. The very strongest symbols deal with apparently "primordial" and "parochial" experiences that are purportedly derived from and that purportedly validate everyday life.[47]

Except among social scientists, emotional subjective validity often counts for more than empirical objective validity. From the mid-1960s to mid-1970s, the *felt* validity of their sidestream ethnicity counted more than it previously had for many people, and we must try to understand why rather than ask whether the symbols that were honored at that time were "really real." The latter is a technical, factual matter and reveals a detached, external perspective rather than an idea that provides insight. The phenomenon that we are trying to explain, moreover, is largely subjective and requires, at least in part, an appreciation of internalized feelings and goals rather than merely the external dating of customs and social boundaries.

Deutsch's Contribution to Studies of Nationalism

Karl Deutsch's main contribution to the study of nationalism was to take it out of the hands of historians and to place it more squarely in the hands of social scientists, particularly social scientists with quantitative inclinations.[48] However, more substantively important (and more apropos to our sociolinguistic interests) was Deutsch's interpretation of nationality as "the ability to communicate more effectively and over a wider range of subjects"[49] among a "large number of individuals from the middle and lower classes, linked to

---

46. Edward J. Lazzerini, "Ethnicity and the Uses of History: The Case of the Volga Tatars and Jadidism," *Central Asian Survey*, vol. 1 (1982), pp. 67–70.

47. Edward Shils, "Primordial, Personal, Sacred and Civil Ties," *British Journal of Sociology*, vol. 8 (1957), pp. 130–45; Edward Shils, *Tradition* (Chicago: University of Chicago Press, 1981); and Ali Mazrui, "Africa Between Nationalism and Nationhood: A Political Study," *Journal of Black Studies*, vol. 13 (1982), pp. 23–44.

48. Peter Calvert, "Karl Deutsch and Political Science," *Political Studies*, vol. 30 (1982), pp. 445–48.

49. Deutsch, *Nationalism*, p. 96.

regional centers and leading social groups by channels of social communication and economic intercourse."[50]

This insight altered the focus on nationalism from intellectual positions and historical events to social processes more generally and to language and communication in particular. His stress on "the middle and lower classes linked to . . . leading social groups" would probably be restated today in ways that would be less oriented toward central and eastern Europe of the late nineteenth and early twentieth centuries, but his stresses on "ability to communicate effectively," "regional centers," "leading social groups," and "economic inter- course" have become the building blocks of most nationalistic theories and studies since his own.

Just below the surface in Deutsch's stress on "social communi- cation" are the basic notions of urbanization (core and periphery), dislocation (social and cultural change), elites (change agents), and economic interests (material modernization), all of which are ingre- dients that figure in my own and numerous other even more recent theories of nationalism.[51] Some theorists have introduced additional formulations or refinements (mobilization, modernization),[52] and I have paid particular attention to "ethnic consciousness" as the crucial distinction between ethnicity and nationalism.[53] Basically, however, we have all merely rearranged, documented, and expounded upon one or more of Deutsch's original notions. Thanks to these notions and their revisions, we can now demonstrate the cultural and ideo- logical innovation and "consciousness raising" that literally creates a nationality where before there was only a passive, unrealized, unac- tivated ethnic potential.

In the aforementioned process, language is not only inevitably used, but it becomes a symbol of the mobilization on behalf of which it is used, as well as the natural arbiter of those who can be reached and included. Of course, nationalism involves a new use of language (for new purposes), as well as new varieties of language; but the

---

50. Ibid., p. 101.

51. See, for example, Imanuel Wallerstein, *The Modern World System* (New York: Academic Press, 1974); Michael Hechter, *Internal Colonialism: The Celtic Fringe in British National Development, 1536–1966* (London: Routledge and Kegan Paul, 1975); D. Chirot, *Social Change in a Peripheral Region* (New York: Academic Press, 1976); and Eugene J. Weber, *Peasants into Frenchmen: The Modernization of Rural France, 1870– 1914* (Stanford: Stanford University Press, 1976).

52. See, for example, Ernst Gellner, *Thought and Change* (Chicago: University of Chicago Press, 1964); and Tom Nairn, *The Break-Up of Britain: Crisis and Neo-Nationalism* (London: New Left Books, 1977).

53. Fishman, *Language and Nationalism*.

result is that the most sophisticated symbol system available becomes both symbolic of and an ingredient and index of the mobilized, modernized consciousness on behalf of which it is employed.[54] The part (that is, language) not only stands for the whole, but renders the whole conscious; it binds the whole together and implements the whole. In the process (a process that takes time and effort and is far from being as inevitable, "natural," and unidirectional as it later appears to be), an awareness of identity is created that often overrides the other interests (religious, economic, and political) of the population involved. Once created, a nationality may be self-perpetuating (which does not mean fixed or unchanging) until and unless it is overcome by forces greater than those that it has mobilized. Mexican-American ethnic consciousness and the role of the Spanish language in that consciousness are, therefore, both means and goals, processes and products.

Critique of Deutschian and Neo-Deutschian Theory

Of the several alternative (and, in part, complementary) versions of Deutschian theory, the Hechterian version is currently most popular.[55] Hechter is primarily concerned with the mobilization along ethnic lines of late-modernizing peripheral areas.[56] His data pertain to Welsh and Irish nationalism and their varying and wavering electoral appeals to their potential constituencies *over a period of generations.* He interprets the support of nationalist efforts as constituting a belated awareness and rejection of "internal colonialism." Thus, ethnic revivals of the Hechterian type are responses of peripheral and late-modernizing ethnic groups that struggle for the rectification of their basically economic grievances with respect to the established "ethnic diversification of labor."

Hechter's interpretations of ethnic revivals are clearly Deutschian, but they are more conflict-oriented, whereas Deutsch's views are more competition-oriented. Hechter also stresses the earlier stages of the industrialization-urbanization-modernization continuum as being most conducive to ethnic revivals, whereas Deutsch and others stress later stages. Much research on the most recent period of the ethnic revival among Belgian Flemings reveals that Flemish causes appeal most to

---

54. Joshua A. Fishman, "Language and Culture," *Social Science Encyclopedia* (London: Routledge and Kegan Paul, in press).
55. See, for example, Beer, *Unexpected Rebellion.*
56. Hechter, *Internal Colonialism.*

urban middle-class professionals rather than to workers.[57] This research implies that stalled, urban midmodernization (rather than late, peripheral modernization) provides the dynamics for mobilizing people along ethnic lines in order to advance basically economic goals.

At the other end of the modernization continuum is Eisenstadt's analysis, which focuses on ethnic revivals in various African settings in which modernization has been "defeated."[58] The economic and technological collapse of modernization leads to a return to regional ethnic identities over and above the prior thin veneer of integrative national identity.

All the Deutschian studies, regardless of the particular stage in the modernization process on which they focus and regardless of their conflict-competition differences, rely on a basically economic dynamic. They view ethnic revivals as elitist-manipulated programs for attaining economic goals. Undoubtedly, such revivals do occur and, even more undoubtedly, economic goals and grievances do play a role in ethnic movements[59] and in ethnic survival,[60] just as they do in religious and secular movements and experiences of all kinds. Many ethnic groups are obviously class-defined as well ("ethnoclasses," as Milton Gordon calls them) but, equally obviously, ethnicity has come to mean something different for middle- and lower-class Americans of Mexican, Polish, and Italian origin.

More dubious, however, is the implication that economic issues are somehow at the core of the human drama in general and of ethnic revivals and experiences in particular.[61] Those who posit

---

57. For similar conclusions about earlier periods, see R. van Alboom, "Aspecten van de Waalse Beweging te Brussel (1877–1914)," *Taal en Sociale Integratie*, vol. 6 (1982), pp. 3–106; and L. Jansegers, "Onmachtspositie van het Brusselse Flamingantisme (1884–1895)," *Taal en Sociale Integratie*, vol. 6 (1982), pp. 107–40.

58. S. N. Eisenstadt, *Revolution and the Transformation of Societies* (New York: Free Press, 1978).

59. See, for example, R. Blauner, "Internal Colonialism and Ghetto Revolts," *Social Problems*, vol. 17 (1969), pp. 463–72; Nathan Glazer, *Ethnic Dilemmas 1964–1982* (Cambridge, Mass.: Harvard University Press, 1983); Charles F. Keyes, ed., *Ethnic Change* (Seattle: University of Washington Press, 1981); and Rothschild, *Ethnopolitics*.

60. Edna Bonacich and John Modell, *The Economic Basis of Ethnic Solidarity: Small Business in the Japanese American Community* (Berkeley: University of California Press, 1981) and Margarita B. Melville, "Ethnicity: An Analysis of its Dynamism and Variability Focusing on the Mexican/Anglo/Mexican American Interface," *American Ethnologist*, vol. 30 (1983), pp. 272–89.

61. Note the disappointment of Susan Olzak, "Ethnic Mobilization in Quebec," *Ethnic and Racial Studies*, vol. 5 (1982), pp. 253–75, when such is *not* found to be the case. Note also the constant need of most confirmed empiricists to ponder other variables. See, for example, Jeffrey Reitz, "Language and Ethnic Community Survival,"

economic primacy a priori (not unlike those who claim that ethnicity is imaginary and that only social class is real) inevitably wind up viewing ethnicity as a "mere by-product of more basic forces" and, therefore, as expendable if not entirely unnecessary and even undesirable.[62] Culture per se becomes an epiphenomenon. Unfortunately, "Marx and Engels left no clear theoretical guideline for conceptualizing the phenomenon of nationalism."[63] Their followers are left therefore with "no explanation of how to deal theoretically with the ethnic divisions of mankind when confronted with divisions based on class,"[64] and few of these followers have had the temerity to strike out on their own to seek out an explanation.[65] Instead of seeing ethnicity as a factor in interaction with others (class, sex, age, religion), influencing others, and being influenced by them in complex fashions that always require *empirical* elucidation, these people believe ethnicity is explained away as an economic residue.

This view, of course, is in conflict with Berlin's view, according to which the ethnic revival of the mid-1960s to mid-1970s was a rejection of the heartless, soulless economic determinism in modern life, which required that we disguise our true feelings and beings for the sake of maximizing the efficiency of the modern marketplace.[66] Most seriously, however, the economic emphases that derive from Deutschian studies (as well as from the countless Marxist and neo-Marxist studies whose ultimate appreciation of ethnicity is infinitely less than that of the Deutschian school) do not agree with the basic thrust of our evidence-anchored view (arguable though it may still be) of the ethnic revival in the United States. This view sees the U.S.

Canadian Review of Sociology and Anthropology, vol. 11 (1974), pp. 104–22; and Stanley Lieberson, *A Piece of the Pie: Blacks and White Immigrants Since 1960* (Berkeley: University of California Press, 1981).

62. See, for example, Howard F. Stein and Robert F. Hill, *The Ethnic Imperative: Examining the New White Ethnic Movement* (University Park: Pennsylvania State University Press, 1977); and Steinberg, *Ethnic Myth.*

63. Turner, *Marx and the End of Orientalism,* p. 60.

64. Leszek Kolakowski, "Marxist Philosophy and National Reality: Natural Communities and Universal Brotherhood," *Round Table,* no. 253 (1979), p. 48.

65. Note, however, Tom Nairn, "The Modern Janus," *New Left Review,* no. 94 (1975), pp. 3–30; Michael Lowy, "Marxists and the National Question," *New Left Review,* no. 96 (1976), pp. 81–100; and A. Jakubowicz, "State and Ethnicity: Multiculturism as Ideology," *Australian and New Zealand Journal of Sociology,* vol. 17 (1981), pp. 4–13, who have called for more initiative along these very lines. See also the variety of views covered by Horace B. Davis, *Nationalism and Socialism: Marxist and Labor Theories of Nationalism to 1917* (New York: Monthly Review Press, 1973).

66. Isaiah Berlin, "The Bent Twig: A Note on Nationalism," *Foreign Affairs,* vol. 51 (1972), pp. 11–30.

ethnic revival as a generalized response over and above any economic differences between the groups that manifested it.[67]

The non-American, nonimmigrant contexts of the Deutschian and neo-Deutschian research we have just reviewed present yet another hurdle in successfully applying it to the ethnic revival in the United States. In America we are dealing primarily with postmodernization rather than with modernization, problematics.[68] Instead of having indigenous minorities wavering between central integration and peripheral autonomy, the United States has primarily immigrant minorities reassessing their original identities in a country with no deeply historical, "indigenous" ethnic center—indeed, immigrational diversity *is* the center in this country. Instead of being a Deutschian programmatic and politicized opportunity, the ethnic revival in the United States was more of a diffuse counterreaction to mainstream characteristics and blandishments (rather than restrictions) in the context of particular events and opportunities. Instead of being an example of Deutschian ideological and cultural innovation and transformation, the recent ethnolinguistic revival in the United States— among Mexican-Americans as well as among other minorities—was primarily a rearrangement of identifying priorities and components. Instead of being the byproduct of Deutschian proto-elite initiatives, the ethnic revival in the United States, including that of languages other than English, was largely an instance of leaderless drift. Instead of having a Deutschian stress on autonomy in matters of language, religion, education, and economy, the U.S. ethnic revival stressed self-understanding, self-righteousness, self-acceptance, and perhaps even self-indulgence. Instead of finding a progression from ethnicity to nationality to nation, we generally find among United States ethnic groups no more than an acknowledged interest in ethnicity that remains far below the level of intensity necessary to sustain the nationality and nation stages.[69]

---

67. Fishman, "Mother Tongues Claiming."

68. See Amitai Etzioni, *The Active Society* (New York: Basic Books, 1968).

69. As used here, the term *nation* is used to mean a political entity, that is, a politically bounded collectivity with the relative autonomy, resource allocation, decision-making, sanction-imposing capacity, and boundary maintenance power that political means provide. *Nationality* implies consciousness of ethnicity, programmatic ethnicity in terms of goals, aspirations, obligations, and imperatives. *Ethnicity* entails only the implementation of part-culture, of folk culture, of little culture, that is, of the daily rounds of life in traditioned (including creatively traditioned) ways. The last mentioned level, ethnicity, is the first to consolidate and be transformed into the second, nationality, by dint of consciousness-raising experiences, usually under the leadership of consciousness-raising elites. The transition from ethnicity to nationality is not inevitable, and the transition from nationality to nation even less inevitable. The correlations

Indeed, if the transition from ethnic group to nationality is rather dubious in the case of the ethnic revival in the United States, the transition from nationality to nation is almost entirely absent, both in ideological as well as in concrete organizational or practical terms.[70] Even the virtual absence of much-feared ethnic politicization[71] in connection with the ethnic revival in the United States (which is not to say that there was no ethnic politics, a veritable staple of the American political scene since the days of Benjamin Franklin)[72] cannot be attributed to the factors usually involved in the absence or presence of politicized nationalism in Deutschian theory. Normally such politicization is attributable to the impenetrability and hostility of the established power structure. Accordingly, the absence or shrinkage of politicization should be attributable to the presence of an easily penetrable and accommodating power structure.[73] However, in the American case the absence of serious ethnic politicization[74] was due to the noninstrumental nature of the ethnic revival per se and to the

---

between degrees of consciousness, purposefulness, and boundary regulation are high indeed for human ethnocultural collectivities, but the progression or even direction of development between any one stage and the next is historical (determined by concrete experience) rather than developmental or programmed.

70. See Edward Sagarin and James Moneymaker, "Language and Nationalist, Separatist and Secessionist Movements," in Raymond L. Hall, ed., *Ethnic Autonomy: Comparative Dynamics* (Elmsford, N.Y.: Pergamon Publishing Co., 1979); and Arline McCord and William McCord, "Ethnic Autonomy: A Social-Historical Synthesis," in Hall, *Ethnic Autonomy.*

71. See, for example, Charles R. Foster, ed., *Nations Without a State: Ethnic Minorities in Western Europe* (New York: Praeger, 1980).

72. See L. Estrada, "Language and Political Consciousness among the Spanish-Speaking in the United States: A Demographic Study," in D.J.R. Bruckner, ed., *Politics and Language: Spanish and English in the United States* (Chicago: University of Chicago Center for Policy Study, 1980), pp. 13–22; and Shirley Brice Heath, "Our Language Heritage: A Historical Perspective," in June K. Phillips, ed., *The Language Connection: From the Classroom to the World* (Skokie, Ill.: National Textbook Co., 1977); Isidoro Lucas, "Political Demands of Spanish-Speaking Communities in the United States," in Bruckner, ed., *Politics and Language;* Michael Waltzer, "Pluralism in Political Perspective," in *Harvard Encyclopedia of American Ethnic Groups* (Cambridge, Mass.: Harvard University Press, 1980), pp. 781–87; and William Spinrad, "The Politics of American Jews: An Example of Ethnic Group Analysis," in Joseph B. Maier and Chim Waxman, eds., *Ethnicity, Identity and History: Essays in Honor of Werner J. Cahnman* (New Brunswick, N.J.: Transaction, 1983), pp. 249–72.

73. Karl Mayer, "Ethnic Tensions in Switzerland: The Jura Conflict," in Foster, ed., *Nations without a State;* and F. Pristinger, "Ethnic Conflict and Modernization in the South Tyrol," in Foster, ed., *Nations without a State.*

74. See Michael Parenti, "Ethnic Politics and the Persistence of Ethnic Identification," *American Political Science Review,* vol. 61 (1967), pp. 242–70, and note his critique of Raymond Wolfinger, "The Development and Persistence of Ethnic Voting," *American Political Science Review,* vol. 59 (1965), pp. 896–908.

weak role of any intelligentsia in the revival as a whole, notwithstanding the general rise in ethnic saliency.

Certainly there is no ground for singling out Mexican-Americans for a discussion of ethnic politics and ethnic loyalty, as some theorists have done.[75] If anything, the continuing depoliticization of Mexican-American community life is more noteworthy than its politicization. For a group of its size, its concentration, and its absolute and relative disadvantage in socioeconomic terms, the political quietude of the Mexican-Americans deserves more inquiry than it has received. Not only are political separatism, terrorism, or other extremism virtually unheard of, but even political organization along traditional ethno-American lines is rather weak and ineffective. The number of Mexican-American governors, senators, representatives, state legislators, and mayors is far smaller than would be expected purely on a pro rata basis and, what is more, most Mexican-Americans express little urgency to overcome such underrepresentation and their consequent lack of influence in the decision-making arena. Although the lack of political influence is bound to be overcome in the next few decades, Mexican-American loyalty to general American political institutions and processes will almost certainly be furthered rather than weakened as a result.

The dramatic growth of ethnic study programs at colleges and universities was a crucial aspect of the ethnic revival per se, but these programs did not prepare "new men" to join with already politicized proto-elites in the acceleration and expansion of nationalist activism in the manner so convincingly demonstrated by Hobsbaum for various European settings.[76] Higher education, on the whole, may have remained the enemy of ethnicity and of sidestream ethnic continuity that it traditionally has been in America. Thus the ethnic revival entailed a detachment on the part of "ethnolinguistically interested" college students from the total higher education experience of preprofessional training, just as the revival per se entailed their detachment from the values, goals, and processes of the mainstream more generally.

Even among Hispanics or American Indians, where more "new men" *did* come into being and where a new leadership *was* trained on American college campuses (a leadership far different in makeup from that which preceded it), frustrated careerism was hardly an

---

75. Bruckner, *Politics and Language.*
76. E. J. Hobsbaum, *Age of Revolution* (New York: World Publishing Company, 1962); and Hobsbaum, "Inventing Traditions."

ingredient in the overall makeup of these new leaders. Unlike the assumptions of Deutschian models, the protest of Hispanics and American Indians was not against a mainstream or central system that excluded them (as detailed by numerous authors who overstate the role of disappointed elites and proto-elites in ethnicity movements).[77] On the contrary, their protest was against a society that eagerly included them as exemplars of "affirmative action," that is, against an establishment that "transethnified" more than it gratified in any material way.

Instead of breaking with internal traditional forces (ethnic churches and ethnic schools), the revival ultimately dug in around these very institutions of daily life. As a result, none of the three stages proposed by Hroch with respect to the life of all nationalist movements—(1) small groups of ideologically innovative intellectuals, (2) wider networks of patriot-agitators, and (3) serious popular mobilization— usually developed, and the latter two, by and large, were totally absent.[78] The ethnic revival occurred during a period of relatively easy social advancement, rather than a period of curtailment; it was, therefore, partially a rejection of such advancement as the be-all and end-all of meaningful life. What Nairn calls "righting the balance of uneven development" does not seem to have been widely involved.[79] Indeed, neither the absence of nor the experience of social mobility may have been involved so much as the downgrading of such mobility from its previous position as the pinnacle of triumph and the attainment of the good life. The revival was neither a "liberal education for traditional individuals" nor "a kind of professional education for individuals on the move into the bourgeoisie."[80] It was neither a questioning of loyalty to America nor a search for a higher loyalty. Indeed, it was far too innocent and disorganized to even be an ethnic revival!

All in all, therefore, this review of Deutschian and neo-Deutschian concepts and theories has served to highlight the contention that the ethnic revival in the United States represented an ethnic process that

---

77. Anthony D. Smith, *The Ethnic Revival* (New York: Cambridge University Press, 1981); and Bud B. Khlief, "Ethnicity and Language with Reference to the Frisian Case: Issues of Schooling, Work and Identity," in Koen Zondag, ed., *Bilingual Education in Friesland* (Franeker, the Netherlands: Wever, 1982), pp. 175–203.

78. Miroslav Hroch, *Die Vorkämpfer der nationalen Bewegung bei den Kleinen Völkeren Europas* (Prague: Universita Karlova, 1968).

79. Nairn, *Break-Up of Britain.*

80. J. Womack, "Mariateque, Marxism and Nationalism," *Marxist Perspectives,* vol. 3 (1980), pp. 170–74.

was different in type and intensity from that which had hitherto been explored in the research on nationalism. Further exploration of the U.S. ethnic revival may illuminate various aspects of ethnicity trans-formations that are as yet little understood—particularly those going on in postmodernization, immigration-based contexts. The U.S. ex-perience calls into question several previously unchallenged assump-tions concerning the relationship between sidestream ethnicity on the one hand, and on the other social class, liberalism-conservatism, elites, ethnic consciousness, social conflict, and political activism.[81] This inquiry into the ethnic revival in the United States may ultimately help to provide a better understanding of some aspects of modern minority ethnicity everywhere, including Mexican-American ethnicity in the Southwest.

Situational Aspects of Ethnic Saliency

A major problem with Deutschian and neo-Deutschian ap-proaches to variation in ethnic saliency is that they are overly categorical or macro oriented. Even at the macro level, however, they have been criticized as insufficiently predictive.[82] Accordingly, I now turn to the level of middle-range specificity, a level of analysis that is neither overly macro nor micro in orientation. In so doing I shall parallel sociolinguistic theory as it has been developed during the past two decades.

Immigrant-derived ethnicity in the United States today (along with Chicano and American Indian ethnicity in this country and indigenous minority ethnicity in many settings throughout the world) has been implemented largely in a context characterized by inter-ethnic contact and by culture change more generally. It is largely a repertoirial phenomenon, by which I mean that it coexists together with a number of "varieties" of socially patterned behaviors, some of which are derived from sidestream ethnicity, others from mainstream

---

81. See William M. Newman, "A Theory of Social Conflict," in William M. Newman, *American Pluralism: A Study of Minority Groups and Social Theory* (New York: Harper and Row, 1973).

82. For example, it is difficult to explain *when* ethnic competition or conflict will occur relative to the onset of consciousness of disadvantage, internal colonization, or change in central priorities.

ethnicity, and yet others bear the stamp of modern generality that is not (or is no longer) indicative of any particular ethnicity.

The first- and second-generational pangs of conflict and double marginality, documented so tellingly in the 1930s and 1940s,[83] are still present in some cases, but they are much more muted and mellowed. In comparison with earlier periods and with the concerted Americanization pressures that were formerly applied by both mainstream and sidestream institutions, not only is it now possible to "be American" in a variety of ethnic ways, but also sidestream ethnicity per se has become much more modern and American. The spirit of the times has changed, and the vast majority of Americans reveal, within their total repertoire of social behaviors, ways of doing, feeling, and knowing that are associated with sidestream ethnicity.

An American ethnicity, too, is coming into being,[84] slowly but significantly, and is crisscrossed by minority ethnic realizations, just as the latter are totally crisscrossed by American doings, feelings, and knowings. The total repertoire is increasingly experienced as a highly integrated whole (rather than as bits and tatters of inharmonious cloth), although it is made up, as are all modern cultures, of old and new threads of diverse ages and origins. The totality of these threads constitute the total repertoire, but they are never implemented totally, all at the same time. As with repertoires more generally, the ethnic repertoire is selectively (that is, contextually) implemented, on the basis of socioconsensual principles of appropriateness and in pursuit of individual goals within a framework of social norms and expectations.

Identity is a matter of social location, Berger tells us.[85] Accordingly, particular combinations of threads (varieties of behavior) are selectively implemented, sometimes combining sidestream and mainstream ethnicity, and sometimes combining old (arguably "authentic") and new aspects of either or both. As "old bread and new wine" are constantly brought together, newness is less overwhelming and disorienting.[86] The principles of selection between the myriad possible combinations are both macro- and micro-determined.

---

83. See, for example, Irvin L. Child, *Italian or American? The Second Generation in Conflict* (New Haven: Yale University Press, 1943).

84. Joseph Hraba, *American Ethnicity* (Itasca, Ill.: Peacock, 1979).

85. Peter L. Berger, *The Noise of Solemn Assemblies* (Garden City, N.Y.: Doubleday, 1961).

86. Patrick J. Gallo, *Old Bread, New Wine: A Portrait of the Italian-Americans* (Chicago: Nelson-Hall, 1981).

Putting Sidestream Ethnicity into Context

Several theorists have claimed that ethnicity is primarily situational.[87] In accord with well-established principles for the use of one language (or language variety) or another within a bilingual community, the implementation of ethnobehavioral varieties can be conceptualized at various corresponding levels of abstraction.[88] At the micro level, one can recognize ethnic acts and events. Birth, death, marriage, coming of age, and the like may well be more heavily characterized by sidestream ethnicity behaviors (including more use of ethnic mother tongues) than are most other acts, events, or "scenes" of modern urban life.[89] Certain persons are particularly likely to be dealt with in terms of shared sidestream ethnicity: one's grandmother, the parish priest, the community poet, the teacher of the local ethnic school. Similarly, certain places and their congruent topics and role relationships (the three together being the building blocks of situations) also mark sidestream ethnicity, particularly if they are ritualized (highly predictable or formalized). If asking grandfather to do you a favor when talking with him privately at the big table in the family dining room is a situation that stresses recognizable sidestream ethnicity,[90] then participating in the saint's-day dinner with the immediate family at the same table is even more likely to be so.[91]

Several studies agree that use of the Spanish language by Mexican-Americans is overwhelmingly family related.[92] In addition, these

---

87. See, for example, D. Handleman, "The Organization of Ethnicity," *Ethnic Groups*, vol. 1 (1977), pp. 187-200; Moerman, "Ethnic Identification"; and J. N. Paden, "Urban Pluralism, Integration and Adoption of Communal Identity in Kano, Nigeria," in R. Cohen and J. Middleton, eds., *From Tribe to Nation in Africa* (Scranton, Penn.: Chandler, 1971), pp. 242–70.

88. See Joshua A. Fishman, Robert L. Cooper, Roxana Ma, et al., *Bilingualism in the Barrio*, 2d ed. (Bloomington: Indiana University, 1975).

89. See Tamara K. Hareven, ed., *The Family and the Life Course in Historical Perspective* (New York: Academic Press, 1978); and Martha N. Fried and Morton H. Fried, *Transitions: Four Rituals in Eight Cultures* (New York: Norton, 1980).

90. Gallo, *Old Bread, New Wine*.

91. See David M. Schneider, "What is Kinship All About?" in Priscilla Reining, ed., *Kinship Studies in the Morgan Centennial Year* (Washington, D.C.: Anthropological Association of Washington, D.C., 1972), pp. 32–64; and Shils, *Tradition*.

92. David E. Lopez, "Chicano Language Loyalty in an Urban Setting," *Sociology and Social Research*, vol. 62 (1976); R. L. Skrabenek, "Language Maintenance among Mexican-Americans," *International Journal of Comparative Sociology*, vol. 11 (1970), pp. 272–82; and Alan Hudson-Edwards and Garland D. Bills, "Intergenerational Language Shift in an Albuquerque Barrio," in J. Amastae and Lucia Elias-Olivares, eds., *Spanish in the United States: Sociolinguistic Aspects* (Cambridge, England: Cambridge University Press, 1982), pp. 135–53.

studies reveal that ethnic language use is greater among older persons than among younger ones. Use of the Spanish language erodes with successive generations of increased interaction with and dependence on English language networks. Accordingly, it is within the family context as a whole, rather than in connection with specific events or acts associated with that context, that the transition from the spread of English (which would merely foster bilingualism) to the decline of Spanish (which fosters English monolingualism) must be monitored.

Obviously, one need not conceptualize sidestream ethnicity episodically (even though that may be the level of preferred data collection or of disciplinary reward). Entire slices of social life (domains) may be more colored by sidestream identity and its implementation than are others—for example, religion more than work, home and family more than street and neighborhood, and school more than entertainment.[93] Domains, related as they are to the major institutional channels of society, constitute parsimonious cognitive, affective, and overt behavioral boundaries in the organization of social life. One need not insist that they always be clear-cut and exclusively sidestream or mainstream situational aggregations in order to recognize that they might be exactly one or the other for some networks and in some historical junctures. Clear-cut and uniform or not, they may nevertheless appear to be phenomenologically so for "actors," and they may well constitute legitimate targets of investigation for researchers.

Network types may also usefully differentiate between sidestream and mainstream ethnicity behaviors or particular combinations thereof. In certain closed networks (networks in which individuals are united by bonds of intimacy and shared experience that transcend and override status differences, and ones that are therefore relatively inhospitable or closed to outsiders), sidestream ethnicity may be more salient than it is in open networks. Similarly, in personal interactions (in which shared qualities of the participants are stressed, rather than the transactional or instrumental goals of their particular encounter), sidestream ethnicity may come to the fore much more than it does in interactions focused upon practical outcomes.[94]

Finally, at the highest level of generality, cultural value clusters

93. Joshua A. Fishman, "Domains and the Relationship between Micro- and Macro-Sociolinguistics," in John J. Gumperz and D. Hymes, *Directions in Sociolinguistics* (New York: Holt, Rinehart and Winston, 1972), pp. 435–53.

94. Frederik Barth, *Ethnic Groups and Boundaries* (Boston: Little, Brown and Co., 1969).

provide appropriate contexts for socially patterned behavior. Whereas *gemeinschaft* (life at the level of face-to-face, small-scale, emotionally bonded, putatively kinship-derived community) and *gesellschaft* (life at the level of impersonal, large-scale, rationally and efficiently organized society) most certainly coexist in modern contexts, they are not equally salient on every occasion. Values, primary relationships, feelings of intimacy, sympathy, responsibility, interest, and involvement with one's fellows, face-to-face experience, and emotional commitment to "those of one's own kind"[95] may be much more associated with sidestream ethnicity than the powerful, efficient, productive, and competitive interactions that constitute the effective, achievement-oriented component of modern life.[96] Not surprisingly, the former context may reveal far more sidestream ethnic being, feeling, and knowing (and use of an ethnic mother tongue) among Mexican-Americans as well as among other components of the American sidestream.

Other Aspects of the Ethnicity Repertoires

The contextualization and interpenetration of ethnicities of one kind or another (as distinct from categorical "all or none" ethnicity throughout) do not exhaust the ethnicity repertoire but merely raise the issue of when. Among other issues related to repertoire is the issue of repertoire range. How many and how disparate are the sidestream ethnicity contexts that are recognized by society? For some, the repertoire could be limited to family contexts. For others, it could range from family and religious rituals to educational and occupational domains as well.

An even more fundamental issue involves repertoire compartmentalization—that is, the extent to which mainstream and sidestream ethnicity may be implemented in the same contexts (acts, situations, and so on). Where both sidestream and mainstream ethnicity are permissible in the same situation (that is, compartmentalization is absent or very meager), the blending of the two will proceed more rapidly than in situations in which they are allocated to either one ethnicity or the other. But the compartmentalization of dual ethnicity

---

95. Franz Boas, "Race Problems in America," *Science*, vol. 79 (1909), pp. 839–49; Fischer, *To Dwell Among Friends*.

96. Joav Findling, "Bilingual Need Affiliation, Future Orientation and Achievement Motivation," in Joshua Fishman, ed., *Advances in the Sociology of Language*, vol. II (The Hague: Mouton, 1972).

is generally difficult to maintain in modern, interactive urban contexts.[97]

As a result, dual ethnicity seldom exists at the societal level, and ethnic discontinuity also becomes rare. The daily or festive rounds that typify one ethnicity are increasingly found in the other ethnicity that is present with it in time and place, and this redundancy or parallelism both reflects and fosters the lack of compartmentalization and the ongoing melding. Although modernization of once-rural sidestream ethnicities increases their ability to cope with urban American social, economic, and political realities, modernization also increases the melding potential between modernities. Even if the modernities stem from two different ethnocultural sources or points of origin, boundary maintenance on a cultural basis is a difficult goal when one modernity faces another.[98] Without boundary maintenance, the crucial ability to exercise the "controlled acculturation" that even certain tiny premodern societies such as the Old Order Amish and the Hasidim can engage in becomes impossible even for much larger groups such as most Mexican-Americans and other Hispanics, German-Americans, and Italian-Americans.[99] For modern urban

97. Joshua A. Fishman, "Bilingualism and Biculturism as Individual and as Societal Phenomena," *Journal of Multilingual and Multicultural Development*, vol. 7 (1980), pp. 3–15.

98. On the concept of boundary maintenance, see Harald Haarmann, *Ethnicity and the Role of Ethnic Boundaries in Processes of Ethnic Fusion and Fission* (in press); Raimondo Strassoldo, "Boundaries in Sociological Theory: A Reassessment," in R. Strassoldo and G. Delli-Zotti, eds., *Cooperation and Conflict in Border Areas* (Milan: Franco Angeli, 1982), pp. 245–71; Christina Bratt Paulston and Rolland G. Paulston, "Language and Ethnic Boundaries," *Language Sciences*, vol. 2 (1980), pp. 69–101.

99. See William E. Thompson, "The Oklahoma Amish: Survival of an Ethnic Subculture," *Ethnicity*, vol. 8 (1981), pp. 476–87; and Joseph W. Eaton, "Controlled Acculturation: A Survival Technique of the Hutterites," *American Sociological Review*, vol. 17 (1952), pp. 331–40. Ethnocultural boundary maintenance may be anathema to the liberal disposition with its penchant for untrammeled interaction; indeed, to many it smacks of apartheid at worst and of "separate but equal" at best. However, boundary maintenance is a minimal characteristic of all life, from the most elementary to the most complex. It entails the basic need and right to control inviolability, to define and maintain one's own system and the circumstances under which others may enter it. At the sociocultural level, boundary maintenence is the screening process by which outside values, goals, artifacts, and individuals are evaluated, admitted, or found wanting. It is the sine qua non of the appearance and the experience of cultural continuity. Boundary maintenance is not necessarily antithetical to democratic or egalitarian interaction; it can be relatively situational, contextual, and accommodating, but unless it exists and is under internal control, no system can continue to function. To deny boundary maintenance to minorities as a matter of principle is to deny them the possibility of controlling their own fates as healthy cultural entities, a denial which is the height of totalitarian monism, no matter how it is dressed up ideologically.

minorities, primary institutions are the very sinews of boundary maintenance.[100]

Without politico-territorial boundaries, Mexican-Americans face the difficulty of maintaining ethnocultural boundaries while interacting ever more energetically with the economic and technical mainstream and its ethnocultural byproducts. Without boundary maintenance (between groups) or compartmentalization (within groups), ethnocultural and ethnolinguistic separation undergoes inevitable attrition—even among Mexican-Americans, the machos of the current ethnic scene in the United States. In their case, too, the third generation is overwhelmingly anglicized in customs and in language, the efforts and attitudes of activists to the contrary notwithstanding.[101]

Similarities and Differences between Ethnolinguistic and Ethnocultural Transitions

Language is a part of an index of, and a symbol of, ethnocultural behavior. As ethnicities meld, change, or absorb and replace one another, the languages of these ethnicities will inevitably be modified as well.

Languages are, of course, always changing, particularly languages in contact.[102] Ethnocultures, too, are constantly changing, notwithstanding the authenticity claims and experiences of their members. More important to our discussion than language change is language replacement or substitution—that is, the adoption of what is consensually regarded as a new or different language in conjunction with a particular ethnic identity or behavioral realization. I am referring here to the possibility of language shift occurring simultaneously with apparent or experienced ethnocultural constancy. Contra-indicated though they may be in nationalist dogma, such language shifts do occur and have occurred in the United States, and their implications for language and ethnicity, as well as for language and culture more generally, need to be examined.

100. See Michael Hechter, Debra Friedman, and Malka Appelbaum, "A Theory of Ethnic Collective Action," *International Migration Review*, vol. 16 (1982); and Raymond Breton, Jeffrey Reitz, and Victor Valentino, *Cultural Boundaries and the Cohesion of Canada* (Montreal: Institute for Research on Public Policy, 1980).

101. Calvin Veltman, *Language Shift in the United States* (Berlin: Mouton, 1983); and Fishman, "Mother Tongues Claiming."

102. Uriel Weinrich, *Languages in Contact* (New York: Linguistic Circle of New York, 1953). This is true even without the problematic context of the overlap and concurrence of ethnic realizations which we are here examining.

Students of the American ethnolinguistic scene have known for nearly a quarter-century that although both language and ethnicity are capable of multiple transformations, these need not occur in tandem. Indeed, language is far more labile than ethnicity per se.[103] The subsystems of language, as well as whole languages, can change and can be exchanged far more rapidly and discontinuously than can the total ethnicity constellation (although it, too, is constantly subject both to change and to exchange). Up to a point, the language associated with a given sidestream ethnicity is considered to be merely influenced by the language of mainstream ethnicity. After that point a sense of real transition obtains, and the language of the mainstream may be used for sidestream ethnicity in addition to all its other uses. This point is reached more definitively and more consciously in print than in speech.

Thus, no matter how all-embracing language is experienced to be as the vehicle or the symbol of the total ethnocultural package, it is only a part, and a detachable part at that, of that package.[104] This was particularly evident in the case of the American ethnic revival (and the Mexican-American ethnic revival) in which language ideologies and language movements per se were almost entirely lacking;[105] those few for whom language itself took the place of the country they had left came to be considered offbeat even by their closest friends and neighbors. As a result, ethnocultural experiences as interconnected ways of doing, feeling, and knowing have been phenomenologically much more robust than their linguistic accompaniments. The former may and do change and meld tremendously, and yet they can be experienced (and interpreted by outsiders) as "authentic" and as intact continuity phenomena.

A few important rituals, a few foods, a transition commemoration here and there, a dance, a melody—these may be enough to maintain a sense of ethnocultural continuity in the midst of far-flung social change and ethnocultural innovation and melding.[106] The "authentic" community cannot be "saved," but neither need it be "lost."[107] The

---

103. Joshua A. Fishman, *Language Loyalty in the United States* (The Hague: Mouton, 1966).

104. Fishman, *Language and Nationalism.*

105. See Frances Svensson, "Language as Ideology: The American Indian Case," *Etudes de Linguistique Appliquée,* vol. 15 (1974), pp. 60–68; and Sagarin and Moneymaker, "Language and Nationalist."

106. Richard D. Alba and Mitchell B. Chamlin, "A Preliminary Examination of Ethnic Identification among Whites," *American Sociological Review,* vol. 48 (1983), pp. 240–47.

107. Yung-mei Tsai and Lee Sigelman, "The Community Question: A Perspective

ethnocultural self-concept, the notion of group identity, can remain intact and unchanged far beyond any similar experience with respect to language. Indeed, in the case of language, detachments occur, and often consensually so, whereas the total ethnocultural experience— traumatized though it may temporarily be—can recover a sense of stability and continuity.

I am not saying that the replacement of one language by another does not exact a huge price in terms of ethnocultural authenticity and continuity and in terms of societal organization and stability as a whole. I *am* saying that the price is contingent on the degree of internal management and control of the total change process and that ultimately, after the worst is over, a sense of basic ethnocultural continuity and authenticity can be recaptured, notwithstanding the linguistic detachment and replacement and notwithstanding the overall ethnocultural innovation and melding. Learning the ethnic mother tongue as a second language and camouflaging the loss of mother tongue usage by modest institutional "gains" in connection with second language use exemplify the simultaneity and confound-ability of mother tongue loss *and* ethnocultural continuity and change.[108]

The experience of language continuity and the experience of ethnic continuity are both highly attitudinal; however, the latter is a much more robust attitude than the former. Discontinuity and detachment are particularly evident for written languages. For spoken languages, the continuity-discontinuity transitions are less sharp, but the morph-syntactic and phonological systems can bend only so far before they are considered to be "something else." The combination of relative linguistic inflexibility and relative ethnocultural flexibility finally results in the triumph of overall ethnocultural continuity experiences over ethnolinguistic discontinuity experiences, if the latter can be brought under ultimate control.

A hammer is experienced to be the same even though on one occasion the head is replaced and on another occasion, the handle. Thus ethnolinguistic and ethnocultural continuity in the United States are both far greater at an attitudinal level than at an overt behavioral one, whether viewed experientially (from within) or evaluationally (from without). In addition, the latter (ethnocultural continuity) is greater than the former (ethnolinguistic continuity). The ethnic revival consisted of a rise in the saliency of both ethnocultural and ethnolin-

---

from National Survey Data—The Case of the USA," *British Journal of Sociology*, vol. 33 (1982), pp. 579–88.
  108. Fishman et al., *The Rise and Fall.*

guistic continuities at both attitudinal and behavioral levels, even though the former was already much weakened and the latter much transformed, from an external evaluation point of view. The revival did not compensate for or overcome either the weakness, on the one hand, nor the transformations, on the other. Although the ethnic revival neither triumphed nor stabilized, it was nevertheless an unexpected and significant occurrence.

On the language front, the ethnic revival was generally related to increased institutional concern for language and increased retrospective acquisition of the mother tongue (second-language learning at best), rather than to genuine language movements or renativization. Mexican-Americans, particularly those in urban centers, reveal a somewhat slower process along these lines, because of their greater numbers, concentration, and recency of arrival, but thus far they have *not* developed a pattern of stable, intergenerational language maintenance. Some of the most traditional communities, however, prove capable of the most "radical" steps on behalf of language maintenance via boundary maintenance in those urban areas where third-generation and even longer-established Mexican-Americans are encountered.[109]

Mexican-American ethnolinguistic activists believe—even more so than the other major Hispanic populations in the United States (Cubans and Puerto Ricans)—that they can maintain their ethnicity without maintaining the use of the Spanish language (45.4 percent of Mexican-Americans versus 22.7 percent among Cubans and 37.5 percent among Puerto Ricans).[110] Accordingly, Mexican-Americans are becoming convinced that their communities have more important problems than language maintenance (95.4 percent versus 90.0 percent and 62.3 percent). Thus, although linguistic assimilation is eschewed and the Spanish language can still often be acquired in the general community (because of the omnipresence of recently arrived monolingual Spanish speakers) even when it is not acquired in the family, reliance on Spanish is weakening ideologically, attitudinally, and overtly at only a somewhat slower rate than have mother tongues among other ethnolinguistic minorities in the United States.[111]

---

109. See Craig J. Calhoun, "The Radicalism of Tradition: Community Strength or Venerable Disguise and Borrowed Language," *American Journal of Sociology*, vol. 88 (1983), pp. 886–914; and Robert St. Clair and William Leap, *Language Renewal among American Indian Tribes: Issues, Problems, and Prospects* (Rosslyn, Va.: National Clearinghouse for Bilingual Education, 1982).

110. Lowy et al., "Ethnic Activists."

111. Veltman, *Language Shift.*

The extent of third-generation Spanish language maintenance in the United States today is lower than French language maintenance among third-generation French-Canadians in Ottawa. Even where both Hispanic parents are still bilingual, only 45 percent of the children aged four to seventeen are bilingual and 99 percent of them speak English as their usual language.[112] Navaho children, by contrast, are 90 percent bilingual, while 84 percent speak English as their usual language. Finally, the percentages for all other third-generation children in the United States are 26 percent bilingual, with 99.9 percent speaking English as their usual language. Thus, the degree of language maintenance among third-generation Hispanics is more similar to that of the majority of ethnolinguistic third generations in the United States than to either the Navajos or the tiny francophone communities in Ottawa. Any claim that Mexican-Americans are not learning English is unjustified. The Hispanic interest in bilingual education has various political, economic, and professional ramifications, but it does not have any serious language maintenance consequences. Language maintenance among minorities depends on the maintenance of cultural boundaries and the intactness of primary ethnocultural institutions—family, neighborhood, and perhaps church. In the Mexican-American case, all these institutions are moving perceptibly in the direction of mainstream America.

If migration from Mexico succumbs to restrictive regulation, we can expect an acceleration of the widespread process of ethnocultural continuity (notwithstanding substantial change in this area) and of sidestream ethnicity as a way of being American. Mexican-Americans are already American "in their own fashion" and will probably be even more fully so in the future—particularly in the language arena.

The Ethnic Revival and the Formation of the American People

The ethnic revival in the United States shares certain characteristics with most other ethnic revivals that occurred at approximately the same time. They all reflected a pervasive (but ultimately muted) alienation from the central ethos and institutions of mainstream society. Given the shallower depth and greater plasticity of American

---

112. Ibid. See also, Calvin Veltman, "Anglicisation in the United States: The Importance of Parental Nativity and Language Practice," *International Journal of the Sociology of Language*, vol. 32 (1981), pp. 65–84.

ethnicity, however, the U.S. revival was also a formative experience in the continuing saga of the formation of the American people.[113]

German ethnicity in Germany has lost any daily awareness of primordial Germanic tribal differentiation. Late as it was in fully consolidating, largely because of Germany's slowness in achieving political integration, a unified and unfragmented German ethnic identity has been achieved for well over a century. This German ethnicity is unaware of a preunified, let alone a pre-German, past in terms of ethnocultural identity and ethnocultural relevance for today or tomorrow. This is even more true in France, which has long been marked by far more political centralization and centralized culture planning than Germany. The transformation from preromanized Celts, to romanized Celts, to Franks, to Christianized regionals, to integrated Frenchmen (with the possible exception of the very last transition for those of "peripheral regional" origin) did not involve changing a personally or societally felt ethnocultural identity. German and French ethnicity are now experienced as primordial verities, historically deep and authentic realizations of time and place. American ethnicity is still largely unfinalized, uncrystallized, unattained, and perhaps even unattainable in such terms, although it has a partial validity, shared with other ethnocultural identities.

Consider for a moment the American view of religion. Religion is nonspecific, nonfunctional, and is not goal-oriented for American society as a whole, yet it is all-pervasive, comforting, and altogether approved and desired by most Americans. Therefore, religion is an integrative force notwithstanding the diversity of religions.[114] Religion in America is neither lower class nor upper class; it is neither liberal nor conservative. It no longer controls law, education, government, health, business, or culture, and yet it is a recognizable ingredient and determinant of all of them in the daily lives, happiness, and well-being of the majority of the population. Without controlling very much, it has become a verity.

Americans expect each other "to be religious"; any religion will do and all religions are equally valid.[115] Religion (but not any particular religion) has become part of the common, overarching "American

---

113. Herbert J. Gans, Nathan Glazer, Joseph R. Gusfield, and Christopher Jencks, eds., *On the Making of Americans: Essays in Honor of David Riesman* (Philadelphia: University of Pennsylvania Press, 1979).

114. See Berger, *Noise of Solemn Assemblies;* Richard K. Fenn, "Toward a New Sociology of Religion," *Journal of the Scientific Study of Religion,* vol. 11 (1972), pp. 16–32; and Philip E. Hammond, "Religion and the 'Informing' of Culture," *Journal for the Scientific Study of Religion,* vol. 3 (1963), pp. 97–106.

115. Andrew M. Greeley, *Unsecular Man: The Persistence of Religion* (New York: Schocken, 1972).

experience." To have no religion is, in the eyes of most Americans, to be both suspect and impoverished. Some religions are more exotic than others, but, in contrast to earlier days, any religion is distinctly better than none in the popular estimation.[116] De Tocqueville's analysis in this connection rings truer today than when he originally wrote it: "If it be of the highest importance to man, as an individual, that his religion should be true, it is not so to society. . . . Provided the citizens profess a religion, the peculiar tenets of that religion are of little importance to its [American society's] interests."[117]

Thanks to the ethnic revival, sidestream ethnicity has come to play a public role very similar to that of religion in American life.[118] A sidestream ethnicity is recognized as being not only natural but humanizing and strengthening in some very general sense, and the people who implement or display such ethnicity situationally are not outsiders in urban America.[119] Although ethnicity completely controls no domain of behavior, it is "a good influence" and makes for a more interesting, colorful, rooted life. It relates to family stability, neighborhood stability, and personal stability. Americans now expect one another to have some sidestream ethnicity; any sidestream ethnicity will do and all ethnicities are equally good (almost) because their role is no longer to help or hinder "being a success in America"[120] but to provide "roots"—that is, give meaningful cultural depth to individual and family life. Thus, a sidestream ethnicity as part of one's background (rather than any particular sidestream ethnicity) has become part of an enriched and overarching American experience in ways adumbrated by Handlin and Greene.[121] There is no need to hide it. In fact, it would be churlish and putting on false airs to do so. What is worse, it would be denying an aspect of American identity.[122]

---

116. R. Laurence Moore, "Insiders and Outsiders in American Historical Narrative and American History," *American Historical Review*, vol. 87 (1982), pp. 390–412.

117. Alexis de Tocqueville, "Principal Causes which Tend to Maintain the Democratic Republic in the United States," in his *Democracy in America*, vol. 1 (1835) (New York: Vintage Books/Random House, 1945), p. 314.

118. David M. Schneider, "Kinship, Nationality and Religion in American Culture: Toward a Definition of Kinship," in Robert F. Spencer, ed., *Forms of Symbolic Action* (Seattle: University of Washington Press, 1969).

119. David Sibley, *Outsiders in Urban Societies* (Oxford: Blackwell, 1981).

120. Thomas Sowell, *Ethnic America: A History* (New York: Basic Books, 1981).

121. Oscar Handlin, *Race and Nationality in American Life* (New York: Little, Brown and Co., 1957) and Victor R. Greene, *For God and Country: The Rise of Polish and Lithuanian Ethnic Consciousness in America, 1800–1910* (Madison: State Historical Society of Wisconsin, 1975).

122. Charles Shanabruch, *Chicago's Catholics: The Evolution of an American Identity* (Notre Dame, Ind.: University of Notre Dame Press, 1981); and Alba and Chamlin, "A Preliminary Examination."

Mexican-Americans have also embarked on this path. Barring fundamental distancing in the future (a war with Mexico, Mexican terrorism transplanted into the United States, nativistic exclusion of Mexican-Americans from the coming development of the Sunbelt Southwest, nativistic excesses in the restriction of immigration), they can be expected to remain on that path for the foreseeable future. Their loyalty will be American; their politics will be American; their language will be American. But their identity will be Mexican-American, and in particular situations they will be staunchly so, accompanied by appropriate ritualized phraseology in Spanish. Major and exacerbating ethnolinguistic distancing from the mainstream is a reciprocal process; it does not depend on Mexican-American dynamics alone. It is not Mexican-Americans alone who must be examined, weighed, investigated, and pondered in order that their identity, loyalty, and language may be better known. In all these respects, "it takes two to tango," and the Mexican-American situation cannot be understood without focusing on the U.S. mainstream as a whole and, indeed, on the international developments that will impinge on its equanimity, permissiveness, and fidelity to American democratic and egalitarian principles.

But, of course, a shared, "common American" ethnicity is growing too (as is the shared American civil religion), particularly among the young.[123] The liberal dream of a modern society in which ethnicity is secondary to the central social processes and to individual aspirations and involvements is being approximated via innumerable and mighty mainstream forces. This is, of course, a case of ethnogenesis,[124] rather than of the "disappearance of ethnicity," as liberals had mistakenly hoped and believed because of their association of ethnicity with the sidestream alone. This shared ethnicity proceeds via the fact that the two, the sidestream and the mainstream, are not greatly compartmentalized and, indeed, are both present not only in most domains but in most situations as well. The family, the church, the school, and the mass media—all are appropriate contexts for implementing,

---

123. Philip Gleason, "American Identity and Americanization," in *Harvard Encyclopedia of American Ethnic Groups* (Cambridge, Mass.: Harvard University Press, 1980), pp. 31–58.

124. Yulian Bromley, *Soviet Ethnology and Anthropology* (The Hague: Mouton, 1974); J. T. Gallagher, "The Emergence of an African Ethnic Group: The Case of the Ndendeuli," *International Journal of African Historical Studies*, vol. 7 (1974), pp. 1–26; Frank A. Salamone, "Becoming Hausa: Ethnic Identity Change and Its Implications for the Study of Ethnic Pluralism and Stratification," *Africa*, vol. 45 (1975), pp. 410–25; and L. Singer, "Ethnogenesis and Negro Americans Today," *Social Research*, vol. 29 (1962), pp. 419–32.

combining, and innovating either or both ethnicities. As a result, the extent of overlap and of parallelism between the ethnic mainstream and sidestream increases.

The boundaries between the two are far less clear than they would be in Europe where historically deep indigenous ethnicities come into contact. Moreover, because the concept of "American ethnicity" is still quite plastic, the sidestreams more easily become part of the mainstream. Indeed, they become tributaries and variants or versions of the mainstream itself—even among Mexican-Americans—rather than arriving at a stable, dual ethnic compartmentalization vis-à-vis the mainstream.[125] The ethnic revival in the United States has, therefore, contributed to a simultaneous broadening of the permissible limits of the notions of "American" and of sidestream ethnicity, making both notions more all-inclusive, more all-embracing, more similar than they were before. The ethnic revival has hastened ethnic change rather than halted it.[126] Instead of becoming a major source or arena of conflict (a charge, as Dubnow revealed long ago, usually made by establishments against aggrieved minorities),[127] ethnicity has become simply another legitimate interest among many. In modern America, ethnicity is most often a behavioral or attitudinal repertoire experience rather than an all-or-none boundary or category. Increases in its saliency or implementation involve hardly any corresponding "identity" changes or accommodations elsewhere in the repertoire. The two streams, mainstream and sidestream, are symbiotically implemented in the lives of the majority who are in the mainstream rather than apart from it. Bromley contends that in the Soviet Union the various nationalities have become more similar to each other while retaining their individuality.[128] The ethnic revival simultaneously brought about both these conditions in the United States.

On the language front, the ethnic revival in the United States from the mid-1960s to the mid-1970s accomplished even less, in any overt sense, than it did on the broader front of ethnocultural behaviors more generally. Use of language other than English did not increase, and there was no more concerted approach to maintenance of non-

---

125. Paul Kutsche, *The Survival of Spanish American Villages* (Colorado Springs: Colorado College Studies, no. 15, 1979).

126. Michael Banton, "The Direction and Speed of Ethnic Change," in Keyes, *Ethnic Change*.

127. Simon Dubnow, "The Ethics of Nationalism 1906," in Koppel S. Pinson, ed., *History: Essays on Old and New Judaism* (New York: Atheneum, 1970).

128. Yulian Bromley, "Ethnic Processes in the Modern World," *Social Sciences* (Moscow), vol. 14 (1983), pp. 98–114.

English language than there had been before the revival. There were no language "struggles" (at least none that would not have occurred without the revival), no real language movements, no surge to language consciousness or beyond language consciousness to language use. At the attitudinal level so closely allied with identity definition, claims of non-English mother tongues did rise dramatically in the late 1960s. But this constituted claiming of a heritage, of family roots, of mainstream deidentification. It was an attitudinal gesture with only indirect and institutional consequence. By the late 1970s, this identification with a non-English mother tongue was largely dissipated among the grandchildren and great-grandchildren of older immigrant extractions. It could return, but even if it did, it would still be a long step away from increased use of a language other than English. Mexican-Americans differ from other ethnic groups in that youngsters whose parents fail to pass on their ethnic language as a mother tongue can still acquire it in the neighborhood, on the street, and in community institutions as a second language. Yet whether as a first or second language, Mexican-American use of Spanish remains minimal and generally decreases with each generation.

It is hard to imagine that the mid-1960s and mid-1970s were only a decade apart. From a time of plenty and conspicuous rejection of the establishment on the part of the young, the United States had entered a period of new concerns: gasoline shortages and gluts, high unemployment, substantial inflation, and a new seriousness (and materialism) on the part of the young. College cohorts became more grade-conscious, more job-conscious, and more propriety-conscious in dress and in public behavior. Public ethnicity emphases withdrew somewhat into their former private recesses.

In the early 1980s, a bill to establish a national commission for utilization and expansion of language resources (H.R. 4389), which proposed to "utilize the more than 28 million people in our nation" who speak languages in addition to English, died in committee; and the entire bilingual education Title VII edifice was threatened.[129] Mainstream comforts, positions, rights, and privileges became more important again, particularly among the age groups that had previously deprecated them, perhaps because their availability was now uncertain. Claiming of non-English mother tongues plummeted, particularly in those groups in which its attitudinal base was furthest

---

129. Henry B. Gonzalez, "National Commission on Foreign Languages," *Congressional Record*, August 4, 1981, E 3902.

removed from overt language use.[130] Once more, we face liberal predictions that the "end of ethnicity" is upon us, temptations to trumpet the "triumph of straight-line theory,"[131] and the uselessness of an ethnicity that is "purely symbolic."

Apparently, the cultural time, cultural space, sense of history, and quest for unique dignity of minorities are not easily appreciated or kept in mind. Most social theoreticians have functional expectations of ethnicity that are different from those of the ethnic minorities themselves, and, without sympathetic sensitivity, the "death wish" vis-à-vis ethnicity will once again come to the fore. It is happening among Mexican-Americans as well, Richard Rodriguez being the most prominent spokesman along those lines.[132] Most social scientists are professional liberals; unfortunately, few of them have sensed that "what is illiberal is homogenization in the name of liberalism,"[133] something that Dubnow and other minority spokesmen realized many decades ago.

The Future of Sidestream Language and Ethnicity in America

The future of sidestream ethnic phenomena is difficult to predict because they carry within them the seeds of their own regeneration. Because these phenomena function in the United States at the private and attitudinal levels (even more so than at the public and overt behavioral levels), it is easy to assume that they have ceased to exist merely because they are not visible to the outside, particularly to the unsympathetic outside observer. Furthermore, because they flourish in direct proportion to distancing and alienation or detachment from the mainstream (but not only because of unmet economic or career expectations, as claimed by Marxists, Deutschians, and their derivative schools) there is a major historical or unique component in their occurrence.

---

130. Fishman, "Mother Tongues Claiming."

131. See Herbert J. Gans, "Symbolic Ethnicity: The Future of Ethnic Groups and Cultures in America," in Gans et al., *Making of Americans*. The theory was reclaimed but endlessly qualified in Herbert J. Gans, "Preface," in James A. Crispino, *The Assimilation of Ethnic Groups: The Italian Case* (Staten Island, N.Y.: Center for Immigration Studies, 1980).

132. Richard Rodriguez, *Hunger of Memory: An Autobiography, The Education of Richard Rodriguez* (Boston: Godine, 1981).

133. Michael Novak, *Further Reflections on Ethnicity* (Middleton, Penn.: Jednota Press, 1977).

Will there be another period when indigenous and immigrant minorities in Europe, and ethnic as well as counterculture identities in the United States, are treated in very similar ways and in which sidestream identity is publicly proclaimed again as more colorful, touching, praiseworthy than losing one's self in the mainstream? Who can tell? But sidestream ethnicity will bloom again and again to the extent that (1) massive disappointment is inevitable in modern urban life,[134] (2) modernization is its own worst enemy (as all of the great founders of modern sociology have claimed), (3) *gemeinschaft* has learned to cope with and to "work around" *gesellschaft*, (4) the adversity of *gesellschaft* is itself a prime factor in the pursuit or creation of *gemeinschaft*,[135] and (5) ethnic social institutions and structures remain (indeed, even increase) when cultural assimilation obtains.[136] (Therefore, the former continue to provide channels for cultural memories, aspirations, and revivals, far more than has been appreciated,[137] particularly given the intellectual penchant to artificially separate structure from culture.)

Berlin's metaphor of the pent-up force of the "bent twig" that ultimately snaps back all the more forcefully (to break loose from the oppressive mainstream pressures of modern life) may, on occasion, be quite appropriate. But ethnic revivals need not be the backlash that Berlin implies, any more than they need to be economically inspired in the trite Marxian sense. They can be unfocused, unchanneled, unpoliticized, and relatively unexploited in any material sense. That they can still occur three and more generations after immigrant incorporation into a relatively open and mobile society has begun is testimony to the emotional depths that revivals plumb, and to the length of the hibernation that even remnants of sidestream ethnicity can survive.[138] All in all, I expect the demise of "Mexican-American-

---

134. See Marshall Berman, *All That Is Solid Melts into Air: The Experience of Modernity* (New York: Simon and Schuster, 1981).

135. See Hannah Levin, "The Struggle for Community Can Create Community," in Art Gallaher, Jr., and Harland Padfield, eds., *The Dying Community* (Albuquerque: University of New Mexico Press, 1980), pp. 257–78; and Gallo, *Old Bread, New Wine*.

136. George Pierre Castile and Gilbert Kushner, *Persistent Peoples: Cultural Enclaves in Perspective* (Tucson: University of Arizona Press, 1981).

137. See Milton Gordon, *Assimilation in American Life: The Role of Race, Religion and National Origins* (New York: Oxford University Press, 1964); Robin Stryker, "Religioethnic Effects on Attainments in the Early Career," *American Sociological Review,* vol. 46 (1981), pp. 212–31; and Patricia Ann Taylor, "Education, Ethnicity and Cultural Assimilation in the United States," *Ethnicity,* vol. 8 (1981), pp. 31–49.

138. Peter L. Berger, Brigitte Berger, and Hansfried Kellner, "Modernity and its Discontents," in their *The Homeless Mind* (New York: Random House, 1973).

dom" even less than I expect its intransigent politicization, which I expect not at all.

But perhaps the major lesson of the ethnicity revival in America is that terms such as "emotion" and "hibernation" are basically unjustified in connection with it. Ethnicity revivals are precisely ethnicity repertoire changes—changes in repertoire saliency, range, compartmentalization, and discontinuity or contrasts. They do not return to life that which was dead. In that sense, they are really not revivals at all. They are awakenings and reforms (or at least reformulations) in a very long and honorable progression of revivals, awakenings, and reforms that have led to new visions of America in the past.[139]

The social science vocabulary referring to sidestream ethnicity has tended toward conceptually impoverished good-bad, active-passive (live-dead) polarities. Obviously fresher, more diversified and conceptually more integrated approaches are needed, with respect to both indigenous and immigrant minorities.[140] This is particularly so since so much of sidestream ethnicity is situational, attitudinal, and private, constantly interacting with the mainstream and changing it as well as being changed by it.

The "American dream" has included the promise of assimilation,[141] the promise of ethnolinguistic self-maintenance,[142] and the promise of freedom to choose between them.[143] However, when major shocks, disappointments, and barriers to cultural syncretism occur (as they must, even in relatively open and affluent societies), the private often becomes more public; the attitudinal, overt; the quiescent, active; the interactive, exclusive; the accepting, rejective; the background, salient. Periphery and core, sidestream and mainstream always coexist, and many factors (rather than just one) are capable of changing the focus from one to the other. When viewed on a worldwide scale, the limits and intensities of ethnicity in the United

139. William G. McLoughlin, *Revivals, Awakenings and Reform: An Essay on Religion and Social Change in America, 1607–1977* (Chicago: University of Chicago Press, 1978).

140. Daniel E. Weinberg, *Ethnicity: A Conceptual Approach* (Cleveland: Cleveland State University, 1976); and William Petersen, "Concepts of Ethnicity," in *Harvard Encyclopedia of American Ethnic Groups* (Cambridge, Mass.: Harvard University Press, 1980), pp. 234–42.

141. Rodriguez, *Hunger of Memory;* and Arthur Mann, *The One and the Many: Reflections on American Identity* (Chicago: University of Chicago Press, 1979).

142. Vine Deloria, Jr., *We Talk, You Listen: New Tribes, New Turf* (New York: Macmillan, 1970).

143. Richard Pratte, *Pluralism in Education: Conflict, Clarity and Commitment* (Springfield, Ill.: Thomas, 1979).

States must be considered restricted indeed, and I predict they will remain so and gain thereby more than they lose.

To predict the future course of sidestream language and ethnicity in the United States would require us to do the impossible: to predict America's future. That is clearly a task beyond anyone's capacity. The number of possible intervening variables between characteristics of the sidestreams and characteristics of the mainstream are simply too numerous to contemplate. Historical contingencies and cohort influences represent the unpredictable borderline between humanistic and social scientific endeavor.[144] But given the special nature of mainstream "American ethnicity"—its historical shallowness, plasticity, and permissiveness—it seems safe to say that it will be host to and influenced by myriad sidestream ethnicities almost indefinitely. Non-English languages may generally be expected to play weak functional roles in most sidestream ethnicities on the American scene past the first generation. (In this connection, racially recognizable and recent Hispanics, South and Southeast Asians, and Pacific islanders may constitute the chief exceptions for the rest of this century.) Such languages, nevertheless, can continue to be notably present at an attitudinal level (and, consequently, they are the recipients of community institutional attention).

Sidestream ethnicity has been discounted all too often in the past. Indeed, it is virtually impossible for those who desire and predict the death of minority ethnicity—and this group has included most of the major thinkers of modern liberal sociology—to admit only to being somewhat surprised at what they consider to be mere "momentary blips," rather than concluding that their conceptions of ethnicity are fundamentally mistaken. Otherwise, they would have to admit that to once again predict the general demise of minority ethnicity is not only a mistaken view, and not only a statement about the prognosticators, but a blinder that hides from vision a part of the process that needs to be better understood. But sidestream ethnicity is a phoenix in modern life; it constantly rises anew from its ashes, and the ashes are more apparent than real. If western Europe can accommodate both increased regionalism and increased extraregionalism (not only in terms of the European Economic Community, but also in terms of increasingly being a periphery to an America-centered

---

144. Andrew J. Cherlin, "Explaining the Postwar Baby Boom," *Social Science Research Council Items*, vol. 35 (1981), pp. 57–63.

world),[145] America itself can accommodate both its own sidestreams and its mainstream as interactive systems. We can better appreciate both the longevity of sidestream ethnicity and the difficulty faced in predicting its future if we recognize sidestream ethnicity as (1) being situationally governed (rather than as categorical, or all or none, in nature); (2) being a continuing and often innovative cultural process of boundary maintenance and reconstruction;[146] (3) going through stressed and quiescent phases (with either direction of development possible,[147] rather than only the progression from quiescent to stressed that the Deutschian school has fixed upon); (4) being purposefully rational, comforting, reassuring, orienting in culturally meaningful time and space and, therefore, internally stabilizing[148] rather than primarily irrational, manipulative, combative, or externally destabilizing;[149] (5) reflecting sidestream-mainstream relations in generalized and affective terms, rather than only in focused and instrumental respects;[150] and (6) being related to cultural identity and cultural democracy[151] rather than related only to incivility and conflict.

Ethnicity is "a far more durable and powerful phenomenon than is usually depicted, . . . it draws on far deeper historical roots and

145. Bud B. Khlief, "Ethnicity and Language in Understanding the New Nationalism: The North Atlantic Region," *International Journal of Comparative Sociology*, vol. 23 (1982), pp. 114–21.

146. Donald L. Horowitz, "Cultural Movements and Ethnic Change," vol. 433, *The Annals* (1977), pp. 6–18.

147. See, for example, Edmund R. Leach, *Political Systems of Highland Burma* (London: Bell, 1954) and Charles F. Keyes, ed., *Ethnic Adaptation and Identity: The Karen on the Thai Frontier with Burma* (Philadelphia: Institute for the Study of Human Issues, 1979).

148. George De Vos and Lola Romanucci-Ross, "Ethnicity: Vessel of Meaning and Emblem of Contrast," in George De Vos and Lola Romanucci-Ross, eds., *Ethnic Identity: Cultural Continuities and Change* (Palo Alto, Calif.: Mayfield, 1975), pp. 363–90; Francis L. K. Hsu, "The Cultural Problem of the Cultural Anthropologist," *American Anthropologist*, vol. 81 (1979), pp. 517–32.

149. See, for example, Joseph J. Parot, *Polish Catholics in Chicago, 1850–1920: A Religious History* (DeKalb: Northern Illinois University Press, 1981); Melvin G. Holli, "Teuton vs. Slav: The Great War Sinks Chicago's German *Kultur*," *Ethnicity*, vol. 8 (1981), pp. 406–51; Carl H. Chrislock, *Ethnicity Challenged: The Upper Midwest Norwegian-American Experience in World War I* (Northfield, Minn.: Norwegian-American Historical Association, 1981); and Franjo Tudjman, *Nationalism in Contemporary Europe* (Boulder, Colo.: East European Monographs, 1981 [distributed by Columbia University Press]).

150. Abner Cohen, "The Lesson of Ethnicity," in Abner Cohen, ed., *Urban Ethnicity* (London: Tavistock, 1974), pp. ix–xxiv.

151. Joel J. Chrisman, "Ethnic Persistence in an Urban Setting," *Ethnicity*, vol. 8 (1981), pp. 256–92; and George Klein and Milan J. Reban, eds., *The Politics of Ethnicity in Eastern Europe* (Boulder, Colo.: East European Monographs, 1981 [distributed by Columbia University Press]).

sociological conditions" and here, one might add, goes through many more transformations, overt and attitudinal, "than many would allow."[152] This would not be nearly so surprising if modern liberal thought had not pretended to the contrary for so many years (and not only in the United States but in Europe as well, as Krejci and Velimsky have shown).[153]

Probably there is no "non-ethnic tomorrow" in the offing, not even in the "post-separatist world"—only a tomorrow in which the ethnic and the supra-ethnic (the sidestreams and the mainstream) will be more intimately linked and identified with each other, as they are in the United States today.[154] Just as the stress of ethnicity in recent European history has rarely aimed at political separatism,[155] so its recent quiescence in the United States does not presage its demise.[156] Minority ethnicity is constantly restructuring and recreating itself and its future all around us, well into and beyond the third generation.[157] Because so many social scientists—particularly sociologists and political scientists—have recognized only one extreme of sidestream ethnicity or the other (either strivings for political separatism and disturbances of civility or amalgamation into the mainstream and total disappearance), most of the more moderate and subtle dimensions of postmodern sidestream ethnicity have been little understood.[158]

Like most other aspects of culture, ethnicity waxes and wanes and changes in response to more powerful and encompassing developments. Like most other aspects of culture, it does not follow a straight line. If our attention to the ethnic revival in the United States of the mid-1960s to mid-1970s has (1) highlighted some of these generally overlooked considerations, (2) spotlighted the pan-human nature of symbolic and attitudinal, nonprogrammatic ethnicity, and (3) placed the complexity and subtlety of such ethnicity more squarely

---

152. Smith, *Ethnic Revival.*

153. Jaroslav Krejci and Vitezslav Velimsky, *Ethnic and Political Nations in Europe* (London: Croom-Helm, 1981).

154. Elise Boulding, "Ethnic Separatism and World Development," *Research in Social Movements, Conflicts and Change,* vol. 2 (1979), pp. 259–81.

155. Allardt, *Implications of the Ethnic Revival;* and Colin H. Williams, ed., *National Separatism* (Vancouver: University of British Columbia Press, 1982).

156. Joan Rollins, ed., *Hidden Minorities: The Persistence of Ethnicity in American Life* (Washington, D.C.: University Press of America, 1981).

157. Richard L. Benkin and Grace DeSantis, "Creating Ethnicity: East European Jews and Lithuanian Immigrants in Chicago," *Sociological Focus,* vol. 15 (1982), pp. 231–48; and Crispino, *Assimilation of Ethnic Groups.*

158. Ronald Cohen, "Ethnicity: Problem and Focus in Anthropology," *Annual Review of Anthropology,* vol. 7 (1978), pp. 379–403; and Hsu, "Cultural Problem."

on the agenda for further empirical attention and theoretical elaboration, it has been an eminently worthwhile effort. If, in addition, Mexican-American political and linguistic phenomena can also be seen from this point of view, perhaps both their current American character and their future trends within the American context will be better understood and more accepted as being well within what the body politic can accommodate.

CHAPTER THIRTEEN

Comparer, c'est comprendre. (French Proverb)

While the ethos of this proverb was the justification for the project that culminated in this volume, in common with other maxims it clothes its truth in overstatement. Lack of adequate analogues stands in the way of understanding. The proverb must itself therefore be viewed in comparative rather than absolute terms, as a statement that the comparative method, with all its imperfections, remains the best, though not an ideal, method for imparting balance to and extracting meaning from socioeconomic data.

In previous chapters the contributors have suggested how a comparative perspective might be brought to bear upon the Mexican-American community with regard to assimilation, the potentiality for intergroup conflict, stratification, "transborderdom," migration, political distinctiveness, loyalty, political mobilization, language retention, language profile, and implications of the ethnic revival. Without attempting to summarize the multitude of observations and conclusions contained in those essays, Walker Connor notes an important common consensual thread running through all the analyses. He also draws attention to two significant dimensions of the Mexican-American drama that were not addressed in this volume.

CONCLUSIONS

Through a Comparative Prism Darkly

Walker Connor

As noted at the outset, this volume is the result of an experiment, an attempt to determine whether a comparative approach might shed additional light on issues involving the Mexican-American community. The goal was a better understanding of the Mexican-American condition in the mid-1980s, not the making of recommendations for public policy. The policymaker would unquestionably find it profitable to cull the preceding essays for guidance, however. Examples might include Rosemarie Rogers's point that the creation of an industrial zone in the Mexican sector of the border region is more apt to serve as a way station attracting Mexican migrants than as a terminal. Or her comment that as a cumulative result of the circular and one-way migration across the U.S.-Mexican border, we may be unwittingly moving toward something of a regional free labor market, a pale reflection of the European Economic Community and the Nordic Common Labor Market. Or the conclusion that both she and Myron Weiner arrived at from quite different sets of data, namely, that immigration cannot be explained simply as a response to economic differentials but may result from or be perpetuated by noneconomic factors, such as an established pattern of migration or "a culture of migration." This conclusion suggests that proposals to curtail immigration from Mexico by investing heavily in job creation there may be predicated upon highly questionable assumptions.

Public policymakers might also heed the conclusion of both Donald L. Horowitz and Myron Weiner that federalism, by compartmentalizing issues, makes them more manageable than is true in a system in which every issue is decided at the center. This conclusion suggests the advisability of allowing state and local governments a greater role in accommodating immigrant problems. They might also heed John Stone's illustrations of how policies such as busing can be indicted as "radical" or "liberal" in one environment and "conservative" or "reactionary" in another. This paradox suggests that pejorative labeling should be avoided and policies decided on their merits, preferably after looking at how similar policies have fared in other societies. Indeed, Stone's closing admonition would serve as an excellent guide to all policymakers—namely, to view all aspects of any issue as part of an integrated, interacting whole.[1]

Perhaps the most important insight that this volume offers policymakers is that the Mexican-Americans are not a single, homogeneous group—not ethnically, socioeconomically, nor politically. For this reason it is unwise to predict future behavior on the basis of the overall number of Mexican-Americans. J. Milton Yinger, for example, notes that the size of an immigrant community is inversely related to its rate of assimilation. Mexican-Americans can therefore be expected to assimilate more rapidly if they perceive themselves as constituting a series of smaller, ancestrally related units.[2] Donald L. Horowitz discusses the large and growing gap in income and status between generations of Mexican-Americans. As in the case of black Americans, such variations in income should be of major concern to policymakers. Thus the criticism leveled against a number of affirmative action programs—namely, that they have redounded to the benefit of the more advantaged black Americans rather than the black American "underclass,"—applies with equal validity to the Mexican-Americans. Finally, Rodolfo de la Garza and Harry P. Pachon catalogue a broad spectrum of values and political orientations among Mexican-Americans. Particularly noteworthy are the sharp differences between perceptions held by citizens and noncitizens. Policies reflecting an ascription of the attitudes of a segment of Mexican-Americans to the entire group are therefore bound to have mixed results.

Awareness of the diversity that characterizes the Mexican-Americans should put policymakers on guard against those who claim to speak in the name of the entire group. Comparison with the black

---

1. Note particularly Stone's statement in his chapter: "No realistic policy aimed at eliminating racial or ethnic disparities can consider one set of institutions in isolation from the others or neglect the complex patterns of causal interconnections between them."

2. The potential consequences of the multiethnic character of the Mexican-Americans are so far-reaching and the policy dangers of equating them with a single ancestrally related people, such as Polish-Americans, are so great that a new descriptive term for them should be coined. Since "people of Mexican origin" runs the same risk of conveying common ancestry, "people of Mexico origin" would be preferable. The perniciousness of terms commonly used to denote groups is well exemplified by the term *Hispanic*. Although the term conveys a sense of a people sharing significant characteristics and sentiments, it in fact embraces persons of different racial, ethnic, and linguistic (many Hispanics cannot speak Spanish) characteristics. Its use as a statistical category has served more to obscure than to enlighten.

American experience is again instructive. During the late 1960s, black militants held center stage: the Rap Browns, Eldridge Cleavers, Stokeley Carmichaels, and Huey Newtons were considered the valid voices of black America. A host of opinion surveys and other data indicating that, even collectively, these individuals spoke for only a small fringe of the community were ignored by policymakers. Similarly, Shirley Brice Heath notes that policymakers have been influenced by Mexican-Americans interested in cultural and linguistic maintenance, despite evidence that most Mexican-Americans are primarily interested in language transition.[3]

In addition to not being oriented to policy formulation, this volume has not been concerned with the view from Mexico City. We have concentrated on the Mexican-American community and its role within U.S. society. This compartmentalization is somewhat artificial because the policies and actions of the Mexican authorities will certainly influence a number of the topics we have addressed. The level of future immigration, for example, will necessarily be affected by the Mexican government's view of emigration. Keeping the border porous is obviously in the best interest of that government. Although the exodus has not been able to offset Mexico's problem of excess population relative to economic capacity, the situation would be much worse without this emigration and without the dollar flows that it generates. Moreover, U.S. concern with undocumented immigration has provided Mexico City with an argument for depicting increased U.S. investment in Mexico as being in the U.S. interest.

The loyalty issue has also been treated in this volume solely from the U.S. perspective. The common conclusion of Myron Weiner, Nathan Glazer, and Rodolfo de la Garza is that there are no visible grounds for concern about the loyalty of Mexican-Americans to the United States. A separate but related issue that we did not address is the degree of detachment of the Mexican-Americans from Mexican politics. Could segments of the Mexican-American community become involved in political opposition to a government in Mexico, thereby creating a problem in Mexican-U.S. relations? Rosemarie Rogers provides illustrations of earlier immigrants to the United States who brought the politics of the old country with them. Granted, the

---

3. For an excellent account of the manner in which self-appointed ethnic leaders claiming to speak for the entire Mexican-American community dominated official U.S. language policy through the late 1960s and early 1970s and led it in a direction not favored by the community at large, see Abigail Thernstrom, "Language Issues and Legislation," in Stephen Thernstrom, ed., *Harvard Encyclopedia of American Ethnic Groups* (Cambridge, Mass.: Harvard University Press, 1980). Particularly p. 623ff.

Mexican political system has been relatively stable for decades. Nonetheless, this issue is a valid one for inquiry, given (1) the recent spread of revolutionary movements throughout the cordillera from Chile to neighboring Guatemala, (2) recent symptoms of serious sociopolitical unrest within Mexico,[4] and (3) the large number of circulating migrants who consider Mexico, not the United States, to be their permanent residence. If such political issues were to develop among Mexican-Americans, their level of involvement would likely be more intense than that of other American residents whose political sympathies concern foreign countries at some geographical distance, not an immediately adjoining country. The potential exists for U.S. territory immediately across the border from Mexico to be used for political sanctuary and intrigue of a kind found along such far-flung borders as separate French and Spanish Basqueland, Northern Ireland and the Irish Republic, Angola and Namibia, Ethiopia and Somalia, Turkey and Iran, Iraq and Iran, Afghanistan and Pakistan, India and Burma, Burma and Thailand, Thailand and Malaysia, Indonesia and Papua New Guinea, Honduras and Nicaragua, and Nicaragua and El Salvador.

So much, then, for what we did not attempt. What did we hope to accomplish by our comparative approach? We did not expect the unearthing of great revelations from soil already thoroughly plowed by specialists. But we did assume that placing the available data on Mexican-Americans into a broader framework should provide somewhat different evaluations of the data's implications. A distant vista has often produced new insight, as we are reminded by those two most celebrated analyses of the U.S. political system produced by a Frenchman, Alexis de Tocqueville, and an Englishman, Lord James Bryce.

We undertook this project in full realization that the Mexican-American phenomenon possessed several characteristics that would make it difficult to discover adequate analogues. Among the more glaring of these were that the United States was an immigrant, nonhomeland society, that the issue involved a state immediately adjacent to the United States, and that the border between the two states marked a first world-third world divide. But, properly conducted, comparative analysis is as concerned with uniqueness as with commonality. Preoccupation with the latter often leads to improperly

---

4. In 1983, for example, in an area in which the Zapotec Indians predominate, the municipal government of Juchitán was forcibly removed from office by the central authorities. In late 1984, armed troops were still considered essential to keep the peace.

facile analogies. However, preoccupation with the former not only risks overlooking commonalities but also risks not fully appreciating the implications of uniqueness. As Donald L. Horowitz responds in his paper to the contention that the United States cannot be productively compared with other states because of its unique features, the very differences that emerge from cautious and informed comparisons between the United States and other societies in themselves furnish greater insight for evaluating the likelihood of successfully accommodating the latest wave of immigration within the particular environment of the United States. In short, it is only through comparative analysis that we learn what something is *not*, as well as what it *is*, and the former may be as important as the latter. Thus, to learn that Mexican-Americans do not consider themselves to be a single, ancestrally related group calls into question the signification of all statistics that treat Mexican-Americans as a single entity.

Given the great concern that the authors in this book have demonstrated toward unique features of the Mexican-American community, perhaps the greatest surprise is the consensus among them that the data demonstrate that the Mexican-Americans are following an integrationist pattern not qualitatively dissimilar from that followed by earlier immigrant groups. Although not ruling out the possibility of significant deviation in the future, the authors suggest that alterations in the pattern have thus far reflected differences of tempo rather than of direction.

J. Milton Yinger's balance of assimilative and dissimilative influences at work on the Mexican-Americans is clearly weighted in favor of the assimilative forces, particularly over the long term. Donald L. Horowitz marshals a welter of attitudinal and socioeconomic data in painting a complex portrait of a people in rapid flux with regard to geographic distribution, status, and income; while he notes the remaining gaps between Mexican-Americans and the larger community, the trend he describes is most certainly integrative in direction. Myron Weiner, while demonstrating that issues of loyalty and non-integration almost congenitally surround transborder groups, finds no evidence of this syndrome operating with regard to Mexican-Americans. Nathan Glazer details a number of structural elements that differentiate the case of Mexican-Americans from those of earlier immigrant groups, but he concludes that there is no evidence that these differences have spawned an anti-integrationist trend. Rodolfo de la Garza's research indicates no lesser commitment to the United States and its institutions among Mexican-Americans than among other U.S. inhabitants; and, in their growing diversification, he finds

Mexican-Americans becoming more like a microcosmic reflection of the American electorate. Harry P. Pachon stresses the danger of comparing groups across different time frames, and echoes Glazer and de la Garza in noting a number of structural changes that make political integration more difficult today. Although therefore maintaining that the Mexican-American experience cannot be expected to be a Xerox copy of that of earlier immigrant groups, Pachon concurs with de la Garza that voter turnout and other indicators of political integration among Mexican-Americans now compare favorably with those of other groups. Shirley Brice Heath and Joshua Fishman both note the attritional losses of Spanish to English. Although contending that Spanish may prove more enduring than have other non-English languages, Reynaldo Macías does not fundamentally disagree with Heath and Fishman concerning the trend toward fluency in English.

The consensus of these authors, therefore, is that when all unique features have been properly inserted into the equation, the forces working for assimilation (which is not to be equated with obliteration) still enjoy a decided edge. There is, however, a single factor that could disturb this equation: continuing high levels of immigration could vitally affect all of the analyses in this volume. Indeed, there is little question but that the Mexican-American community would not be the recipient of the immense attention currently turned upon it (including the publication of this collection) were it not for the anticipation of its vast enlargement as a result of continuing massive in-migration from Mexico.

The number of Mexican-Americans is already large. The 7.7 million persons identified as Mexican/Mexican-American/Chicano in the 1980 census outnumber the populations of more than half of the independent states in the world, including many that often figure prominently in the world news—such as Denmark, El Salvador, Finland, Guatemala, Honduras, Ireland, Israel, Jordan, Lebanon, Libya, New Zealand, Nicaragua, Norway, and Switzerland. On the other hand, Mexican-Americans accounted for only 3.4 percent of the total U.S. population in 1980. More important than the absolute number of Mexican-Americans in 1980, however, is the rapid growth that this figure represents. Between 1970 and 1980 the number of Mexican-Americans nearly doubled, making them the country's fastest-growing element.[5] Moreover, spokesmen of the U.S. Immigration

---

5. In the perception of those who accepted the larger estimates of undocumented migrants, the community had more than tripled during the period.

and Naturalization Service openly acknowledge that they have been unable to slow the inflow of migrants, an indication that this growth is continuing.

Given the large percentage of newcomers among the Mexican-Americans, the consensus of the authors in this volume on the integrationist pattern being followed by that community is all the more remarkable. Without exception, they agree that great leaps along the integration continuum correspond to generational change. Income, status, political mobilization, language switching, outmarriage, and the multitude of subprocesses comprising assimilation all undergo significant rates of increase between generations. Whatever the attitude of the parental generation, Americanization has been a swallower of youth. But can it be safely assumed that what is past is prologue? What would be the result if, over a long period of time, the number of newcomers should exceed the number integrating? What if the rate of influx should exceed the rate of acculturation and assimilation?

Such questions warn of the danger of projecting past and present trends into the future. Much of our insight into the processes of assimilation in the United States is drawn from the experiences of earlier immigrant groups whose rate of immigration relative to the country's population as a whole, after a period of consequence, underwent a sharp decline. From the 1840s through the 1890s, for example, annual German immigration into the United States averaged more than one-fiftieth of the country's total population. This rate subsequently underwent a rapid and permanent decrease, but had it continued unabated, it is not at all improbable that the German-language public schools of the nineteenth century would still be with us. Indeed, given the fact that people of German ancestry accounted for 26.14 percent of persons reporting their ancestry in the 1980 census, compared with 26.34 percent for persons of English ancestry, had the rate of German immigration continued unabated for another five decades, German might well be today a coequal language with English, and U.S. culture and institutions be quite different from what they are.

Attempting in the late twentieth century to project developments within the Mexican-American community is not totally dissimilar from attempting to project developments within the German-American community from the vantage point of the mid-nineteenth century. So much hinges upon the inestimable rate of future immigration from Mexico. Moreover, estimates of immigration rates even for the recent past vary widely. From the vantage point of the mid-1980s,

we can only make the following two observations: (1) no radical
change either in immigration policy or in the introduction of measures
for effectively policing the border appears imminent;[6] and (2) in the
absence of such changes, there are reasons to presume that undocumented immigration will not only persist but increase. Given Mexico's
large population and high fertility rate, combined with the massive
discrepancy in economic opportunities between that country and the
United States (the per capita income ratio between the two countries,
respectively, is roughly one to five), the push-pull effects of migration
flow will continue to exert massive influence across this third world—
first world common border.

Rosemarie Rogers quite properly warns against stressing proximate causes of migration, such as income differentials, rather than
more structural factors such as the system of land tenure or rural
population pressure. But in these matters also, the signs augur
accelerated migration. Pressure on the land is reflected in the fact
that Mexico currently has less than one arable acre per capita (as
contrasted with more than two per capita in the United States), a
figure that takes on added gravity in light of the 41 percent of the
labor force engaged in agriculture (as contrasted with 2.7 percent in
the United States). Moreover, discrepancies in quality of life between
the two countries, as reflected in life expectancy, health services, and
educational opportunities, further support a projection of increased
migration. Finally, both Myron Weiner and Rosemarie Rogers point
out that once a pattern of migration becomes well established, it tends
to perpetuate itself even in the absence of discrepancies between the
originating and culminating points, and such a pattern is certainly
now well established between areas of Mexico and points in the
United States.

Assuming, then, that undocumented immigration is destined to
continue, it should be recognized that its impact upon attitudes toward
integration will not be limited to the Mexican-American community.
Integration involves not only the attitudes of the newcomers toward
the host society; it is a synthesis of the interaction between these
attitudes and those of the hosts toward the newcomers. If history can
be a guide, the perpetuation and acceleration of immigration might
well give rise to a more hostile atmosphere. From Benjamin Franklin's
attack on Germans in Pennsylvania to the successful demand for the
exclusion of Orientals and an immigration formula intended to protect

---

6. In the election year of 1984, Congress rejected proposed legislation (the
Simpson-Mazzoli Bill), whose impact upon future immigration would at best be indirect.

"Americans" from mongrelization by any people from outside north-western Europe (a formula dropped only two decades ago), spurts in immigration have frequently been met with outbreaks of xeno-phobia.

Rodolfo de la Garza notes that an irrational note can be detected in the current debate concerning immigration from Mexico. In particular, he points out that opponents of immigration continue to aver, in the face of contrary evidence, that immigrants are taking jobs from citizens.

Meanwhile, rather than contributing to a climate of dispassion and moderation, the public utterances of some key political figures have seemed better designed to raise apprehension and anxiety. In 1983, U.S. Attorney General William French Smith informed the Congress: "We have lost control of our border. Failure to act can only result in further illegal migration, greater public frustration . . . and the negative effects . . . of a large number of persons living outside the law."[7] The following year, in the midst of a presidential campaign, Ronald Reagan tied the immigration issue to the very survival of the United States: "The simple truth is that we've lost control of our borders, and no nation can do that and survive."[8]

The possibility of continuing transborder migration giving rise to a more inhospitable atmosphere is therefore not to be overlooked. But as of this writing, public opinion apparently remains relatively untouched by or tolerant toward the issue. According to a poll conducted by Gallup for *Newsweek* in June 1984, 55 percent of all respondents agreed that immigration was a "very important" issue, but placed it well behind unemployment (84 percent), inflation (73 percent), and nuclear war (70 percent) in this regard, and slightly behind environmental protection (57 percent). Significantly, respond-ents living near the Mexican border did not differ appreciably from the norm, 63 percent agreeing that the issue was very important. In answering other questions, the respondents indicated a high degree of ambivalence toward immigration. Although 61 percent agreed that immigrants displace U.S. workers, 80 percent agreed that "many immigrants work hard—often taking jobs that Americans don't want." And whereas 59 percent agreed that "many immigrants wind up on welfare and raise taxes for Americans," 61 percent agreed that "immigrants help improve our culture with their different cultures and talents."

---

7. *Christian Science Monitor*, March 1, 1983.
8. *New York Times*, June 15, 1984.

Despite their inconsistency, these opinions do not reflect the broad-based nativist impulse that periodically manifested itself before World War II. A number of contributors to this volume warn against analogizing across time-frames, and the matter of public attitudes toward immigrants seems to be a case in point. As we have emphasized, ethnic consciousness and prejudice have played a prominent role throughout American history. As reflected in the popular tendency to use the acronym WASP to describe prerequisites of status and power within U.S. society, ethnic heritage has historically been a critical criterion of acceptance. These same ethnic attitudes have historically shaped opinions concerning which peoples do or do not make acceptable immigrants. However, the surge in interethnic marriages during the past two decades signifies a remarkable change in popular attitudes away from ethnic exclusivity. Although ethnic prejudice has certainly not disappeared from U.S. society, it is far less a barrier to acceptance. And as data presented in this volume confirm, the surge in intermarriage has extended to Mexican-Americans. What all this suggests is that although undocumented immigration may well give rise to a popular reaction against this transborder immigration per se, the reaction is far less likely to be imbued with the sort of fervid ethnic prejudice that characterized pre-World War II reactions to "the immigrant threat."

To recapitulate: The closing of the immigration valve had a pronounced effect upon the rate of integration of former immigrant groups. We cannot predict the future level of transborder immigration or the impact that it will directly and indirectly exert upon the attitudes and behavior of Mexican-Americans. However, our contributors convincingly demonstrate that Mexican-Americans to date have been treading an integrationist path not dissimilar in essence from that traveled by earlier immigrant groups.

ABOUT THE AUTHORS

Walker Connor is the John R. Reitemeyer Professor of Political Science at Trinity College in Hartford, Connecticut. Currently visiting professor of political science at the National University of Singapore, he has published extensively in the fields of comparative nationalism and national movements. His most recent book is *The National Question in Marxist-Leninist Theory and Strategy* (1984).

Joshua Fishman, Distinguished University Research Professor of Social Sciences, Ferkauf Graduate School, Yeshiva University, is widely known for his work on language loyalty, nationalism, and bilingual issues. His most recent book is *The Rise and Fall of the Ethnic Revival* (1985).

Rodolfo de la Garza is associate professor of government at the University of Texas at Austin, where he directs the Center for Mexican American Studies. He has written numerous articles on Mexican politics and Mexican-American political involvement; he also is the author with F. Chris Garcia, of *The Chicano Political Experience: Three Perspectives* (1977).

Nathan Glazer is professor of education and sociology at Harvard University and coeditor of *The Public Interest*. His most recent book is *Ethnic Dilemmas* (1983).

Shirley Brice Heath is an anthropological linguist in the School of Education at Stanford University. Among her extensive publications on ethnography and language use is *Ways with Words: Language, Life and Work in Communities and Classrooms* (1983).

Donald L. Horowitz is professor of law, public policy studies, and political science at Duke University. He is the author of numerous books and articles on racial and ethnic relations and on the role of the courts in policymaking. His book *The Courts and Social Policy* won the Louis Brownlow Prize of the National Academy of Public Administration. His latest book is *Ethnic Groups in Conflict* (1985).

Reynaldo Macías is assistant professor of education at the University of Southern California and director of the USC Center for Multilingual, Multicultural Research. The author of numerous articles and books on bilingualism, language policy, and education, he has just completed work on a monograph, of which he is the principal author, *Estimating the Number of Language-Minority and Limited-English-Proficient Persons in the U.S.: A Comparative Analysis of the Studies.*

Harry P. Pachon is associate professor of public administration at Baruch College, City University of New York. He is also executive director of the National Association of Latino Elected and Appointed Officials (NALEO). His long-standing interest in politics and public policy relating to Mexican-Americans is reflected in his most recent book, written with Joan Moore, *Hispanics in the United States* (1985).

Rosemarie Rogers is a professor of political science at the Fletcher School of Law and Diplomacy, Tufts University. She has worked extensively on migration, migration policy, and the settlement of immigrants in host countries. Her latest book is an edited volume, *Guests Come to Stay: The Effects of European Labor Migration on Sending and Receiving Countries* (Western Press, forthcoming in May 1985).

John Stone is a reader in the Department of Social Science and Administration, Goldsmiths' College, University of London. He is the editor of *Ethnic and Racial Studies*. His interests include racial and ethnic dynamics in western Europe, social change in Southern Africa, and theoretical explanations for racial conflict in contemporary society.

Myron Weiner is Ford International Professor of Political Science at the Massachusetts Institute of Technology. He has worked and published extensively in the areas of ethnicity in the Third World, and ethnicity, migration, and political behavior in developing countries. His most recent books include *Sons of the Soil: Migration and Ethnic Conflict in India* (1978) and *India's Preferential Policies: Migrants, The Middle Classes and Ethnic Equality* (1981), written with Mary Fainsod Katzenstein.

J. Milton Yinger is professor of sociology and anthropology at Oberlin College. Over the past decades his work has focused on the sociology of religion, on countercultures, and on minority groups, discrimination, and prejudice. The fifth edition of *Racial and Cultural Minorities,* written with George E. Simpson, has just been published (1985).

PARTICIPANTS IN THE CONFERENCE

(With Affiliations at the Time of the Conference)

Rodolfo Acuna
*California State University at
Northridge*

Tomas Almaguer
*University of California at
Berkeley*

Carlos Arce
*National Coordinating
Council on Chicano Higher
Education*

Azril Bacal
*University of the Americas,
Mexico*

Nedra Bickel
*Southern California
Association of Governments*

Max Camarillo
*University of California at
Santa Cruz*

Gilberto Cardeñas
University of Texas at Austin

Guadalupe Compean

Walker Connor
Trinity College

Dr. Wayne Cornelius
*University of California at
La Jolla*

Rodolfo de la Garza
University of Texas at Austin

Manuel de la Puente
General Accounting Office

Morris Densmore
Weingart Foundation

William Diaz
The Ford Foundation

Thomas Espenshade
The Urban Institute

Leo Estrada
*University of California at
Los Angeles*

Joshua Fishman
Yeshiva University

Joanne Freilich
*Southern California Association
of Governments*

Nathan Glazer
Harvard University

Manuel Garcia y Griego
Colegio de Mexico

Shirley Brice Heath
Stanford University

David Heer
*University of Southern
California*

Elizabeth Hirsch

Donald Horowitz
Duke University Law School

Frank Hotchkiss
*Southern California Association
of Governments*

John Huerta
*Mexican-American Legal
Defense and Education Fund*

Gail Jensen
*Southern California Association
of Governments*

José Limon
University of Texas at Austin

Lydia Lopez

David Lopez
*University of California at
Los Angeles*

Dennis Macheski
*Southern California Association
of Governments*

Reynaldo Macías
*University of Southern
California*

Don Manson
The Urban Institute

Margarita Melville
*University of Houston, Central
Campus*

Gary Meunier
*Southern California
Association of Governments*

Joan Moore
*University of Wisconsin at
Milwaukee*

Rebecca Morales
*University of California at
Los Angeles*

Diana Morris
The Ford Foundation

Thomas Muller
The Urban Institute

John Oshimo
*Southern California
Association of Governments*

Harry Pachon
City University of New York

Amado Padilla
*University of California at
Los Angeles*

Mary Pardo
*California State University
at Northridge*

Fernando Peñalosa
*California State University
at Long Beach*

Sol Price
Weingart Foundation

Gerald Resendez
*California State University
at Northridge*

Rosemarie Rogers
Tufts University

Georges Sabagh
*University of California at
Los Angeles*

Ciro Sepulveda
*California State University
at Northridge*

Peter Skerry

Rodolfo Stavenhagen
Colegio de Mexico

John Stone
University of London

Diego Vigil
*University of Southern
California*

Harry Volk
Weingart Foundation

Benji Wald
National Center for Bilingual Research

Myron Weiner
Massachusetts Institute of Technology

J. Milton Yinger
Oberlin College

00